Walking the H

Olli Rehn

Walking the Highwire

Rebalancing the European Economy
in Crisis

Olli Rehn
Helsinki, Finland

ISBN 978-3-030-34591-4   ISBN 978-3-030-34592-1   (eBook)
https://doi.org/10.1007/978-3-030-34592-1

Cover illustration: © "On Driftwood", 1991, by Tuula Juti

This Palgrave Macmillan imprint is published by the registered company Springer Nature Switzerland AG
The registered company address is: Gewerbestrasse 11, 6330 Cham, Switzerland

"Muddling through can prevent you from tumbling down."
—A proverb in Eastern Finland

Foreword

I have known Olli professionally for the best part of a decade. We have become very close even though we have been far apart. When Olli took up the office of European Commissioner for Economic and Monetary Affairs in February 2010, he was thinking about Greece and I was in Iqaluit, in the Canadian arctic co-hosting the G7 Finance Ministers and Central Bank Governors meetings. We met at the IMF spring meetings in April, as the Greek debt crisis intensified. In the months and years that followed, we discussed Europe's evolving response as the sovereign debt crisis spread dangerously. By the time Olli stepped down from his role in 2014, many of the most critical tactical, strategic and institutional measures had been enacted, and Europe was well on the path to recovery.

Olli rightly sets Europe's evolving response in the context of the constraints of the incomplete financial and institutional framework within the Euro area at the onset of the crisis. Olli was one of a handful of policy-makers responsible for finding a way through. He not only helped shape the course of events but also reinforced the very foundations of the Euro. The book therefore provides a unique insight on how decisions were arrived at, the ideas that were discarded and those that have been left for another day. Olli sets the record straight on what was and was not possible at the time and also exposes the fault-lines that remain unaddressed today, and setting out an agenda for future reform.

Over time, the Euro area crisis forced policy-makers to address a number of critical gaps in its institutional framework:

- *Financial backstop*: The Euro area entered the crisis without a backstop for member states that had lost market access and a display of overwhelming force was required to regain the market's confidence. The Euro area now has a European Stability Mechanism (ESM) for member states in financial difficulty, and the European Central Bank has the ability, through Outright Monetary Transactions, to protect the integrity of the Euro by purchasing bonds of distressed countries (subject to their meeting commitments entered into as part of an ESM programme).
- *Banking union and macro-prudential framework*: As Olli accepts, it took far too long to address weaknesses in the banking sector. The missed opportunity of the 2010 stress tests, not remotely credible in the eyes of outside observers, underlined the need for change. Though there remains further to go, a step change has been achieved with the set-up of the Single Supervisory Mechanism, the Single Resolution Authority and European Systemic Risk Board. Left for the future though are the risk-sharing elements—a bank resolution fund and a common deposit insurance scheme.
- *Debt-sustainability*: The absence of a comprehensive backstop and resolution regime for banks took away the option of restructuring debts as the crisis emerged. But as these were put in place Europe has developed the ability to restructure failed banks.
- *Macroeconomic policy*: Perhaps difficult have been reforms to the framework to support fiscal sustainability and to encourage coordination between macroeconomic policies. The innovations have been a "six pack" of reforms to economic governance to identify and correct imbalances in 2011 supported in 2013 by the "two pack" which gave the commission more powers to police them. The focus on structural reforms and on creditor countries as well as debtors is a welcome step forward. However, with imbalances in the Euro area still looming large today, with large current account surpluses in Germany and the Netherlands it remains to be seen whether these reforms will prove sufficient.

Having to develop the Euro-area's financial and institutional framework on the hoof, only as the crisis emerged, proved to be incredibly costly. It left a painful and enduring legacy of high public debt. As the crisis took hold, time was lost building the political support for a comprehensive financial framework with delay leading to a Euro area wide recession that "could have been avoided". Knowing what we do today it is easy to imagine as Olli does, a more aggressive and rapid sequencing of reform that might have limited the fall out for the economy, for jobs and livelihoods. But it is always easier with the benefit of hindsight and if one abstracts from the time it can take to build political consensus across multiple jurisdictions.

Drawing on his experience, Olli lays out a comprehensive agenda for further reforms.

Reflecting the challenges we face today, I will pick up on one aspect of unfinished business—macroeconomic policy. Paraphrasing a comment I made back in 2015, it is difficult to avoid the conclusion that, if the Eurozone were a country, fiscal policy would have been substantially more supportive over the past decade. It is not clear that the bias towards tighter fiscal policy has yet been fully addressed. Today—with interest rates at the short and long end of the curve at records lows—the strain placed on monetary policy is still plain to see.

This is not just about the sum of individual fiscal stances, though that was undoubtedly influential. It is also about the absence of a fiscal risk-sharing mechanism. No major monetary union is as decentralised as the Euro. In my view (and largely consistent with the Five Presidents Report), this is a critical component of Europe's financial architecture.

Olli is right to diagnose part of the problem as one of weak investment and to point to structural reform as a lever alongside fiscal policy.

I would make a link here to need for Europe to develop further its capital markets union and to extend its leadership in responding to the challenge of combatting climate challenge. Moving to a carbon neutral economy will require trillions of Euros of investment across the public and private sectors. It has never been cheaper to raise finance. A concerted focus on deepening markets in green finance and mobilizing sustainable investments can put Europe on the path back to strong, sustainable and balance growth both now and in the distant future.

To understand the present, you need first to understand the past. There are few better guides to how the Euro area arrived with the set-up that it has today than Olli Rehn. This book will prove to be an invaluable read, both to students of a crucial phase in European economic history and to those seeking to understand better today's challenges and opportunities. I hope that you enjoy it as much as I have.

Mark Carney
Governor of the Bank of England, 2013–2020, and
the Bank of Canada, 2008–2013

Preface

This book is a story about walking the highwire of the euro crisis and the subsequent rebalancing and recovery of the European economy in 2010–2014. The political context of that time was coloured by the rising wave of populism in Europe and the accelerating Brexit debate in Britain, both of which had evident interfaces with the euro crisis. The essential challenge for the Eurozone policy-makers in those years was to contain the burning banking and debt crisis and to stabilize the economy, and thus to lay a sturdy foundation for sustainable growth and job creation.

Why have I written this book? Over the years, I have received requests and encouragement from many colleagues, stakeholders, citizens and friends to write my crisis memoirs. So in the summer of 2014, soon after I finished my ten-year service as a European Commissioner and was freshly elected to the European Parliament from my native Finland, I started to organize my files, collect material and write the first drafts for book chapters. There are many ways of spending one's summer breaks—I've spent the past five summers in part with this book.

To those who worry about it, I can ensure that this is not one more book in the genre "how I saved the world"—it couldn't even be, as we know. My motive is different. One inspiration has been Robbie Robertson, who was Bob Dylan's first lieutenant in Dylan's greatest years and lead guitarist of the Band. Robertson states bluntly why he wrote his memoirs: "There is so much stuff written about this period, about the Band and about me and Dylan—and a lot of it is a bunch of crap. Just not true. They don't know. They weren't there. I was there! So I felt like I needed to testify".[1]

So, to paraphrase Robertson, I felt I needed to testify on crisis management and on the reform of economic governance in the Eurozone during the crisis. There is much stuff written about the crisis—some pretty good stuff, but some only a bunch of crap, which needs to be corrected. Two particular issues of misunderstanding stand out in the history debate of the euro crisis. First, the policy constraints that stemmed from the badly broken financial sector and the severe risks of sovereign defaults were fundamental, and they limited policy space much more than is usually recognized in retrospective analyses. This concerned especially fiscal policy in the years 2010–2012, i.e. prior to the European Central Bank fully launching its monetary stimulus, which gradually but over time profoundly changed the policy-making landscape and facilitated a better policy mix to fight the liquidity trap and boost growth and jobs. Second, the institutional or political economy constraints are also typically not recognized. These are mostly related to the misperception that the Eurozone rescue operations would have followed the Community method, which works through the EU rules and institutions. However, in reality most of the time they had to be conducted by the intergovernmental method, in which decision-making is dominated by the larger member states. And the intergovernmental method reduces the space for common decisions and increases the number of veto points, which by nature leads more often to second-best rather than first-best policy outcomes.

Besides correcting these misperceptions, there is also another, deeper reason to write this book. I find it crucial for the future of the euro as a single currency and for the European Union as a political community that we draw analytically correct and evidence-based lessons of those tough times when Europe's single currency and real economy were at the brink of collapse. In those crisis years I served as Member and Vice-President of the European Commission, responsible for economic and monetary affairs, and I take it as my duty to analyse the essential lessons of the crisis for the next Eurozone reform, for the sake of future generations of Europeans, with the hope that current and future policy-makers in Europe would find these reflections useful for their decision-making. Europeans deserve better decisions than what they got during the crisis—but first they need to be aware of and come to terms with the need to reform the Eurozone architecture to get us there.

The creation of the precursor of the European Stability Mechanism, the European Financial Stability Facility, in 2010 is a clear-cut case in point. The new institution was crucial in taming the crisis. What lessons can we draw from its creation?

It was past midnight on Sunday on 9 May 2010 in Brussels, already turning into Monday 10 May. I was busy talking with my colleagues in the corridors of Justus Lipsius, the architecturally sterile and even blunt building of the Council of the European Union close to the *Rond-point Schuman*. The EU finance ministers had been desperately looking for an agreement over the weekend on a European financial firewall to contain the unprecedented turbulence in the financial markets. All the Commission's proposals had been rejected until then, and we were on the last timeout, badly on injury time. The crisis was exploding, and a decision was needed before the stock markets opened around the globe. The first one would be the Asian market in Tokyo at 2 a.m. Central European Time.

There was a fair amount of historical irony that the first rock bottom of the euro crisis had to take place on the Schuman Day, which commemorates the Schuman Declaration of 9 May 1950 that launched the very process of European integration, and is hence also called Europe Day. It was not the best but certainly the most memorable Schuman Day I can recall, having not lived the one in 1950. Besides, it was Mother's Day—no offence to my late Sweet Mama!

As we needed to make the very last effort, I called my key civil servants and experts to a small and shabby meeting room at the end of the corridor. I said to them: "Guys, you know we are stuck. There is no more time for first-bests, as we've tried them all, and they've dried out. Have we really turned every stone? Give me finally even a sketch of an idea that could fly, no matter how much outside the box!"

After some long and painful moments of silence and collective meditation in the small room, Maarten Verwey, a senior Dutch civil servant and chair of the Eurogroup task force on stability issues, asked whether we could consider a special purpose vehicle (SPV) to construct a stability fund. The SPVs had gotten a bad name during the financial crisis, since they were intrinsically linked to securitization with subprime loans that substantially contributed to the crisis—but never mind this time: *nécessité fait loi.* We had a quick discussion about how it could be constructed, based on sliced ("pro rata") member state guarantees, instead of a joint community guarantee. I thought that this model just might fly with the Northern countries. "Let's focus on that. Would you mind going and asking whether such an SPV would finally be acceptable to Germany?" I asked Maarten. Off he went.

Little did I know at the time how many times I would have to repeat the very same question in the course of the crisis, although I had started to get an idea about the things to come. Germany had increasingly become the locomotive of the European economy and of the Eurozone financial rescue operations.

When I posed the question, Schuman Day had already turned to Monday 10 May. It was past midnight, around 1.15 a.m., and the Asian markets would open in 45 minutes. The previous week had been terrible for European assets, and Friday had ended in a sour mood, promising a withering storm on Monday morning, as the market forces were seriously doubting the will and ability of the euro area to safeguard financial stability. And now, after three days and a few nights of continuous conferencing behind us, EU member states in the Council were still deadlocked and could not agree on a way out. We were heading into a stone wall, unless a solution was found.

Hence, we simply had to reach a sufficiently bold decision that could convince markets and investors. Then, we could prevent European assets being slaughtered first in the Asian and then in other stock exchanges, which would undoubtedly drive the real economy of Europe—growth and jobs—into recession. I suddenly recalled what the Fed Chair Ben Bernanke had quipped in 2008: he would name his memoirs *"Before Asia Opens"*. The US policy-makers had felt the same gruelling pressure from the financial markets two years previously that we were facing now. However, I was not much comforted by his sharp wit, as I felt the free fall of the European economy in my stomach and spine and bones and, perhaps wishful thinking, in my brains as well.

So Maarten went. This time he came back soon. The German delegation was exceptionally led in that long night by Interior Minister Thomas de Maizière, who was called urgently to duty to replace Finance Minister Wolfgang Schäuble. The latter had been hospitalized upon his landing to Brussels earlier on Sunday afternoon, like a bad omen. Despite the short notice, de Maizière was admirably well versed in the matter. His answer was now finally and quickly affirmative. I had a deep breath of relief. We had scored a crucial goal, at the last second of the injury time.

Next, I went to talk with Elena Salgado, then finance minister of Spain and chair of the Ecofin Council, and suggested to her to reconvene the meeting before Mrs. Merkel changes her mind, as soon as possible. So the 27 ministers gathered again at 1.30 a.m. and made their final touches to the crucial decision in less than half an hour. At 2.08 a.m., Salgado declared the decision adopted. Europe's big bazooka of 500 billion euro was thus born, with its midwives quite worn. Together with the agreed share of the International Monetary Fund, the bazooka now amounted to 750 billion euros. No mean achievement, finally, I thought.

To break the news, we had to rush to the Council press room with Elena Salgado. We could only have a quick word on the main messages on our way. At 2.15 a.m., we started explaining the ECOFIN decision in the Council press room: "A firewall of 750 billion euros is thus created, with the key 2:1 between the EU and IMF, by the EU committing 500 and the IMF 250 billion euros".

After the press conference, at around 3.00 a.m., I was on my way back home in the suburb of Auderghem in Eastern Brussels. My phone rang. It was the US Treasury Secretary Tim Geithner who called me at 3.15 a.m. and wanted to know details of the solution and my take of it. After my summary, he congratulated us Europeans for achieving an important decision, and then, with his tongue in cheek, offered to provide us with some consultative advice, if we ever needed such... the US financial firewall, like our EFSF in 2010, had been created in 2008 only after a fierce political battle. I had a tired but deep laugh, thanked him and promised to come back shortly. I continued home, had a cold beer and hit the sack after the three-day jamboree.

That was the first turning point of the Eurozone debt crisis, and the financial environment calmed down for a while. But there were many more rock bottoms and balancing acts yet to come. We were now truly walking the euro crisis highwire. And the outcome of the highwire walk was by no means predetermined. This book aims at explaining why and how the euro was nevertheless saved. It is a story in the political economy of the euro: its origins, crisis, reform, recovery.

In the past 70 years, we have been better in unifying Europe than communicating it. To do better, we need a well-informed debate in civil society, not only among policy wonks. So let's practice what we preach and make Europe understandable for our citizens. I've followed George Orwell, who combatted doublespeak and jargon which made him the perhaps unwilling hero of my journalism classes. I may not have fully succeeded, but I hope the reader still appreciates the effort.

Helsinki/Mikkeli, Finland   Olli Rehn
August 2019

Note

1. Robbie Robertson as quoted in the *Financial Times*, 17/18 December 2016, Life & Arts section, p. 13.

Acknowledgements

Needless to say, I have written this book in a purely personal capacity. Neither the European Commission, which I served for one and a half decade in total, nor my current institution, the Bank of Finland, should be held responsible for its content.

Producing this book would not have been possible without the help of many colleagues, collaborators, commentators, editors and friends. I would like to warmly thank all of them for their efforts to assist in getting this work done.

While most thankful to all those who helped me to improve the volume, I alone am responsible for the views expressed here and any shortcomings and possible errors that remain.

I am particularly grateful to Dr. Juha Tarkka, Professor Vesa Vihriälä and Professor Emeritus John Zysman, who so generously shared their expertise, read various versions of the manuscript and provided invaluable comments, which helped to improve the analysis and storyline. I owe big thanks to research analyst Dafna Pearson who helped in editing the introductory chapter and posed tough questions that improved its logic. My warmest thanks to Professor Emeritus Charles Goodhart who kindly reviewed the whole manuscript, provided insightful comments and encouraged to publish the text. Likewise to the external reviewers Professor Panicos Demetriades and Dr. George M. Georgiou for their thoughtful comments.

My former cabinet members Thomas Krings, Taneli Lahti, Timo Pesonen and Peer Ritter read an early draft and provided most insightful and useful comments. I want to thank all the members of my cabinet in 2004–2014, especially Stephanie Riso, Karolina Leib, Amadeu Altafaj and

Simon O'Connor who were among those who carried the toughest responsibility during the crisis years with unwavering commitment and formidable distinction.

Lauri Poutanen organized my files in Brussels in 2014–2015 when I was starting to write this book while working full time and running two electoral campaigns. Lauri's thoughtful commentary along the way has greatly contributed to the final product. My colleagues Marja Nykänen and Tuomas Välimäki read the text and provided most valuable comments, especially on legal considerations by Marja and on monetary economics by Tuomas. So did Hanna Freystätter, who also helped me in producing charts, together with Pasi Ikonen and Lauri Vilmi.

Jeromin Zettelmeyer and other participants of the World Economic Forum's Council on Public Finance and Social Inclusion provided highly valuable comments on Chapter 17 that analyses the causes of the double-dip recession in 2011–2012. Jeromin has been a great discussion partner in preparing ground for further Eurozone reform, and he read various other chapters as well and provided constructive criticism, which I have at least partially taken into account.

There are many other people who have contributed to the book through comments and criticism, the provision of material, or other kinds of support. For that, I want to warmly thank Erkki Alaja, Julie Bolle, Tuula Juti, Lauri Kajanoja, Juha Kilponen, Mikko Kontti, Jarmo Kontulainen, Iikka Korhonen, Jaakko Koskentola, Giles Merritt, Pekka Morén, Bert Musial, Elisa Newby, Timo Pylvänäinen, Kari Reijula, Martin Selmayer, Antti Suvanto, Katja Taipalus and Petri Uusitalo.

Big thanks to Marco Buti, Servaas Deroose, Maarten Verwey, Sean Berrigan, Gerassimos Thomas and all the other officials of the European Commission's Directorate-General for Economic and Monetary Affairs (DG ECFIN) for their everyday policy advice in 2010–2014, which is apparently traceable in the book.

I would like to warmly thank my friend Professor Alpo Rusi and my late friend Professor Tuomo Martikainen for their continuous encouragement, comradeship and intellectual curiosity in sharpening the analysis.

For technical assistance and helping keep my files organized, I am very grateful for Mari Hämäläinen, Nelli Rentola, Irma Martinmäki-Tuikkala and Jonna Sjögren. My parliamentary assistants in Brussels, Pekka Eskola, Tatu Liimatainen and Emilia Pernaa were valuable sparring partners on European issues.

Special thanks to my producers Rachel Sangster at Palgrave Macmillan for the English edition and Juha Virkki at Docendo for the Finnish one, as well as to the translator Tatu Henttonen and the publisher Juha Janhonen at Docendo. Many thanks to Ilkka Korhonen, who earlier helped in translation, and to Silva Rehn, who edited my occasionally clumsy English at the final stage and contributed to the cover design by her ideas.

This book has been written over several summers by Lake Puula in Mikkeli, Finland, in the North-Eastern corner of the European Union, as well as over numerous weekends in Brussels and Tervuren, Belgium, and in Helsinki, Finland. My warmest thanks go to my wife Merja and daughter Silva who witnessed the production of yet another printed work, and still stood by me. They know my commitment to participate in the making of a better Europe at the time of present formidable challenges. I hope the reader shares the sentiment and determination.

Contents

List of Figures

List of Boxes

Part I

Setting the Scene

1

Introduction

The euro area debt crisis erupted in full force over a decade ago. In late 2009, hardly a year since the collapse of Lehman Brothers, the euro crisis was triggered by the explosion of Greek public finances and a heightened risk of widespread defaults. It quickly became the most dangerous aftershock of the global financial crisis, and the past decade has been a profound stress test for Europe and its single currency. As the economic historian Adam Tooze put it, "The Eurozone crisis was a massive aftershock of the earthquake in the North Atlantic financial system of 2008, working its way out with a time lag through the labyrinthine political framework of the EU".[1] The perception and nature of the euro crisis changed fast. What was initially perceived as a sovereign debt crisis in a few member states quickly transformed into a euro area-wide systemic crisis in the course of 2010–12.

The systemic crisis was caused by a combination of factors: severe macroeconomic imbalances in many euro area member states, such as excessive private and public indebtedness and unsustainable current account deficits, an interwoven nexus of banks and sovereigns, neglect in preserving financial stability, and the absence of crisis-fighting tools in the original Maastricht construction of the economic and monetary union (EMU). As confidence in sovereign finances of several member states collapsed, a damaging financial contagion spread throughout the euro area which at the time consisted of 16 member states (19 to date). A financial bush fire turned into a forest fire that almost burnt the euro as a currency.

© The Author(s) 2020
O. Rehn, *Walking the Highwire*, https://doi.org/10.1007/978-3-030-34592-1_1

Those of us involved in crisis management walked a highwire, trying to prevent the failure of the euro and simultaneously seeking to address the systemic shortcomings of the euro system. Both dimensions—putting down financial fires and reconstructing the Eurozone architecture—were necessary and became the core job of the second Commission of President Jose Manuel Durao Barroso in 2010–14. I recall vividly when, in the summer of 2010 during the early stage of the crisis the former European Commission President Jacques Delors, one of the founding fathers of the euro, said in an interview: "Now the firemen have done their job. Hence, it is time to call on the architects". Delors wanted to seize the moment and move quickly to reinforce the EMU. Journalists asked me about this, and my answer was: "Yes, I certainly agree with Delors – but only halfway!" I said very clearly that it was not the right time to sack the fire-fighters yet, no matter how much I wanted it, and no matter how much I wanted to get out of the fireman's job myself.

True, since then the architects have definitely been needed to redesign the institutional foundations of the euro. However, the financial wildfires did not disappear, but instead returned time and again in Ireland and Portugal, Italy and Spain, Cyprus and elsewhere, in the course of 2010–13, and still again in the hot Greek summer of 2015. At some point even the break-up of the euro was a perceived threat, and this re-denomination risk led the sovereign bond yields of Italy and Spain to sky-rocket in 2011–12. Thus, it is evident that post-2010 we still needed an even sturdier fire brigade—and we will continue to need one, just in case. At the same time, a well-functioning, ergonomic architecture of the euro is of paramount importance to help prevent any future crisis and enable the Eurozone to enjoy economic stability and sustained growth.

While the very survival of the euro was in danger, there were critical moments and sometimes desperate rock-bottoms. Yet the euro was saved through painful decisions that laid a foundation for coalition building and ignited positive policy spirals. As a result of crisis management and economic stabilization, the Eurozone has been on a continued path of recovery and growth since 2013.

It is critical that we draw proper evidence-based lessons from this grave period when Europe was at the brink of collapse—for the sake of the euro as a single currency and the EU as a political community. In order to explain why and how the euro system was created in ways that set it up for vulnerability to imbalances and made it prone to crisis, without providing any instruments for crisis management, we need to first look at the economic and political context in which the euro was created.

Understanding the Construction of the Highwire

The euro was created as a key part of the great wave of economic and political transformation that spread across the world in the 1980s and 1990s. In Europe, it took the form of deepening and widening the integration of the European Union. In that period of change, economic globalization and financial liberalization were redefining the functioning and rules of the world economy. In the Western world, the economic liberalism of Ronald Reagan and Margaret Thatcher turned the pendulum from the state to the market. The market-liberalizing reforms of Deng Xiaoping in China brought hundreds of millions of his compatriots to the domain of the capitalist world economy and to its labour force. The fall of the Berlin Wall and the collapse of the Soviet Union ended the Cold War, liberated Central and Eastern Europe, and set up the process that led to the unification of the continent—into a Europe whole and free.

The reunification of Germany meant that she became first politically and over time also economically stronger, especially in relative terms to its neighbours. Meanwhile, the French were reluctant to accept German reunification without a compromise that would anchor Germany deeper into European political structures. Hence, the exchange of the German Deutsche Mark for the euro has often become regarded as a key political demand and necessary condition for the French accepting the German reunification. It was commonly perceived, especially in France, that this would not only diminish the sovereign monetary power of Germany but also advance the French pursuit of political equality. Thus, in that context, the euro emerged as a basic bargain necessary for German reunification, a corollary of the European Single Market and a symbol of European unity.

While political in the first place, there was also a substantial economic and financial component in the Franco-German reconciliation and in the European project. The common, though diversely perceived, goal was to create an EMU. The German approach was essentially the one represented by Hans Tietmeyer, the former leader of the Bundesbank and Finance Ministry: instead of some endogenous convergence, the euro was seen as the "crowning" of the integration effort—the German logic went along the lines that "first a political union, then an economic union". The French had a very different, more *volontariste* idea of how to move into an economic union, which included a strong "economic government" as a counterweight to an independent central bank of the monetary union.

Whether the euro would have been born without the fall of the Berlin Wall and the prospect of German reunification is an interesting counterfactual question. In June 1988, the European Council had already made the key decision on the progressive realization of the EMU. By April 1989, the Delors Committee had prepared a concrete action plan to realize a single currency based on three evolutionary stages: first, the full liberalization of capital movements; second, meeting by member states of the convergence criteria like public debt and deficit and exchange rate stability; and third, the permanent locking of exchange rates and the creation of the single currency as the sole unit of account in 1999. The Committee's deliberations were driven by the then still recent economic stagflation and currency turbulence in Europe in the 1980s, including competitive devaluations by countries out of balance, and the creation of the single market, which according to many economists and policy-makers of the time required the creation of a single currency in parallel, or immediately following.

Ten years after the euro was enshrined into the Treaty of Maastricht, the former prime minister of France, Edouard Balladur, forcefully illustrated the nature of the single currency as a result of a Franco-German compromise and underlined Chancellor Helmut Kohl's historic role in its creation:

> Could Kohl have, without the prestige he had acquired during the peaceful reunification of his country, persuaded himself and his European partners to sacrifice the Deutsche Mark and all the other national currencies on the altar of the euro? The Deutsche Mark had to give the example, otherwise nothing would have been possible...Did Kohl make it through European conviction, for fear of his own nation and its passionate and unpredictable ways, for the sake of his historic legacy, or in order to compensate, balance and constrain the over-power that reunification brought to Germany? Be that as it may, he did so: he put the political and moral force of the reunification that was so quickly and brilliantly achieved into the service of European unity.[2]

While Balladur exercises formidable rhetorical elegance, it is nevertheless both pertinent and fair to conclude that the EMU was the result of the politico-economic dynamics of the time and of bargaining between Germany and France, with the latter in the driver's seat but the former controlling the navigator and thus the destination. The outcome of the Franco-German negotiations has often in historical analysis been regarded as an outright *quid pro quo*—"one for you, one for me"—implying that the German reunification was allowed to happen in return for a seat for France at the Bundesbank table. In my view, this is too straightforward and simplistic of an interpretation. Rather, the creation of the euro, against many odds, was the result of a joint European policy reaction to the economic and political transformations of the 1980s and early 1990s, enabled by the strategic political orientation of the German and French leaders, especially Helmut Kohl, Hans-Dietrich Genscher and Francois Mitterrand, and systematically pushed forward by supranational policy entrepreneurship, especially by the European Commission and the Governors' Committee, chaired by Jacques Delors in 1988–89.[3] But it is of course impossible to determine whether a counterfactual scenario where the euro was born ***without*** German reunification could have been realized.

Facing the Crisis III-Prepared

In Europe, the global collapse of financial stability in 2007–8 was a crucial factor that triggered market turbulence and uncertainty. The most intense period of the Eurozone crisis occurred between the years 2010 and 2013. Despite the overall recovery that began in spring 2013, which has helped create by now 11 million net new jobs, the crisis had a long shadow in terms of high unemployment in many countries. Overall, the crisis unfolded in three stages, as illustrated by Fig. 1.1.

1. As a prologue, the global financial crisis started in August 2007 and entered its most intense phase in September 2008 with the collapse of Lehman Brothers. It hit the Eurozone hard and reduced its GDP by a

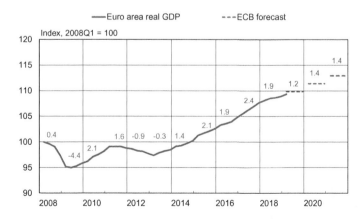

Fig. 1.1 GDP and its growth in the euro area, 2008–21 (*Source* Eurostat, ECB, and Macrobond. *Notes* Euro area, changing composition. Figures next to the line are annual growth rates)

dramatic 4.5%. Between 2008 and 2009, the crisis hit money market funds and strangled interbank lending. However, thanks to the effective global policy coordination mostly in the G20 framework, substantial monetary and fiscal stimulus packages like the European Economic Recovery Plan were agreed on, which helped the world economy and world trade recover in the course of 2009 and 2010.

Yet, the unemployment rate in the Eurozone jumped from 7.5% in mid-2007 to 10.0% by late 2009.[4] Towards the end of 2011, the unemployment rate started to rise again peaking at 12% in the beginning of 2013. These developments led to high and persistent unemployment, and thus to deep social and human scars in many parts of Europe. Since 2013, employment has recovered and the seasonally adjusted unemployment rate in the euro area stood at 7.7% in March 2019.[5]

2. After a brief interlude, the second phase of the crisis, the sovereign debt crisis, hit Europe with full force from October 2009 onwards and ran wild from 2010 to 2012. As said, it was a major aftershock of the global financial crisis which had its breeding ground in the financialization of the world economy and in the interbank credit and sovereign-bank linkages of the global financial system.

This phase of the crisis was characterized by rising bond yields of sovereign debt, prohibitive costs of sovereign lending in vulnerable countries due to the perceived break-up risk of the euro (= "redenomination risk"), and lockouts of some sovereigns from market funding altogether (this happened to Greece, Ireland and Portugal, while Spain and Italy were close calls). The spread of government securities, or sovereign bond yields, and thus the difference in borrowing costs between the vulnerable countries and Germany widened dramatically.

By February 2010, the threat of Greece's default and a possible Grexit were perceived as major contagion risks for the whole Eurozone. This prompted the Eurozone policy-makers to decide on emergency lending for the vulnerable member states. The first conditional financial assistance programme for Greece was finally decided in May 2010 and amounted to 110 billion euros, to be financed roughly 2/3 by the Eurozone and 1/3 by the IMF. The May programme indeed helped to stop the financial turbulence—but only for a day. It led to the creation of the European Financial Stability Mechanism (EFSM) and European Financial Stability Facility (EFSF) only a few days later on 10 May 2010. This was subsequently— some years later in 2012–13—followed by the creation of the permanent, well-capitalized international institution, the European Stability Mechanism (ESM).

At that stage in May 2010, or more accurately from October 2009 to June–July 2011, the crisis was still mostly a matter of small states. Thanks to the new tools that were created, the small states' bush fires were successfully prevented from turning into continent-wide forest fires. Soon, however, Ireland (in November 2010) and Portugal (in April 2011) also requested a conditional financial assistance programme.

3. The Italian and Spanish crises of 2011 and 2012 coincided with the deterioration of the Greek political situation. They were creeping, protracted confidence crises that rapidly accelerated and reached an even more dangerous stage than the Greek one. Both countries faced immense market pressure and very high bond yields, which led to credit rating downgrades and threatened the sustainable service of their public debt. Even France was touched by these headwinds. This was where the euro area debt crisis turned into a truly systemic crisis, with the perceived risk of the euro area break-up, and was at its most dangerous phase.

The credit downgrades and the increases of non-performing loans in the banking sector in Italy and Spain had negative ramifications to the lending capacity of these countries' banks. This in turn led to a credit crunch and to a damaging decline in private lending to enterprises, especially small- and medium-sized ones, in most of Southern Europe.

This profound problem choking growth in the euro area was related to the differences in dealing with the clean-up of the banking sector and restoration of lending to households and businesses. While the United States succeeded in cleaning up its banking sector in 2008 and 2009, Europe's financial repair was only properly done from 2012 to 2014, and in some ways it remains unfinished business.

Eurozone growth performance began to substantially weaken relative to the United States in the second half of 2011, coinciding with a widening gap in the long-term interest rates between the Eurozone and the United States. Part of that is accounted for by the increase in the ECB policy rates. But an even more important factor was the intensification of the euro area banking and debt crisis, felt in the financial markets and reflected in the significant increases of the spreads of the bond yields between the so-called vulnerable member states and the core countries (see Fig. 1.2).

This development aligns closely with **the financial accelerator theory**, which was developed by Ben Bernanke when he was a leading scholar of the Great Depression—long before becoming chairman of the US Federal Reserve. He defines its basic idea in that "recessions tend to gum up the flow of credit, which in turn makes the recession worse". Consequently, credit becomes constrained, which hits household purchases and business

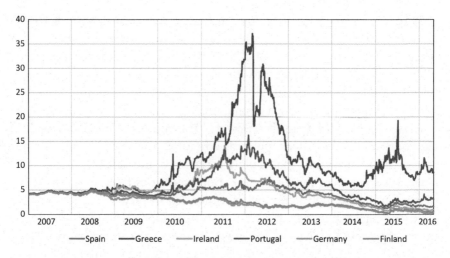

Fig. 1.2 10-year sovereign bond yields, 2007–16 (*Source* Macrobond)

investments, thus amplifying the recession. All this puts economic activity in a reverse gear.[6] This will be discussed in-depth in Chapter 17.

In the Eurozone in 2011–12, the higher sovereign bond yields had a damaging impact on growth in the countries concerned, not only through the standard interest rate mechanism where yields of financial instruments are an opportunity cost for real investment, but also—and perhaps primarily—through the impact on the availability and cost of financing to the private sector. The refinancing costs of the banks increased and asset values decreased, which in turn weakened the availability of collateral and led to more rapid deleveraging and caused a financial squeeze in the private sector. In addition, a vicious circle set forth in public finances: higher yields increased the public sectors' financing burden, accentuating insolvency fears, as well as fears that the sovereigns could not guarantee the functioning of the banking sector should it face serious solvency problems.

To a large extent, the financial accelerator theory, in this case actually a financial *decelerator*, does explain the Eurozone's protracted recession and weak growth performance. When the crisis hit, the response vacillated, acted in slow motion and with too little financial firepower. Hence, the financial system was out of oxygen for too long to support credit and the crisis was seriously worsened.

Not that financial repair hadn't been attempted earlier. Yes, this was done namely with the bank stress tests of summer 2010. But the Eurozone's fragmented and weak confederal bank supervision of that time, without any community-level powers of intrusive supervision nor verification of results, and the related *financial nationalism*—to use the expression invented by Nicolas Véron—of the Eurozone member states did not make success plausible then.

As one of the early lessons of the crisis, the European Commission in January 2011 called for a comprehensive crisis response by the Eurozone, in which a set of parallel and sequential policy measures was suggested: first, to reinforce the financial firewalls (EFSF/ESM) to make the Eurozone sturdier to withstand turbulence from speculative attacks; second, to pursue the recapitalization of banks once the EFSF/ESM had been reinforced and tentatively tested; third, to pursue the consistent consolidation of public finances, with focus on structural fiscal balance over the medium term; and last but not least, to drive economic reforms for sustainable growth and job creation.

It didn't quite work out like that. As Mario Draghi rightly pointed out at the end of 2011, after a particularly dangerous crisis phase: "Ideally, the sequence ought to have been different. We should have had the EFSF in place first. This would have had… a positive impact on the capital positions of the banks with sovereign bonds in their balance sheets… That may exert pressure on banks to achieve better capital ratios by simply de-leveraging. De-leveraging means two things: selling assets and/or reducing lending… the second option is by far the worst".[7]

When we look at the course of events with the wisdom of hindsight, it was a missed opportunity by us Eurozone decision-makers collectively. It turned out that such an economically reasonable sequence was not politically achievable within the Eurozone's unfinished institutional framework. It is a no-brainer to say that the financial decelerator played a major role in killing growth, especially in the period of 2010–12.

Another lesson is that when there is an emergence or a major threat of recession or deflation, or both, monetary policy must be forcefully used to bring back higher employment and normal inflation. At times the ECB was slow to act, but it did so decisively in the autumn of 2008 and again in the summer and fall of 2012, when it finally started to fully act as the lender of last resort for the euro area financial system. In April and July 2011, the ECB's premature rate hikes contributed to the choking of the economy at the hinge of recession. On the positive side, the quantitative easing or the major asset purchase programmes from 2015 onwards were successful in fighting the then very serious menace of deflation and critically supported the recovery.

All in all, there were significant institutional and policy-related constraints. One stemmed from the intergovernmental structure of decision-making. The other was grounded in the rather conservative policy legacy of the European Central Bank.

The Impossible Triangle

Managing the crisis meant negotiating between countries with very different agendas. And behind the agendas were their national goals and constraints. On this, I follow Susan Strange: "What I am suggesting here is a way to synthesize politics and economics by means of structural analysis of the effects of states – or more properly of any kind of authority – on markets and, conversely, of market forces on states".[8]

In that context, the Commission became a proactive broker of compromise among three key players: the German Federal Government in Berlin, the ECB in Frankfurt and the IMF in Washington, DC. These three centres had (and mostly still have) the financial chips—funds or money, directly or through financial or monetary policy instruments—and thus, they were empowered to call the shots. More often than not, they were not rowing in the same direction, but rather were at loggerheads over the preferred course of policy action, either over substance or simply over principle or procedure. In 2010, I started to call them the Eurozone's "*Impossible Triangle*" (Fig. 1.3).[9]

The Triangle is of course a simplified analytical scheme and certainly not intended to offend any of its corners, nor to underestimate the other Eurozone member states. Obviously, France has traditionally been a driving force of European integration and could—or even should—be included in the Triangle, especially as part of the German–French tandem during the era of Chancellor Merkel and President Sarkozy. But at the time its weaker economic standing constrained its role during much of the Eurozone debt

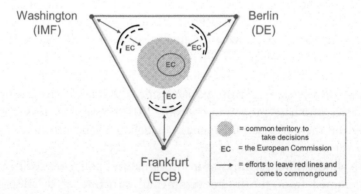

Fig. 1.3 The Eurozone's "Impossible Triangle" (*Source* Author's original sketch in December 2010)

crisis. In any case, one could add around the triangle the other 18 member states of the Eurogroup, as well as the ESM and the European Parliament in the policy areas where they have treaty-based competences.

The "impossibility" should not be taken literally, but nevertheless seriously. It refers to the simple fact that if it were the case that each of these actors stuck to its own rules, principles and policy goals, no solution would be attainable within the triangle. Take, for example, the so-called haircuts of Greek public debt (i.e. "private sector involvement"), which became the key issue in agreeing to the second rescue programme in 2011 and 2012. The IMF was supportive of the haircuts, as it was a matter of respecting its rules which require debt sustainability as a necessary condition. Conversely, the ECB was against the haircuts as a result of the mandate to preserve financial stability in the euro area and especially in the banking system. For Germany, the Bundestag's parliamentary prerogatives and its political aim to reduce the taxpayers' burden oriented the country in favour of haircuts.

Of course, many similar conditions and constraints were valid for other Eurozone member states, including the countries that requested and used conditional financial assistance, i.e. Greece, Ireland, Portugal and Spain. For countries in Southern Europe, it was a matter of contagion, thus they opposed haircuts (for long). For France, it was about the banking system, and so it also resisted them. For the Netherlands and Finland, it was a matter of saving taxpayers' money instead of a bailout, and thus they approved of the haircuts.

The Commission sought to build bridges across this European Disunion. It meant engaging in a continuous and forward-looking negotiation process with the euro area member states and other institutions, bilaterally and multilaterally. As a result of this triangular drama, the Eurozone air was often thick with so-called red lines—absolute conditions or obstacles to decisions—which none of the key actors wanted to compromise on. At one rock-bottom of the crisis, at a Eurogroup, ECB and IMF meeting, this prompted me to proclaim: "These red lines prevent us from finding a common territory and making a decision – please turn your lines at least into *pink* ones, so that we can cross them and finally reach a solution".

In this context, the role of the European Commission became different from how it is often perceived in public. On the one hand, the Commission was present and active in virtually all European and international instances of decision-making that mattered: President Barroso represented it in the leaders' Eurozone and G8 and G20 Summits, while I did so in the Eurogroup, the G7 and G20, as well as the IMF, at the level of finance ministers and central bank governors. Our bilateral communication with President Barroso was seamless and continuous to maximize our external impact and to ensure internal coordination in the Commission. On the other hand, while the Commission had policy influence as a result of its perceived expertise in economic analysis, its statutory mandate in economic governance, and as the leading member of the EU-IMF "Troika", it however had no substantial money to put on the table.[10] Hence, in the real world of "show me the money", the Commission did not have substantial direct financial leverage, only (at most) indirect. Thus, the Commission's role became that of a proactive broker and compromise-builder to create the required common territory for decisions within the Impossible Triangle and in the Eurozone, so as to facilitate or enable a solution and action.

More often than not, these institutional constraints meant that the available solutions were second-bests. In other words, they were politically feasible, rather than economically optimal. But in most cases, even a second-best solution was better than no solution. The obvious downside was that this meant that the Eurozone was often perceived as acting "behind the curve" and seen as "kicking the can down the road", i.e. postponing crucial decisions or decisive actions, for which it was constantly criticized. A prime case in point is the protracted process that started with the creation of the temporary EFSF and gradually led to the creation of the permanent ESM in 2010–13.

The Silent Transformation of the ECB: From BuBa to Fed

The monetary (or financing) constraint stemmed from the 1990s bargain on the imperfect institutional design of the European Central Bank. The ECB was recognized to play a role as the last reserve of liquidity for the banking system, against good collateral. But the combination of the fact that the ECB was forbidden to engage in monetary financing of sovereigns and the lack of a Eurozone stability mechanism for the sovereigns laid the vulnerable member states open to financial market turbulence, even outright market panic. Yet, to contain financial turbulence in the time of crisis, the principles that Walter Bagehot (1826–77) defined for the central banks' lending to financial institutions are generally valid. According to "Bagehot's Dictum", central banks should, in times of financial crisis and in order to contain panic, (1) lend to banks early and freely, i.e. without limit; (2) to solvent depository institutions; (3) against sound collateral; and (4) at interest rates high enough to dissuade those banks not truly in need.[11] At the outbreak of the crisis, the ECB was understandably hesitant to engage in sovereign bond-buying programmes, which nevertheless became necessary in order to contain financial turbulence, particularly as there was no independent/ultimate mechanism to serve as a financial firewall at the outset of the crisis in 2009–10.

The ECB's unwritten doctrine, however, started to change towards a more activist approach. First, this happened in late 2008 with a switch from controlling the quantity of central bank reserve lent to banks to controlling the price of the lending, and with the currency swaps that it did mostly with the US Federal Reserve, which began to play an important role as a global lender of last resort to the global financial system when the interbank lending suddenly dried out after the fall of Lehmann Brothers in September 2008.[12] The next step was taken in 2010, when the ECB started to experiment with a bond-purchase programme of government securities (the Securities Market Programme, or SMP), followed by the three-year long-term refinancing operations of banks (or LTROSs) in December 2011. Its monetary policy approach and method was finally profoundly changed from summer 2012 onwards with the Outright Monetary Transactions programme (= OMT, in existence since September 2012 although never put in use). This was followed by the introduction of negative interest rates since 2014 and the large-scale asset purchase programmes since 2015.

The silent transformation of the ECB "from a Bundesbank to a Federal Reserve"[13] over the years 2010–15 will be a recurring theme and undercurrent in the book. Bundesbank, the highly respected German central bank, symbolizes classical stability-oriented central banking, while the Federal Reserve works here as a shorthand for a more activist counter-cyclical approach to monetary policy. The ECB's transformation was mostly an incremental and gradual change, more by pragmatic steps than by a grand design, but it also turned, underneath, into a silent philosophical transformation in monetary economics and European central banking. As Philip Hartmann and Frank Smets conclude, "the ECB has adjusted its monetary policy to the changing and challenging circumstances over time, making effective use of its strategy and framework… broadening its tools over time it has become more similar to its peers as well".[14] The ECB's transformation will be dealt with further in Chapter 17.

What consequences did the ECB's transformation have? It had two rapid effects, which affected both the financial system and sovereign states.

First, it simply but crucially helped to restore financial stability and return confidence to the banking system. The ECB—or more precisely the Eurosystem, since it is the national central banks that extend last-resort finance to banks in their respective jurisdictions[15]—was regarded as the lender of last resort to the banks and the financial sector, in line with Bagehot's principles. But it did not do the same job for the member states, as lending to sovereigns would equal monetary financing that was forbidden by the EU Treaty. For instance, the asset purchase programmes since 2015 are based on the objective derived from monetary policy to bring inflation upwards to the ECB's price stability target "below but close to 2%", in a situation where underlying inflation (excluding energy and food prices) have been stubbornly around or even below 1%. Lending to the sovereigns was left to the ESM. However, the essential game-changer was the ECB's OMT commitment in 2012, as the Eurosystem in reality took the role of the lender of last resort with regard to the Eurozone in its entirety, *but with the essential caveat that it did so only in a situation where a systemic re-denomination risk, or the risk of a break-up of the euro, occurred.* In this context, it should be recalled that it was only possible for the ECB to accept becoming the lender of last resort after it could genuinely and credibly be convinced of the sustainability of the member states' fiscal policies, and of the Commission's will and ability to ensure it.

Second, the ECB's bold actions gradually created a whole new landscape for fiscal policy after August–September 2012 by bringing down the bond yields and helping to eliminate the immediate threat of sovereign defaults and market lockouts in the Eurozone. Hence, it helped to reduce the over-burdening fiscal pressures on the member states and enabled the Commission to focus less on nominal fiscal targets to convince the markets, and more on the structural balance of public finances over the medium term, which no doubt is a more reasonable way of conducting fiscal policy—if you can afford it in terms of confidence. The focus on medium-term fiscal sustainability was made the policy guideline by the Commission in spring 2012.

But the Commission had to proceed cautiously, for both economic policy and political reasons. In regard to economic policy, it was better to be safe than sorry and avoid the risk of premature relaxation of the consistent consolidation of public finances, which was bringing the Eurozone's fiscal deficit in aggregate down from 6–7% in 2009–10 to 3% by 2013, and thus helping to restore confidence in the Eurozone by 2012–13. Five years later in 2018, the government deficit in the euro area was down to 0.5%, and the euro area public debt has been stabilized at the level of 85.1%.[16] As to politics, this policy shift was not welcomed in the key creditor countries, like Germany, the Netherlands and Finland, who had been calling for fiscal rigour and whose support we needed to maintain. Therefore, it was advisable to proceed with prudence and in a tactically smooth manner.

The ECB's policy shift was the critical turning point in the crisis—or should we say the *critical learning process*. Thanks to the ECB's OMT decision, supported by other unconventional policy measures, the immediate existential threat to the Eurozone gradually vanished. Since then it became possible to pursue a more balanced policy mix in the Eurozone and in the member states to support sustained growth and job creation, without compromising the necessary survivalist goals in fiscal policy.

But there is an important caveat: even the ECB's policy action would not have worked alone—the stabilization of public finances and the creation of EFSF/ESM, both in 2010–12, were critical in the early stages of the crisis in containing the recurring financial turbulence and restoring financial stability. They were also important for the political acceptance of euro area stabilization policies. It is worth recalling that it was both Germany and the ECB who in late 2011 called for the fiscal compact, which was even more rigorous in terms of fiscal rules than the then very recent six-pack reform of economic governance. The Commission though applied the better-constructed six-pack rules in economic and fiscal surveillance, which will be discussed in Chapter 9.

In my view, the evolution of the ECB's approach underlines the importance of policy coordination, especially in a currency union like the Eurozone. Coordination is by no means contradictory to independence of any institution. I witnessed the ECB's vigorous guard of its independence as the Commission's (non-voting) representative at the Governing Council's table in 2010–14 and can willingly testify to that. Since July 2018 as a member of the ECB Governing Council, I am practising what I preach in these lines. But it is a simple fact—almost a no-brainer—that smooth policy coordination matters for a better policy mix.

The Real Issue: How to Manage Macroeconomic Imbalances?

At a deeper level, this is a story of the eternal fundamental question of postwar European economic and monetary cooperation: How to manage macroeconomic imbalances—that is, how to deal with the unsustainable current account surpluses and deficits between EU member states, so that it enables strong, sustained growth and improves employment? This issue of *macroeconomic* imbalances, the best proxy of which are *current account* imbalances, rather than "only" the one of *fiscal* imbalances, has been and should be seen as the key metric (even though the fiscal imbalances undoubtedly also contributed to the macroeconomic ones).

It should be underlined that both the extra- and intra-European macroeconomic imbalances were indeed not a "new" issue. They did not surface in Europe only after the 2008 Lehman shock, when the large and unsustainable macroeconomic imbalances within the euro area were revealed. Instead, they have accompanied the whole evolution of the European economic, monetary and trading system as a key policy issue since at least the foundation of the European Payments Union in 1950 and the European Economic Community in 1957.[17] This was also the case in the 1980s and 1990s, two decades that saw the gradually growing pursuit of creating a European monetary union, as Harold James has maintained:

> [T]he large cumulative imbalances... convinced Europe's policymakers that a monetary union was the only way of avoiding the risk of periodic crises with currency realignments whose trade policy consequences threatened the survival of an integrated European market.[18]

In this sense, the creation of the euro was a matter of internalizing international monetary spillovers and exchange rate movements within Europe. It was thus another kind of mechanism to adjust macroeconomic imbalances. In fact, any currency regime—be it a gold or silver standard, a flexible or fixed exchange rate, a currency union or something else—should be seen as a better or worse mechanism for economic adjustment, both in relation to capital flows in the global financial system as well as international trade flows in the real economy, and to their inherent interaction. It can be seen as a way of trying to optimally channel the economic flows of international trade and capital movements between countries. In post-war Europe, this has largely been a matter of how to rebalance the European macroeconomy between the German current account surpluses and French current account deficits, so that growth and jobs will not suffer, but rather gain.

It is said that generals always prepare for the previous war—recall the Maginot Line of France in 1940. Likewise, the monetary policy-makers easily take decisions in the light of the lessons drawn from previous depressions or recessions. The fact that "monetary generals" base their thinking on the latest battles is natural and oftentimes reasonable, since the laws and problems of economic policy are quite similar and universal over time and space, at least in market-based economies. The Fed—and the world—were lucky to have Ben Bernanke as Chair during the global financial crisis, as he had in his previous incarnation as scholar thoroughly studied the causes and remedies of the Great Depression of the 1930s. Seldom does the optimistic logic "this time is different" work—this has been the popular phrase to illustrate the supposed changes in the laws of economics since time immemorial, or from the Dutch Tulipmania in the seventeenth century to the Roaring Twenties, from the new economy and dot-com boom in the late 1990s to the Greenspan Put and subprime and banking boom before the global financial crisis. Carmen Reinhardt and Kenneth Rogoff have illustrated this elegantly in their historical study, sarcastically entitled *This Time Is Different: Eight Centuries of Financial Folly* (2009).

On the other hand, each currency regime brings with it its own side effects and problems, which can partly be seen beforehand, but partly only over time, often related to the evolution of the economy and society at large. This is what happened to the nineteenth-century gold standard, which could not survive the birth of mass democracy and growing strength of trade unions after the First World War, as demonstrated by Barry Eichengreen in his modern classic treatise *Golden Fetters: The Gold Standard and the Great Depression, 1919–39* (1992).[19] Other factors contributing to the credibility loss of the gold standard after 1918 were the emergence of a hegemonic vacuum—or the loss of leadership—in the world economy, the erosion of international economic policy coordination and the shifting conceptual frameworks on policy goals with the Keynesian revolution.

In recent decades, the structure and functioning of the world economy have again changed, as have internal values and institutions in member states. All these changes have had an impact on the functioning capacity of the chosen currency regime. Without trying to belittle the current problems in the EU, it is useful to compare today's Europe to the one 25–30 years ago. That world was not quite problem-free, either. It is easy to forget that the euro was created under circumstances where quasi-permanent monetary instability had eroded the conditions of sustained growth, and where productivity and competitiveness had badly suffered due to the long period of "stagflation", the combination of stagnation and inflation—or the *Eurosclerosis*, as it was commonly called. Price and monetary stability were regarded as missing elements, which the single currency was expected to provide (even if the paramount importance of *financial* stability was neglected). Of course, the euro also required different policies and more internal economic flexibility of its members, especially in the labour market, but that should have been known from the start. Some countries have been able to live with the euro better than others, which has largely been a matter of national policy choice, without forgetting the systemic problems of the Eurozone at large.

Against this backdrop and in the light of the large and unsustainable macroeconomic imbalances in 2010, the rebalancing of the Eurozone economy became the critical issue, especially after the immediate fire-fighting. That's why the European Commission analysed and prepared reports on macroeconomic imbalances, which focused particularly on excessive current account deficits and surpluses, and also on the housing markets and households' indebtedness. We raised them regularly as a critical policy issue, both in the context of the governance reform and in policy recommendations. The six-pack reform of 2010–11 on economic governance included the Commission's initiative on a Macroeconomic Imbalance Procedure, which after an intensive and heated debate was adopted in the end of 2011. The impact of these institutional changes and policy efforts was limited, but certainly more than nothing.

In retrospect, we see that it was only or at least mainly the deficit countries that adjusted, which is a regrettable second-best outcome. This can be seen below in Fig. 1.4: the blue bars represent the combined current account balance of the "surplus countries" and the red ones of the "deficit countries", based on their standing when the crisis hit in 2008. The surplus countries include Austria, Belgium, Germany, Finland and the Netherlands, while the deficit countries include France, Italy, Spain, Portugal, Ireland and Greece.[20]

The graph testifies to the very substantial effort in economic adjustment in deficit countries like Spain, Portugal and Ireland: by 2013, their combined current account was in balance and turned to surplus in 2015. In 2015–18, the Eurozone as a whole has scored a current account surplus of over 3%. At the same time, the combined surplus of the surplus countries reached over 6% in 2015–18, and in recent years Germany has had a current account surplus of over 7%.

What are the economic and policy implications of the rebalancing process? It depends on the school of thought you subscribe to.

On the one hand, if you have strong trust in international policy coordination, you would argue that a better-coordinated Eurozone policy stance should bring more optimal outcomes in sustainable growth and job creation. From that standpoint, you could say that there is still plenty of slack—or untapped economic potential—in the Eurozone economy, which should be released by a better policy mix, especially by the Keynesian recipe of more optimal aggregate demand management.

On the other hand, if you have less trust in international macroeconomic policy coordination, and especially if you underline more the "ordoliberal" importance of structural competitiveness, fiscal sustainability and legal certainty, you might argue that it is at the end of the day up to each and every member state to carry out policies that ensure sustainable growth and job creation. From that standpoint, you could say that there is now

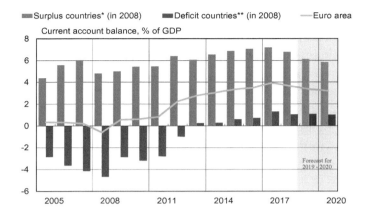

Fig. 1.4 Rebalancing of the Eurozone economy, 2007–20 (*Sources* European Commission and Macrobond. *Surplus countries: AT, BE, DE, FI, NL. **Deficit countries: FR. IT, ES, PT, IE, GR)

more resilience in the Eurozone economy, especially thanks to the improved structural and cost competitiveness that will provide better outcomes in terms of jobs and growth in the medium-to-long-term.

In my view, it would have been preferable to pursue a third way, i.e. a more even rebalancing of the Eurozone economy, where the deficit countries pursue structural reforms and fiscal consolidation, while the surplus countries boost productive investment and domestic demand. This was the policy mix that the European Commission recommended in the annual growth surveys and policy initiatives, especially once the Macroeconomic Imbalance Procedure provided the legal base and some tools for it, beginning in 2012.

Nevertheless, a word of caution is required, since the relationship is anything but straightforward. Because the Eurozone is not a closed but a large open economy, which trades a lot with the rest of the world, the intra-Eurozone impact is smaller than many intuitively think. This implies, for instance, that one euro more spent in German investment spills over only to a very limited extent into the Greek economy. In fact, the trade channel impact is much less important for the rebalancing than the potential reflationary impact through the real exchange rate, which is influenced by wage increases and public spending in the surplus countries. But even the reflationary argument may get more complicated, since reactions of monetary policy to such reflation through higher interest rates might weaken its impact and relativize this argument.

This will be another recurrent theme of this book. In particular, Chapter 14 deals with the rebalancing efforts in relation to the two largest

Eurozone economies, Germany and France. In Chapter 18, I will discuss some misadventures of the beloved but "dismal" science of economics, such as the insufficient attention to capital flows and macroeconomic imbalances before the euro was created and during its first booming decade in existence. On this deficiency of policy and economics, I concur with Waltraud Schelkle who has maintained, "In the set-up of the Eurozone, it was anticipated that a common monetary policy would require national adaptation and fiscal demand management [would] have cross-border effects, but the externalities of financial-sector regulation and integration were underestimated".[21]

In Search of First-Best Solutions and Reforming the Eurozone

What about the future of the Eurozone? Much has been done already to make the Eurozone sturdier and more resilient, especially with the reform of economic governance and the creation of the ESM in 2010–12, and by creating the banking union since 2012. We don't have to start from the scratch, and no revolutionary reform is needed.

Based on experiences of the past crisis years, however, it is a simple fact that the Eurozone can no longer afford sub-optimal decision-making. Its policy-makers should seek genuinely first-best solutions, meaning institutional reform and internalizing the benefits and costs that were previously victims of sub-optimization, if they envisage making the Eurozone sufficiently resilient to survive the next crisis and to enable stronger, sustained growth and job creation. That's why it is vital to build a sturdy bridge between the North and the South of Europe, or between the creditors and debtors in the surplus and deficit countries. It must link countries in pressing need of economic reform, such as France and Italy, to countries that could have fiscal space for boosting domestic investment, such as Germany and some of the Northern countries. And it should keep on board the central bankers who still tend to be suspicious of wasting monetary expansion on an unreformed landscape.

The policy mix and reform of Eurozone governance will be my focus in Part IV where lessons learnt from the euro crisis will be discussed.

Before dwelling into the in-depth story on the Eurozone financial and debt crises, the next chapter outlines the evolution of my mental map of Europe and ponders why and how a peripheral Finn like me ended up as one of the chiefs of the Eurozone fire brigade during the crisis. I will provide the reader with the full freedom of choice to either enjoy Chapter 2 as a scene-setter for broader European endeavours—or to jump over it directly to Chapter 3, *Fire Brigade to Athens*. If choosing to skip the next chapter, my only regret will be that you may not learn to appreciate why peripheries tend to love Europe more than the centre does, which is key to understanding the very essence of the EU.

Notes

1. Adam Tooze, *Crashed, How a Decade of Financial Crises Changed the World*. Allen Lane, 2018, p. 14.
2. Edouard Balladur, *Les Aventuriers de l'Histoire*, 2001, p. 283.
3. On the role of strategic political orientation in the economic and democratic transformation of Europe by Germany and France, see Magnus Ryner and Alan Cafruny, *The European Union and Global Capitalism: Origins, Development, Crisis*. Palgrave Macmillan, 2017, p. 10. On supranational policy entrepreneurship by the European Commission, see Wayne Sandholz and John Zysman, 1992. Recasting the European Bargain. *World Politics*, 41(1): 95–128, 1989.
4. Eurostat, Euro area unemployment at 9.6%. This is calculated as weighted average for the 19 Eurozone members of 2017. Press release 2 March 2017. See: http://ec.europa.eu/eurostat/documents/2995521/7895735/3-0203201 7-AP-EN.pdf/8a73cf73-2bb5-44e4-9494-3dfa39427469.
5. https://ec.europa.eu/eurostat/documents/2995521/9628005/3-01032019-B P-EN.pdf/fdee8c71-7b1a-411a-86fa-da4af63710e1.
6. Ben S. Bernanke, *The Courage to Act: A Memoir of a Crisis and Its Aftermath*. W. W. Norton, 2015, pp. 35–36. See also Ben S. Bernanke, *Essays on the Great Depression*. Princeton University Press, 2000, pp. 5–38; 70–160.
7. Mario Draghi, interview in *The Financial Times*, 14 December 2011.
8. Susan Strange, *States and Markets: An Introduction to International Political Economy*. Pinter Publishers, 1988, pp. 13–14.
9. Every economist recognizes the original *impossible trinity* (or *trilemma*) in international monetary economics by the Nobel Laureate Robert Mundell, which argues that it is impossible to pursue all three elements, the free movement of capital, independent monetary policy and fixed exchange rate, at the same time. The central bank can only choose two out of these three, while opting for all three together at the same time is impossible. I have chosen to name it "only" as an impossible *triangle*, in order not to confuse it with a "real" trilemma where only two out of three goals can be achieved.
10. I use the term EU-IMF Troika as the shorthand for the three institutions, i.e. the European Commission, the European Central Bank and the International Monetary Fund; the Troika's set-up was in 2010 formulated

as "the Commission in liaison with the ECB, together with the IMF". The Commission had most influence on the use of the EFSM (European Financial Stability Mechanism), which was a community instrument based on extra space the EU budget and providing the budgetary ceiling of 60 billion euros. Decisions of the EFSM could be taken by qualified majority, in principle. However, after the creation and initial activation of it in 2010–11, the UK refused to accept its use, which essentially froze this option.

11. Cf. Paul Tucker, Bank of England, speeches in 2009. Quoted in Wikipedia. See also Brian Madigan, *Bagehot's Dictum in Practice*. Speech at Jackson Hole in August 2009.
12. Adam Tooze, *Crashed: How a Decade of Financial Crisis Changed the World*. Allen Lane, 2018, pp. 9–10.
13. Olli Rehn, *Myrskyn silmässä*. Otava, 2012.
14. Philip Hartmann and Frank Smets, *The First Twenty Years of the European Central Bank: Monetary Policy*. ECB Working Paper Series No. 2219, December 2018.
15. I am referring to the Emergency Liquidity Assistance (ELA), which is provided by Eurozone national central banks with the permission of the ECB Governing Council.
16. https://ec.europa.eu/eurostat/documents/2995521/9731224/2-230420 19-AP-EN/bb78015c-c547-4b7d-b2f7-4fffe7bcdfad (on deficit) https://ec.europa.eu/eurostat/documents/2995521/9731224/2-23042019-AP-EN/bb78015c-c547-4b7d-b2f7-4fffe7bcdfad (on debt).
17. Harold James has convincingly shown the role of long-standing imbalances in his seminal work *Making the European Monetary Union: The Role of the Committee of Central Bank Governors and the Origins of the European Central Bank*. The Belknap Press of Harvard University Press, 2012.
18. James 2012, p. 12.
19. Eichengreen, *Golden Fetters: The Gold Standard and the Great Depression, 1919–39*. Oxford University Press, 1992, Introduction.
20. In fact, Finland is statistically a "special case" here, as it turned from a surplus country to a deficit country in 2011 and continued as such until 2017, then turned back to surplus for a while, but according to the latest revised statistics, is again producing a small current account deficit. For the sake of analytical and statistical consistency, it is kept in the previous category.
21. Waltraud Schelkle, *The Political Economy of Monetary Solidarity: The Euro Experiment*. Oxford University Press, 2017, pp. 303–304.

2

A Peripheral Finn in the Capital of Europe

"Mais qui est Olli Rehn?"—"Who is Olli Rehn?" This is the question the Belgian Socialist Minister Paul Magnette brawled out in the aftermath of his country's stabilization programme in early 2012. It was just after the formation of a new Belgian government—or after 541 days without a democratically mandated one—by the Socialist leader Elio di Rupo, who was Magnette's mentor. I had put quite a lot of effort into supporting Belgium in bringing together a budgetary coalition in the parliament, which soon turned into a government coalition. It was done for the unity of the country, which Magnette also supposedly cared about.

Anyway, the question Paul Magnette posed is a reasonable one. I assume he didn't in the first place refer to me personally, but rather as a representative of my institution, the European Commission. The question of legitimacy of the Commission's mandate in economic governance is a well-grounded one. And there is a solid answer: the Commission's mandate in economic governance has been decided jointly by the member states in the Council and the European Parliament and is anchored in EU legislation. *Pacta sunt servanda.* "Let us respect the agreements". That's where the Commission's legitimacy in economic policy coordination stems from, even if in practical politics it is often challenged.

On the other hand, we are all flesh and blood, human beings. There is plenty of what the sociologist Emile Durkheim calls "a yesterday's person" in all of us, through the historical evolution of societies and its conscious and subconscious impact on individuals. Thus, the question of Magnette could be reformulated as follows: "Why was a peripheral Finn steering the

© The Author(s) 2020
O. Rehn, *Walking the Highwire*, https://doi.org/10.1007/978-3-030-34592-1_2

European Commission's fire brigade in the capital of Europe during the worst crisis of the euro? Why not an Alsatian, a Berliner, a Florentine, an Austrian, a Parisian, a Roman – or a Walloon?"[1] Well, part of the answer is that not everybody in the continent has yet realized that today's European Union is no more the cosy club of the European Economic Community of 1958.

An Accidental Firefighter

Life is full of accidents. I was by no means supposed to be one of Europe's firefighters during the Eurozone debt crisis—quite on the contrary. My native country Finland was not yet even a member of the European Community when the Euro was conceived in the Dutch town of Maastricht in 1990–92.

There is no doubt that Finland is perceived as a geographical and some-times geopolitical periphery from the perspective of Continental Europe. One might think that living in the periphery of Europe would qualify you less of a European. But it may actually work the other way around. "The periphery loves Europe more than the centre", jested Professor Loukas Tsoukalis once, and he is not completely wrong—even though many of his compatriot Greeks might not agree with him today.

You could also replace the word "periphery" by the word "small state": for small states, the value of European integration can be more naturally and easily understood than for larger member states. In the EU, might is not the only right. And it's not only that: let's recall that even the largest EU mem-ber states are in fact small states in the globalized world where the relative weight is moving to Asia. Some of them have just not yet realized that they are, too, small states in the global governance.

We Finns embarked on a deeper European journey as soon as the Cold War started to unravel. Finland applied for membership in the European Union on 18 March 1992 and joined on 1 January 1995. I recall it well as I worked intensively for our EU membership and in April 1991 participated in the drafting of the new Government Program, which took a major step for preparing the membership application. And as a Member of Parliament I was voting for the decision to apply for EU membership and chaired the Finnish delegation to the Council of Europe in 1991–95.

But in fact the Finns had moved towards Europe much earlier still, by join-ing the European Free Trade Association through a special arrangement in 1960, as well as by signing a free trade agreement with the European Economic Community in 1973, despite Soviet suspicions and original opposition to it.

The Nordic Spirit and Talkative Finns

I saw the Cold War and Europe of the 1960s and 1970s through a child's eyes. My parents spent their midsummer 1961 by camping in Stockholm's archipelago: I was born nine months later, but with one week's delay, on 31 March 1962. So I got some pretty fundamental Nordic spirit into my veins even before I was born. Why not, since one thing I am proud of is the Nordic legal, social and cultural heritage, which defines Finland as well as her sisters and brothers in Scandinavia. Some decades later, my Old Man jokingly suggested that my special interest in international relations and security policy stems from his good timing of my birth in-between the Berlin crisis (June–November 1961) and the Cuban missile crisis (October 1962).

My family originates from Mikkeli, in Eastern Finland. The region is called Southern Savo (or Savonia). Mikkeli is the capital of Lake District, which is the region where most folks have a summer cottage and a sauna by a lake, and where a large portion of Helsinki's population move during the summer weekends and holidays. The lakes are pure, they freeze in winter but tend to get warm in the summer, and nature is unspoiled. The region is not overly wealthy, and it is quite dependent on the "green gold" of forests, so the new emergence of bio-economy plays a big role there.

By accident—or not—the Savo region has produced all the three Finnish EU Commissioners that have taken office before the 2019 European elections. My predecessor Erkki Liikanen and I hail from the same town, and our families crossed paths in the same township, Pitkäjärvi. My successor, Jyrki Katainen, Commission Vice-President in 2014–19, hails from Northern Savo.

Perhaps one reason for the rather strong European presence of the Savo region is that its people do not fully fit to the stereotype of taciturn Finns. Before the digital age in the last millennium, there was a popular postcard up for sale in Brussels describing "The Perfect European" as a combination of cheeky national stereotypes, so that they should be "Humorous as a German", "Cooking like a Brit", "Sober as the Irish", "Humble as a Spaniard", "Flexible as a Swede", "Driving like the French", "Organized as a Greek"—and most discourteously, "Talkative as a Finn"!

But that's not the whole story. In the country I know best, there is a saying: "Even a funeral in Eastern Finland is a more joyful event than a wedding in Western Finland". We Eastern Finns are the Mediterraneans of the country with a more easy-going attitude to life—and we seldom respond to a question with a straight answer, rather by a counter-question. In that sense, the linguistic mentality of Eastern Finland gets close to Yiddish and the Jewish culture. Sarcastic realism and self-depreciation are part and parcel of the life in Eastern Finland—probably for good reason. The motto of this book, "muddling through may prevent you from tumbling down", is just one illustration of the survival tactics in the tropics of Eastern Finland.

Meanwhile, the Western Finns are the serious Scandinavians who get things done in industry and business, academia and administration, and enhance productivity and prosperity of the whole nation. Or that's what they believe—seriously.

Combining Western Values and European Bridge-Building

The Stone Sacristy of my native town Mikkeli reflects Finland's geopolitical position and Western heritage. It was constructed in the late Middle Ages as a sacristy of the Catholic church. With the Reformation, it was turned into an Evangelic-Lutheran one. The Sacristy—which is situated just to the west of the 1323 border between Sweden and Russia—is a symbol of Finland's security equations. It also reflects the long unity of Sweden and Finland as one state since 1153–56 after the Catholic pilgrimage arrived in Northern Europe. Since then Finland was an organic part of Sweden until 1809, and we share a strong legacy of the rule of law, civil liberties and democracy. Sweden lost Finland to Russia during the Napoleonic Wars, and Finland became part of the Russian Empire as an autonomous Grand Duchy for over a century in 1809–1917.

During the Cold War, Finland practised the policy of neutrality. With Russia, we Finns have the same railway gauge, but a different value base. Democracy and the rule of law are deeply anchored into Finnish DNA. So are the rights of small nations. The harsh conditions of the armistice with the Soviet Union in September 1944 were regarded as a bitter end by many Finns, as illustrated by the realism of Private Rahikainen, an Eastern Finn and a key character in Väinö Linna's magnum opus *The Unknown Soldier* (1954): "They and their goddamn speeches. When you're all out of gunpowder, it's better to keep your mouth shut than to go spouting about the rights of small nations. A dog raises his hind leg on them".

I recall the discussion I had with my maternal grandfather, Ville Valjakka, in the afternoon of the referendum day, 16 October 1994. I called him from Helsinki to ask if he had already voted. His answer was as telling as it was straightforward: "Of course I voted. And of course I voted 'yes'. I spent five long years looking to the East – since then I've only been looking to the West!"

For my Grandpa, it was a choice of values. He was born in 1912 as a crofter's son and worked hard all his life, first as a mason, then as a taxi driver, later on as a small-property developer and insurance manager. A war veteran, he fought as reserve sergeant in the Winter War 1939–40 and the Continuation War 1941–44. He abhorred communism and defended freedom and democracy—and certainly the rule of law and especially (his) private property—and was determined to join the EU, which for him meant finally fully joining the West. This was the majority view among the war veterans, then still a numerically and politically powerful force.

Joining the EU was a logical step in that process of seeking security and sustained socio-economic development. The Finns wanted to join a broader European political community as it played an important role for collective security.

The ordinary Finns also felt strongly about the fate of Eastern European nations. There was spirited sympathy for the Czechs and Slovaks after the Prague Spring was crushed in 1968. Six years old then, it took me some years before I fully understood why my Old Man and his brothers cheered so emotionally in front of the TV when Vladimir Nedomansky's Czechoslovakia beat the Soviet Union's "Red Machine" in the ice-hockey world championships of 1969—the hope of the Prague Spring and its crushing by the Soviet tanks still lived in vivid memory.

For a neutral country in a difficult geopolitical corner of Europe, developments in the European political and security scene always had very important consequences. Helsinki was the seat of the SALT talks on the reduction of strategic nuclear arms in 1969–72 and of negotiations on the Conference of Security and Cooperation in Europe (CSCE, now OSCE) in 1969–75. The CSCE Final Act was signed in Helsinki in the hot summer of 1975. Recalling that he was doing his military service at the time of the CSCE Final Act, the German Federal President Frank-Walter Steinmeier elegantly expressed the following at the Kultaranta Conference of June 2019: "It was – as we know with the benefit of hindsight – one of those pivotal moments in history that leave their mark on an entire generation. The wisdom and ingenuity of a great Finn, Urho Kekkonen, was indispensable to make it happen. He pursued the interests of his own country, Finland, but he did so with a broad vision and a deep understanding that fostered peace and security on the entire European continent and beyond". The CSCE played at least as important a role in tearing down the Wall as did Ronald Reagan—even though this is not often recognized, least of all in the United

States—thanks to both its first basket, which dealt with security and cooperation, and its third basket, which dealt with human rights. West German Chancellor Willy Brandt's *Ostpolitik* was obviously pivotal for the *rapprochement*, and it was the German sibling of the European CSCE process. In essence, success of the West was based on a combination of containment and cooperation.

This was the topic of a dinner meeting I had with the late Hans-Dietrich Genscher, a European statesman and the longest-serving foreign minister of Germany, near Bonn in the summer of 2009. Then aged 82, he was as sharp as ever, and humorous and hearty. I was the liberals' candidate for the EU foreign minister post. We had our dinner on a restaurant terrace in the mountains of Petersburg, admiring the midsummer sunset and beautiful scenery over the valley. He recalled his personal journey as a member of the liberal party of East Germany in 1945–46, then emigrating to the West. We discussed European security, German unification, Russian history, European and German liberalism. Genscher pondered warmly about the CSCE, Helsinki and Kekkonen: "The CSCE has been the most important peace process in European history. Without it, Germany could not have been re-united, nor could Eastern Europe become liberated from real socialism. The role played by the Finnish initiative and President Kekkonen was crucial". My cabinet member Thomas Krings had organized the dinner meeting, and him and I had a most memorable evening with a true European statesman.

So since my school years I started to follow and live with the European political evolution. Later on, it was only natural to delve into these European issues, which have been part and parcel of my life for over 35 years now.

School, Spare Parts and Small-Town Life

In school, my favourite subjects were mathematics and history, with Finnish and English next in line. I enjoyed reading from an early age. Books have remained a permanent love. Yet my first priority was not school, but rather spare parts—odd though it may sound—and football, which probably is a more natural inclination for a kid.

The spare parts stem from the fact that I am an entrepreneur's son. My father Tauno Rehn (1930–2006) was a self-made man, born in a sauna as a crofter's son. He became an orphan during wartime at the age of 10 and had to quit school and take on farm work. At the time, social policy in the countryside of the relatively underdeveloped Eastern Finland was not overly generous. Soon, he left for town and after some spring-boy jobs became a spare parts salesman in mid-1940s and later was promoted to manager in a company that had several car dealerships. He started his own business in 1965 and ran it mostly successfully until his death in 2006.

His father was born in 1893—in the same year the painter Eero Järnefelt realized the painting below, describing the burning of a forest to cultivate the land, or the slash-and-burn cultivation method which was then still used for agriculture in some parts of Eastern Finland. The blond girl with black circles around her eyes, probably not yet 10 years old, could thus well have been my grandpa's big sister (Image 2.1).

Of course, my Dad was also my role model, and I learned to value hard work and enterprise from him. It also meant that—although there was never any direct pressure—I started to work in his company since I was 12 years old. Counting exhaust pipes for inventory in –25C, cycling deliveries to gas stations and repair shops, learning the 10-digit Bosch spare part numbers by

Image 2.1 Eero Järnefelt: "Slash and burn" (1893) (*Source* EERO JÄRNEFELT (1863–1937); Under the Yoke (Burning the Brushwood); 1893; Oil; 131.00 cm x 164.00 cm; Finnish National Gallery/Ateneum Art Museum; Photo: Finnish National Gallery/Yehia Eweis)

heart, and later negotiating deals with repair shop owners over the counter. All that led me to respect hard work, enterprise and the real economy. It was also good hands-on training for negotiations in Brussels, Frankfurt, Moscow, the Balkans and elsewhere.

All that also included a fair deal of romantic belief in economic progress that characterized the post-war decades—it was the time of *das Wirtschaftswunder* or *les Trente Gloriouses* that dominated the economy and popular psyche of continental Europe and was felt in our Eastern Finnish periphery as well. I still recall the warm and sunny summer day in 1966, when I was a four-year-old boy, when my father drove a brand new West German Opel Kadett to our yard, replacing his third East German Wartburg—that's when I realized we do belong to the West! As far as automobiles went, Opel was simply in a totally different technical class, which I admit further strengthened my Western orientation.

I also learned to appreciate the working man: the spare parts salesmen were the working-class heroes of my youth. Our salesmen became my good friends, and thus, I learned to respect the employee rights and care for social justice, and to take a positive view on employee participation at workplaces.

But I also had all the reasons to respect strong women, thanks to one very close by, at home. My mother Vuokko (1938–2011) was the first gymnasium (high school) graduate and the first university student of her extended family. After graduating in 1960, she worked as an English and Swedish teacher for many years, as well as a "school steward" or a local activist in the teachers' trade union, OAJ. Later on, she became the marketing manager of our company—and was elected a Member of Parliament after me in the mid-1990s. I am most grateful to her for encouraging me to study social sciences, as she saw it was my field.

Basically, my hometown Mikkeli was a safe and stimulating place to live and grow in the 1960s and 1970s. I led a rather ordinary, mostly happy life as a child and as a youngster. But that was ruptured on one January morning in 1987, when the news came that the car that was taking my sister Sirpa to the Finnish skiing championships crashed. I took the first flight to Kuopio and its University Hospital to be with her. She never regained consciousness, and eleven days later, she was dead.

It is impossible to describe the sorrow we felt. My parents never recovered from it. Sirpa was a talented, hard-working engineering and business student at the Helsinki University of Technology, now known as Aalto University, and would have made a great entrepreneur. After the funeral, I used to spend a lot of time at her grave talking with her. My conclusion was that I should try to lead a meaningful life by working for justice and fairness and making the world a better place. This may sound naïve on paper, but that's how it was and still is. Deep sadness can be turned into realism and then to reform and revival. That's how public service became my vocation.

Thus, after a rather easy-going childhood and youth, the mood in my life suddenly turned melancholic in 1987. I battled against that feeling mostly by working hard. If any of my companions or friends then felt neglected or offended, I do regret that. Only since I met my wife Merja in 1993 and married her in 1995, and once our daughter Silva was born in 1998, my mood turned first to a neutral and then to a positive though permanently no-nonsensical territory.

Football: A Lifetime Affair

Alongside spare parts, football has been my other passion, which also contributed to my mental map of Europe. In Mikkeli, the local football club MP (Mikkelin Palloililjat) organized a European league for Under-11 as part of its football school, which probably today would be called a (very rudimentary) youth academy. I made my debut in Manchester United in 1968 at the age of six. In the following years, I played for Tottenham Hotspur and Benfica, and then moved to Real Madrid and captained it for two years, before being compelled to retire from the European League in 1973 at the age of 11. Those were happy days. Since then, I did not make it to the European leagues until having a chance to play for the Finnish Parliament and the European Commission (Image 2.2).

But I continued to play in the youth teams and went onto the first team at the age of 17, believing I could pass like Johan Cruyff and score like Gerd Müller—no lack of self-confidence. We were fighting to qualify into the Finnish Premier Division, and succeeded in the following year. Our team was technically skilful and tactically savvy, but quite inexperienced, and despite our (at best) entertaining attacking style, our vitrines were not filled by major trophies. During my military service two years later, I gradually got alienated from serious semi-professional football, not as a player but as a career. It was a matter of both push and pull.

Push, as I realized I had reached the limits of my talent. In September 1981, we played in Oulu, the capital of Northern Finland. FC Oulun Palloseura (OPS) had drawn 1-1 against Liverpool in the European Cup at their home stadium some weeks before. Now we reached a 2-2 draw against OPS, and I managed to score into the very same goal as the legendary

Image 2.2 Stretch it to the limit! Priming a goal in the match Mikkelin Palloilijat vs. Tapiolan Honka 2-2, Premier Division Qualifiers, Mikkeli Sports Stadium, 1981 (*Source* Timo Pylvänäinen, Länsi-Savo)

Scotsman Kenny Dalglish. It was definitely the most I could possibly achieve with my limited footballing talent!

Pull, as I had become more and more interested in how society and the economy around me functioned. Instead of sitting in the back of the team bus for hours on away matches, playing card games like stud poker for some pocket money, I dropped out of the core group and concentrated on reading fascinating books on economics, politics and history in the middle of the bus. Respect to my teammates who understood that!

As a lifetime affair, football has nevertheless ever since been my lifeline in getting into new social settings, which makes me associate with immigrants who are seeking for ways to integrate into the local community. Both at Macalester College in Minnesota and St. Antony's College at Oxford, we had nine nationalities in the starting squad of eleven, which made these teams true melting pots. And I remember with special warmth and gratitude the victories we scored for the Finnish Parliament in the European parliamentary tournaments. Defeating the formidable team of the German Bundestag has been a particularly sweet and consistent treat.

Just for the record, and to avoid any misunderstanding: I am not a football fan—for me, football is just the way of life.

Today, I play with my veteran friends in Helsinki normally twice a week, mainly for mental health. Our team FC Soppa[2] plays with the scoring rule "one-touch and straight from the air", which requires some technique, and reduces aggression. And afterwards we have a regular sauna and occasional beer. Our team includes many immigrants and is thus doing its part to integrate the newcomers into Finnish society. Probably, the only thing in football I regret is the xenophobic or even racist behaviour of some "ultras" who have not internalized the essence of the art—there should be no space for that in the great game. On equal rights and anti-racism, I do fully subscribe to what Gary Lineker, the football legend and the studio host of the BBC's Match of the Day programme, said in an interview some time ago:

> Footballers are… the least racist of all because they've just grown up with different races and different people from different countries with different-coloured skin. You look round a dressing room; you don't look at him and go, he's black, he's Asian, he's… you go, he's a good player, he's all right, he's not. You don't see other things.[3]

Lineker may not be Martin Luther King or Nelson Mandela, but to my ears that sounds as good as or, in its realism, even better than the United Nations Universal Declaration of Human Rights. Respect! No to racism! No à racismo!

Studying Social Sciences, Engaging in Politics and Policy-Making

While I had been interested in politics and history ever since I was a kid, my political involvement started in earnest, strange though it may sound, towards the end of my military service in 1981–82. In politics, it was a very intensive time both in Europe and at home. The Cold War was going through its last really tense period, although we didn't know it yet. In Finland, President Urho Kekkonen resigned after 25 years in office, and the country was preparing for a crucial presidential election in January 1982. It led to a landslide for Dr. Mauno Koivisto, the social-democratic prime minister and central banker, and a war veteran.

I recall an event during my military service that profoundly related to the European security context. We had just started Class 168 at the Reserve Officer School (RUK), located in the town of Hamina, the

South-Eastern-most corner of Finland. We arrived at the garrison from our brigades from different parts of the country on Saturday 20 November 1981. On Sunday 21, the whole South-Eastern military district was put on red alert. We were given hard ammunition, including the anti-tank and artillery companies, and sent to the forest facing the East. Why?

Our guess was because the Finnish Armed Forces wanted to signal that Finland was ready to defend its sovereignty and territory no matter what. There was the threat of a conflict in Central Europe, with a possible spillover in the North. The situation in Poland was very tense, which shortly led to the declaration of martial law. The Solidarity movement was challenging the legitimacy and even the survival of the Soviet-backed Communist government, led by General Jaruzelski.

The memories and fears of 1956 and 1968 were still very much alive everywhere in Europe. Although there might have been some exaggerated symptoms of "Finlandization" in Finland in the 1970s and 1980s, those symptoms never reached the army command who ensured that our readiness to defend the country was kept intact and made clear. Thus, we spent some memorable time with my fellow officer students and our weapons in a chilly, slushy forest in South-Eastern Finland. We were shivering with cold and wet feet, and thinking of Poland.

This memory has often come back to my mind, not least when the first free elections were held in Poland in 1990 or when Poland joined the EU in 2004. In fact, Poland's EU accession and the process leading to it are a strong reminder of the EU's now underperforming soft power—not underestimating the role of Solidarity and domestic political forces. In that case, the Solidarity clearly had more divisions than the Red Army, to paraphrase Stalin's quip "how many divisions does the Pope have". Against the backdrop of that difficult democratic battle, it is indeed saddening that Poland is today struggling with fundamental freedoms.

It has been said that the RUK is the most important management school in Finland. For better or worse—mostly for better—there is more than a grain of truth in that saying. Finnish military training is based on individual initiative and teamwork of the conscripts, not (only) formal discipline, so the leadership courses at RUK had a fairly modern twist as far as management training is concerned. For me it was a formative experience, in the sense that as a 19-year-old lad I was elected to the board of the student union, which included mostly 25–30-year-old "seniors"—lawyers, engineers, business folks, historians and priests, some with Ph.Ds.

So while we had our "105 glorious days" of very cold and snowy winter warfare training in the RUK (by coincidence, the reserve officer class is

105 days long; the Winter War lasted 105 days), everybody else in the country was talking about presidential politics. You can add the economic crisis, nuclear power and the birth of the green movement to the list. So I pondered political issues a lot. I have regarded myself as a centrist liberal as long as I can remember, but at the time there was no obvious party choice. The Liberal Party, which had a glorious past and was my father's political home, had long ago lost its political compass and virtually disappeared from the scene. The Social-Democratic Party, which I read a lot about and followed closely, was too left-leaning and semi-socialist in the 1970s, at least for my social-liberal mindset. The National Coalition Party still had a rather conservative outlook. The Centre Party, or the Peasant Union until 1965, was the pacemaker of the Finnish republican and (at best) progressive heritage and had an entrepreneurial and socially radical line. But it was still quite rurally based. The Greens were yet to be born, and the pre-Green social movements were still in the fringes as far as the big national questions of foreign and economic policy were concerned—and if they were treated at all, the pre-Greens looked more like Fundis than Realos. And I definitely wanted to participate and leave my mark on the core issues of foreign and economic policy.

After some time of reflection and studying the policy programs of the political parties, in spring 1982 I decided to participate in the activities of the Centre Youth Union, which combined a deep ecological commitment to social justice and strong civil liberties. I was particularly active in issues related to Finnish foreign policy and developmental cooperation. In due course, I was made responsible for its solidarity campaign for the African National Congress, which is among my best memories of political activity. We lost many votes by roughly 3900 vs. 100 in the party congresses in the 1980s, but we were nevertheless part of an international movement that called for a trade embargo and fought the apartheid. South Africa has had its share of setbacks since then, but it was memorable to be part of the international movement chanting "Free Nelson Mandela!"

During my military service, I felt a need to expand my horizons, especially since my promising career of a semi-professional footballer seemed to be over before it had truly started. Without any specific plan, I applied for a university scholarship from a Finnish-American fund, created after Finland had as the only country paid back all its wartime loans to the United States. Passing the exams, I was accepted for scholarship and got a few offers to study from some colleges. I decided to opt for Macalester College in St. Paul, Minnesota, thanks to its academic record and inspiring curriculum.

Thus, in September 1982 I ventured for the first time looking for America and flew to Minneapolis through New York's JFK airport. I majored in economics and international relations and studied some journalism during the academic year 1982–83. Teaching at Macalester was competent and inspiring, and I studied hard. For a political economy nerd, it was a wonderful combination of macro- and microeconomics, political science and international relations. *Macroeconomics* by Rudiger Dornbusch and Stanley Fischer, *The Post-Industrial Society* by Daniel Bell and *The Essence of Decision* by Graham T. Allison were my favourites. In journalism, we learned to write plain, simple English with the help of George Orwell's *Politics and the English Language* and Strunk and White's "the little book" *The Elements of Style*. Our journalism professor Ron Ross, a former Vietnam correspondent, coached us to avoid meaningless jargon. And we internalized the sixth rule of George Orwell: "Break any of these rules sooner than say anything outright barbarous".[4]

Recently, I was glad to note that in 2016 Macalester College was ranked second among the "The 25 best US colleges for students who want to change the world" by the World Economic Forum and the Princeton Review. They argued as follows: "Macalester is built upon a commitment to civic leadership and engagement. Students have several opportunities to get involved on campus through the Civic Engagement Centre, primarily in community service, social action and advocacy, and political engagement". I wouldn't mind being 20 and doing it all over again.

In Search of the Liberal Centre in Finland and in Europe

However, full-time student life was over for me earlier than I thought. I returned to Finland to study economics and international relations at the University of Helsinki. At the end of 1983, the leadership of the Centre Youth approached me and asked if I would like to join its staff as part-time international secretary. So I started political work in January 1984—part-time in theory, full-time in practice—which continued in different positions for over three decades.

The mid-1980s was when the Centre Youth wing began gathering green and liberal steam to reform the party, which we thought had plenty of progressive potential but had become too conservative. In 1987, the Centre Youth elected me as the chair of the organization. Our work culminated by the bicentennial of the French Revolution in May 1989 with the adoption of the Centre-Liberal Manifesto, in which we called for liberalizing the economy for entrepreneurship, for social justice through citizen's basic income, for ecologically sustainable economy and for pursuing Finland's active role in Europe. We were the driving force behind the Centre Party joining the Liberal International and the European Liberals and Democrats (ELDR, now ALDE). Our program reflected civic and social liberalism in the pursuit of justice as fairness, inspired by *A Theory of Justice*, the modern classic of John Rawls. I may soon be getting middle-aged, but I still stand broadly by these Rawlsian goals.

I pursued academic work in parallel with political activity. In 1989, I was recruited as an assistant at the Department of Political Science and finished my master's thesis on social movements and political parties in the post-industrial welfare state. My master's thesis focused largely on the Greens and built on classics like Robert Michels and Antonio Gramsci. I crammed through Joschka Fisher's writings on the German Greens in Goethe's language, which did indeed call for some stamina. Some decades later, it was a great honour and delight to work with Joschka when he was Germany's highly respected foreign minister.

When the Berlin Wall was coming down, to my regret I was not there, instead preparing a scholarship application to the British Council. Subsequently, I was admitted to the University of Oxford to write a doctoral thesis—called D.Phil. there—in international political economy. So in September 1990 I moved to Oxford, with the aim of completing my D.Phil. thesis in 2–3 years. I did so finally in 1996, as quite a lot happened in the meantime, both in European affairs and in my personal life. I truly enjoyed the seminars at Oxford where you could freely exchange views and let the best argument win. My thesis dealt with the relationship between corporatism and industrial competitiveness, and through that prism, analysed the evolution of economic strategies of small European states. It focused largely on the interaction between economic and monetary policy, on the one hand, and the functioning and flexibility of the labour market, on the other. In retrospect, it was a useful education for my later duties in economic affairs, both in Finland and in Europe.

The main intervening event was the decision of sufficiently many Helsinki voters to elect me to the Finnish Parliament in March 1991. That was unexpected, but I was indeed motivated to work for the renewal of our country which was in economic free fall and in search of its place within the European transformation. We inherited vast macroeconomic imbalances from the previous government, and when the coalition talks took place in April 1991, the economy was plummeting, contracting with the speed of minus 7% growth per year. Together with the sudden collapse of bilateral Soviet trade in the year end 1990–91, the policy mistakes of the late 1980s led to a banking crisis, two devaluations and rocketing unemployment. So the next couple of years I spent as MP and in 1992–93 as policy advisor to Prime Minister Esko Aho, who did a huge deal in order to restore the economy and pull the country and its people towards EU membership.

Europe was my mission, and I wrote both analytical and political articles on integration. One of my first pieces on EMU, a lengthy article in Finnish in 1993, was entitled "*The General Theory of Employment, Money and Integration*"[5]—again, no lack of self-confidence, when paraphrasing the main work of John Maynard Keynes!

Subsequently, I was actively involved in organizing the Yes campaign for EU membership in a citizen movement that later on became the European Movement in Finland. While that campaign was successful—or rather, as the Finnish people knew what historic decision had to be made—I saw my own political position soon eroding, since the Centre Party was split on the issue of Europe.

This led to both a victory and a defeat in the party congress in June 1994. It has been said that the Centre Party has the third largest party congresses in the world, after the Chinese Communist Party and the US Democratic Party—it may be a slight exaggeration, but there are around 4000 delegates across the country, usually in an ice-hockey rink, taking decisions in a very republican manner. As Deputy Chairman still before the congress, I had proposed that the congress first votes on EU membership, and only then on party leader—implying that a "no" on the EU issue would lead to the resignation of the party leader and fall of the government. That angered the euro-sceptics, as this order helped persuading the majority to support EU membership, which indeed happened. So while the delegates in June 1994 on Saturday voted 2/3 in favour of EU membership, on Sunday they voted me out of the party leadership, as a revenge. That's democratic politics—no appeals.

Since my political influence in Finland had thus eroded, I was ready to follow my European conviction and at the end of 1994 was chosen to the European Parliament, where I served as vice-chair of the Liberal Group and leader of the Centre delegation in 1995–96. After I lost my seat in the by-election of 1996, and after having been a "professional evolutionary" for over a decade, I left politics, turned to academia, and started a project to set up the Centre of European Studies at the University of Helsinki in 1997. At the invitation of Commissioner Erkki Liikanen, I became his head of cabinet for the period 1998–2002.

Upon my return to Finland in January 2002, the Centre Party was in the middle of a leadership contest. As one of the leaders of the liberal wing, I had to enter the campaign. I enjoyed the half-year campaign and reached a good second place. Not good enough for the top, but well enough to consider candidacy in the parliamentary elections in March 2003. However, that did not work out, for reasons very hard to rationally explain. One of the strangest incidents that have ever happened to me was when my close friend and liberal soulmate, Dr. Alpo Rusi, in 2002–3 was accused of spying for the GDR in the late 1960s and early 1970s. Alpo was the foreign policy advisor of President Martti Ahtisaari in 1994–99, and one of the key people in the Sarajevo Summit and Kosovo peace talks in 1999.

Before any real investigation and following apparently organized leaks, Alpo was brutally and publicly crucified by the Finnish elite and media— not their finest hour. Once I realized that he was being made into the scapegoat of all the sins of Finlandization and was being politically assassinated in front of my eyes, I thought I had to defend him in public with some investigative journalism that 99% of Finnish journalists had regretfully neglected. MEP Heidi Hautala and Tapani Ruokanen, the editor-in-chief of *Suomen Kuvalehti*, were among the few friends who joined the battle for the rule of law and historical truth. We got plenty of support from ordinary Finns who were not that easily fooled, which gave some hope as to the future of the nation.

Based on my investigations, I was soon able to prove that the Finnish Security Police, Supo, had mixed two brothers and left a number of probable culprits without any examination. But it took unnecessarily long for Supo to admit its mistake and confess that Alpo was innocent. The debacle ended with Alpo being freed of all charges in June 2003 and the state prosecutor declaring him innocent. I had to pass the parliamentary elections of March 2003 because the case was still open and I could not mix politics with my defence of Alpo. We wrote a book called *The Cold Republic* (*Kylmä tasavalta*, 2003), which revealed the investigative cover-ups and journalistic catastrophe, and suggested a parliamentary oversight of the Finnish security police in line with the principles of Western liberal democracy.

While I was considered a *persona non grata* and a politically dead man walking in my own country in 2002–3, I was nevertheless appointed— against most political odds—to be the Finnish Commissioner a year later.

Those events were fresh in my mind when I started as Enlargement Commissioner in 2004. It is thus no surprise that I put human rights, the rule of law and press freedom into focus with Turkey and the Western Balkans. Our good efforts to build bridges of civilizations with Turkey by way of EU accession negotiations ended up with a train wreck due to overwhelming scepticism in both Europe and Turkey. The work for stabilization in the Western Balkans was more consequential and rewarding. Croatia joined the EU in 2013. Serbia is on a European track. So are Albania and Macedonia. Kosovo got its independence and moves on. The border dispute on Piran Bay between Croatia and Slovenia was solved, at least to the extent that it did not become an obstacle to overall stabilization and progress in the region. Bosnia-Herzegovina has not become a functional federation, but has maintained peace. On war crimes, there has been justice and reconciliation. It was a long battle, together with ICTY Chief Prosecutor Carla Del Ponte and many EU member states, to get the war criminals Ratko Mladic, Radovan Karadzic and others to face justice. It is pivotal for the EU to hold on to its core values and work with the Western Balkan people to help them stay on a European and not illiberal path.

A Personal Stress Test

The Eurozone debt crisis also turned out to be a personal stress test for everyone who spent many years in its epicentre. That's how the former US Treasury Secretary Tim Geithner describes his experience during the global financial crisis in the US financial fire brigade in his memoirs *Stress test* (2014).[6]

I have never shied away from demanding professional challenges, as long as they are meaningful. But I have to admit there were moments during the crisis when we felt that the oxygen was running out and we couldn't get our heads back above the water. There was a killer pattern: always when we thought we had made it and turned the tide, new obstacles rolled over that felt even more insurmountable than previous ones. Another rock-bottom— again and again, for years and years.

This I did frankly not know or could not possibly think of as I had a rendezvous with President Jose Manuel Barroso at the end of October 2009, when he was finishing the distribution of portfolios for his second-term Commission for 2010–14.

Having worked intensively with Barroso as Enlargement Commissioner in 2004–9, we had built a very close working relationship, based on mutual trust. Thus, I went to the meeting confident that I would be assigned a meaningful portfolio policy-wise, while I could only guess but not really know what would be his final offer for me. Following my foreign policy work in South-Eastern Europe under the enlargement portfolio, I had been appointed by the Finnish Government and the Alliance of

Liberals and Democrats in Europe (ALDE) as their candidate for the newly created double-hatted post of "EU foreign minister", but by early February 2010 Baroness Ashton had already been appointed for that post, so it was no longer on offer.

After our usual football small-talk, Barroso went straight to business: "We have worked very closely and well together over the past five years. Now, I want to ask you to take responsibility for economic and monetary affairs after Joaquin Almunia, who will move to competition. Yours will be a key portfolio in the coming five years".

It was not a total surprise for me, as I had been substituting for Joaquin Almunia occasionally in the European Parliament when he was on missions. I had also been active since the "Minsky moment" in 2007–8 in the Commission's internal debates to advocate a forceful fiscal and monetary stimulus to support the economy in the form of a European Economic Recovery Plan, which succeeded.

So I felt both joy and burden. Joy, as I had an educational and professional background in the field of international political economy—the subject that is also my lifelong passion. Burden, as I knew we were still living through the global financial crisis and I sensed that something really toxic was brewing in the Eurozone macroeconomic imbalances. I took a deep breath, thought for a second and thanked Barroso for his confidence and promised to devote all my energy and experience to this portfolio: "Appreciated. It will be a tough job but a meaningful mission".

Before we finished, Barroso asked, out of curiosity, what portfolio I had expected he would propose for me. We had become close friends and confidants over the previous years, which was reinforced by both of us seeing the Community method as the best way of pursuing European integration. So I felt no particular need to hold back my thoughts and intuition and said: "I feared you'd propose me the administration. I expected trade policy. I wished for economic and monetary affairs". Barroso had a good laugh and wished me success in my new duties.

After the meeting, I walked through the President's 13th floor in the Berlaymont to take the lift back to my office on the 10th floor. On the way, I remember thinking about the huge economic challenges we faced and what kind of policies it would take to overcome them. Somehow I recalled the maxim which I associated with the great Argentinian writer Jorge Luis Borges: "For a gentleman, only impossible missions are attractive enough".[7] I've never had a gentleman syndrome nor considered myself one in the first place (don't blame Oxford for that!), but I always thought there was something fundamentally tempting in this aphorism.

Somehow we kept on walking the highwire, with both patience and a sense of direction—economically and politically, and even personally. In the light of today, while halfway through 2019 and witnessing Europe's recovery on its seventh year but in an increasingly uncertain world, I feel we've made reasonable progress—but cannot rest on our laurels. Judge it for yourself in the coming chapters.

Notes

1. My last name could as well have been translated "Peripheral" or "Sideliner", as it was originally "Syrjäläinen" in Finnish, unless a Swedish officer in the eighteenth century failed to pronounce it and renamed one of my ancestors with a Swedish soldier name Rehn.
2. The name "Soppa" literally translates to "soup". The abbreviation in this context derives from the Finnish words "Pallokentän Sosiaalipalloilijat", est. 1990 ("The Social Footballers of the Football Stadium"). Its senior section is called FC Cremonese.
3. *Lunch with the FT*: Gary Lineker. 30 December 2016.
4. George Orwell, *Politics and the English Language*. Penguin, 2013 (originally 1945).
5. Olli Rehn, Työllisyyden, rahan ja integraatio yleinen teoria: Euroopan rahaliitto ja Suomi. In Petri Lempiäinen (ed.), *Suomen ulkosuhteet 1990-luvun Euroopassa* (Finnish external relations in the 1990s Europe). Edita 1993. Revised version in Olli Rehn, *Pieni valtio Euroopan unionissa* (Small State in the European Union). Kirjayhtymä, 1996.
6. Timothy F. Geithner, *Stress Test: Reflections on Financial Crises*. Crown Publishers, New York, 2014.
7. I must admit remembering the saying incorrectly at that spontaneous moment. The correct quote is "A gentleman is interested in lost causes only", which obviously has a somewhat different twist. Thanks to my daughter Silva for correcting this—well, that should be expected, as Jorge Luis Borges is one of her favourite authors.

Part II

Managing the Crisis

3

Fire Brigade to Athens

My very first day in office as European Commissioner for Economic and Monetary Affairs, 10 February 2010, started with Greece. Jean-Claude Juncker, then president of the Eurogroup, joined me in the mid-morning to lead a conference call of Eurozone finance ministers from my office in Berlaymont, the headquarters of the European Commission. We had long ago agreed that the first substantial Eurogroup discussion on Greece should take place immediately when the new Barroso II Commission could formally start working. It was a friendly encounter between us two and our teams in my Berlaymont office. By contrast, the Eurogroup conference call was a very serious and intensive negotiation of 16 finance ministers over the phone lines.

Juncker is a sharp and witty human being with a big heart and strong social conscience, and firmly committed to Europe. I share his fundamental but realistic conviction on Europe as well as his taste for witty humour, even though I must admit he is the master and I am still an apprentice. So it is no wonder that we started to work well together straight from the beginning of the crisis and my term in office, which was indeed necessary, as we were to face tough times together.

The economic mood in Europe—which we were obviously very concerned about—was in those days very nervous, fragile and turbulent. Greece was in a free fall, as a consequence of her past fiscal irresponsibility and statistical fraud that had begun to surface to public awareness. Financial stability of the whole Eurozone was soon seen in danger, as the Greek bush fire threatened to turn into a European forest fire, with damaging ramifications

© The Author(s) 2020
O. Rehn, *Walking the Highwire*, https://doi.org/10.1007/978-3-030-34592-1_3

to the nascent recovery and weakened employment—and there was no existing fire brigade, nor fire extinguishers. Even worse, we had just experienced the most severe global financial crisis since the 1930s, which had badly damaged growth and jobs and led to an increase in fiscal deficits and public debt. All, or almost all, European economies were vulnerable.

It is worth recalling what was the rather triumphant stance and tone of the European Council, the EU's highest decision-making body of the national leaders, in Feira, Portugal, in June 2000, when Greece was accepted to the Eurozone:

> The European Council congratulates Greece on the convergence achieved over recent years, based on sound economic and financial policies, and welcomes the decision that Greece will join the Euro area on 1 January 2001 which constitutes an additional positive step in the monetary integration of the Union.

Now the mood among the other Europeans was indeed very different. In the conference call, my first and foremost objective was to convince the Eurozone member states that the situation was extremely serious and required a decisive response by the Eurogroup. I had had "enough" time to prepare for the endeavour, because the Barroso II Commission started its work in office seven months [sic!] after the European elections, effectively four months later than expected. The reason was that the European Parliament delayed the vote on the Commission President from July to September, and then some Commissioners-designate did not pass the parliament's hearings and had to be replaced by another person of the same nationality.

The only upside of all this exaggerated and unnecessary political drama was that I indeed had time to dwell deep into the new portfolio responsibility, spending my Christmas holidays 2009–10 thinking about policy options and getting ready for my parliamentary hearing, as well as shadowing my predecessor Joaquin Almunia from November 2009 until the start of the Barroso II Commission on 10 February 2010. The dramatic unfolding and rapid progression, or regression, of the Greek fiscal crisis overshadowed and dominated the preparatory phase.

At that stage, various policy options were considered to deal with the Greek crisis. Of course, we didn't know exactly the scale of the challenge, not least since the Greek accounts were totally unreliable due to the statistical fraud that had started to come into open. But we knew enough to understand that the situation was extremely serious for Greece and for the Eurozone, and the incoming information from the statistical clean-up only increased our degree of concern.

One option to avoid a default of Greece that was considered was a bridge loan without additional outside policy conditionality (at least no more than the normal EU economic surveillance). However, this was soon and understandably turned down by some of the member states in the core ad hoc crisis group, which was composed mainly of the G7/G20 members of the Eurozone and representatives of the Commission and the Eurogroup.

At the other end of the spectrum stood the option of debt restructuring, or the "Voldemort" option whose name should not be pronounced. At the time and in that context of the substantial risk of financial contagion, this was considered too risky because of the vulnerability of other Eurozone member states to the likely or in fact practically certain contagion effect that this option would create, especially without any convincing and credible financial firewall or lender of last resort.

The de facto rejection (at that stage) of both the "softest" and the "hardest" options thus left the option of IMF-style conditional financial assistance programme to the table as the least unrealistic solution to the Greek rescue. We knew then that there would be several obstacles on the road, such as the so-called no-bailout rule of the EU Treaty which stipulates that "The Union shall not be liable for or assume the commitments of central governments, regional, local or other public authorities, other bodies governed by public law, or public undertakings of any Member State, without prejudice to mutual financial guarantees for the joint execution of a specific project". Nevertheless, this was the option we geared the Commission's preparations, and the same mood seemed to gain ground in key member states. We knew that no perfect solution was at our disposal.

As was to be the case in most of the important decisions during the crisis, there was little time to spare. Herman van Rompuy, former Belgian prime minister and now president of the European Council, a reflective economist and shrewd negotiator who over the crisis years played an important role in getting Europe's act together, had called the Eurozone Summit for the next day, Friday 11 February. Any decisive response would require the creation of some sort of a stability fund or at least a bridge loan for Greece to contain the financial bush fire. This was supposed to be combined with rigorous action to stabilize the public finances by the Greek government and with the supervision of European and possibly international creditors. This was the immediate challenge and it was related to Greece. But the Commission did not hide its view that the crisis was considered systemic and that the fundamental weaknesses of the Eurozone were structural, and thus the policy agenda should also include the creation of a permanent financial firewall and enhanced economic policy coordination within the Eurozone.

Who were then members of the unofficial financial "fire brigade" that was set up in early 2010? It was a combination of leaders from the EU member states and European institutions, as well as key officials of the IMF.

Starting with member states, the German Chancellor Angela Merkel and Finance Minister Wolfgang Schäuble had to assume leadership roles. Other key members in this fire brigade included people from all Eurozone countries, ministers and their staff, from the smallest to the largest. Besides Germany, obviously France as a founding partner of the euro had a particularly crucial role, which was illustrated by the active stance of President Nicolas Sarkozy and Finance Minister Christine Lagarde, as chairpersons of the EU and the G20 during the first years of the crisis in 2010–11. The inauguration of Mario Monti and François Hollande at the helm of Italy and France, respectively, brought about a new kind of dynamics in crisis management, where the German–French duo was replaced by a more multipolar model—for better or worse—and where the role of Germany as the economic *primus inter pares* was increasingly central to the financial rescue operations.

The roster of the fire brigade also included representatives of the EU institutions, such as the European Commission, the Eurogroup, the European Council and of course the European Central Bank, as well as their competent staff committed to and working hard for saving the Euro. In the Commission, President Jose Manuel Barroso was intensively involved in crisis management, and I was his right-hand or left-hand man. His interface was the European Council and the principals, mine was the Eurogroup and finance ministers. The European Council, which has over the past decades increasingly taken the policy lead in the EU, in line with the principal-agent method, convened in the format of the Euro Area Summit close to twenty times during the crisis years. In addition, the fire brigade made use of the IMF, International Monetary Fund, as its consultant and second (sometimes first!) fire engine. The European Parliament functioned as the democratic interface essential for gaining EU-wide support for our actions, although it has been said that it was "frustrated when EU crisis management takes place outside its reach".[1] The national parliaments carried their democratic and budgetary responsibilities with rigour—sometimes with such rigour that tied the hands of the fire brigade too tightly at critical moments.

The Greek Tragedy: Lost Competitiveness and Statistical Fraud

The simple but basic issue in the case of Greece was living above one's means, both generally in the economy and especially in the realm of public finances. Year after year, Greece kept spending more than it earned. Greece's current account deficit had reached the staggering 15% of GDP in 2008. The fiscal deficit was exploding. Upon taking office as prime minister, George Papandreou stated that the Greek fiscal deficit was at least double compared to the 6% pursued at the time (previously, the goal had been 3.7% of GDP for the fiscal year 2009). Ultimately, the deficit turned out to be—for many unbelievable—15.4% of GDP, which became clear only later on when the national accounts were revised, completed, verified and validated by Eurostat.

Once Papandreou brought this fact in October 2009 to the cold light of day, revealing the systematic falsification of statistics, investors woke up to the risk attached to the sovereign bonds of the Eurozone's peripheral countries, which risk, according to the universally accepted dogma, "was not supposed to exist". The revelations had also another effect, as Martin Sandbu points out: "Papandreou and his ministers took the opportunity to air the state's financial and dirty laundry while they could still blame their predecessors for both the mismanagement and its cover-up. In their counterparts' eyes, however … these revelations strengthened the feeling that the Greeks could not be trusted, regardless of the government at the helm".[2]

Papandreou's announcement caused a shock in the financial markets and stupefied political decision-makers. The yields on Greek sovereign bonds began to rise to unsustainable levels. In May 2010, the yield spread (or premium) on 10-year bonds versus Germany was bordering on a record-high 1000 basis points or 10%; i.e. the market yields on Greek sovereign debt rose to over 10 percentage points above the interest rates paid by Germany. This is an unbearably high price for sovereign borrowing, and Greece would no longer have been able to finance its public expenditures at that interest rate level. Therefore, investors considered Greece to be de facto in default, and the country's government did not have many options: Greece had its back against the wall in financial terms. Greece was facing either a default, or the presumably politically humiliating fact of resorting to international loan funding from the EU and/or the IMF.

The contagion effect was soon also felt in the other vulnerable countries: in addition to Greece, Portugal and Spain also saw their credit ratings downgraded in March–April. The crisis was widening and deepening with accelerating speed.

A member state of the Eurozone facing a potential default would have dramatic effects to the Maastricht construction of the economic and monetary union. Namely, there was no crisis management mechanism foreseen in the Maastricht Treaty that established the EMU in 1992. From the start of my preparations to take office, this was an issue in our internal discussions in the Commission. I recall one preparatory meeting on 14 December 2009 when one of my senior officials said that Greece may force the EU to "call off the Maastricht bluff" of no bailout option. In the same meeting, it was decided to intensify our internal reflection in the Commission on the use of Article 122 of the EU Treaty as basis of rescue operations. The second paragraph of Article 122 states: "Where a Member State is in difficulties or is seriously threatened with severe difficulties caused by natural disasters or exceptional occurrences beyond its control, the Council, on a proposal from the Commission, may grant, under certain conditions, Union financial assistance to the Member State concerned". We thought a case could be made that Greece was now in "severe difficulties caused by exceptional occurrences beyond its control"—it was considered fair to say that an external event, the global financial crisis, had created exceptional occurrences, even if domestic reasons were undeniable.

Moreover, in the same meeting on 14 December 2009 we came to the tentative conclusion that the design of the future Eurozone stability mechanism (which in our firm view there was to be) could be similar to the balance of payments (BoP) facility, which was an EU budget fund with a solid legal base that could be used for non-Eurozone members of the EU, and was or had indeed been used for Hungary, Latvia and Romania. It was based on funding from the EU budget, or rather the budgetary framework, as it would have used the funding space under the own resources ceiling but outside the then approved budget (which was lower than the ceiling). I instructed preparations to the effect. This decision to prepare ground for a stability mechanism had far-reaching consequences and turned out to be most useful on the weekend of 7–10 May 2010, when the EFSM/EFSF was conceived.

Even in Greece, the economic crisis was not only due to the problems in public finances, but due to the intertwined loss of price competitiveness. I want to underline the "intertwined", because the continuous ballooning of the public sector and its rise into wage leadership raised wage costs to comparatively high levels and crumbled the price competitiveness of the private sector, particularly the export sector, which had remained too small. This became apparent when comparing the development of unit labour costs in

Greece and Germany during the initial phases of the euro: in 2000–8, the unit labour costs in Greece increased by 18% while Germany's unit labour costs *decreased* by 13% compared to the euro area average. In other words, the debt crisis of the Greek public economy was preceded by a collapse in the competitiveness of the country's national economy: labour costs had spun out of control and were the main cause for a massive macroeconomic imbalance, which was reflected in the country's considerable trade and current account deficits.

Financial crises typically have a turning point, where growth peaks and the decline—or nosedive—begins. The euro area debt crisis was brewing in the accumulated imbalances, but it was sparked when the Greek fiscal deficit spun out of control. Much in the same way as subprime housing loans triggered the financial crisis in the United States. In the words of British economist Roger Bootle, "Attributing the disaster of 2007/9 to subprime is rather like saying that the first World War was caused by the assassination of Archduke Franz Ferdinand in Sarajevo in 1914. Given the state of the financial system, if the subprime crisis hadn't happened, something else would have".[3] Be that as it may, the disclosure of the Greek budget deficit in October 2009 was this kind of a tipping point, which triggered the debt crisis that had been building up for quite some time in the euro area.

Underlying the increasing indebtedness of the Greek public economy was the reckless expansion of the public sector, which had continued since the 1980s. Furthermore, Greece had falsified its statistics, first to gain membership in the euro in 2001, and subsequently, to avoid pressures by other Eurozone countries and the Commission to balance its economy and public finances before being accepted to the euro. At the outset of the Greek crisis, I was shocked to hear in a meeting from a previous finance minister who had been sitting in the table in the Ecofin Council in 2000 where Greece was welcomed to the Eurozone that "all of us around the Ecofin table certainly knew Greece did not meet the EMU criteria, but we nevertheless made a unanimous decision to accept Greece as a member".

At that time, Eurostat, or the European Statistical Agency in Luxembourg, had no authority to audit accounts in the member states. The Commission had actually proposed this in 2005, but the proposal was rejected by the member states in the Council. Hence, the operation of the EMU with respect to the monitoring of public finances was based on trust, not control—that is, trust in the member states to declare their own budgetary deficits and debt levels accurately and reliably. That did not quite work out, as we have witnessed. The system functioned as well or badly as would function a football team whose head coach doubled as the referee of the match!

When I learned out about these quandaries, I started working to reinforce Eurostat's audit authority and committed to this endeavour in the hearing at the European Parliament at the beginning of January 2010. When Barroso's second Commission finally took office in February 2010, its very first legislative proposal in its very first formal meeting was indeed the proposal to provide auditing powers to Eurostat. This time the Council and the Parliament processed the proposal quickly, so the new powers entered into force in August 2010.

In September 2010, Eurostat's auditors delved into the Greek national accounts and began to reform its statistical institution Elstat. For the following year's assessment, Eurostat verified the reliability of the operations of the Greek Statistical Authority and the accuracy of its statistics. Presently, Greece's statistics should be as reliable as those in any normal member state, and Eurostat normally validates them without reservations. In the light of these achievements, it is very difficult to comprehend the accusations against the post-2009 chief of Elstat, Andreas Georgiou. He did what any honest civil servant should do and certainly should not have been prosecuted but commended for his actions.

A Moving Train Heading for a Collision

Greece's predicament worsened rapidly over the winter 2009–10, and the free fall continued in February–March 2010. The situation was not helped by the fact that the Commission did not have a mandate to work.

After twists and turns lasting for several months, President José Manuel Barroso's second Commission finally got the European Parliament's approval on 9 February 2010. We held the Commission's first unofficial meeting in the evening—the official inauguration would not be until the following day—and had a low-profile group dinner in Strasbourg. Neither the delay in the approval of the Commission in the parliament nor the serious economic circumstances gave grounds to a very festive event. Barroso made a speech that was peppered with humour but was serious in terms of content. Tackling the debt crisis that was then emerging and becoming overwhelming was on top of the new Commission's agenda.

On the following morning on 10 February 2010, I took an early bird flight from Strasbourg to Brussels and, as previously explained, prepared for my first Eurogroup teleconference, where I would also make my first appearance as a Commission representative to the finance ministers. This was not going to be a soft landing to a new job on the very first day.

The teleconference produced an analytical but critical and tough debate on the situation in Greece. Besides Juncker and Jean-Claude Trichet, president of the ECB, on substantive policy issues the discussion was steered by Christine Lagarde, finance minister of France. Wolfgang Schäuble of Germany was playing libero.

After its bond yields, or interest rates, had gone sky-high, Greece was expected to balance its economy rapidly. In addition, any funding programme would be strictly conditional. This would be carried out in accordance with Article 136 of the Treaty, according to which decisions concerning economic policy are to be made by the Council among the Eurozone countries by a qualified majority, without participation by the country subject to the measures (in this case, Greece). The ministers also emphasized their preparedness in general to take other common determined actions to safeguard financial stability.

So we prepared a draft statement for the Eurozone Summit, which was held on the following day 11 February 2010 and which voiced its unanimous support to the Greek stabilization measures that had been decided recently. At the same time, the heads of euro area member states, led by Chancellor Merkel and President Sarkozy, reassured they would do "whatever it takes" to safeguard financial stability. This phrase was to be repeated time and again in the course of the crisis. It took quite some time and some "big bazookas" before the markets believed us.

First Mission to Berlin

In some leaked recordings at the possession of the Financial Times that were made when preparing his crisis memoirs, *Stress Test*, the former US Treasury Secretary Tim Geithner has (supposedly) described the attitudes of the European participants in the G-7 meeting in Iqaluit, Canada, just south of the Arctic Circle, in early February by saying that "the Europeans wanted to crush Greece". I cannot have any personal memory of that meeting, as I was not present (the Commission was represented by Joaquin Almunia). But I recall well the subsequent period when the rescue operation was started. While there was certainly plenty of criticism and mental agony over Greek profligacy, nobody certainly "wanted to crush Greece"—claiming that is absurd. In reality, the European Commission did precisely the opposite: we wanted to convince the reluctant member states on the merits of rescuing Greece. Likewise we needed to convince the Greek government and political class of the merits of requesting a financial assistance package rather sooner than later. The Greeks were afraid of opening their books and facing policy conditions, while the other member states were concerned about the moral hazard and turning Greece into a bottomless pit where one would have to throw new money after the old, over and over again.

But the critical thing was to get Berlin's support for a financial rescue operation of Greece. That's why I wanted to go there for a mission immediately once I had taken office. As Enlargement Commissioner in 2004–9, I had made regular missions to the Chancellery and the Ministry of Foreign Affairs in Berlin, and I wanted to continue the productive practice of talking with the Germans well in advance. The mission in February 2010 turned out to be most useful—more on it below.

Personally, however, I had some mixed feelings. Over the winter, I had physically managed one portfolio, enlargement, and mentally prepared for another, economic and monetary affairs. I had been preparing for my new position and the forthcoming parliamentary hearing at the end of December 2009 and beginning of January 2010 so intensely that my Christmas holiday was cut to invisible. So I had imagined that I had earned a few days of skiing holiday in February during the European School's holiday week, which tended to shape our family's common schedule.

Thus on Thursday 17 February, I was spending the first day of my short skiing holiday in Mikkeli with my family, when I received a call from Christoph Heusgen, my former colleague from Brussels, now acting as foreign policy advisor for Chancellor Merkel: "The crisis is escalating. We are considering our options. Would you have the time to stop by Berlin any time soon?" Our family was planning to stay in the wintery scene and ski tracks of Southern Savonia until Sunday, so I asked, if the coming Monday or Tuesday would be alright. "Can't you make it this week, say Friday? We have a situation". What can you say to that? Well, I knew we have a "situation"! So I promised to arrange myself somehow to Berlin for Friday, next day.

The purpose was for me to meet some of the leading officials of the Chancellery and Ministry of Finance under the radar screen, without any publicity. This way we could brace ourselves entirely for the measures required for containing the crisis and prepare the decisions to be made. Previously, there had been unwanted tensions between Germany and the Commission, but this time we could not afford them—smooth co-operation would be needed.

I instantly organized a small team from the Commission to Berlin, so that we could talk things through at once with the Germans, to the extent possible. I was joined by Antonio Cabral, President Barroso's economic advisor, Servaas Deroose, the Deputy Director General of DG Economic and Financial Affairs, and Stéphanie Riso, the Deputy Head of my Cabinet. This was a strong team, with both experience and fresh power. Servaas Deroose did subsequently lead the preparation of many programmes under difficult circumstances from Greece to Spain. Antonio Cabral is a long-time economist and trusted economic policy advisor to President Barroso. Stéphanie Riso, now with Barnier in the Brexit tream, is a one-person brainstorm and a gutsy Frenchwoman, who was named *La Combattante*, The Fighter, by Jean-Claude Trichet after one particularly tight Eurogroup meeting. Quite accurate.

The mission proved very useful. In the meetings with Uwe Corsepius, Director of EU affairs at the Federal Chancellery, and Jörg Asmussen, secretary of state, we developed a plan combining the results of preparations made by the German administration and the Commission. I also had a very productive Saturday morning meeting with Jens Weidmann, then economic policy advisor of Chancellor Merkel who was later on appointed president of the Bundesbank.

The Germans gave reassurance of their commitment to the euro and readiness for actions required to salvage it. In return, the foundations of the economic and monetary union would have to be reformed in the spirit of the German stability culture. Many of the decisions subsequently made by the Eurozone, such as the comprehensive reform of EMU economic governance, the conditionality of the Greek programme and the lightening of its debt burden, IMF's participation in the Greek programme, and the establishment of a stability fund for the euro area, were discussed already in these meetings. We agreed on many issues, not all of them.

Befitting the nature of the crisis, the journey involved all kinds of mishaps. I intended to complete the visit as a one-day trip on Friday. However, as all the airplanes in the Central European sky—apart from the winter-resourced Helsinki airport—were delayed due to the tough winter conditions, I had to reroute via Munich, and I did not arrive in Berlin until late Friday evening. Some of the meetings were rescheduled to Saturday morning. When I returned to Mikkeli to pick up my family on Saturday evening, a proper wood-heated sauna felt super-sweet after three days of travel. I was feeling wistful as I had to steer my car towards the Helsinki-Vantaa airport already around noon on Sunday. Back to the firemen's boot camp in Brussels!

Fire Brigade on a Reconnaissance Mission to Athens

Next, ten days on, I was off on a mission to Greece. It was planned carefully with the ECB. I had originally planned to go there alone with my own Commission team, but that didn't work out.

A few days before my departure, the ECB President Jean-Claude Trichet insisted that the ECB should be part of the mission. As I was talking with him over the phone from the corridors of the new Commission's kick-off seminar somewhere in the Belgian countryside, I received a hairdryer talk à la Sir Alex Ferguson from him over the phone line. I ensured that my voice was likewise very clearly heard and stated that I am ready to take an ECB representative along, on the condition that Trichet makes it clear to his representative that I am the leader of the delegation and will steer the work on the ground—I had my suspicions. That was agreed, but Trichet said the ECB had reservations on precise measures—no prob. Next we agreed that we'd use the formula "the European Commission in liaison with the ECB".

Soon we were however told that, by the member states' demand, a representative of the International Monetary Fund, IMF, would insist to join the delegation. Well why not. Thus, the formula had to be expanded "The European Commission in liaison with the ECB and together with the IMF". The Troika was born.

We left for Athens on the evening of Sunday 28 February 2010. At that stage, there were still confusing messages as regards the IMF participation. On Sunday morning Barroso called me to express his support for the mission and the method: "The participation of the ECB and IMF is OK, but you lead". Late afternoon he called again, as I was already at the airport. He had talked with Chancellor Merkel, who was very worried that the German Constitutional Court might oppose a financial assistance programme on the grounds that it would amount to monetary financing of a euro area member state and thus break the "no-bailout clause" of the EU Treaty.

Still, Merkel was willing to contribute financially, "but it would be very difficult". At that stage, I got the impression that the Chancellor was more leaning towards a Community instrument, or at least a coordinated instrument, since it would most probably avoid the constitutional problems related to bilateral loans.

The first actual working day was Monday the 1st of March. First, we had a long talk with the finance minister, George Papaconstantinou, who was in charge of the reform programme of the public economy and communication with the team of the three institutions consisting of the Commission, the ECB and the IMF, which was soon labelled as the "Troika", like it or not—I don't, but the name regrettably stuck, and will be used in this book when necessary and for the sake of clarity to the reader.

George Papaconstantinou is a very capable economist with a Ph.D. from the London School of Economics and an effective operator, who took great pains to ensure Greece's survival in difficult conditions. I also met other ministers and George Provopoulos, the central bank governor. Towards the evening, I had a tête-à-tête with Prime Minister George Papandreou, whom I knew well from previous political contexts, mainly concerning the stabilization of the Balkan region. Papandreou was the chairman of the Socialist International who admires Nordic social democracy and is a devout proponent of international co-operation and European integration.

I got a good impression of the resoluteness of the Greek government, and this view was shared by Jürgen Stark, member of the ECB's executive board and Poul Thomsen, Director of the IMF. Over the following days, the Greek government committed to making decisions on new measures to reduce the budgetary deficit. Greece had only in January 2010 presented a plan to reduce the budget deficit from 13% to below 9%. Since then, economic developments had been worse than expected, market reactions strong and tax revenues lower than anticipated. Therefore, Greece was preparing for further measures to cut the deficit, which meant that the impact would be felt by most Greeks. We knew the task would be extremely hard, considering the social tensions in Greece and the threat of disorder.

We got a taste of the political and social tensions in Athens while negotiating in Papaconstantinou's office. The meeting had to be suspended due to the very loud noise from the demonstrations. You could not hear what the other party in the room was saying. At least no one can complain that we wouldn't have heard the voice of the streets! But we had to move elsewhere to continue working.

In the run-up to our trip to Athens, tensions had increased, particularly between Germany and Greece. Jürgen Stark had made some strong comments about Greece's finances, while Theodoros Pangalos, the deputy prime minister, also famous or rather infamous from Finland's EU accession negotiations, had demanded Germany to compensate for the costs of the German occupation in 1941. The atmosphere was charged with tension. Our trip was to be rounded off by a lunch among our delegation and Pangalos. I was waiting for it somewhat anxiously, but the lunch in fact proceeded in agreeable and even humorous terms. It was the policy issues and public statements that did the arguing, rather than the people—these were all professionals and acted accordingly.

But in the public debate, political tensions across the euro area were heating up, particularly between the Germans and the Greeks. The air was dense with accusations of the "lazy Greeks" and "stingy Germans"—or "frugal Finns". The crisis was beginning to mentally and politically divide Europe.

Preparations for supporting Greece through a conditional financial programme continued undercover, although this had to be denied in public. Together with the member states' representatives, the Commission was preparing a European stability fund that would enable the provision of coordinated support, if it was requested and deemed necessary.

The ECB played a central role in the preparations, in line with the above-mentioned Troika formula "the Commission in liaison with the ECB…" that President Jean-Claude Trichet used to cite amicably. The ECB was of course needed firmly on board, both because of its formidable expertise in the banking and financial matters and because of its sole powers to authorize a national central bank—here the Greek central bank—to provide the liquidity lifeline for the Greek banking system through the Emergency Liquidity Assistance (ELA). The latter issue came to play an increasingly important role when the debt restructuring was contemplated in 2011–12 and in the rock-bottoms of the Greek crisis in 2012 and 2015.

Early March, German Finance Minister Wolfgang Schäuble made a proposal to create a European Monetary Fund. It had been prepared for a long time in the German administration, the Ministry of Finance in particular. The economists Daniel Gros and Thomas Mayer had published a policy paper on the creation of an EMF in early 2010.[4] Schäuble used to be a trusted advisor to the "Unification Chancellor" Helmut Kohl, and a longtime European big-league player, who was the other author of the Lamers-Schäuble paper outlining the "core Europe" in 1994. Now he was paving its foundations. Especially when the German media was firing the questions, I gave broadly constructive comments on Schäuble's proposal. The EMF would be of assistance, also in the preventive sense in future, even if its effectiveness depended on the concrete details. To be sure, I underlined that only the Community method could provide decisions that are simultaneously de facto effective and legitimate to the citizens.

Now the German approach was getting more clarity. Schäuble was still firmly against IMF funding, and his proposal on the EMF should be seen in that light, as an alternative to the IMF. On the other hand, and also for the real or supposed constitutional reasons, the model should be coordinated bilateral assistance. Hence, our first-best or Community instrument would face an uphill struggle.

At the Eurogroup meeting on 15 March, I reported on the situation in Greece based on our visit and presented the work done to prepare for a loan or stabilization mechanism. I explained that finance granted through the mechanism could be implemented in two ways: either (1) by loans guaranteed jointly by the euro area or (2) bilateral loans between Eurozone countries implemented in a coordinated way. I said the Commission considered the first alternative to be the better and more convincing one. But I added that in the context we were in, the main thing was to reach an agreement, so we were receptive to either one.

In a press conference in the evening, I stressed that in addition to the inevitable crisis management measures we had to look further. The Greek crisis and its management had shown that there was an urgent need for closer coordination of economic policy within the euro area. This need had already in principle—though not in practice—been acknowledged, and its legal basis was created in the Treaty of Lisbon. The Commission would prepare legislative proposals on the matter based on Article 136 determining the economic policy for the euro area.

I said I was striving for the Commission to be able to make a proposal on reinforcing the Eurozone economic governance by mid-April. As it turned out, we did not quite make this schedule, since many issues got more complicated down the line and messed up our clear plans.

But in May, after intensive debates in the Commission, we came up with an initiative and presented a communication that set the terms of debate in the reform of Eurozone economic governance and later became the basis for discussion of a working group led by Herman van Rompuy and the legislative package approved subsequently by the Council and the Parliament. This package is known by the nickname "six-pack", and it finally entered into force in December 2011.

Greece Drifts Towards an EU-IMF Stabilization Programme

In March and April, the situation in Greece became even more critical. However, to our astonishment among the Commission and Eurogroup officials, the Greek government was not yet ready to ask for financial support, since it wanted to retain the largest possible leeway and was afraid for its own sovereignty, or authority. At the same time, other Eurozone countries had their own political problems. Many important regional *Land* elections were being held in Germany over the spring. Looking back, it is clear that Greece should have been encouraged to enter an adjustment programme earlier, before the crisis had escalated and spread through the contamination effect over the entire euro area.

I asked Marco Buti, the Ecofin Director General, to call me after the Euro Working Group meeting on 8 April 2010 at 19h and give his sounding. His view was blunt: "It's now the moment for Greece to make a request; things are getting from bad to worse". I certainly agreed and said I would talk to Papaconstantinou still the same evening on the matter. Later on that evening I called Papaconstantinou and said that looking at the rapid deterioration of the situation—with the deposit withdrawals increasing by the hour—my responsibility as Commissioner for Economic Affairs was to pose the question, "should you not submit your request for financial assistance from the EU right now?". He answered: "We must know if we get the money. Otherwise we are in the worst of all worlds. I keep getting phone calls from the IMF if we were ready to move to a precautionary mechanism – need more details on that". So there was no movement by the Greeks yet, much to my regret. We agreed nevertheless to talk again the next day to judge the situation in the light of both markets and politics, especially the EWG soundings.

I said to Stephanie Riso afterwards, "My hunch tells me that the Greeks and the Germans must have agreed behind our back: no request before 10 May [= the date of the next regional elections in Germany, North-Rein-Westphalia, editor's note], after that OK". In case I was wrong, which may be the case, I have to apologize to both sides. But it is always better to be even over-anxious than be outright fooled.

Anyway, the work towards a financial assistance programme continued under the radar screen. The EWG had already pretty much agreed the pricing and other elements for a loan agreement. Germany was very cooperative. In my phone call with Dominique Strauss-Kahn, it was confirmed that the IMF was promoting a precautionary arrangement, which was either a pursuit to enter into the European territory or—more astutely—an effort to pressure the Europeans to agree on a deal.

While private entrepreneurship continued in some quarters, that day it became clear that any deal on Greece would be on a single and fully fledged joint programme. "Single and fully-fledged" meant that it would cover structural reforms, fiscal policies and the financial repair. "Joint" meant it would be indeed a joint effort of Eurogroup (= the Eurozone member states), the Commission, the ECB and the IMF.

In the so-called inofficial meeting of the Ecofin Council in Madrid in mid-April, the debate was overshadowed by disagreements on the future course of action, and especially heated up when the Eurogroup discussed Greece and the strengthening of economic policy coordination within the euro area.

Our meeting was also overshadowed by very concrete natural clouds—there was a cloud of volcanic ash emanating from Iceland. It prevented our return flight, so we rented a minivan with Stephanie Riso and drove it through Spain and the Basque country all the way to Bordeaux where we rested. In the morning, we took a train to Paris to meet Christine Lagarde at Bercy and from there onwards to Brussels. The whole "interrail mission" to Madrid took six days.

During the trip to Madrid, I could again go and see Pablo Picasso's most impressive work, *Guernica*, which made me reflect on various European destinies in the past and the present times—Guernica tells an artistic story of a village in the Basque country bombed to the ground by the Nazi German and fascist Italian air forces during the Spanish Civil War. It is a tragic work of art, and a reminder of the heavy historical burden from the twentieth-century Europe. Today's democratic and deeply European Germany has broken with the past of those dark times.

Over the winter, there was some hope—or dream—in some quarters to provide bridge financing for Greece. However, due to the chronic fiscal deficit, there was no willingness in the creditor side to engage in such an exercise. Moreover, that was an obstacle for an outright debt restructuring, as well—certainly not the only obstacle. George Papaconstantinou, the Greek finance minister at that time, puts it well in his crisis memoirs: "Debt restructuring was strictly off-limits. For the Eurozone, giving debt relief to a member state running a 16% annual fiscal deficit would be to condone to fiscal excess; and doing so for a country which had lied about its statistics would add insult to injury".[5]

Greece ended up in a financial lock-out towards the end of April 2010. It happened during the IMF's spring meeting in Washington, where I was representing the Commission. George Papaconstantinou kept me—as always—up to date, and on Wednesday 21 April he told Greece was going to seek support already before the coming weekend. Of course, the formal request came in just as I was having my morning jog between 6–7 a.m. in Georgetown, which is a daily ritual for me during my trips to Washington. Mandeep Bains of my Cabinet was about to start running after me, but she kept her calm and preferred to wait at the hotel lobby for me to return from my jog at 7 a.m.

This also marked the moment when the IMF stepped decisively into the crisis management of the euro area. Initially, especially the strongest proponents of European integration had firmly opposed the participation of the IMF in the management of Eurozone affairs, but soon the heads of the member states aligned themselves to a different position. From the EU's perspective, co-operation with the IMF has been mostly beneficial due to its valuable expertise and credibility.

Early Bird Meeting in Washington: The Deal Is Sealed

Soon after Greece's request arrived, I proposed to schedule a meeting with IMF's Managing Director Dominique Strauss-Kahn on Saturday morning 24 April. We met at 7.00 a.m. sharp on Saturday in his office at the IMF headquarters. The meeting was naturally also attended by Jean-Claude Trichet and George Papaconstantinou. I cannot say "we had been waiting for that moment", since even the most realistic person somehow hopes for a last-minute miracle, but what I can say is that we had made careful preparations for the Greek request for assistance, and the roadmap had been fine-tuned over the preceding weeks.

In the meeting, we agreed on further steps to finalize the EU-IMF programme and particularly the fiscal policy objectives. We also reached a preliminary agreement on the sharing of the burden between the EU and the IMF, although I had already discussed that privately with Strauss-Kahn, based on the information we then had on what our principals, i.e. the member states of our respective institutions, would be ready to agree on. We were fully aware that Germany and France, along with the other Eurozone countries, would prefer the IMF to assume as large a share as possible. We strived for a deal where the IMF would account for roughly a third of the funding of the whole programme. It was limited by Greece's relatively small quota of 1 billion euros in the IMF's appropriations and the fact that the fund had previously never lent more than 10 times the quota.

DSK, as Dominique Strauss-Kahn is known, was on top of his game, as usual, and he delved into the core items of the potential Greek programme, such as the fiscal policy stance and the monitoring of reforms. He was thoroughly prepared to discuss Greece despite his heavy agenda and schedule as the IMF's managing director, which is especially fully booked during the spring and annual meetings of the Fund. DSK stressed that Greece's debt sustainability was a key condition for IMF funding, which was a concern shared by the rest of us. It indeed became one of the key issues and also controversies within the Greek programme over the following years.

The Saturday morning meeting in Washington marked the final stretch of deciding on the first Greek programme. After the negotiations had ended, the Eurogroup was summoned to Brussels on Sunday 2 May. It decided on an aid package comprising a total of 110 billion euros, which was linked to stringent conditions on the balancing of public finances and restoring the competitiveness of the Greek economy and its growth capacity through structural reforms. The euro area would account for 80 billion euros and the IMF for 30 billion of the funding. The funding by the euro area would be granted as bilateral loans, which was the second-best option, as an agreement was not reached on joint euro area loans.

Recalling the European Council's triumphalism on Greece joining the euro as expressed in the above-quoted Feira conclusions in June 2000, now ten years later in May 2010 there was a radically different tone in the Eurogroup statement:

> The Eurogroup Ministers concur with the Commission and the ECB that market access for Greece is not sufficient and that providing a loan is warranted to safeguard financial stability in the euro area as a whole. Following a request by the Greek authorities, euro area Ministers unanimously agreed today to activate stability support to Greece via bilateral loans centrally pooled by the European Commission under the conditions set out in April.

Contrasting Sentiments in Berlin and Athens

In the evening after the Greek deal had been struck and the press conference was over, I hurried to Brussels airport. Together with my advisor Dr. Vesa Vihriälä, I travelled to Berlin, where we arrived before midnight. On Monday morning in Berlin, I presented the deal to the executive committee of the SPD, *die Sozialdemokratische Partei Deutschlands*, then the leading opposition party in the Bundestag. I had been invited by the chairman of the SPD parliamentary group, former Foreign Minister Frank-Walter Steinmeier, who is today Germany's Federal President, to help gain support for the Greek package among his own ranks and peers in the SPD. I had learned to highly appreciate Steinmeier with whom we had worked closely together in enlargement policy and in the pacification of the Western Balkans. Although the SPD was in the opposition, it recalled its European convictions and did not look to weasel away from its European commitment.

We had a tough but fair discussion with the SPD's executive committee. In addition to Steinmeier, both Sigmar Gabriel, the party chairman, and Martin Schulz, the leader of the alliance of Socialists and Democrats in the European Parliament, were active in the debate. SPD, as the traditional beacon of European social democracy, wanted banks and bankers, in addition to taxpayers, to share the burden of funding the Greek debt programme through private sector involvement. This position was understandable, but I underlined to the SPD's leaders the concern that it might also speed up the contagion effect to other vulnerable member states, as investors would become wary of investing in their sovereign debt due to the risk of capital loss.

As a concrete demand for its support, the SPD insisted on making a push for a financial transaction tax. The SPD remained consistent on this issue and in June 2012 a financial transaction tax became a part of the mutual agreement between the German federal government and the SPD-led opposition in the context of the ratification of the EU's fiscal compact. Prior to that, in autumn 2011, the Commission had made a legislative proposal for implementing a financial transaction tax. It has not been approved, not to speak implemented, due to many practical implementation problems and active political opposition in its way.

Meanwhile in Athens, the post-1974 social and political consensus following the military junta's fall was about to unravel. The Greek Parliament was expected to vote on the bill endorsing the programme and the economic reforms and fiscal measures it included. Street demonstrations condemned the programme from the start, even before it was being voted, not to speak implemented. A very bad omen.

Even worse—and a major nasty surprise, at least for me—was that the conservative opposition party, *Nea Demokratia*, had decided to vote against the bill that endorsed the measures required for the rescue package. Nea Demokratia had itself been in power in the preceding years and was not quite innocent to the precarious fate of the Greek economy. But the new leader of Nea Demokratia, Antonis Samaras, didn't feel any need to build national consensus, which became a dramatic defect in the Greek programme. Bridges were burning all over. It is easy to agree with George Papaconstantinou who writes as follows: "Starting in that day and for the following two years, Greece became the only one of the bailout countries without cross-party support for the adjustment effort – and the country paid dearly for this populism".[6]

The bill passed in the Greek Parliament with 172 votes out of 300. Technically, it was enough. Politically—and perhaps mentally in the Greek society—we knew the big drama was only just brewing.

Notes

1. Luuk van Middelaar, *Alarums & Excursions: Improvising Politics on the European Stage*. Agenda, 2019, p. xv.
2. Martin Sandbu, *Europe's Orphan: The Future of the Euro and the Politics of Debt*. Princeton University Press, paperback edition, 2017, p. 53.
3. Johan van Overtveldt, *The End of the Euro: The Uneasy Future of the European Union*. Agate Publishing, 2011, p. 82.
4. Daniel Gros and Thomas Mayer, *How to Deal with Sovereign Default: Towards a European Monetary Fund*. CEPS Policy Brief 202, February 2010. See also Thomas Mayer, *Europe's Unfinished Currency: The Political Economics of the Euro*. Anthem Press, 2012.
5. George Papaconstantinou, *Game Over*. Papadopoulos Publishing, 2016, p. 126.
6. Papaconstantinou 2016, p. 138.

4

Big Bazooka by Night

The market forces are indeed a very unreliable ally. As President Bill Clinton's policy advisor James Carville put it in 1993, "I used to think if there was reincarnation, I wanted to come back as the President or the Pope or a .400 baseball hitter. But now I would like to come back as the bond market. You can intimidate everybody".

In spring 2010, the market forces were in a full intimidation mode, especially the bond market. After the Eurogroup's agreement on the conditional rescue package for Greece was finally reached on Sunday 2 May 2010, the market turbulence was expected to settle down, at least for a while. This is what indeed happened. But the timeline *for a while* just turned out to be *only one day*!

Monday was a reasonably calm day. But as early as Tuesday, market turbulence re-emerged and soon escalated to new heights. By mid-week, it was clear that we would be forced to hold a new crisis meeting as soon as possible to agree on additional measures to contain the turbulence. President of the European Council, Herman van Rompuy, called a Eurozone Summit for the following weekend.

The Eurozone Summit on Friday 7 May 2010 was originally supposed to focus on taking the final decision on the Greek rescue package. However, as the market turbulence got worse and worse during the week, its agenda transformed towards the establishment of a European stability fund. The Summit discussed the issue but failed to reach a concrete solution. Therefore, the heads of European governments threw the task to their finance ministers and to the Ecofin Council. The decision to hold an

© The Author(s) 2020
O. Rehn, *Walking the Highwire*, https://doi.org/10.1007/978-3-030-34592-1_4

extraordinary ministerial meeting of the Ecofin Council was finally taken only at half past one on the night between Friday and Saturday. When we had confirmation that the finance ministers would convene on Sunday—I would have to prepare the Commission's proposal for a decision for the meeting—I realized that I would immediately have to spearhead the internal preparations in the Commission and liaise with the member states and the ECB.

Earlier during the week, I had agreed to a television interview on the Saturday morning show of the Finnish Broadcasting Company, which now would not happen, of course. I had also agreed to "hitchhike" to Helsinki on the corporate jet of Prime Minister Matti Vanhanen and the Finnish delegation, which had a seat reserved under my name. On the spot, I called Jari Korkki, a reporter who was fast asleep, and subsequently on Korkki's advice to Petri Kejonen, another reporter who was in equally deep sleep and on duty the following morning. I asked if they were OK with the idea of having Prime Minister Vanhanen on their show instead of me. They agreed of course. Thus, a few hours later PM Vanhanen was on screen, professionally as always explaining contents of the Greek package and the decisions concerning the prospective establishment of a European stability fund.

By that time, I was already in Berlaymont after a few hours of deep sleep in my bed, followed by a quick shower. I had convened a meeting with my key personnel for 8 a.m. on Saturday morning. They included my Head of Cabinet Timo Pesonen and Deputy Head of Cabinet Stéphanie Riso, as well as my advisor Vesa Vihriälä, Director General Marco Buti and the ECFIN Directors Sean Berrigan and Gerassimos Thomas. Black coffee was consumed by the litre. My impeccable personal assistant Irma Martinmäki-Tuikkala managed the office and logistics with her usual smooth but firm grip.

I opened the meeting by reporting on the discussions of the previous day and night and the expectations attached to the Commission:

> Our job is to prepare a package that is ambitious in terms of restoring the credibility of the euro area, but at the same time realistic with respect to gaining the approval of the member states. And it needs to be ready tomorrow, on Sunday, first for the college of commissioners and next to the finance ministers to make the decision. We are given no clear-cut instructions for preparation by the European Council, and hence no restrictions either. We need a sufficient counterforce for the market speculations. Joint European bonds would be the most effective solution model, but are the member states ready for that? After all, they require unanimity. I could imagine other models, too – based on a divided country-specific liability – but they are not as effective. Any ideas where we start untangling this bundle?

The finance ministers' Ecofin Council meeting was scheduled for 3 p.m. on Sunday 9 May. On Saturday morning, I talked to Commission President José Manuel Barroso, who decided to convene the Commission extraordinarily at 1 p.m. on Sunday. Those Commissioners like Budget Commissioner Janusz Lewandowski that could not physically attend the meeting would participate through a video link. At the same time, we agreed that I would meet Barroso at 11 a.m. on Sunday. Hence, we had 27 hours to make an "ambitious and acceptable proposal" to set up a European stability fund. Of course, we realized the historic significance of the moment. In fact already during my day-long skiing holiday in February, standing on the cold patio of our summer cottage and talking to Marco Buti on my cell phone, we had semi-seriously concurred that what we were now building up was indeed a European monetary fund, to be called the EMF.

I dug up alternatives sketched during the winter and spring from the desk drawer. We were lucky to have outlined different stability fund models well ahead, as they came in handy now, as we started to compare the alternatives against each other. In the course of that Saturday, we began to lean towards a proposal based on the balance of payment (BoP) programme for non-eurozone EU member states, which had already been tested in Hungary, Romania and Latvia. Our proposal first leaned on guarantees granted on the EU's budget. These would amount to about 60 billion euros. I gained the Budget Commissioner Janusz Lewandowski's approval for this proposal following tough but very constructive negotiations. Furthermore, we proposed that any funding beyond 60 billion euros would be based on loans jointly guaranteed by all of the 27 EU member states. We expected that such common European loans would be best able to minimize financing costs, alleviate the pressures on sovereign bonds and hence effectively calm down the sovereign debt markets that were going on overdrive.

First I talked to Barroso who after some questions endorsed the proposal, and then the rest of the colleagues who did likewise, and then the Commission proposal was adopted. Thus I had a strong mandate. The Commission's meeting ended five minutes past 3.00 on Sunday afternoon. We made the final polishing touches to the actual legal text in my office, and I left for the other side of the street to the Council's Justus Lipsius Building to the Ecofin Council meeting. At Justus Lipsius' door, I made statements as soothing as possible in order to give reassurances that the stability fund could be set up on the basis of the Commission's proposal. Deep down, I was not quite that certain.

There was additional drama in the meeting of the Ecofin Council as the German Finance Minister Wolfgang Schäuble had taken ill on the way and had to be driven to hospital directly from the airport in Brussels. I considered Schäuble an important ally in creating a European stability fund, as he had proposed a "European Monetary Fund" in February and stated very clearly his position: "Eurozone members could also be granted emergency liquidity aid from a European Monetary Fund to reduce the risk of defaults". So I became even more concerned about the German support.

On the spot, Schäuble's secretary of state Jörg Asmussen, the experienced and always creative economic-policy trouble-shooter, called Chancellor Merkel in Berlin, who said she would send a minister-level replacement for Schäuble. As Merkel could not reach Rainer Brüderle, the outspoken minister of economics who happened to be on a flight somewhere—I don't know how hard she might have tried—she turned to her trusted person, Interior Minister Thomas de Maizière, who was alerted to the trip in the middle of his Sunday hike in the forest. Within a few hours, de Maizière was flown in Brussels by the German Air Force, well briefed and ready to step in the negotiations on the solutions for the stabilization of the euro area.

This marked the final stretch of the first phase of the counter-fires lit to suppress the debt crisis. The euro-area decision-makers—finance ministers in the meeting room, prime ministers, governments, parliaments and their EU affairs committees in the capital cities, as well as the citizens watching the crisis and the meeting—were under unprecedented pressures. I took the floor first and decided to be as outspoken as I could. George Papaconstantinou has afterwards written that I was "no longer the imperturbable Finn". I don't know if I ever have been such, but this time there could be no restraint. I stated loud and clear that we are in a profound systemic crisis and we have been badly behind the curve so far—now we need to get ahead of it. I tried to be as explicit as possible: "Portugal and Spain need to announce new measures – today! We need a credible financial backstop – today!" When looking at the ministers around the table, I felt the message went across, and we got strong support in most of the interventions.

However, there was one big shortcoming and another big question mark in our approach. Both stemmed from the extremely short time span to prepare the initiatives.

The shortcoming was that we didn't know how high a number in euros for the backstop the member states, particularly Germany and France, were ready to accept, as we had not gathered credible intelligence from the Merkel-Sarkozy talks. We had an idea of a high figure, but we couldn't raise a number without knowing where the member states could stretch, because leaks from the meeting were commonplace and we couldn't afford giving an impression of a failure. In any case, the Commission's proposal consisted of two parts, first 60 billion euros up to the ceiling of EU budget, and beyond that "joint and several guarantees" (i.e. Eurobonds of some kind) when exceeding the ceiling. Due to the uncertainty on the acceptable size of the fund, I decided to leave the exact figure open in my introduction, assuming that this would be discussed after the initial round, which actually happened. The Swedish Finance Minister Anders Borg criticized me heavily for this omission—this time his criticism was not without justification.

The big question mark was the ECB's plans and readiness to take action in terms of buying government bonds of the distressed sovereigns, like Portugal and Spain, maybe Italy as well. I discussed over the weekend with ECB President Jean-Claude Trichet and with some other members of the Governing Council, including Mario Draghi, Erkki Liikanen and Axel Weber. They all wanted to know—maybe for different reasons and with different goals in mind—what the Commission would be proposing on a stability fund and whether the Council or the member states would be expected to come along. Meanwhile, I got a broad idea of what the ECB was planning as regards to buying government securities of the stressed member states, which led to the effectively parallel decision on the Securities Markets Programme (SMP). Every institution guarded its independence, but there had to be some form of coordination.

Likewise, we were in constant contact with Dominique Strauss-Kahn, the managing director of the IMF. Prior to the decisive meeting, I also had conversations with some key non-euro members of the Ecofin Council. The outgoing UK Treasury Secretary Alistair Darling (Labour had just lost to the Conservatives in the general election of May 2010) said that he could not commit the UK to contribute financially to any Eurozone rescue operation. This remained the UK position, even though the relatively limited Community instrument of 60 billion euros, the European Financial Stability Mechanism, was created on 10 May 2010 and actually used in the early phase as the first fire extinguisher, which the UK did not oppose. Anders Borg provided useful policy advice from the Swedish experience of banking crisis and encouraged to go for a massive big bazooka to calm down the market turbulence.

President Trichet was chairing the ECB Governing Council as a continuous conference call from Basel, Switzerland, in connection to the meeting of the Bank of International Settlements, which is the "central bank of the central banks" and based there. In the course of the evening, we spoke several times over the phone, and I got the impression that the ECB was ready to move, but only on the condition that the member states moved first by creating a credible financial stability fund. This led later on to an unfortunate but unintended communication accident from my part in the early-hour press conference, of which something below—the central bankers of the ECB were not happy, even though as a silver lining my accident actually served to strengthen the collective credibility of the Eurozone.

The solution had to be hatched before the Asian markets opened at 2 a.m. on Monday morning 10 May 2010. The talks were tough and even bitter at times, not least when it came to the new role of the European Central Bank. The ECB President Jean-Claude Trichet told me over the phone that the finance ministers had until midnight to "bear their responsibility and make decisions" and spoke with key ministers as well. I also spoke to DSK several times during the night to check if the IMF and indirectly the United States were on board with a parallel decision.

The Commission had proposed a big bazooka leaning on a joint guarantee from the EU budget and the member states, such that would awe the markets and—so we thought, could pacify the turmoil and outright panic prevailing in the markets. However, our proposal did not pass in its original form, mostly on account of opposition from the countries with the highest credit ratings. During the afternoon and the evening, we tested various alternatives, but none of them amassed the unequivocal approval of the member states that was needed for a decision.

Late at night, in a burst of probably excessive creativity, I even proposed a (retrospectively desperate) solution where the funding would be either based on loans or loan guarantees, so that each member state could decide which option to use. Germany would have accepted that, but this was not good enough for the countries with low credit ratings. They were afraid of higher interest expenses and a further downgrade in their ratings, and therefore, they wanted a uniform solution.

After many failed rounds, in the course of the night between 9 and 10 May, things finally started to move at Ecofin. Following lengthy discussions and yet another stalemate, during a break in the meeting after midnight, I brought together a small emergency team to think "outside the box", as nothing inside it seemed to fly. The team included Stéphanie Riso, Marco Buti and Gerassimos Thomas from the European Commission and the Dutch official Maarten Verwey.

As described in the preface, I asked these brightest economics and market minds in the Eurozone fire brigade to rapidly think up a creative solution outside the box that would unlock the stalemate and enable reaching an agreement. In this meeting, Verwey, who had been chairing the preparations of a European financial firewall at the level of officials, reminisced that in the course of the preparations, the use of a Special Purpose Vehicle (SPV) had been considered as an option for the financial assistance programmes. I said this sounds possibly viable and why not try it now, as all other alternatives had been exhausted and rejected by different parties. "Could you go and ask the Germans if they could support this", I asked Maarten who went away. Verwey had a discussion with the Germans and came back after 15 minutes: "And yet it moves". A big relief—the gridlock might begin to disentangle!

After the reconnaissance action and the message from the Germans by Verwey, I went to talk to the energetic Ecofin Chair Elena Salgado, who was relieved that a solution was now emerging in the horizon. She convened the ministers back in the conference room with the aim of reaching a decision and adjourned the meeting. The atmosphere was tired and tense, with some desperation in the air. Yet, the mood was also anticipatory: Could there be a model that would bring an end to the stalemate? Could we finally agree on a European stability fund?

A European Stability Fund Made Out of Three Components

When the meeting was re-convened, everyone was waiting first for the Commission's proposal and next Germany's reaction to it. I presented the compromise proposal on the Commission's behalf. The ECB's Vice-President Lucas Papademos gave positive comments and endorsed the proposal. Next, Germany's representative, Thomas de Maizière, took the floor to support the compromise proposal. A sigh of relief spread over the conference hall: there had been a breakthrough. Hence, birth was given to the European Financial Stability Facility, or EFSF, which became the precursor of the European Stability Mechanism, ESM.

At the time of creation, it didn't and probably couldn't cross anyone's mind that the 440 billion euros reserved for this EFSF would later shrink to around half of it, to a bit over 200 billion euros in terms of actual lending capacity. This was due to the aim of ensuring the highest AAA credit rating for the EFSF borrowing in its entirety and the fact that the guarantees by all member states were not equally valuable in respect of this aim. The triple-A countries had to double guarantee the guarantees provided by the other member states.

This episode illustrates how profoundly important it would have been to prepare for the worst already when the Euro was conceived. I was not at Maastricht in 1990–92, but I get the impression that the neglect of a crisis management facility at the talks there was intentional: Maastricht's (unrealistic) aim was to guarantee stability by rules and market discipline, not by financial safety nets—and the no-bailout clause reflected this ordo-liberal thinking. This was in sharp contrast to what the international community did in 1944, when the IMF was created for the crisis prevention and stabilization purposes as a core building block of the Bretton Woods system. From another angle, the episode also shows the importance of the EU decision-making process under the normal Community method, where the voice of all member states is heard and decisions are reached under qualified majority, not unanimity with numerous veto points.

The decision of the Ecofin Council contained several elements. It highlighted the determined implementation of the Greek programme and the commitment of all member states to the balancing of their public finances, and it specifically mentioned Portugal's and Spain's commitment to the new measures. In return, a European stability fund was set up, with the announced total volume of 500 billion euros. It consisted of two parts, as 60 billion euros came from the Community fund (EFSM), guaranteed with the EU's budget, and 440 billion euros came as guarantees by the member states (EFSF), which would be divided (or "sliced" as "pro rata") by the customary ECB capital key among the member states in proportion to their gross domestic product and population.

In addition, the IMF was prepared to participate for half of the EU's share, or 250 billion euros. I spoke about the matter over the weekend on several occasions with DSK of the IMF. He confirmed that this $2+1$ solution or $500+250$ billion euros had the backing of the US Treasury Secretary Tim Geithner.

The decision by the European Central Bank to launch the SMP, the purchasing programme of sovereign bonds of the distressed countries Greece, Ireland and Portugal, and later on of Italy and Spain too, was a key element in the Eurozone's programme to overcome the crisis. However, it was a publicly unspoken part of the programme, since of course only the ECB spoke of matters of the ECB, although it was in fact linked with the member states' EFSF solution. The SMP decision was reached after some apparently dramatic turns in a teleconference of the ECB's Governing Council on Sunday night 9 June 2010. It had been prepared at the Governing Council's dinner in Lisbon on 6 May. The launch of the ECB's bond-purchasing programme together with the establishment of the euro area stability fund EFSM + EFSF initially calmed down the markets over the following weeks. It was as close to the big bazooka as we could get. However, the decision by the ECB later on contributed to the resignation of the Bundesbank's President Axel Weber.[1]

The legal basis of the decision by the Ecofin Council was determined to be Article 122.2 of the Treaty, which makes reference to "natural disasters or exceptional occurrences". The community instrument EFSM (60 billion euros) thus created included all 27 member states, and decisions on its use would be in principle subject to a qualified majority at the Commission's initiative.

In contrast, the intergovernmental EFSF (440 billion euros) only included the Eurozone member states. Its decisions would require unanimity of the Eurogroup. This later resulted in several hindrances that slowed down the decision-making, since every member state had the right of veto. For example, the IMF can take its critical decisions on conditional financial assistance programmes subject to a qualified majority of 85% of the votes at the executive board, which facilitates sufficiently fast decision-making in crisis situations.

Budgetary power of the parliaments is sacred. That's partly why the crisis created severe political tensions, which were soon felt in the national debates in the Eurozone. Often all eyes were on the German Bundestag, but these tensions were very much alive and kicking in many other parliaments as well, including in the Finnish parliament, and in her parliamentary elections of 2011.

Back in the meeting, the final polishing touches to the Ecofin decision were made in the grand conference hall of the Council's Justus Lipsius Building between 1.30 a.m. and 2 a.m. at night. The decision that was acceptable to everyone was reached at 2.08 a.m., which is eight minutes after the Asian markets had opened. Together with Salgado, I went to the Council's press room at 2.15 a.m., where we held a press conference and explained the solution. I left for home after 3 a.m.

On my way home, passing Brussels' Woluwe ponds at 3.15 a.m., Tim Geithner called to my mobile phone: "My warmest congratulations. This was a very important decision to contain the crisis". And he added, with a tongue in cheek, "If you need any consultative advice in the future use of the stability fund, don't hesitate to turn to me or my folks. You know we have some experience of the TARP arrangement..." Geithner's voice had a combination of joy and self-irony so typical of him—the TARP, or the Troubled Asset Relief Programme used to bail out banks, was certainly not easy to get approved by the US Congress. At any rate, I appreciated his call and in general his consistent support to the Eurozone during the crisis.

Geithner's call made me think: Could this be the "Hamilton moment" of the Eurozone? In the United States, the first Treasury Secretary Alexander Hamilton, the same guy who's now dancing in Broadway, created the foundation for a strong national economy thanks to the deals made in 1790 with Thomas Jefferson, when they agreed on the assumption of the states' war debt by the federal government in exchange for setting the capital to the swamps of the Potomac River, the site of today's Washington, DC. In retrospect, it is clear that my imagination had taken me to a turbo drive and firmly into the air. Especially after the fragility of the EFSF lending capacity was revealed, we saw the economic and political limitations of the May 2010 deal.

White Clouds in Pori Prior to the Next Downpour

Regrettably, by now most of the issues on the table were dividing Europe into the North and the South. The Belgian (Flemish) Economist and Financial Journalist Johan van Overtveldt, later to become the country's finance minister (2014–19), talks about the "German camp", in which he counts the Netherlands, Austria and Finland (and probably his own Flanders!), and the "French camp", which would include most of the other member states, especially of Southern Europe.

Many of the discussions on that Sunday, daytime and night-time, as well as the numerous similar discussions that were yet to follow, became a continuation to the tensions prevailing especially between Germany and France already when the economic and monetary union was being moulded. The Commission sought to overcome these boundaries and combine the best and most viable elements of the proposals, with the aim of reaching common solutions.

Germany called for a stability culture and wanted to restore budgetary discipline. France emphasized solidarity and the ECB's political role. These debates had heated up on Friday 7 May. Now, a basically synthetic resolution was sought with a fresh method. The partly improvised outcome of 7–10 May 2010 talks have been described by Luuk van Middelaar, an astute political science-cum-philosophy-oriented observer of European politics, as follows: "The Eurozone countries had also given themselves what looked like a European monetary fund.... This was judicial jerry-building, but it worked. The markets were surprised in a positive sense this time. The situation stabilized. The improvisation was a success."[2]

A few days after the critical meetings, in an interview the German Interior Minister Thomas de Maizière described Germany's approach towards the Eurozone stabilization measures as follows:

Germany wants to provide its loan guarantees on the basis of its own cred-itworthiness, and not to take on some unlimited liability. All Germans have worked hard to achieve better financing conditions. If we provide loan guar-antees for a country that is in trouble, we want to provide those guarantees on the same conditions that we encounter, as Germany, on the markets. We don't want to turn the EU into a transfer union. France is not as strict as us. The French said it would send a strong signal to the market and facilitate French financing possibilities if we used an average European financing rate. That was not our position and that is why the negotiations went on so late in the night.

From the perspective of rescuing the euro area in the long term, the origi-nal initiative presented by the Commission, which combined proactive eco-nomic supervision and stronger common stability facilities, would have been better and more convincing. This would have immediately created the big bazooka that would have been able to pacify the market turmoil.

On the other hand, it is regrettably typical of perceived European balance of power that de Maizière saw the decision-making only as a bilateral deal, as a wrestle between Germany and France. This was the usual dynamic for dec-ades in the EU, and at its best it served as the locomotive of European inte-gration. However, despite Germany's veto being critical, this time there were in fact many participants who contributed to the solution during the pro-cess. But de Maizière is right when he says that the outcome leaned towards the position represented by Germany, something which would be typical in the subsequent Eurozone rescue operations, as well.

When developing our proposal, I calculated that we could count on the European commitment of Wolfgang Schäuble, who as the finance minister of Germany would play a key role in the decisions-making to set up a new stability fund. As noted, Schäuble had presented his proposal for a European Monetary Fund only a few months before, in February, and by moulding his proposal into a Community-based initiative for a European stability fund we thought we might just about be able to get the Germans on board. It was at least worth trying, since all the other alternatives for a big bazooka were essentially weaker. Thus we opted for a sturdy fund that would have the financial backing of, in the first place, guarantees from the EU budget, and once those would be possibly consumed, of joint and several guarantees of the EU member states. If classical Eurobonds (that have never existed, so far) would have been the first-best idea from the standpoint of finan-cial stability, this was probably "the best of the second-bests", went our thinking then.

However, it didn't work out like that, as we now know. Unfortunately, Wolfgang Schäuble was hospitalized on the very day of decision-making. But probably even that did not matter, as the German red lines were firmly prepared—if not set in stone—in by the Chancellery and the Ministry of Finance, where there was always enough of continuity. Moreover, the German position was shared by the Dutch and the Finns, probably by the Austrians and Luxembourgers, as well. Consequently, we had to get back to the drawing board and use all the possible creativity to put together a model that would both do the job and gain unanimous support.

Initially, the EFSF was convincing, and the markets had faith in it. 750 billion euros was in the calibre of a big bazooka, and a larger fund than the IMF. Gradually over time, however, the image began to crumble. There were two reasons for this: as said, the goal of an AAA rating resulted in half of the guarantees going into the buffer, leaving only a good 200 billion euros at hand in net terms from the gross sum of 440 billion euros, which began to erode the credibility from one side. The big bazooka shrunk into a mere hand grenade. Meanwhile, the German Bundesbank challenged the ECB's bond purchase programme, which began to erode the deal from the other end. Following a respite lasting through the summer, stormy clouds began to gather again on the euro-skies as the autumn was drawing nearer.

Before that, the stress tests of European banks were finalized in July. Their implementation and publication started well. Soon, however, doubts emerged, and the credibility of the tests was called into question during the summer holiday in August. There was no effective European verification mechanism, so the national financial regulators protected their own banks by withholding their true state, which was financial nationalism of serious sort. At the same time, the situation of the Irish economy, and banks in particular, began to deteriorate rapidly. Unnerving premonitions gained ground in August–September 2010.

After mid-July, I spent a couple of days in Pori at the Finland Arena discussion forum and the jazz festival, as I usually do every year. That year, the main performer was my permanent favourite John Fogerty, the vocalist and songwriter of the Creedence Clearwater Revival, whom I had never seen in a live concert before.

On Friday night 23 July, before Fogerty's concert, however, I had to take part in a G7 teleconference, in which I would introduce the stress test results on the EU's behalf. For this purpose, we rented a cabinet at Hotel Vaakuna, where, dressed in my summer shorts, I presented our assessments about the shape of European banks. Luckily there was no video feed!

I made the presentation rather to-the-point in order for us to make it to the concert. After the teleconference ended more or less in schedule, we arrived as the second set was just about to start, and John Fogerty started singing his classic song "Who'll Stop the Rain?" It was the right question, befitting the market situation. Who would stop the debt crisis and make the rainy clouds over the market go away? I found myself pondering that under the still rather light sky of the late evening in Pori.

But in no time, we came to find that "A Hard Rain's A-Gonna Fall".

Notes

1. The Italian economist and journalist Carlo Bastasin has presented a detailed account of the events of those days in his book *Saving Europe.* Brookings Institution Press, 2012.
2. Luuk van Middelaar, *Alarums & Excursions. Improvising Politics on the European Stage.* Agenda, 2019, p. 37.

5

Deauville Doomsday and Voldemort in Ireland

"How did you go bankrupt?"—"Two ways. Gradually, then suddenly". The classic line of Ernest Hemingway in *The Sun Also Rises* forced itself to my head when thinking about the financial turbulence in late 2010. As autumn 2010 was drawing nearer, the mood in the financial markets began to deteriorate again, gradually at first and then faster. There were several intertwined reasons. More and more doubts arose concerning the stress tests conducted on European banks. There was increasing uncertainty about the shape of the Irish and Spanish banks. As a consequence, a visible gap was emerging in Ireland's public finances, and the markets knew that this also would undermine the credibility of the country's economic policy.

Uncertainty created by the fact that the exact size of the gap was not known at the time itself contributed to the emerging panic in the Irish sovereign debt market. It was a classic case of a banking crisis turning first to market panic and then to a sovereign debt crisis—the diabolic loop between the banks and the sovereigns.

According to an old wisdom, the markets are a good servant, but a bad master. In autumn 2010, the market forces were running amok and dragging democratically elected leaders around like a dog on a leash. Certainly, the market forces were panicking as well, and the situation was slipping out of everyone's hands.

In his classic portrayal of the Second World War, *The Unknown Soldier* (1954), the Finnish author Väinö Linna described the feelings of the Finnish soldiers lacking modern anti-tank weapons as they were overpowered by Soviet tanks in 1944: "They'll flatten us!" This was the mood also among the Eurozone leaders in fall 2010. This time round, there were no

© The Author(s) 2020
O. Rehn, *Walking the Highwire*, https://doi.org/10.1007/978-3-030-34592-1_5

anti-tank defences, either especially not the badly missed "big bazooka", which could have stopped the avalanche of the market forces. In Linna's novel, Lieutenant Koskela managed to contain the attack for a while, but finally a satchel charge was not enough to stop the modern tanks and Koskela got himself killed over nothing, before the bazookas arrived. Was it the Eurozone that was now being flattened—and the defences were for nothing?

Ireland's Gauntlet Run

I recall vividly when my cell phone flashed at the kitchen table in our home in the Auderghem suburb of Brussels at 8.30 a.m. on a cold and snowy Sunday morning, the 21st of November 2010. I had brewed my usual strong black coffee and was just about to enjoy it with my full-fibre black rye bread and two fried eggs, in order to kick-start my body before my regular Sunday morning football training match.

The caller was Irish Finance Minister Brian Lenihan who, after a short small-talk, told me that the night before the country's government had decided to apply for financial support from the EU and the IMF. It was a secret decision for the moment. Lenihan wanted to give me a heads up that the government's letter on the request for aid would arrive later that day and then become public. Lenihan's call was not a total surprise, as he had warned me on Friday about Ireland's intentions.

On the spot, I called the ECB's President Jean-Claude Trichet. The call went to voicemail, so I left a message. Next, I warned my cabinet and director general. Then I left for an hour and a half to play football with Finland United on the frosty lawn of the Park Cinquantenaire in Brussels. In the middle of the training match, my cell rang—Trichet wanted to get the latest update on Ireland. I described the situation and we agreed that we would get in contact once Ireland's application had arrived. In spite of the frosty weather, I did not feel my sweat drying nor my shirt freezing on my back. Adrenaline was pumping through my veins.

Lenihan broke the news in an interview with the Irish broadcasting company RTE around noon. For the evening, the Eurogroup had already been summoned to a teleconference. The ECB had been actively pushing for an EU-IMF programme for Ireland, since the uncertainty there was undermining the credibility of the whole EU's financial system and threatened to stop the region's emerging economic growth, and it wanted decisive action to correct the country's macroeconomic imbalances in return for emergency liquidity assistance, which was vital for its banks. Arthur Beesley, an Irish Times journalist, later reported: "The secrets, lies and denials were at an end. Ireland's rescue was finally out in the open."[1]—To Beesley, I'd point out that requesting a financial rescue package is very much like conducting a currency devaluation—and it is definitely not customary to publicly announce devaluations in advance, either. We Finns know it well, with a 61-year-long history of major devaluations between 1931 and 1992.

Ten days earlier I had called Brian Lenihan from Seoul, South Korea, where the G20 group's finance ministers were holding their meeting. After the official G20 meeting, at around midnight local time, the finance ministers and central bankers of the Western countries' G7 group convened an informal crisis meeting concerning Ireland's rapidly deteriorating situation. The Irish bond yields had already exceeded the critical threshold to face market lockout at 7%—no iron law, but a rule of thumb, and as such quite informative. In the early days of November, before my visit to Dublin, they had climbed to nearly 8%, compared to less than 5% three months before, and by mid-November they were already approaching the level of 9%. The banking front was likewise under huge pressure, with deposit and other fund outflows of around 2 billion euros in just four days. The aggravating situation in Ireland posed a threat to the stability of the entire euro area and to the tenuous recovery of the global economy that was going on at the time. The intensifying rumours and leaks of an Irish rescue that were stimulated from somebody somewhere did not help at all.[2]

I had requested to hold a late-night G7 meeting after the G20 working dinner, which was welcomed by others. I opened the meeting with a presentation of Ireland's situation to my G7 colleagues. The colleagues shared my concern that Ireland's situation could get out of hand and result in a collapse of confidence in the European banking system. Jean-Claude Trichet especially was very worried. Tim Geithner and Dominique Strauss-Kahn promised the support of the United States and the IMF to any European efforts to calm down the Irish situation. Geithner kept his composure as usual and suggested that we should immediately contact the Irish government. At the end of the meeting, we agreed I would call Brian Lenihan in Dublin right away and tell him about the mood at the meeting—essentially suggesting handing in the request without any further delay.

I went to the hotel's hallway and found a quiet corner. I looked up Lenihan's name on my cell and pressed the green button. "Good evening, Brian. It is midnight in Seoul. The situation has changed", I said to Lenihan. This was our code, which meant that the time was ripe and support ensured to file the request for financial support. I knew he understood it, as we had discussed the way forward so many times, referring to the "changing situation" as a euphemism for moving to a financial rescue. Lenihan asked whether the United States and the IMF would be fully on board. I responded that I assumed them indeed to be. Already a few months earlier, when the catastrophic condition of the Irish banks was revealed, I had concluded that the probability of Ireland being able to avoid drifting into an EU-IMF programme was ultimately very low.

I know that in Ireland the Korean events and contacts from there to Lenihan created big questions on the right order of things in a democracy, as described by Kevin Cardiff in his account of the Irish crisis, *Recap*.[3] On the other hand, the Irish situation now threatened the whole Eurozone, which required rapid action.

Banking Crisis Caused by the "Celtic Tiger" Running Wild

But let us not get ahead of ourselves. How did Ireland end up in an economic nosedive in the course of 2010?

First, we have to ask: Where did Ireland's descent begin? Actually, from its ascent. What I mean is that after the creation of the euro, and the resulting decline in the interest rates in the peripheral member states, Ireland experienced a rapid credit expansion and consequently, a huge real estate bubble. This doping whipped the "Celtic Tiger" to an even more awe-inspiring growth spurt on top of the growth that was fast to begin with. This is how the columnist Fintan O'Toole described the Irish state of mind in 2011, during the height—or trough—of the Irish crisis:

> The Celtic Tiger wasn't just an economic ideology. It was also a substitute identity… embraced with fervour, and its sudden demise has been a psychic, as well as an economic, shock.[4]

The Irish setting was not without its paradoxes. Before the crisis, Ireland was generally considered a European success story. Ireland had been able, from its initially underdeveloped state, to catch up with the rest of Europe, especially during the 1990s, in terms of economic development. Ireland's gross domestic product only amounted to 80% of the euro area average in 1993, but in purchasing power parity terms, it had reached as much as 134% in 2007.[5]

I had joined the club of Ireland's admirers as I wrote the following in my book *Suomen eurooppalainen valinta* (Finland's European Choice), published in 2006:

> When Ireland joined the European Economic Community in 1973, it was a poor and backward country. Now, its GDP ranks as the second-highest in the EU. One of the factors underlying this fantastic success story is that Ireland has, during the three past decades, skilfully taken the advantage of the opportunities of the common policies and benefitted from regional funding.[6]

Should I cancel my past statements in the light of the crisis that troubled Ireland in the early 2000s? Maybe not all of them, since there is still—or rather again—plenty of truth in the story, as Ireland has been growing strongly over the past years since 2012. Especially the part which describes Ireland's economic and modernization over several decades is still valid. But in another respect I might do well to reconsider my words: I refer to Irish economic policy in the first decade of this millennium, which no longer stood on sustainable grounds. This was due to the housing credit boom and subsequent bust, and excessive dependency on foreign capital inflows.

After all, Ireland's crisis was not primarily an impasse resulting from reckless public finances, but a banking crisis emerging from macroeconomic imbalances and the overheating of the real estate markets, which ultimately brought the public economy to its knees. The Irish credit bubble and banking crisis were in many ways very similar in nature to the severe banking crises in Finland and Sweden in the 1990s.

The crisis had brewed for a long time, but it did not explode until global financial crisis hit following the US real estate bubble and the Lehman bankruptcy in 2007–8. The needle that finally burst this bubble in Ireland was the all-encompassing deposit guarantee—the "blanket guarantee"—granted by the government in September 2008 on all deposits and investments with Irish banks. While initially successful, the Irish government thus took on such massive commitments which it was not ultimately capable of managing on its own. This deposit guarantee scheme also covered two banks operating under suspicious practices, the Anglo Irish Bank and the Irish Nationwide Building Society, which have been described as "no more than casinos for property developers".[7]

When the Irish banking crisis was revealed in all its ghastliness in autumn 2010, from the perspective of the European economy—and not just the euro area—it involved potentially an even more explosive charge and worse consequences than the Greek crisis. The Irish financial system was a highly interconnected part of the European financial system. This constituted such a large threat also to British financial stability and the country's financial capital, the City of London, that Britain (as well as Sweden) joined in the rescue operation of the Irish economy which was otherwise executed and funded by the Eurozone and the IMF.

The situation was made more difficult by the disproportionately large size of the Irish banking system relative to its whole economy. Before the crisis, the accounting assets (= balance sheet) of Irish banks amounted to as much as 1700 billion euros, a staggering 1060% of the country's GDP. As much as 70% of the total balance sheet was held by the Irish subsidiaries of foreign banks or such banks that were only registered in Ireland but operated mainly overseas. Although the Irish economy only constitutes 2% of the euro area economy, its banking system corresponded to 10% of the euro area whole, and, therefore, the second-round effects of a sovereign default and subsequent banking bankruptcies would have been very damaging for the entire European economy.[8]

Banks' Stress Tests Became a Lost Opportunity

As discussed in the previous chapter, the stress tests conducted in spring and summer 2010 were a long-overdue opportunity to provide the public, and investors in particular, a true and fair view of the shape of European banks. The stress tests conducted in the United States a year earlier had materially strengthened confidence in the country's banks at a critical time. All in all, the tests in the EU concerned 91 banks in 20 countries. The test covered 65% of all assets and liabilities held by the banks, which was a sufficiently broad coverage.

Initially, the stress tests were received well by the markets, but soon doubts began to emerge. Only seven banks failed the test and had to commit to increasing their capital in order to strengthen their stress tolerance. Only one German and one Greek bank in addition to five Spanish savings banks were unable to demonstrate that they would have sufficient capital reserves to sustain a capital ratio of at least 6% relative to their outstanding loan stock in the context of a recession and a debt crisis. Hence, the total recapitalization need was deemed to be only 3.5 billion euros, which was only about one-tenth of the general estimation by the markets, i.e. 30–40 billion euros—and this time the market participants were probably closer to the correct estimate. At the other or higher extreme, the investment bank

Barclays Capital had assessed the total recapitalization in the European banking sector need to be as high as 86 billion euros.[9]

As time passed, defending the stress tests with a straight face was not the easiest of tasks, but I did so for as long as we had together agreed to do so. However, as the criticism mounted and proved justified, even the poker face did not help any longer. Together with my colleague Michel Barnier, who was in charge of banking regulation and supervision, we were thoroughly frustrated and subsequently concluded that it would be inevitable to find more robust and convincing institutional solutions for European banking supervision.

The fundamental reason behind the failure of the stress tests conducted under common rules of the game was that their execution had relied too much on national authorities, without a common, strong European financial supervision. In the absence of anything better, the coordination of the tests was managed by a relatively loose common monitoring conducted by the CEBS, Committee of European Banking Supervisors. At the time, we did not yet have the present EBA, European Banking Authority, which has materially stronger powers, nor the Single Supervisory Mechanism of the ECB, which is the engine of the present banking union. According to Nicolas Véron, "Financial nationalism prevented the tests from being credible or really useful. Nations view the bank tests as a competitive game among countries and not as a way to ensure the common good of European financial stability".[10] No doubt he was right on how things stood then.

The national authorities had the tendency to give an overly positive a view on the shape of the banks in their own country. Only a few countries went too far with this bias, but that was enough to crumble the overall credibility of the tests. This was one of the reasons why we in the Commission had started making preparations to create closer common European banking supervision in connection with the ECB.

Ireland's Banking Mess Undermines the Confidence of the Markets

None of the Irish banks failed the stress test, which soon constituted a serious problem to the credibility of Irish banking supervision. According to the prevailing perception in the markets, many Irish banks were weakly capitalized, and no one believed in the clean bill of health they had received. Ireland had been in the danger zone for a long time. The gauntlet run began in September 2010, when doubts emerged about the shape of the banks and the interest rates rose.

Right at the beginning of September, I met with my colleague Joaquín Almunia, the Commission vice-president in charge of competition and thus also of banks' government subsidies. As an experienced economic policy-maker, Almunia was well informed about the state of Irish banks, since he had managed the economic and monetary affairs portfolio before me up until February 2010. We talked about how Ireland could reorganize its banks, run down the unviable ones, implement an asset management company, or a "bad bank", and recapitalize the viable banks.

Rumours were running wild in Dublin, especially about the losses of the Anglo Irish Bank falling on the taxpayers' expense, and these rumours were beginning to spread to the markets. On 6 September, I received a worrying report from my officials about the condition of the Irish economy and banks. My senior advisor Vesa Vihriälä, an expert in banking crises, and the Commission's country desk director Istvan Szekely kept me closely in the loop on the situation in Ireland. By the end of August, Ireland's credit rating sunk, deposits were fleeing in a steady flow, and the inflow of worthless mortgages into Nama, the bad bank, meant a sizeable increase in the banks' recapitalization needs. This in turn entailed an increase in Ireland's budgetary deficit, which served to repel investors from Ireland's sovereign bonds.

In mid-September, Ireland's crisis deepened further, as the yields on sovereign debt reached the critical level of 6%. The yield on Ireland's 10-year sovereign bonds never sunk below that again during the crisis. Generally, an interest rate level of 6–7% is considered dangerously high, and rates over 7% tend to break the camel's back fast.

It was a vicious circle, the Keynesian "animal spirits" yours truly in action. The market pressure was rapidly becoming a self-fulfilling prophecy. As the distinguished economic historian Charles Kindleberger put it some decades ago:

> The theory of rational expectations assumes that investors' expectations change more or less instantaneously in response to each shock and that investors immediately see through to the impacts of each shock on the long-run equilibrium prices... In contrast the insight from financial history is that expectations change slowly at some times and rapidly at others as various groups realize... that the current forecasts of prices and values in the distant future differ from earlier views of these same prices and values.[11]

So Ireland had entered the danger zone and seemed increasingly unable to get out of it on its own. At this stage, we were monitoring Ireland closely, together with the European Central Bank. The ECB was pushing for swift solutions to cut the deficit, in order to restore investors' confidence. However, there was a fresh problem of another scale: the fiscal deficit was threatening to soon reach truly astronomical proportions due to the banking sector recap needs.

In mid-September, I concluded that the process with the Irish had to be speeded up. I called Minister Lenihan and scheduled a secret meeting with him in Brussels on Wednesday evening 22 September 2010. This time the word "secret" was no exaggeration, since the meeting remained a secret for a long time and it was not until a year after the meeting that *The Irish Times* reported on it in its thorough account of the preparation of the Irish EU-IMF programme.[12] We held an afternoon meeting at Berlaymont, which was also attended by Joaquín Almunia and Jürgen Stark, the ECB's Chief Economist and a member of its executive board. During the meeting, we did an "X-ray scan" of the Irish economy and banking sector. At that point, there was not yet open discussion about a funding programme. In this context, "open" means any number of eyes more than "four eyes only".

After the meeting, I sat down together with Lenihan and we agreed I would keep the IMF informed about developments in Ireland—just in case. Lenihan also implied that, as a country within the sphere of Anglo-American culture, the Irish kept close contacts with Washington and would not cringe at IMF participation. At this stage, the IMF was not particularly focusing on Ireland, as its attention was rather centred on keeping abreast with the developments in Spain and Portugal.

The time bomb went off only a few days later. My officials reported to me that by the end of September, Ireland would publish a plan for winding down banks and also present an estimate of the costs. Especially the Anglo Irish Bank, which had inexplicably passed the stress test in the summer, would cause immensely inflated costs, and increase the total bill to the Irish taxpayer from 17 billion euros to at least 45 billion, possibly even to 50 billion euros.

This had two consequences: first, the Irish banks were rapidly consuming the collateral approved by the ECB, as corporate clients' deposits were fleeing the country fast in large amounts. Irish banks were kept standing only by funding provided by the Eurosystem. Secondly, the government's costs resulting from the recapitalization of banks would raise the Irish budgetary deficit sky-high. Even without the banking mess, the deficit would have amounted to 12%, but with the mess it ultimately reached 32% of GDP. To a non-specialist, it is worth pointing out that this indeed was the annual deficit, not the total debt accumulated over the years. Hence, public debt rose to around 100% of Irish GDP. Before the crisis, Ireland's public debt had only amounted to 27% of GDP at its lowest.

Lenihan participated in the Eurogroup meeting on 30 September via telephone from Dublin. In half an hour, he described the elements and estimated costs of the Irish bank programme. There was a deadly silence in the room. The mood was as frustrated as sombre. However, together with the Eurogroup's President Jean-Claude Juncker, we had to stand by the Irish programme in public. Led by France, a loud opposition had emerged against Ireland's corporate taxation of 12.5%. This was understandable, but the timing was not optimal, to say the least—you don't help a fellow who is already on the ground by kicking him to his underbelly! At the end of our meeting on Friday, the Irish sovereign yield stood at 6.64%, so the 7% threshold was dangerously close. At the Commission, we intensified our preparations to be ready when Ireland would drift into a rescue programme.

Next things started to move fast. In connection with the IMF's annual meeting in Washington on 8 October, I informed Managing Director Dominique Strauss-Kahn about the situation in Ireland. We acknowledged the need to raise the level of alert and intensify our joint work in monitoring the country. Now the IMF became actively involved. In the evening of that same day, at a G7 meeting for finance ministers and central bank governors, Ireland was at the epicentre. On 12 October, the Commission's delegation landed at Dublin airport and began a fact-finding mission in the country's Ministry of Finance and the Central Bank of Ireland.

In mid-October 2010, Ireland's economic state was bleak to begin with, but it soon turned even more horrendous. This was due to the weekend meeting by German and French leaders in the coastal town of Deauville, which set private sector involvement as the mainstay of the EFSF, repelling even the last investors from Ireland. Market literacy was in short supply that weekend.

The Deauville Double Deal—A Real Double Whammy!

I admit that the Deauville deal came right out of nowhere for me and for the Commission—it came totally from the bushes. Our reconnaissance utterly failed. So was it for the then other 14 Eurozone member states. Having said that, the agreement between France and Germany was such a surprise that I could not have envisioned or imagined it even in my nightmares before I had to witness it.

What was it all about? There had been serious disagreements between Germany and France about the solutions required to tackle the debt crisis.

These can be crystallized into two questions. To implement budgetary discipline, Germany demanded automatic sanctions to those breaching the Stability Pact, while France was opposed to them due to its own high debt levels. In addition, Germany demanded the private investors' involvement in sharing the financial losses, while France was against that, partly because of contagion, partly because of its vulnerable banks. Private sector involvement—or "haircuts", in the popular language—would imply that the private creditors of governments would be forced to bear their investor risk and pay for it through debt restructurings or haircuts in loan principal.

President Sarkozy had invited Chancellor Merkel to France to the traditional beach and spa resort town of Deauville to discuss crisis management and reconcile their positions. The meeting began on Sunday evening the 17 and continued on Monday, 18 October. It became one of the turning points of the crisis.

Information about Merkel and Sarkozy's accord came to the other member states and the Commission in a very peculiar way. The Task Force on Economic Governance led by the European Council's President Herman van Rompuy convened on Monday morning 18 October in Luxembourg. Its constitution was essentially the same as the Ecofin Council, a majority of the members being finance ministers. I represented the Commission in the Task Force.

After van Rompuy's opening remarks and mine, Christine Lagarde asked for the floor first and presented France's position. In the beginning, its content was not a surprise, but soon we heard something that forced us to listen to her more closely. Lagarde proposed that we forfeit the semi-automatic sanctions pushed by the Commission to the violators of the rules. Furthermore, private sector involvement should be implemented as soon as the EFSF was turned permanent. Next, the floor was given to Germany's state secretary Jörg Asmussen, who replaced the still hospitalized Schäuble and who—laconically and briefly—delivered the German position: "Germany concurs with France's position as presented by Minister Lagarde". I knew him well, and for me his body language indicated that as a financially most literate person he was less than comfortable with the deal. The other members were flabbergasted about the sudden turn.

The gist of the Deauville deal was that Germany accepted the watering down of the semi-automatic sanctions and France in return accepted private sector involvement in the agreement on the European Stability Mechanism—debt restructuring was a long-standing goal of Germany. Both parts of the Deauville deal actually point towards the "market discipline" strategy of economic governance.

After we got over our initial shock, we launched a one-day very civilian urban guerilla war with a few like-minded finance ministers against the Deauville deal. The usual German allies in the Eurogroup, Jan Kees de Jager of the Netherlands and Jyrki Katainen of Finland, distinguished themselves particularly in this operation.

The Deauville compromise would have meant the dilution of the sanctions and delay of related decisions into a process of about two years, which would have rendered the whole procedure—and the Stability and Growth Pact with it—meaningless. What De Jager and Katainen did on the spot around the table was to refuse approving Germany and France's joint proposals before they received the Commission's approval for those amendments. Decisions in the Task Force required unanimity from the member states, so we were able to bring back many elements, including to save the sanctions mechanism and to shorten the timeline in making the decisions to a tolerable few months (France wanted delay in years).

Hence, the damage caused by the Deauville Doomsday for the six-pack and the reform of economic governance was mostly remedied during the high-pressured and turbulent but historic meeting that lasted some 12 hours. Subsequently, the European Parliament fixed the rest in the summer of 2011, when the final wrestling about the six-pack legislation was done between the Parliament and the Council.

The foundations had been laid by the Commission's initiatives, or communications, in May and June 2010 on a comprehensive reform of the economic and monetary union and on reinforcing economic policy coordination and country-specific surveillance. The two initiatives broke new ground for European economic governance. This reform package also created the agenda for the Task Force led by Herman van Rompuy. Without the Commission's legislative proposals and the Community method, there would have been no results.

However, we were unable to fix the other issue, private sector involvement, since it was more clearly a decision requiring unanimity among the member states. The ECB's President Jean-Claude Trichet criticized the resolution forcefully both on the spot at the meeting and soon also in public.

On behalf of the Commission, I proposed that the decision on private sector involvement should not be made there and then—in the middle of the crisis—but it would be advisable to wait until the following year and discuss the matter in a calmer moment. If the stability mechanism could be built on a clean slate, without the presence of an acute crisis, private sector involvement could be an effective way to prevent moral hazard and free riding in advance. But in the middle of a crisis, it would only repel investors from sovereign bonds, and vulnerable countries would no longer be able to raise funding in the markets.

Carlo Bastasin has called Deauville "a sophisticated way to commit suicide".[13] With respect to the semi-automatic sanctions, our corrective action succeeded. But as regards private sector involvement, i.e. discussing debt restructuring publicly, the damage was done on the Deauville weekend, and it could not be easily fixed: contagion was on the run. As Jean-Claude Trichet put it in the end of 2010: "Before Deauville, Greece was on its way back to private markets".

What is the essential political conclusion of these events? My view is simple. Germany and France are the key drivers of European integration. Without them, the EU does not function. But the necessary lesson of the Deauville deal is that Europe is too valuable to be left to Germany and France alone. Let us not forget either how Germany and France together connived the breach of the Stability and Growth Pact in 2004, when they watered down the pact, with Italy's support. It is the EU institutions' duty to keep every party involved and decisions collective. This is called the Community method, which keeps Europe legitimate and moving on.

Ireland's Dead-End and the Mission to Dublin

The Deauville deal sealed Ireland's fate. The country might have ended up in the EU and IMF's purse anyway, but that we don't know. Within few days after Deauville, Irish interest rates exceeded the critical 7% mark. I met Lenihan in Brussels on Monday 25 October right on the weekend after the G20 ministers' meeting held in Gyeongju, Korea. Despite minor jetlag and full and heavy G20 agenda, I needed to focus on the balancing of Ireland's public finances and the spending cuts in the 2011 budget, which I had studied on the return flight from Korea. Jürgen Stark of the ECB also participated in the meeting.

On 4 November, Lenihan announced expenditure cuts worth 6 billion euros in order to balance the budget. This was a considerable amount by Ireland's measure, and reaching an agreement within the government was not easy. At the ECB's press conference, Trichet gave his support to Ireland's efforts in a rather evasive way by saying that the magnitude of the cuts "is not insufficient". Soon, Irish sovereign yields surpassed 7.5% for the first time, peaking at 7.8% and closing the day at 7.66%. Ireland would not survive for long at interest rates that high. The ECB was also becoming increasingly convinced that Ireland would need external lending.

On 8–9 November, I made a long-prepared mission to Dublin. The air was charged with political tensions. I met with not just members of the government but also the opposition parties, as well as representatives from the trade union confederation and the employers' association. In addition to Lenihan, I had a mostly cordial discussion with Prime Minister Brian Cowen and a lengthy substantive meeting with Michael Noonan, who was an experienced political stalwart in the then largest opposition party, Fine Gael. Noonan was predicted to become the finance minister should his party win the elections in 2011, which indeed happened soon. Over the years, I very much learned to respect his consistency and safe policy hand, and his combination of economic literacy and political experience.

To close the day, I had a late supper privately with my old liberal buddy Pat Cox, a former president of the European Parliament and also of the Liberal Group there. He was a top man in both positions. Pat did not beat about the bush in recounting why and how the Irish economy had ended up in the impasse. Topping his list were the close connections between leading politicians and real estate speculators. Pat described the social impacts of the crisis by sharing the experiences of his six children and their friends at university, in working life or in finding a job. It made the regrettable human costs of the crisis very concrete and tangible.

During my Dublin mission, instead of preaching, I tried to do as much listening as possible. If anything, I encouraged the Irish to find a common chord, which has helped small countries to conquer their hardships. I told my counterparts about Finland's experiences in overcoming our deep depression in the 1990s. I underlined the position of small countries and the role of community policy in the EU, in which context the Finns and Irish will easily find affinity with one another. In terms of mutual domestic understanding, Ireland proved a different case to Greece, where internal harmony was not found, and perhaps was not even truly sought. Although Ireland was preparing for elections and there were customary disputes about internal politics, the ability of the Irish to find mutual agreement on the key objectives of saving the economy was crucial and admirable—and greatly benefitted the country.

Before arriving to Dublin, I was invited to give a speech at Ireland's Institute of International and European Affairs. I used that occasion to convey a very clear and unequivocal message of the EU's support to the Irish in their hardship. The event was crowded and sweaty, for me and for the audience. Even many of the senior officials I knew had to remain standing, as the hall with dense air ran out of seats.

I wanted to lift the fighting spirits: "It might feel a small consolation at times like these, but I have no doubt that Ireland will overcome this crisis. You are smart and stubborn people. Time and again you have proved you can overcome adversity. And this time you do not face the challenges alone. Europe stands by you".

On the next morning, the Irish Times wrote that the lecture hall of the Institute was not quite as close to bursting even during the visit of President Mikhail Gorbachev. I am not sure if that should be taken as a compliment.

No Voldemort in Dublin

During my visit, there were not yet candid or detailed negotiations about the EU-IMF programme, although this Voldemort—"he-who-must-not-be-named", as everyone who has read her Harry Potter will know—was hanging in the air during my meetings and press conferences. Ireland had not yet presented a request for financing support, so formally speaking such negotiations could not have been conducted, although the position of the country deteriorated by the day. But in the meeting with Brian Lenihan we discussed a rescue programme as a possible scenario. He knew that I was in favour of a programme, but he said that Ireland was still well funded and it was not clear a programme would be needed. Yet, even without the Voldemort in public, everybody knew what we were up to and shared information with us, which greatly helped the mutual and rapid preparation of a programme.

After weeks of preparations, we were getting close to full preparedness at the Commission to launch the preparation of the final steps for a programme, should the request come. We considered we had no alternative and it was our duty to prepare for it, since the likely ramifications of the Irish crisis could otherwise be damaging not only for Ireland but also for the entire European economy.

In the meantime, the collective mood within the Eurogroup was changing regarding the critical issue of life after Deauville. Soon the notion began to gain ground, among the finance ministers and their secretaries of state in particular, that the blunt announcement of private sector involvement in the faces of investors had not been such a carefully considered move, and the situation needed corrective action. The repair operation was launched a few days after my trip to Ireland, now in Seoul, South Korea, in connection with the G20 Summit.

Together with the EU countries' secretaries of state, we prepared a draft for a statement that the finance ministers of Germany, France, Italy, Spain and Britain decided to issue together. The gist of the statement was to underline that private sector involvement would only relate to possible future lending programmes, and it would not be applied to the present holders of sovereign bonds. This did not however pacify to any great extent the pension funds, employment pension funds and other investors that had begun to dodge Irish, Portuguese, and increasingly also Spanish and Italian, sovereign bonds.

The question of investors' responsibility is a complex one. If the euro area could have been built in 2010 on a clean slate and without the massive sovereign debt burden in many member states, clear rules on investors' responsibility could have provided with stronger market discipline and hence force the Eurozone countries to a more responsible management of their public finances. How so? Because investors would probably flee and interest rates would react earlier on, if there was a threat of public finances straying from the sustainable path.

Unfortunately, we did not live in such a fantasy world, but in the cruel reality, where the debt burden of the Eurozone countries and other EU member states too had risen in only two years from 60 towards 90%. Under such circumstances, constant active discussion of investors' responsibility by taking so-called haircuts on their bonds, and of debt restructuring by responsible leaders, is akin to an economic policy suicide. Having said that, I know well that the citizens, or taxpayers and voters perceive investors' responsibility as necessary, in order to make the banks and other investors who made mistakes carry their share of the responsibility and take losses. A true dilemma, to which I return in later chapters.

Applying elementary financial literacy, talking loud and clear about investors' responsibility in the middle of the crisis meant that such investments that were previously perceived practically risk-free now turned suddenly very risky indeed, since a debt restructuring would cut away a significant proportion of the capital invested. From the individual investor's point of view, it then made sense to avoid investments in the sovereign bonds of the Eurozone countries that had suddenly turned very risky, which led to reduced demand and higher yields—or to an outright buyers' strike. The end result was a complete lockout of several countries from the markets, as we witnessed during the debt crisis. The case of Ireland in fall 2010 was a textbook example of this effect.

The internal decision-making of the Eurozone was asymmetric in one important sense: the position of those pushing for stronger private sector involvement was stronger for the simple reason that they only had to keep talking about it, and the snowball kept rolling and growing almost by itself as the rumours spread. Then after a certain stage, it was no longer possible to stop the avalanche, which had to be terminated by debt restructuring. In Greece, this point was reached in early spring 2011. It was expedited by Greece's internal discord and shortcomings in the implementation of the stabilization and reform programme. Externally, it was hastened by mounting internal political pressures in many Eurozone countries that were averse to lending to Greece.

The case for public discussion about investors' responsibility is similar to the one about devaluations: handle with care! It is not appropriate for decision-makers in charge to talk about it out loud, since mere talk about investors' responsibility stirs panic in the market and easily creates a self-fulfilling prophecy. However, when the facts so require, private sector involvement may have to be implemented on a case-by-case basis to restore the debt-servicing capacity of an individual country—in this case, Greece. Initially in 2010–12, this had to be considered without any ex ante mechanism. With the ESM in place since 2012, the collective action clauses (CACs) in the ESM programmes provide rules on how any possible debt restructuring could be decided. In the future, further developing the CACs may be part of a reinforced European Stability Mechanism.

At the Eurogroup meeting on 15 November 2010, Lenihan, who was the last one to arrive due to the thick fog at Brussels airport, was put under heavy pressure by his colleagues. The message of his Eurogroup colleagues was clear: go back to Dublin immediately and ensure that your government immediately announces it will seek support. Otherwise, the consequences of the fall of the Irish financial system will be dramatic for the entire European economy. So Lenihan went back.

After Ireland filed its application, the Eurogroup convened on the phone on Sunday evening to discuss the matter, and it gave its support to negotiating the programme. We launched the official negotiations right away. Thanks to the preparations made under radio silence, the final programme was approved within a week. The Troika, or the EU Commission, the ECB and the IMF, were prepared for what was coming, as they had discussed the essential elements of a prospective rescue operation closely with the Irish government. The deal was signed on 27 November.

The agreement made with Ireland consisted of an 85 billion euro programme, 35 billion of which would be used to recapitalize banks after the dead wood had been cleared, the banking system reorganized and the Anglo Irish Bank run down. According to a report made by the bank restructuring specialist firm BlackRock, the total recapitalization spend at the end of March 2011 remained at 24 billion euros. Ireland itself funded the programme with almost 20 billion euros from its pension fund reserves. The EU countries' share of the funding amounted to approximately 50 billion euros and the IMF's to slightly less than 20 billion euros.

There was one major problem, which had to wait to be solved at a later stage. When the loan support to Ireland was first announced, it was to be provided at an interest rate that was so high—at around 6% when converted to fixed-rate funding—that it seemed to undermine the objective of the exercise. We were aware of the problem in the Commission and argued for a lower rate in the Eurogroup, but without initial success. We raised the issue again in March 2011, and subsequently discussions in the Eurogroup moved on, and the problem was corrected later on in 2011. It was the same story as in the cases of Greece, Ireland and Portugal (especially the first two): because of the urgency to contain the financial market turbulence, it was necessary to get the rescue programme—and especially the financing—under way; the main creditors at that stage still insisted on an excessively high interest rate, under pressure from their parliaments—and electorates. You may call it parliamentary democracy.

On Ireland, there was the further complication of the German–French initiative to insist increasing its 12.5% corporate tax rate as condition. However, once things started to calm down, there was a more rational realization that these issues should not be linked, and the interest rate should be made reasonable.[14]

No surprise, the Irish banking crisis led to a political crisis and the resignation of Prime Minister Brian Cowen's government and the defeat of his Fianna Fail party in the elections. In early 2011, a new coalition government consisting of the centre-right Fine Gael and the centre-left Labour Party took office. After the elections in 2011, Ireland has been characterized by political stability, which has been a key prerequisite for the country's impressive economic recovery.

The country's government aimed to return to the markets in autumn 2012 and start raise funding from private investors. The European Council in the end of June 2012 made important decisions concerning this goal, as it began cutting the toxic linkage between banks and governments by enabling the direct recapitalization of banks when the ECB assumes banking supervision and by refraining from emphasizing investors' responsibility within the ESM. As a result, Ireland managed to return to the markets already in July 2012 when it completed a sale of a five-year-bond, the first new issue of long-term debt since September 2010.

Brian Lenihan: Personal Courage and Public Service

On 10 June 2011, sad news arrived from Dublin. Brian Lenihan, who had pancreatic cancer, passed away at the age of only 53 years. He was very much appreciated and missed by his EU colleagues and fellow ministers of finance. I wrote a letter to Brian's widow Patricia and gave an interview to Ireland's public broadcasting company, RTE:

> Brian showed great personal courage, strength and dedication to the management of common affairs during a time which was extraordinarily challenging for Ireland and Europe. In placing his duty to the nation above his personal difficulties, Brian Lenihan has provided us with an outstanding example of public service. Patricia's loss is shared by the many people across the European political arena, who had the privilege of knowing Brian Lenihan as a politician and a person.

By 2012, Ireland was recovering: its exports were strong, industrial output rising and the economy growing for the second consecutive year. However, unemployment remained high and the long shadow of the crisis with its social ramifications would still fall on Ireland for a long time. However, the necessary adjustment and correction of imbalances were moving on. Ireland's growth continued in 2013 and it exited its adjustment programme in December 2013. By 2018, Ireland's economy is continuing to grow at 3–4% per year, employment has been substantially improving, and its deficit continues on a downward path. With this progress, it seems safe to say that the Celtic Tiger is getting back in shape, hopefully though as a somewhat wiser and slightly less aggressive cat than before the crisis.

I must say I enjoyed working with the no-nonsensical Irish officials and people over the years, knowing that it was the toughest of times for them, even though I also got my fair share of criticism. Maybe our special relationship stems partly from the fact that I've always loved Irish rock and folk music, to the extent that our wedding "waltz" was not actually a traditional waltz, but Van Morrison's "Someone like You".

To some extent, the sentiment seemed reciprocal. Kevin Cardiff, the former Secretary General of Ireland's Department of Finance, writes in his crisis memoirs some words which I carry warmly in my heart:

> Over the years we dealt with Olli Rehn, he was regarded rightly as a good European and a friend to Ireland.[15]

No further comment on my part. Let's just keep up the friendship and move on.

Notes

1. Arthur Beesley, Dark Days: Behind the Bailout. *The Irish Times*, 19 November 2011. http://www.irishtimes.com/newspaper/weekend/2011/1119/1224 307810593.html.
2. Kevin Cardiff, *Recap: Inside Ireland's Financial Crisis*, 2016, pp. 147–190. Cardiff's book includes a detailed and, to my recollection, accurate account of the difficult road towards the Irish EU-IMF programme.
3. Cardiff 2016, pp. 150–153.
4. Fintan O'Toole, *Enough Is Enough: How to Build a New Republic*. Faber & Faber, 2011, p. 3.
5. Carlo Bastasin, *Saving Europe: How National Politics Nearly Destroyed the Euro*. Brookings Institution Press, 2012, p. 229.
6. Olli Rehn, *Suomen eurooppalainen valinta* (*Finland's European Choice*, not translated in English, only in Finnish), 2006, p. 88.
7. O'Toole 2011, p. 7.
8. Bastasin 2012, p. 231.
9. Bastasin 2012, p. 227.
10. Overtveldt 2012, pp. 106–107.
11. Charles Kindleberger, *Manias, Panics, and Crashes: A History of Financial Crises*, sixth edition. Palgrave Macmillan, 2011 (1978), p. 84.
12. Beesley 2011.
13. Bastasin 2012, p. 233.
14. I am grateful for Professor Charles Goodhart for drawing my attention to the importance of this episode. See also Cardiff 2016, pp. 194–195, 221–222.
15. Cardiff 2016, p. 125.

6

Comprehensive Crisis Response

By the summer of 2010, it eventually became clear to virtually everybody that the Eurozone debt crisis was a systemic one, not cyclical, random or sporadic. This reminded me of the words of John Maynard Keynes in his *General Theory* in 1936:

> I have called my theory a general theory. I mean by this that I am chiefly concerned with *the behaviour of the economic system as a whole*... And I argue that important mistakes have been made through extending to the system as a whole conclusion which have been correctly arrived at in respect of a part of it taken in isolation.[1]

In the Commission, we started to prepare a systemic response immediately after the Barroso II Commission had taken office in February 2010. The events and critical decisions of May 2010, i.e. the conditional financial rescue package to Greece and the creation of the European Financial Stability Mechanism/Facility, only underscored the urgency of a systemic response.

In addition to the measures by individual Eurozone countries, it was high time to begin correcting the systemic shortcomings remaining in the structures of the euro by strengthening the economic union and by speeding up the creation of such a permanent stability fund that would be able to calm down the constant turbulence.

Quite soon, these issues came together under the working title "Comprehensive Crisis Response", thus named because action was required on all policy fronts. My cabinet quickly christened the comprehensive crises response as the "CCR", in due reference and certainly also in due

© The Author(s) 2020

O. Rehn, *Walking the Highwire*, https://doi.org/10.1007/978-3-030-34592-1_6

reverence to the Creedence Clearwater Revival, the legendary American blues-rock band from the 1960s and 1970s, which was led by the great singer-songwriter John Fogerty. Well, better the CCR than, say, "Status Quo", "Mötley Crüe", or "Crazy Horse"!

Of course we were also aware that we would have adjust the CCR on the basis of learning by doing. It was worth keeping in mind the proverb of Mike Tyson: "Everyone has a plan 'til they get punched in the mouth". We got enough punches to the mouth to understand the paramount importance of adjusting the plans.

In May 2010, we took the initiative and presented a Commission communication on reinforcing the Eurozone economic governance. Following the mostly positive feedback, the subsequent legislative package was decided by the College of Commissioners on 29 September 2010. It soon came to be known with the nick-name "six-pack", thanks to the six pieces of legislation it included. The package was broadly well received in the EU at that time, across the left-centre-right political spectrum in the European Parliament (if not counting the euroskeptics), and both in the North and the South—though the consensus did not last long (Image 6.1).

Image 6.1 Commission President Jose Manuel Barroso with Michel Barnier and the author, presenting a package of reform proposals in the Commission press room in June 2010

Spicy and Humid Dinner in Justus Lipsius

To prepare prospective reforms of economic governance, President van Rompuy called a dinner meeting on reinforcing EMU economic governance for the evening of Monday, 19 July 2010. It took place in the 8th floor dinner room of the Council, in Justus Lipsius. The participants included van Rompuy, Barroso, Jean-Claude Trichet and me. Each of us had one policy advisor along. I was accompanied by my deputy head of cabinet, Stephanie Riso.

In retrospect, the hot and humid dinner in the summery Brussels (+30C) turned out to be quite important for the future fire-fighting, since it over time significantly helped to improve policy coordination among the various EU institutions in the pressing context of the raging existential crisis within the euro area. With President Barroso, we had initially responded to van Rompuy's invitation with a certain degree of hesitation and scepticism, since the event could be taken as an imperial move by the European Council President in one of those classic but so useless turf wars in Brussels. However, the discussion turned out to be not only frank and open but indeed also most productive and useful that over time paved the way for smoother decisions on several policy measures and coordination and stabilization mechanisms.

One observation was that van Rompuy had taken steps backwards as to the biting semi-automatic sanctions (the so-called reversed qualified majority), which we assumed was the result of French influence. In the end of the meeting we however agreed, as the request of van Rompuy, that the Commission will prepare a policy paper on options for the Task Force.

Even more worrying was the open scepticism of van Rompuy and Trichet as regards the Commission's capacity to deliver on economic governance and fiscal surveillance in line with the Stability and Growth Pact. Barroso and I called for fairness and defended the Commission's track record. "The member states have been the problem, not the Commission; recall 2003–5 with France and Germany". That was a reference to the breach of the Pact by the two most powerful Eurozone member states, which had critically eroded its credibility.

In reality, I felt that van Rompuy was clearly concerned about the fact that the Commission seemed to be emptying the contemporary policy agenda: the legislative package on six-pack would cover all essential novelties of governance that could be carried through under the existing EU Treaty. That's why he was looking for his "own" profile issue for the Task Force: it was originally supposed to be a crisis management mechanism, but the

9 May decision on EFSM/EFSF had obviously made its creation outdated as a political issue. Now the profile issue was seemingly to create a supreme fiscal council in the Eurozone, which would be in direct competition with the Commission, making it practically redundant.

At the end of the dinner, van Rompuy made a proposal to agree on a high-level "economic government" for the Eurozone, composed of himself as European Council President, Barroso, Trichet, Juncker and me in our respective institutional responsibilities; thus all the key Eurozone institutions would be represented and contribute. He proposed that this informal body would meet always before the Eurogroup and Ecofin meetings. Barroso was at first clearly not in favour of this arrangement, as he thought this would be an institutional oxymoron. Trichet followed suit, but softer: "maybe a teleconference".

In due course I was glad to confess that my suspicion had not been realized and admit that van Rompuy's initiative turned out to be a very important institutional innovation, for which he must be given fair credit. It became a regular practice that always before the Eurogroup meetings and often before the Eurozone Summits this composition of people met in order to coordinate positions and aim at ensuring that the outcomes would be closer to first-best than purely second-best ones. It was certainly not an economic government, but nevertheless a very useful body to ensure that the Eurozone would take common positions rather than be divided. For me, it became a very useful forum to efficiently sound out the views of the key players of the "impossible triangle": Juncker had usually touched base with the Germans and the French, and thus knew the basic position of the member states "with chips"; the Commission kept close contact with the ECB, and I personally with both Trichet and Draghi; the only key player missing from this particular table was the IMF, but that was not a real problem since the Commission as the chairing institution in the Troika usually was well informed of the Fund's positions.

Over time it became somewhat easier to try overcome the red lines of the triangle. This goes also for the interplay between fiscal and monetary policy. As Tommaso Padoa-Schioppa, the former ECB and Commission official and Finance Minister of Italy, remarked: "It would be unfortunate if [the ECB's] independence were to be confused with loneliness".[2] In my view, the ECB Governing Council is always fully independent to decide whatever it deems right within its mandate, but for the ECB and the Eurozone a bit of coordination in policy matters would do no harm.

After the dinner, we had a debriefing by chatting with Barroso, standing at the parking lot of Justus Lipsius. It was still +30C at 11 p.m., and the political air was equally hot and humid. We agreed we might come halfway to van Rompuy's direction in terms of procedure, which meant waiting with our legislative package until the Task Force had given its report in the end of September. I said to Barroso: "If there is going to be an independent fiscal body providing ex-ante assessments on member states' fiscal policies, I can close the shop and ask for the multilingualism portfolio from the President…!" Barroso had a good laugh and promised to consider that favourably.

After several weeks of haggling and bouncing ideas back and forth, we found a solution. I wanted to seek Trichet's support on how to strengthen economic governance. We agreed to meet immediately after the summer break. So I flew to Frankfurt and we met in his office in the Eurotower in Frankfurt on 2 September 2010. I presented three key points for reinforced economic governance:

1. Reinforce the Pact by introducing the rule of reversed qualified majority and thus turn around the burden of proof. With this change, the Commission's proposals under economic governance would stand, unless there is an active 70% opposition of the votes in the Council to take a contrary view, which would be very rare.
2. Separate technical analysis and political discretion through a Commissioner who would be equipped with the same kind of competences as the Competition Commissioner holds in the enforcement of competition and state aid policies.
3. With certain conditions, consider a wise persons' group.

After listening to our plans and posing some critical questions, Trichet said he can fully support these basic lines and underlined that close cooperation between the Commission and the ECB is a precondition for a solution. He wanted to know in most concrete terms, how the "Competition Commissioner Model" would be realized and how the powers of the Economic Affairs Commissioner were to be reinforced.

Now the common points of departure of the Commission and ECB were brewed and agreed for the concluding round of deliberations in the Task Force chaired by van Rompuy. The ECB-Commission cooperation had substantial and substantive impact on the final report of the Task Force. It also paved the way for the creation of the post of Commission Vice-President responsible for economic and monetary affairs and the Euro, which came to concern me in due course. So I was negotiating on my own job description, but was not yet aware of that.

Gathering Storms Towards the End of 2010

The fall of 2010 in the Eurozone was dominated by the rescue of Ireland, the legislative work on the six-pack, and the talks in van Rompuy's Task Force, as described in Chapter 5. One positive outcome of the Task Force was its recommendation in its report of 21 October 2010 to establish a permanent crisis management mechanism, which we had been calling for. This led later on to a separate decision on the transformation of the EFSF to the permanent European Stability Mechanism (ESM). The Eurogroup endorsed this in its meeting on 28 November 2010 and the European Council took a decision in principle on it on 16–17 December 2010. The decision provided guidelines for the finalization of the ESM Treaty, such as the unanimity requirement, the preferred creditor status and the introduction of collective actions clauses to the euro area government bonds from June 2013 onwards (which would facilitate managed debt restructuring, if needed in future). Moreover, the European Council agreed to amend the EU Treaty with the simple procedure to create the legal base for the ESM.

I spent the Finnish Independence Day 2010, the 6th of December, in a Eurogroup meeting in Brussels. The Finnish Broadcasting Company *Yleisradio* interviewed me with Finance Minister Jyrki Katainen before the meeting at the ground floor lobby of Justus Lipsius. It was difficult to come up with anything uplifting to say to the Finns, as the crisis went on and on, in spite of all the vast counter-fires. Besides, the people back home were focused, as the tradition goes, on viewing the Independence Day gala reception broadcast from the Presidential palace on their TVs at home.

Between 6 December and Christmas Eve of 2010 was the deepest abyss of the euro crisis, until then. But many were yet to follow. By December 2010, the Irish crisis program had been approved. In addition, strengthening of the economic and monetary union had received a positive response by the EU's legislative bodies, the European Parliament and the Council, which represents the member states. On the other hand, the constant public speculation about private sector involvement (PSI), or investor responsibility, seemed to scare off investors and to raise sovereign yields to sky-high levels. Information from the markets did not even hint that interest rates in the financially vulnerable and distressed countries might be coming down. After Ireland had requested assistance, the hardest pressures on sovereign bonds were felt in Portugal and Spain. Both countries were faced with the threat of the end of market-based funding, which would drive government finances into an impasse.

International community was broadly supportive of Europe's effort of stabilization—some more than others. One positive surprise was China, which all through the crisis provided consistent support for the Eurozone and didn't resort to blame games, unlike some Americans. For China, Europe is the world's largest economic area and thus critical for her export industries—and no doubt they certainly had the issue of market economy status in the WTO in mind, as well.

In October 2010, together with Juncker and Trichet we met our Chinese counterparts in the so-called Euro Troika format (yet another one of those three-pronged creatures!) in Brussels. Governor Zhou Xiaochuan, the respected head of the People's Bank of China, referred to recent statements from China's leadership to support with its foreign exchange reserves EU countries facing financing problems, especially Greece, while President Trichet thanked China and expressed appreciation to China's trust in the euro area and its sovereign signatures.

In December 2010, just two days before Christmas, I visited Beijing to meet with officials of the Chinese government under the so-called High-Level Economic Dialogue, which is the formalized method of conducting dialogue with the People's Republic. Vice-President Joaquin Almunia and Trade Commissioner Karel de Gucht were collegial members of the European Commission delegation. Our impressively knowledgeable and witty host was Vice-Premier Wang Qishan, who was then responsible for the economy and finance. Later on in 2012–17, he was responsible for the fight against corruption, a key task under President Xi Jinping, and was elected China's Vice-President in the Peoples' Congress in March 2018.

After our discussions, Wang Qishan said in an interview in the Wall Street Journal that China supports the measures taken by the EU and IMF to financially rescue certain European countries and stabilize the financial markets. He maintained that China hoped the effects of the EU's measures to address the Eurozone debt crisis became apparent quickly. His public comments gave the euro some positive momentum in currency markets. I welcomed his words and China's support and underlined Europe's determination to contain and beat the crisis, exemplified by the recent agreement to replace the temporary rescue fund (expiring 2013) with a permanent financial stabilization mechanism, the ESM.[3] I also met again with Governor Zhou, with whom I had the honour and pleasure to continue substantive discussions on economic and monetary policy over the years.

The CCR with Slow Motion

So the autumn had mainly passed in preparing the Irish program and the new legislation for the reinforced EU economic governance. Along with these tasks, in November 2010, we in the Commission began to prepare the next round of stronger counter-fires to the debt crisis, which was flaming again. In our view, the crisis had turned ever more clearly into a systemic crisis, and therefore conquering it would also require a system-level solution.

Although the ECB had assumed a major responsibility in the management of the crisis, we could not count on it on a permanent basis due to the constraints of its mandate in the EU Treaty and also due to the reservations on a more proactive policy mode by the ECB in its Governing Council. Without a strong permanent stability mechanism, we would inevitably be faced with disintegration of the euro area, either by slowly withering away or by a faster collapse.

The first complete draft of the comprehensive crisis response was prepared in October/November 2010. It was developed to a non-paper by the beginning of December 2010. The Commission non-paper was a combination of economic reforms, fiscal consolidation, financial repair and economic governance. National budgets needed to be brought into more solid footing so that the rebalancing of the entire real economy would not be jeopardized. The implementation of structural reform had to be refocused in order to create the necessary groundwork for economic growth. Bank capital had to be strengthened in order to avoid a credit crunch. The stability mechanism had to be fortified in order to counteract the market turmoil. The reform of the economic and monetary union had to be pushed forward in order to facilitate the prevention of crises proactively.

The rationale of the CCR was both long-term and short-term. While many of these actions concerned mostly about the long-term, it was reasonable to assume that all these together would also increase confidence in the markets in the short term.

While preparations for the CCR went on, several actors, including the German ministry of finance and the IMF, shared information at the civil servant level and worked towards the same goal, though with somewhat different nuances. By and large, the German, Commission and IMF non-papers went into the same direction: all underlined the need to increase the EFSF effective lending capacity and its scope of activities; to create a flexible credit line for the Eurozone; to proceed fast with bank recapitalization and restructuring; and to encourage the vulnerable member states like

Portugal and Spain to intensify their efforts of stabilization and reform. The IMF could also call for the ECB to substantially increase sovereign bond purchases and step up liquidity facilities; the Commission instead used the euphemism "ensuring properly functioning bond markets in the euro area", which meant basically the same thing, but respected the ECB's cherished independence. Even the German finance ministry recognized the systemic nature of the crisis and endorsed giving extra funding to the EFSF to ensure that the amount of 440 billion euros is actually available; moreover, the Germans were clear about the need for Portugal to enter into a full program and Spain into a precautionary one.

The basic content of the Commission's version for the CCR for the Eurozone was a package deal that would offer a solid framework within which vulnerable member states would commit to overhauling their public finances and restoring their competitiveness. The lending capacity of the EFSF was to be raised to 440 billion euros, which was thought to be enough to convince the markets that there were no gains to be made in speculating against the euro countries. By doing this, we should have been able to push down the yields on the sovereign bonds of the vulnerable countries to a level that was at least tolerable.

I discussed the CCR on the basis of our non-paper with various finance ministers in the margins of the Eurogroup in December 2010. At that point, the foremost message was: "We are not ready yet, wait until January". Well, we waited—and waited. It turned out to be a very long wait. Decisions finally started arriving only in the summer and autumn of 2011, by which time it was already too late to avoid another real-economy recession. When unanimity is required, decisions often become hard to come by, especially during times of crisis.

While the crisis was pressing, there were also positive developments for the euro. I spent the New Year's Eve and Day in Tallinn to celebrate Estonia's joining the Euro on 1 January 2011. Estonia wanted to be in the political and economic core of Europe and aimed at enhancing its economic stability in the turmoil of the crisis. Its economic flexibility and entrepreneurial dynamism would fit well to the euro, I thought. I'll discuss the Baltic states road to the euro in more detail in Chapter 14.

The Tallinn New Year was a memorable event with *Eesti Vabariik's* President Toomas Ilves and Prime Minister Andrus Ansip, with whom we took out the first Estonian euros from the ATM in the crispy, frosty winter weather. My colleague Siim Kallas and our spouses Kristi and Merja joined the good-spirited celebrations. Estonia was now quite a different country than in 1982 when I first visited it.

Making the ESM a More Effective Bazooka

On 3 January, I returned to my Berlaymont office and held preparatory meetings on further sharpening the CCR. We had an in-depth briefing and planning session with Marco Buti and Stephanie Riso on 5 January, considering how to beef up the EU financial firewalls and governance. We knew we had to prepare for a long battle.

In the evening of 5 January, we had a working dinner with Barroso in Berlaymont to refine our strategy. On the EFSF I proposed to him: "reinforce the effective lending capacity and widen the scope of activities". In my view, we had reached the point in the crisis when we had to be as bold as possible, and not worry too much about the likely banging we would be getting. I felt Barroso agreed with the stance I proposed. We discussed Portugal and Spain, including the prospects of a rescue program. I understood Barroso was sceptical to their need.

We continued to further specify the CCR the whole following week. But talking about Portugal, on the following Sunday we had a pleasant event in the snowy field of Ixelles, Brussels—a game with Portugal. It was a draw 3-3. I scored 2 goals for Finland United, both one-touch, the first nicely to the top corner. Not bad for a soon over-50-year-old who played with fellow below-30-year-olds. I remember this particularly well as it was my last game to score "seriously" (if not counting the goal against Germany in the 2016 European Parliamentary Tournament!). The Eurozone debt crisis had a very negative spillover effect on veteran football by breaking up the career of a promising 49-year-old striker.

Back in business on Monday 10 January, in order to prepare myself for two important meetings to be held next day. On Tuesday morning, Klaus Regling, an always thoughtful ex-colleague in the Commission and now the managing director of the EFSF/ESM, came to see me in Berlaymont. We had a confidential reflection about the possible ways and means of debt restructuring of Greece. Klaus gave his take on how the buy-back of government bonds á la Brady Plan (in reference to debt buy-backs in Latin America in the late 1980s) could be applied. His scheme had a striking similarity to the subsequent bond buy-backs in Greece. It has always been productive to ponder with Klaus, and continues to be.

In the afternoon, Dominique Strauss-Kahn of the IMF visited me in Berlaymont. Over a cup of coffee, we discussed and fully agreed on the necessity of a CCR and its policy priorities. I requested that he could talk to Ms. Merkel in favour of a flexible use of ESM next day in Berlin, where he was going to meet her. He said he was planning to do so. Of course,

I also had to ask about his presidential candidacy in 2012—his response was a relaxed laughter, and he said that he had not thought it through and was not sure what he would do.

The Commission anyway continued with preparing the comprehensive crisis response and presented it in under the name Annual Growth Survey (the first of its kind) on 12 January 2011. As said, many people outside the Commission were also thinking along similar lines.

An interesting question is whether the idea of a banking union in the Eurozone was already in the plans. The answer is "no" and "yes". In name, it was not yet. In substance, many of its elements were at the core of the CCR: the balance sheet repair, stress tests, recapitalization, regulatory reform, and the new supervisory architecture. Further development of the banking union concept in the critical phase of 2011–13 illustrates the challenges but also successes of the European project, united in diversity. As Waltraud Schelkle has put it:

> The paradox of diversity can also explain why it took the United States more than 150 years and innumerable financial crises before a viable monetary-fiscal constitution became acceptable to the members of the federation. That history was not an exercise in optimization but a trial-and-error process of finding economically stabilizing and politically acceptable ways of governing a single currency.[4] In other words, it was a political economy in action, not pure rational economics.

At the end of January 2011, I visited Berlin again. We met with Wolfgang Schäuble and discussed the pressing policy issues and conditions for a comprehensive programme. I got confirmation for my perception that Germany would be prepared to drive such a programme—at least in some form and in some depth—when the political time was ripe. Jörg Asmussen, Schäuble's deputy and state secretary, had shared with me before Christmas 2010 Germany's core ideas for a CCR. There were many similarities to our views, but the two approaches were obviously not identical. Nevertheless, the essential analysis of both, also of the German position, was that the Eurozone response had thus far been "behind the curve", and both also recognized the systemic nature of the crisis. The German position was summarized: "We are no longer looking at a series of incidents affecting individual businesses, … a crisis within the system. It is *the system itself that is in crisis*". The outcome of the CCR deliberations was, over time, a synthesis of the two, though—which is no surprise to the seasoned Eurozone watchers—it was closer to the German version.

I was also invited to give a speech in the parliamentary group of the German liberal party, the FDP. The meeting was attended by most of the Party's 93 Members of the Parliament, as well as by the ministers, MEPs and a large group of assistants. The reception I received from this smaller government party was sympathetic in terms of atmosphere, but sceptical in terms of substance.

I did the first part of my speech in German, which required hard practice for several days before the mission. Taneli Lahti, a member of my Cabinet, a Doctor of Economics from the Nürnberg University, helped me to draft a solid text in the spirit of the German stability culture. Even that did not seem to help when I moved on to the second part of my speech, the establishment of a stability fund. "Prearranged and rubber-stamped", veteran politician would say of the meeting, since the FDP's positions had already been decided and there was not much leeway to negotiate.

The FDP was no more the motor in European integration as it used to be when the late Hans-Dietrich Genscher was the party leader and Germany's longest-serving foreign minister. Since the electoral defeat of 2013, the party under the dynamic Christian Lindner made an electoral comeback in 2017, but its European orientation remains dualistic—in general terms, it is a pro-European political force, but maintains a sceptical libertarian approach towards economic stabilization.

President Barroso was very concerned about the deterioration of the economic situation in Europe and pushed for the implementation of the comprehensive program actively. In the press conference on the CCR on 12 January, he proposed an enlargement of the capacity of the EFSF and emphasized that this decision was needed already in the Eurozone Summit scheduled on 4 February 2011. Barroso was right, but we didn't score a goal this time. The summit was not the most successful one in other respects, either. Germany and France were calling for a competitiveness pact (the Euro Plus Pact), which sought the right things. But it only leaned on loose intergovernmental cooperation, bypassing the institutions of the Union. This was met with harsh criticism by many small member states. According to the Belgian Prime Minister Yves Leterme, it was a "truly surreal summit".

Following Barroso's proposals, the Commission in turn was severely criticized for excessive activism and for rushing things unnecessarily. "You are rocking the boat!" "That's only very artificial discussion!" There were shots fired at us more or less from every direction. Nonetheless, the Commission kept its enterprising stance under Barroso's lead. I staunchly supported Barroso's initiative on the rapid, necessary enlargement of the lending capacity of the EFSF.

After a particularly long day in mid-January, I noted in my journal:

> We just have to endure this beating. We will not achieve anything if we do not hold the line in public, too. Whether we do this or that, it will always be the wrong way around for someone. If we stay quiet, nothing will proceed, and they will say even the Commission is not making any demands. On the other hand, if we demand decisions, they will say we are rocking the boat and jeopardizing the rescue operation of the euro.

Sometimes, moderation is for the best. But now as the crisis was truly steamrolling over us, it was indeed better to burn out than to fade away or to rust, as the rock-and-roll poet Neil Young would put it. The Commission's duty is to push forward the common European cause, and loudly, too, when necessary, not least during the long-lasting debt crisis, and not to remain quiet in the congregation.

Sequencing Fails—The Wrong Marching Order

Enlargement of the lending capacity of the European Financial Stability Facility, the EFSF, kept dragging on. In order to ensure the highest credit rating for itself, the fund had already been forced to build buffers so high that its actual lending capacity was practically cut down to half. Hence, the credibility of the EFSF was eroded, gradually at first, but soon with ever more rapid strides.

However, in another Eurozone Summit held towards the end of March 2011, the euro area leaders somewhat unexpectedly announced that they would increase its actual lending capacity from 200–250 billion up to 440 billion euros—which was indeed the original objective, but fell due to the problematic financial structure. Unfortunately, the favourable market impact of this decision evaporated quickly, when certain member states, including Finland, began last-minute haggling to water down what had already been agreed on. Not the finest hour.

The final agreement was not reached until October 2011, when a decision was also made to bring forward the launch of the permanent ESM by a year to July 2012. However, by late autumn 2011, this decision was already much too late, since Italy had wound up in a credibility crisis and Spain was also in deep trouble particularly with its banking sector. This procrastination proved costly for Europe, and affected both the unemployed and taxpayers.

Sequence matters in economic policy and financial fire-fighting. In order to achieve the best outcome possible, the measures outlined should have been implemented in the right order. By "the best outcome possible" here I mean strengthening the financial stability of the whole Eurozone by the kind of determined policy that would lay the foundations for sustainable growth and better employment.

What, then, would have been the right sequencing?

First, we should have strengthened the stability mechanism, so as to cut the contagion effect short and to protect the other countries at risk. The next or second thing should have been to push for a strengthening of the banks' balance sheets and capitalization so that their problems and ongoing deleveraging would not result in a credit crunch and suffocate the emerging economic recovery, but that the banks would instead keep their credit taps open for companies and households. The third and final move should have been a managed debt restructuring for Greece, in order to reduce the country's impossible burden of debt. The implementation of "private sector involvement" (PSI), the euphemism for sovereign debt restructuring, should have been done in such a way that it would not drag down the other Eurozone countries when investors exit its government bonds.

The idea underlying this sequencing was to protect the Eurozone from a liquidity trap due to ongoing deleveraging of the banking sector, and to prepare prudently for a managed debt restructuring in Greece. This way, proactive actions could have prevented any negative spillovers of the deleveraging and restructuring on the rest of the euro area.

As we now know, this reasonable objective did not quite succeed. The recapitalization of banks nudged forward first, and as an individual measure, this implied a deleveraging process that threatened to drive the euro area into a credit crunch. Ultimately, the Eurozone was only saved from that by the ECB's long-term refinancing operations (LTROs); that is, the massive three-year re-lending operations launched in December 2011 and February 2012. Next, the managed restructuring of Greek debt was conducted in two phases, first in July 2011 and second, with a larger cut on loan principal, in early 2012. The launch of the permanent stability mechanism and strengthening of its actual lending capacity were left for later. The failed sequence exposed the euro area to a dangerous contamination effect.

I recall the frustration in Berlaymont reaching higher levels than ever. Once, in July 2011 when we discussed the obstacles to and watering down of the comprehensive response, President Barroso told me in desperation: "I don't believe in this. It is only *homeopathy!*" My response: "No, antibiotics!"

But I sure added that we definitely needed a more surgical and genuinely systemic crisis response.

The main reason for the wrong marching order and the procrastination on tough issues is not necessarily to be found in individual decision-makers, but rather in the rigid structure of the decision-making process in the Eurozone. It is cold realism that it was rational in the short term for the governments of individual member states in certain circumstances to minimize political risk, even at the cost of the economic future of the whole euro area, which led to a politically motivated priority setting instead of a factually justified one. Risto Murto, CEO of a major pension fund, coined it well as to Finland's policy stance: "The minimization of joint responsibility in the short term is leading to the maximization of long-term liabilities".

This discrepancy between short-sighted political motivations and long-term economic goals does not relate to only one or two member states, but was a rather universal feature. Yet in which form it appears seems to depend largely on the economic competitiveness and financial position of the member state concerned. Marxists would point to an inbuilt contradiction in the social order. This is the fundamental reason why the euro area was forced to hold a total of 19 crisis summits during the debt crisis in 2010–12. For quite some time, the euro area crisis was no more fundamentally an economic crisis, but a political one—or an institutional crisis of decision-making structures, to be more exact.

Another reason for the misguided sequence was the difficulty of reaching each decision under the unanimity rule, which did not allow for systematic planning of how the whole equation of multiple decisions would be executed effectively—or at least it did not allow one to wait for a systematic implementation of the plans. One had to embrace one by one the agreements that could be reached, cross her or his fingers and pray at least for a mundane miracle, when nothing better was available. Hence, the reality of decision-making in Brussels did not fully correspond to the image of a "Brussels supremacy" so much hated by some. Rather, there were often too many red lines and thus little common territory for compromise solutions.

When using the customary community method in EU's decision-making, in which the Commission has the right of initiative, the Council makes decisions by a qualified majority and the parliament by absolute majority, the ability of the EU institutions to have an influence, and to proactively mediate different opinions into an agreement, is much more potent. This was not the case on this occasion.

The community method is indeed the way in which the Union is able to function and make decisions. When unanimity is required, the ability of the Council to make decisions efficiently and in time is lamentably limited. Unfortunately, historical precedents of this are, rather than warning examples, warning exclamation marks. After all, this was a key factor to the fall of the League of Nations in the 1930s.

Portugal's Turn Before the Second Round in Greece

Towards the end of 2010, Spain and Portugal ended up at the epicentre of crisis. Behind the scenes, there were discussions about a precautionary program for Spain and a fully fledged program for Portugal.

Soon Greece also re-emerged as a problem, as the country's political parties were unable to join forces to implement the reform programme, and the country began to lag behind its fiscal consolidation goals. Discussions about the second Greek program started in March 2011 and they were at full speed by Easter. It had become increasingly clear that, in the context of the second program, private investors would have to bear the majority of the losses, since there was no other way of bringing Greece's massive burden of debt on a sustainable track. But *how* that could be decided was anything but clear.

Differences of opinion surfaced about how to deal with Greece and especially PSI. Some participants such as the ECB were adamantly against any restructuring. Meanwhile, some member states pushed for a heavy "haircut", or large cuts into the nominal principal of Greek sovereign debt. Common ground could not regrettably be found by summer 2011. Vetoes cancelled each other out, and no decision was possible, which led the Eurozone to drift without direction and drain to an unmanaged solution.

Portugal's situation deteriorated in early 2011 on the back of sluggish economic growth and a persistent deficit in public finances. Portugal's actual problem was not so much any reckless management of public finances—though there were sticky and inherited fiscal-structural problems—than the weak productivity and competitiveness of the economy and a long-lasting accumulation of debt in the private sector. Prime Minister José Socrates was not willing to admit the depth of Portugal's problems, although even the Portuguese opposition required the government to turn to the EU and the IMF. At the end of March 2011, the government however lost the vote on the fiscal package in the parliament, which was interpreted as a motion of censure.

The final straw was a public petition by Finance Minister Fernando Teixera de Santos in early April to his own government (sic!) to call for external assistance, including an only superficially concealed threat of resignation. This persuaded—or rather coerced—Prime Minister Socrates to change his mind. On 7 April 2011, Portugal applied for a euro area loan support to stabilize its economy. The timing apparently also reflected the decision by Portugal's largest private banks to refuse to buy any more sovereign bonds, since they considered it too risky. Discussion about PSI in cutting Greece's burden of debt affected investors' perception about risk also in the rest of Europe. Now this contagion effect reached Portugal.

In retrospect, Portugal would have fared better had it sought Eurozone financial assistance earlier, since this would have helped the country on the path of reforms sooner, and the entire package would have been cheaper for the Eurozone. It would have been definitely better also for the Eurozone. For the first time in June 2010, I requested this to Minister Fernando Teixeira dos Santos in private by asking the question, whether Portugal had begun to prepare for an EU-IMF program, since the need for adjustments to regain competitiveness in the country exceeded its own resources. In winter 2010–11, the issue surfaced in discussions of the Eurogroup. Several Eurozone countries saw Portugal's impasse and encouraged the country in the course of the winter to make a rapid request for support. Meanwhile, standing facilities were being prepared in various different quarters for Spain to calm down the markets, but the government of the country did not find it necessary.

A few days after Portugal's plea for support, just before mid-April, I found myself on a mission impossible in an unofficial Ecofin Council meeting in the town of Gödöllő, close to Budapest in Hungary. The Finnish opposition at the time—the Social Democrats and the True Finns—threatened to overthrow the loan support for Portugal by voting against it in the parliament. In any international setting, I had to constantly respond to questions about Finland posed by my colleagues. The image of Finland had received a new tone of colour, and especially a lot higher contrast. This was also the number one topic for the international media, on which I was of course asked to comment on a daily basis, in every context possible.

At the Gödöllő press conference in front of the entire global media, I was forced to answer to the question if the Portuguese package would face a dead-end in the Finnish Parliament. In order to pacify the atmosphere, I had to say that I trusted Finland would eventually participate in the common push by the euro area to prevent Portugal's default and to safeguard financial stability in the euro area. As by Ecofin standards, there was a record-high participation by the Finnish media, the message spread at the same time to Finland. The opposition did not fail to jump at the opportunity to criticize me for disregarding democracy, which was certainly not the case, particularly when a devout *républicain* such as myself was concerned.

The word "trust", which I often use, can be understood, besides as an assessment of the certainty of something, also as an ostensibly concealed expression of will. This time, it meant no doubt both.

For some reason, particularly the Social Democrat Party decided to launch a group attack on me due to my statements. The front-page headlines of the party's newspaper *Demari* (presently *Demokraatti*) screamed on Monday 11th April that I had dictated commands to the Social Democrats. I had not done such a thing, nor was I even capable of doing so. At the same time, as the SDP was firing a broadside towards me, I was engaged in close co-operation on a daily basis with several problem-stricken socialist governments. At the time, the SDP's ideological brothers and sisters were reigning, for example, in Greece, Portugal, Spain and Ireland—and the German SPD was supporting the rescue from the opposition position.

Ultimately, after many twists-and-turns and colourful events, Finland decided in June 2011 to participate in loan-funding the Portuguese reform program with its two-percent share of the total package. This became a key part of the program of Prime Minister Jyrki Katainen's government (2011–14), which included the SDP. Later on, the call for some sort of collateral to cover the Finnish loans in the second Greek package was the condition that the SDP demanded for its support, and got it.

The Greek Debt Restructuring: Act One

When the finance ministers and central bankers from all around the world convened a week later at the IMF spring meetings in Washington in mid-April 2011, the euro area debt crisis was in the epicentre again. The IMF's spring and annual meetings are a biannual "jamboree"—or a sort of party conference for international economic policy-makers, usually with rather direct, analytical and evidence-based discussions about the prospects of the world economy with the aim of coordinating the economic policies of different countries or regions. G7 and G20 tend to convene as well in connection with these IMF meetings. In addition, there are dozens of panels, fringe meetings, seminars and conferences of several organizations.

This time, Portugal was at the top of the public agenda, but underneath—and subject to real policy wrangling—was Greece. At the time, the Portuguese program was finalized to a large extent in terms of content, and it was no longer discussed in Washington, except for the several political uncertainties related to its approval, not least in Finland, where the political atmosphere had turned euro-sceptic.

Meanwhile, Greece was back. In the course of the winter, the mission chiefs of the Commission, ECB and IMF in Athens warned that the Greek program was derailing after a good start. Although the Greek government and parliament had decided to take consolidation measures in their public finances, there were no signs of rebalancing of the country's fiscal position. Even more worrying, the critical part of the program, the pursuit of structural reforms, was failing badly. As a consequence, Greece's debt burden was now expected to rise so high—up to 160% of GDP—that it would be unable to manage the burden without a restructuring.

Since the matter would be discussed in the G20 ministers' meeting, it was crucial to seek a common Eurozone stance. In cooperation with Ramon Fernandez, the very competent secretary of state of the French ministry of finance, we convened the Eurozone state secretaries participating in the G7/G20 group, which eventually became to be known as "the Washington Group" that met subsequently and irregularly to sort things out before many critical decisions. We sat down with them for a long and intense evening in Washington after the official meeting agenda had ended on Wednesday, 13th April. Despite the tiredness caused by the jetlag, we gathered up the remaining energy and sought late at night to find an analytical solution to the persistent problems of Greece. You always need an analytical solution—a strategy—before you can start forging a political solution.

The session of state secretaries had a follow-up a few nights later, when the finance ministers of the G20 Eurozone countries held a meeting chaired by Jean-Claude Juncker, President of the Eurogroup. I participated in the meeting together with Jean-Claude Trichet, the ECB's President. Due to fresh worrisome information received from the representatives of the Troika in Athens, there were serious discussions in Athens for the first time in a year on finding a sustainable resolution for Greece's problems also in terms of debt sustainability.

In May, Greece was discussed in meetings by groups of various compositions around Europe. After initial difficulties, the first steps were taken towards a controlled restructuring to moderate Greece's unbearable burden of debt.

Overall, the situation in the spring of 2011 was still fragile and turning worse especially as regards Italy and Spain. The CCR had moved in some dimensions, but only very partially—therefore the vulnerability of the Eurozone continued and underlined the need and urgency to get decisions made. More on both Greece and the CCR during the summer and fall of 2011 in the next chapter.

Thus, yet another hot summer on the cards. Down on the corner—Bad moon rising! But it was not to be the last hot summer, or even the hottest one, unfortunately.

Notes

1. John Maynard Keynes, *The General Theory of Employment, Interest and Money.* Preface to the French Edition, 1936. Included in the *Collected Writings of John Maynard Keynes: Volume VII.* Macmillan, Cambridge University Press, 1973, p. xxxii.
2. Padoa-Schioppa, Tommaso, *The Euro and Its Central Bank: Getting United After the Union,* 2004, p. 180. Cited in Waltraud Schelkle, *The Political Economy of Monetary Solidarity: The Euro Experiment.* Oxford University Press, 2017, p. 225.
3. Owen Fletcher and Aaron Back, China Voices Support for European Bailouts. *Wall Street Journal,* 22 December 2010, p. 10.
4. Waltraud Schelkle, *The Political Economy of Monetary Solidarity: The Euro Experiment.* Oxford University Press, 2017, p. 2.

7

Summertime Blues in Italy

Spring 2011 culminated in mid-May with a news bomb from New York City. Dominique Strauss-Kahn, the Managing Director of the International Monetary Fund, was arrested on 14 May 2011 at the Kennedy airport, only minutes before he was taking off by an Air France flight to Paris. I got the shocking news by text message from Spain's Elena Salgado, DSK's fellow socialist modernizer, and then checked the news from various websites: DSK had indeed been arrested on charges of sexually assaulting a hotel maid, a very serious accusation if proven true. Later on, apparently after much legal juggling, the charges were dropped, but DSK had to resign immediately.

I had talked with DSK just a few days before, in a very different spirit and in a rather more substantive context, as we discussed a new programme for Greece. He was hurrying the European decisions in a way that would mean the Eurogroup would feel cornered, and unable to decide. He said the IMF was unwilling to commit itself into a second programme, unless the Eurozone will take the ultimate responsibility for lending to Greece. The IMF would block its part of 12 billion euros to be disbursed by the end of June under the first programme, unless the EU was ready to guarantee the funding needs of Greece for the next 12 months. This would have however been very difficult to get suddenly passed in many parliaments and thus would have created unnecessary political tensions and seriously risked the positive outcome.

I was suspicious the French electoral context might have some impact on the hurry and wrote to my notebook after the phone call:

© The Author(s) 2020
O. Rehn, *Walking the Highwire*, https://doi.org/10.1007/978-3-030-34592-1_7

I cannot avoid the impression that DSK is driving the quick option in June in order to get a clean slate by 28 June, when he is – I heard it through the grapevine – planning to launch his presidential candidacy. But with this premature hurry he is pushing the Eurozone into a shitty corner, and the differences of view will surface, even explode, in a much uncontrolled way, which may damage the cause.

These suspicions soon became irrelevant, and we can't know if they were correct or not—there may have been substantive reasons for the hurry from the rather rigid IMF standpoint as well. Anyway the French Socialist Party had to choose another candidate, and in June, the IMF picked another competent French policy-maker, Finance Minister Christine Lagarde, to lead the Fund as Managing Director ("MD" in the Fund's parlance) from 5 July 2011 onwards. The MD post was temporarily carried by DSK's capable deputy, the American economist John Lipsky, with whom we prudently prepared the Greek file for a subsequent decision over the early summer weeks.

Of course, the disappearance of DSK from the helm of the IMF caused a certain delay in the negotiations of the second programme for Greece, although first Lipsky and then Lagarde smoothly picked up the baton. The focus of firefighting was anyway moving to Italy and Spain. In some ways, the summer 2011 was cut in two halftimes: the epicentre was on Greece until July, from July onwards, on Italy and Spain. It is a no-brainer to note that the Greek haircuts in July had something to do with this sequence of events. Those who claim there is no contagion effect from debt restructuring must be blind or have closed their eyes from empirical evidence.

For me, summer 2011 was not spent on holidays, but by then in the already regular duties of the Eurozone voluntary fire brigade. Crisis for all, holidays for some only. Our search for the "lost ark"—the comprehensive crisis response—continued as intensively as ever, though we had no Harrison Ford to jump over the snakes. My traditional cultural missions to the Pori Jazz and Savonlinna Opera Festival had to be cancelled at the last minute due to various crisis meetings.

It was also a very Italian summer for me, but not under the soft sun of Tuscany, nor at the San Siro stadium in Milan, nor in the historic *piazzas* of Rome, nor on the fascinating streets of Elena Ferrante's Naples. Instead, my topmost memory from August 2011 was that I had just started my vacation at our cottage by the lake in Mikkeli when the phone rang—never to stop ringing until the end of August. One moment, I would be standing on the pier by the lake or on the patio with my mobile phone, talking to Mario Draghi, Governor of *Banca d'Italia* at the time, or Giulio Tremonti, the country's finance minister. Next, I would be off to driving on Finland's Highway 5 and flying further to Frankfurt and Brussels, back and forth. Then, the summer was gone. And for a Finn, life is too short to miss even one summer.

Those who doubted that there would be any contagion effect from Greece and Ireland were proven wrong latest in the summer of 2011. The contagion effect was in full steam in July 2011. The uncertainty surrounding Greece, difficulties related to the approval of the Portuguese programme in the parliaments of some member states, Italy's stalling reforms, and the crumbling credibility of the stress tests on German and Spanish banks—all these kept feeding the distrust that began to draw Italy and Spain towards the edge of the cliff. The debt crisis had taken increasingly clearly the shape of a *euro* crisis—it was a truly systemic crisis that would require an equally matching systemic response.

One contributing element was the premature interest rate hike of the ECB to show its rigour in defending price stability. The ECB had been under heavy criticism especially in Germany for its bond-buying programme. As the recovery was moving ahead and headline inflation was rising above 2% (though only very temporarily), and despite the ongoing financial turbulence and debt crisis, the ECB Governing Council started to consider and prepare for a rate hike, which eventually was decided and done twice, in April and July. In retrospect, we know that the recovery had turned very much weaker during the spring and summer, and it was certainly and unfortunately further weakened by the premature rate hikes of 2011.

It was discomforting for many, including me, to learn that the ECB Governing Council was prepared to raise interest rates despite the looming financial turbulence, based only on a relatively short-term upward peak in inflation. It was customary that the Commissioner was not invited to the Governors-only dinner discussions, which preceded the rate-setting monetary policy meetings, especially in the Trichet era, so I was surprised to learn about this in the morning in the formal meeting.

In the plane back to Brussels in the evening, I scribbled to my notebook and wondered if the rate hike was wise, considering the dangerous turbulence in the crisis countries Greece, Portugal and Ireland and in the countries at the edge, Italy and Spain. The game on Trichet's successor was also a factor, making the usual centre ground almost as hawkish as the hawks, since Germany's support was considered crucial to be appointed the next President of the ECB.

Furthermore, the ECB aimed at making a clear distinction between normal monetary policy (= the policy rate) to fight inflation and unconventional measures (= the SMP or the bond-buying programme) to tame the crisis. Soon it became evident that it was too smart tactics, which in due course would give way for a more calibrated strategy, based on the sequencing of both conventional and unconventional policy measures and forward guidance in communication.

Commentators at the time were rather ruthless as to the ECB's decisions. Carlo Bastasin wrote: "The decision by the European Central Bank to stop buying the bonds of Greece, Portugal, and Ireland was a major episode of the tug-of-war between the ECB and the national governments. Both sides underestimated the unintended consequences that their conflict would have on the private economy. It was a fatal mistake".[1] James Surowiecki wrote in September 2011: "The July rate hike was like kicking the economy when it was down".[2]

Apart from the rate hikes, there were two other culmination points in the course of the summer. First, as things were getting from bad to worse, not least due to Greece, a Eurozone Summit was convened on 21 July. Its effect was again short-lived. Second, the ECB decided to re-start the bond-buying programme in early August this time including also Italy and Spain. This was supported by some communication efforts by the Commission. This helped to create a calmer slip-stream, for some time… but finally it turned out to be only a temporary truce. The decisions before and in the July summit failed to convince the markets that the crisis had been brought under control, and the turbulence continued despite the ECB's actions.

For Italy, this meant a scorching summer and autumn. Silvio Berlusconi, the Prime Minister, distanced himself from the policies of his own Finance Minister, Giulio Tremonti. To balance the budget, Tremonti had pushed for further expenditure cuts and tax increases. Interest rates in Italy had jumped over the 5% mark for the first time in three years. Even more worryingly, the Italian interest rates were now on the same track as Greece, Ireland and Portugal had been a year earlier. The bush fire in Greece was expanding into a forest fire over the whole euro area, threatening the Italian and Spanish economies to catch the fire, as well.

In July, there was an avalanche of bad news coming from various parts of the euro area. Portugal's credit rating sunk to the junk category, the ECB raised its policy rate for the second time, and certain euro area politicians began to loudly call for a rough and hard debt restructuring and euro exit for Greece. To add insult to injury, the Eurozone leaders failed to expand the lending capacity of the European Financial Stability Facility (EFSF), which would have been critical to restore its damaged reputation as the "big bazooka", or as a true and sturdy financial firewall. I knew that from then on, we would definitely be walking the highwire of extreme turbulence.

The "Secret" Meeting in Luxemburg

But the scene for the summer turbulence was set already in the spring. By May 2011, it had become clear to all key players that the debt burden of Greece and its trend was unsustainable, even if the ECB was the last Mohican to still resist. The matter was discussed in various meetings in various compositions around Europe.

Eurogroup President Jean-Claude Juncker wanted—rightly in my view, and at the eleventh hour—to get some order in the public cacophony around the second programme for Greece and the very dividing issue of debt restructuring. Therefore, he invited a small group of key ministers and officials to Luxembourg on Friday 6 May 2011 to a small secret meeting— or I should say to a "supposedly secret" meeting, since it was leaked and became public before it had barely started.

Not that we didn't try our utmost to keep it secret. I made my preparations inside the Commission without telling the exact purpose to anybody apart from President Barroso and made the travel arrangements outside official channels, which was easy as we were only driving from Brussels to Luxembourg. The Greek Finance Minister George Papaconstantinou, who took part in the second half of the meeting, took precautions like booking the flight to Frankfurt, to avoid leaks—which in his case succeeded, unlike some others.

It was a sunny and warm Friday afternoon in Luxembourg when we arrived to the government mansion in Luxembourg. Somebody suggested we could kick off the meeting outside at the terrace, and so it was decided. Just when we were about to begin, everyone's phone started flashing or shaking or buzzing, as hundreds of text messages were received asking what the heck is going on. *Spiegel Online* had broken a story and revealed the meeting, with the nasty and completely false spin that the meeting would have been called urgently to discuss a possible Greek exit from the euro. That was of course political dynamite.

First Juncker's spokesman denied the meeting, which didn't go down well with the media—an understatement of the year. After some quick second thoughts and collective reflection, we decided to make a brief statement to control damage, stating that Christine Lagarde (then G20 chair) and Juncker (as Eurogroup chair) had decided to convene the Eurozone ministers of the G20 to an informal meeting to discuss G20 matters and invited the Greek finance minister for consultation. The simple lesson was straight from Communications 101: never lie!

The leak caused understandable anger and anxiety among the participants, and the hidden tensions on substance surfaced in a forced manner. The leak and the way it surfaced didn't really help creating an atmosphere of confidence and solving the pressing Eurozone problems, rather to the contrary. In the halftime, when Papaconstantinou arrived, Trichet left the scene and refused to participate in a meeting even discussing debt restructuring.

In the second half at the restricted small dinner, Juncker went straight to the beef: since Greece had no chance of accessing the markets in 2012, we needed to agree on a new, second programme. I followed up and gave the Commission's take: the programme as such was not failing and substantial reduction of fiscal deficit had been achieved, but implementation should be stepped up, with a stronger focus on structural reforms. I also regretted that the opposition in Greece was not supportive of the programme but rather digging ground under it—Samaras' party *Nea Demokratia* was member of the European Peoples Party, like most of the participants at the table. I appealed to them to urge Nea Demokratia to support national unity. In vain.

Next, Papaconstantinou presented the Greek case by referring to the huge fiscal consolidation achieved and the many reforms done. But for him, the atmosphere around the programme was excessively negative, both in Greece and outside it, compared to the progress made. In his view, the best way forward for Greece would be a combination of an ambitious balancing of public finances with a high primary surplus, on the one hand, and a voluntary offer to bond-holders to lengthen or exchange bonds maturing up to 2020, with no haircuts, on the other.[3]

It was now clear that the Eurogroup's internal divide on debt sustainability and private sector involvement (PSI) was getting ever deeper. I tried to build bridges in Luxembourg between the two camps and turn some of the red lines pink in the Impossible Triangle, simply to move forward in firefighting. I defended the Greek track record by saying that seven (!) percentage points of deficit reduction are not peanuts, while I also underlined the need to reach a substantial primary surplus in 2014. My suggestion on debt restructuring was to recognize the case for voluntary re-profiling: we are not against a Vienna-type initiative, with the rollover of exposure.

Due to the remaining red lines and limited mandates, we didn't however get anywhere on substance. Tremonti lamented that the absence of the ECB from this meeting was tragic. Juncker stated afterwards that our joint message should be: no Greek exit, no restructuring, but re-profiling is open, and we'd work for a reinforced programme. I followed this script in my subsequent communication.

While the "secret" meeting was an immediate failure, it nevertheless achieved something useful that would pay off later on, in fact sooner than we then thought. PSI, popularly known as "haircuts", had been the white elephant in the room, or the real-life "Voldemort" that "should not be mentioned". Now it was at least allowed to internally discuss the Voldemort, and the serious work of analysing the options and next steps in the preparatory machinery of the Eurogroup could finally start making real progress.

Haircuts and Barbers

In the course of the spring and summer of 2011, negotiations on debt restructuring of some form took place between the Greek government and the International Institute of Finance (IIF) that represented her international investors and banks. This international group of investors and banks was steered cunningly by Josef Ackerman, the chief executive of Deutsche Bank and chair of the IIF.

In the Commission, we were concerned about this process triggering a "credit event"—a code word for hard debt restructuring—because we considered it a jump to the unknown and dangerous from the point of view of accelerating the already ongoing contagion. I stated the Commission position in the margins of a FT Deutschland conference in Königstein: "We have been discussing a Vienna-style initiative and in that context we have also examined the feasibility of a voluntary debt rescheduling or re-profiling on the condition that it will not create a credit event".[4] By "Vienna-style", I referred to the public–private Vienna Initiative in 2009 to reschedule loans of Eastern and Central Europe, instead of an outright restructuring or cutting the capital. That helped contain systemic crisis and maintain lending to the real economy in the region. In my view, the time of denying some sort of debt restructuring was over, especially after the May experience in Luxembourg, and it was better to give some reassuring and non-dramatic messages, even if the final haircut could and probably should go deeper than that.

In Athens, things were now moving. By the end of June, after very confrontational discussions, the Greek parliament approved another stabilization package involving major savings measures and tax rises. This was a condition set by the Eurogroup for the approval of the second loan programme. Once progress was made in Athens, at my request Jean-Claude Juncker summoned the Eurogroup to a telephone conference on 2 July, a Saturday night, to make decisions. As I was in a conference in Finland, I did the call at the Commission Office in Helsinki.

On behalf of the Troika, I presented the decisions, which received unanimous but unenthusiastic support from the member states. After the decisions on Greece, I called for the Eurogroup to make the still missing decisions on the CCR before the central European summer holiday season. These would be required especially in respect of strengthening the stability fund, so as to ward off the contagion effects, as well as recapitalizing banks in order to bolster confidence. In this respect however, the meeting was fruitless and frustrating, even depressing.

After the long, dark winter and an equally bleak spring, the prevailing mood among the ministers of the Eurogroup was tangibly tense, which you could sense even over the phone in a conference call. I received my share of the negativity, too—something to which I had already become accustomed. Tired of procrastination, I wanted to make it clear that we cannot wait beyond the summer break with the critical decisions on Greece and a reinforcement of the financial firewall, which should have been taken in July. It was considered "unbelievable" by some ministers that the Commission rushed things in the supposedly member states' domain.

However, in a couple of days the increasing uncertainty and procrastination over the decisions led to a "chaotic spiral" in the markets on 7 and 8 July.[5] Over the weekend of 9–10 July, telephone lines were busy, particularly between Berlin, Paris, Frankfurt and Brussels. Market turbulence was no wonder, as there was much uncertainty in the air. The critical issue was the presumably looming restructuring of Greek public debt, which stands for a reduction in the nominal value of someone's debt (also called "haircut" or "PSI", as previously noted). A more modest version would be re-profiling, which stands for an extension of the maturity of a loan held by a private investor to the distant future, in order to avoid an impossible hump or repayment in the short-to-medium term. As Papaconstantinou correctly writes, "until spring 2011, both 'R' words were banned from Eurogroup meetings".[6] But it didn't mean that it was not discussed elsewhere: in public by the bankers, media and some politicians, in private by policy-makers.

I recall that at some point in the winter of 2010–11, when the debate on debt restructuring was intensifying, I thought we needed really to think outside the box. So I took the matter up with President Barroso in a bilateral private meeting by suggesting to consider calling a long weekend meeting of all member states and EU institutions, in which a decision of substantial debt restructuring of several Southern European countries could be taken, to be announced by Sunday night, and having the decisions take effect on Monday morning. The negative market effect would have to be contained by a sturdy financial firewall, the combined firepower of the ECB and

EFSF. We did a serious thought experiment on this imaginative alternative, but had to conclude that it was an unworkable scenario, mainly because of the deep internal divisions in the EU, which could not have facilitated a rational, effective and sufficiently rapid decision-making. No doubt, there would have been other, more technical hurdles, too. Anyway, the Big Bang idea had to be dropped as unworkable.

The debate now hinged on the issue of debt sustainability of Greece. It needs to be underlined that the only legally valid negotiations took place between the Greek Government and its international creditors, represented by the IIF. But the Eurogroup had a major stake in the outcome because, in the equation of programme funding, reducing the debt burden of Greece had a direct impact on the programme size, which in turn would reduce the need for official lending by other member states. The funding equation was simple: the amount needed for official lending by other member states was the large residual component left over, after the primary surplus or deficit of the public sector was summed up together with the IMF funding and the net reduction of public debt, the latter through a haircut or debt buy-back, or other form of restructuring. Hence, it was only natural that the Eurogroup and Commission provided flanking support for Greece in these talks.

The backdoor discussions had matured by June–July 2011 to the extent that the issue could be taken up confidentially in the EU institutions. The Euro Working Group was then chaired by Italy's market-savvy and always analytical state secretary Vittorio Grilli, who was a year later appointed the finance minister of Italy to succeed Giulio Tremonti. The options on the table included a debt exchange or debt buyback, which was regarded as a condition by several member states to accept a second programme for Greece that the country needed to stay solvent.

On Sunday 17 July, Jean-Claude Juncker called me in the morning. We agreed to meet with Ackermann and the IIF folks on Tuesday in Brussels at the Luxembourg embassy. We also decided that Jean-Claude would call Schäuble and Ackermann, I would talk with Grilli and Dallara.

So I called Grilli who was in close contact with his interface of state secretaries, the Euro Working Group, which had a conference call later in the day. Grilli was quite pessimistic about the crisis awareness in some member states: "The markets do not believe in euro governance. Meanwhile some in member states believe there is no contagion. Soon, after next downgrades, Italy and Spain will drop from the EFSF loan packages, which will be left to AAA only". I have to say Grilli was right in his grounded pessimism, or sensible realism, as the events would soon prove.

We were cautious and of the view that any deal had to be agreed *voluntarily*, so as to avoid causing a "credit event", meaning a sovereign default, which was considered dangerous for financial stability and credibility. The maximum was a "selective default", a softer and shorter version, in the market parlance.

We also had intense contacts with the IMF, not least as John Lipsky had become a close collaborator and Christine Lagarde was one already and becoming ever closer. She sent me a message of encouragement on the night (in Europe) of Monday 18 July, and cordially pushed us European to move on debt restructuring—she had just changed the seat from France to the IMF. I responded to her:

> Many thanks for encouragement, much needed. The air is still too thick with red lines… In fact, I am not and nor is the Commission against the PSI, but it depends on how it would be realized; the key is no credit event. We are pushing for a more comprehensive solution, including the more flexible use of the EFSF (secondary & precautionary) and the reduction of interest rates and extension of maturities… That's the most we can achieve now. More will surely follow, either immediately if the crisis deepens or only shortly if we have a breathing space. I believe your staff could take a closer look at contagion; it is underestimated… What I say may be criticized as muddling through, but it is hard to see a more viable and politically doable alternative for the moment. I'd be glad to change my view, if the facts and circumstances change. I keep an open mind.

So our balancing act on the highwire went on. In the meeting at the Luxembourg embassy in Brussels on 19 July, the mood was cordial but tense, as the stakes were high for all participants. Ackermann concurred with our general assessment that the situation was critical for the European economy: "Nobody in the Middle East, Switzerland, Russia, believe in the euro… We are close to September 2008. We need a convincing package ASAP". But there was no agreement in sight.

The talks continued in the next two days especially between Greece and its international creditors. In the Eurogroup corner, Germany was already thinking about next steps, assuming the one in the making then would turn out to be insufficient. According to Papaconstantinou, this is how the situation was perceived in the Greek government: "Germany was already thinking beyond simple re-profiling, but was waiting for Trichet's term to finish before revisiting the issue".[7]

I talked with Barroso who had concerns about the effect of possible PSI in "contagion countries", i.e. Italy, Spain and Portugal. In order to contain contagion once the Greek haircuts happened, in our view we should first— and before anything else was attempted—reinforce the Eurozone financial firewall, which was in the first place the EFSF/ESM, but could also lean on the ECB action, at least partly. This should be the unequivocal priority in the forthcoming Eurozone Summit.

The Eurozone Summit of 21 July: Steps Forward, but Too Late

Thus, the way was paved for the first round of debt restructuring of Greece. Barely, three weeks had passed since the Eurogroup teleconference of 2 July. By now, the market turbulence had escalated to the effect that the European Council President Herman van Rompuy decided to convene a Eurozone Summit on 21 July 2011.

President Barroso described the situation bluntly but to the point when delivering his opening statement to his colleagues in the Summit:

> So far, we have not managed the crisis effectively. Too many national interests have hampered agreement on a comprehensive solution. If we are to agree on such a solution, we must put these national interests aside. We must find this solution today! The longer we delay, the fewer options we have available.

Barroso maintained that the Eurozone had to focus its attention on a long-term strategic response to the crisis and to start acting and taking decisions immediately, based on seven building blocks:

1. Restoring the sustainability of Greek public finances.
2. Clarifying the terms of private sector involvement (PSI).
3. Reforming and expanding the EFSF.
4. Getting serious about the banking sector repair.
5. ECB committing itself to support liquidity.
6. Agreeing on economic governance.
7. Communicating better and removing the cacophony.

Some significant decisions were achieved in the Summit. In addition to measures designed to alleviate the Greek debt crisis, including the first round of haircuts, the Eurozone leaders agreed on a more flexible use of the EFSF. Based on the decisions of the summit, the EFSF (and the future ESM) was enabled to act on the basis of a precautionary programme by granting a precautionary credit line *à la* IMF to problem-stricken countries. It could also finance the recapitalization of banks under certain conditions through loans to governments, also in the non-programme countries as needed (considered very important for Spain, and potentially for Italy). And it could start purchasing sovereign bonds on the secondary markets (again very important especially for Italy and Spain). All these measures would be strictly conditional on corrective policy actions by the countries concerned.

The July 2011 resolution signified a further financial input of 109 billion euros to Greece. A major part of that came from private investors, as the managed debt restructuring was expected to reduce the funding need of Greece by 54 billion euros over three years. Hence, Greece's debt burden was forecast to drop from an unbearable 160% to a reasonably tolerable 120% by 2020. In retrospect, we know that these goals did not fully materialize, as many bond-holders could avoid the haircuts by holding out from the collective decisions. That was a further complication in striving for a neat and tidy managed restructuring, which was often presented as a simple cure-for-all solution to the euro crisis.[8] Hence, the introduction of effective collective action clauses was and still is ever more important, to facilitate a meaningful way to achieve debt sustainability.

Two interpretations could be immediately made on the outcome. On the one hand, one could consider that the solution was neither final nor sufficient in the long term, but at least the road had been paved towards debt sustainability. On the other hand, one could conclude that the taboo of PSI had been broken, but the outcome was not credible, so the compromise was the worst possible.

This or that, the sequel came faster than anyone expected.

Of course, there was no reason to be overly satisfied with the outcome. The haircuts on Greece were clearly insufficient to be convincing. And the EFSF enlargement was put into the back-burner, which was the surest way of calling for trouble in the markets. I had hard time understanding the lack of market literacy, or sheer complacency. This omission came to haunt us soon, and big time.

By the beginning of August, the situation in the markets had turned from bad to worse, or from serious murmurs to uncontrolled turmoil. Part of the reason was the ECB rate hikes in April and July, and the cessation of bond-buying programme SMP around the midsummer. These were amplified by the lack of fiscal commitment of certain member states. Italy was now at the epicentre of the crisis.

During the years the crisis lasted, it did not respect summer holidays. In the summer of 2011, once I had just taken my third attempt at a summer holiday in the end of July, I had to again immediately return from Mikkeli to Central Europe.

Prior to that, on 1 August Mario Draghi (then still at the helm of *Banca d'Italia*) called me in a very worried mood. He was very concerned about the market pressures and higher yields, as the country was facing substantial bond auctions in September, and asked for flanking support from the Commission for a bolder response by all EU institutions. On the following day, I had a phone call with Finance Minister Giulio Tremonti. In line with the Commission's duty of economic surveillance, I informed him that the Commission could endorse Italy's revised budget and underlined the paramount importance of its effective implementation.

On the same day, a conference call of the EU "institutionals" was organized to take stock of the economic situation and the implementation of 21 July Summit decisions. Presidents van Rompuy, Juncker, Barroso and Trichet and I were present over the phone. I did the call from the office of Länsi-Savo, the regional newspaper where I had once worked as a summer reporter, since they had better equipment for the purpose, and promised to have no listening devices on—sometimes the media can be very constructive and trustworthy!

I said in my intervention that the short-term growth prospects have worsened compared to our spring forecast. The turbulence in the financial markets and damaged confidence was taking their toll. I underlined the importance of full implementation of the Summit decisions. Some progress had been made, as a new EFSF framework agreement had been concluded and the guidelines concerning the recapitalization of financial institutions and the precautionary credit line had been agreed. However, the guidelines concerning interventions on the primary and secondary markets were still under discussion, which was a major handicap at a very critical market moment. I also emphasized the need of completing the reform of economic governance, as the six-pack was still pending in talks between the Council and the European Parliament, one year after the Commission proposal was sent to them for adoption. No conclusions were adopted in the conference call, but the points I raised were generally endorsed as the future course of action.

The ECB Moves to Expand Its Bond-Buying in the Secondary Markets

Next day on, I was on my way to the ECB's Governing Council, which convened in Frankfurt on 4 August. On 3 August, I also phoned Jean-Claude Trichet and privately encouraged the ECB to utilize the Securities Market Programme (SMP) to contain contagion: "The situation is extremely serious and contagion is spreading. The Euro-area Summit's decisions have not worked. Tomorrow's Governing Council is very important. Could you consider giving a signal that the SMP can be activated to provide liquidity? At least not rule that out?"

Trichet was always powerfully defending the independence of the ECB—rightly so, and likewise this time. But after the necessary denials, he went into "meditation", his favoured expression that we learnt to refer to in-depth thinking, and proceeded to criticize the Eurozone governments for the lack of understanding the seriousness of the situation, with a special reference reserved for Italy, where Berlusconi was on his way to take the carpet from under the feet of Finance Minister Giulio Tremonti by cancelling the consolidation actions put forward by the latter. There was an "absolute absence of credibility of governments", according to Trichet. I was not that vocal, but I could well understand Trichet's frustration. On the other hand, he criticized the governments on the Greek haircuts, on which I could not agree. But for the ECB it was considered "a stab in our own back", as it supposedly made SMP totally useless. This was one reason for the discontinuation of SMP purchases.

The setting for the Governing Council meeting was particularly demanding and sensitive. In the end of July, as the negotiations in Washington on the US fiscal cliff ended with no results, global epidemic risk aversion hit in. As a consequence of the Eurozone Summit decisions of 21 July, there were very high expectations in the markets towards the EFSF and particularly towards the ECB.

As the Commission was responsible for fiscal surveillance in the member states, I provided my assessment of the measures taken by Italy and Spain against the backdrop of the Council recommendations. I said that Italy was in the process of doing more on fiscal and structural issues than it had succeeded in communicating, including the latest speech of PM Berlusconi. I gave a relatively positive assessment: "The Commission expected Italy to back up the fiscal targets for 2013 and 2014 with concrete measures, which was now done, and the recent decisions implied that Italy was on track to bring its fiscal deficit below 3% in 2012 and balance by 2014". I thought it was a fair assessment, largely reflecting the substantial efforts by Finance Minister Giulio Tremonti. However, there was going to be a little handicap: as was soon seen, the Government did not live up to these decisions.

But that was not known by the time of the decision, and the ECB could move now. Thanks to the decisions of the Eurozone Summit and Italian authorities, the ECB's Governing Council nevertheless considered that governments had kept their promise of active measures, which enabled the ECB to relaunch asset purchases on the secondary markets and also to expand the

SMP to Italy and Spain, countries which were being choked by punitively high interest rates.

In his regular post-meeting press conference, President Trichet provided the ECB's economic and monetary analysis by underlining the particularly high uncertainty and downside risks amid continued moderate expansion: "Given the renewed tensions in some financial markets in the euro area, the Governing Council today also decided to conduct liquidity-providing supplementary longer-term refinancing operation (LTRO) with a maturity over six months".[9]

Turning to fiscal policies, Trichet stressed the need for "strict and timely implementation of the IMF/EU adjustment programs and the renewed commitment of all Heads of State and Government to the agreed fiscal targets". This was a clear message to Berlusconi and to Prime Minister Zapatero of Spain. Several countries should, according to the Governing Council, announce and implement additional frontloaded fiscal adjustment measures, "with inflexible determination". That implied quite a strong intervention into the governments' territory of fiscal policy by the ECB.

Initially, the ECB decisions led to a decline in interest rates in these countries. However, this came with a price: the ECB's internal unity began to falter. Jürgen Stark, the German member of the Executive Board, threatened to resign due to the secondary-market purchases, since he deemed these actions as monetary financing, in breach of the EU Treaty and against his principles. He lived up to this threat in the autumn, and the resignation took effect at the end of the year. Jörg Asmussen, the secretary of state of the Ministry of Finance, a seasoned and smart policy-maker with deep experience in international financial issues and one of the key members of the Eurozone fire brigade, was appointed in his stead.

Meet the Press in Brussels

From Frankfurt, I flew on to Brussels on the Thursday evening of 4 August 2011. As there were clear problems in our communication, I wanted to organize and lead several preparation meetings, teleconferences and a news conference, which we called to calm down fears and speculations.

Next afternoon, on Friday 5 August 2011, I met a full house of the EU-accredited media in the press room at Berlaymont. I started by admitting that the markets had not responded as expected to the decisions of the July summit. I also admitted that the euro area had had difficulties in communicating the decisions taken.

However, I emphasized that the rise in government bond yields did not reflect the fundamentals of the real economy of the euro area, since a modest recovery was underway, and the stabilization of public finances and the implementation of structural reforms had been put into motion. I underlined the fact that the use of the EFSF was thanks to the Summit being made increasingly flexible to conduct bond purchases in the markets and recapitalize banks. Now implementation of the decisions was underway, in spite of the summer holidays.

I also referred to Italy and Spain, trying to appeal to the common sense of the market forces: "A word on Italy and Spain. The market unrest witnessed in the last days is simply not justified on the grounds of economic fundamentals. It is not as if the fundamentals of the Italian and Spanish economies have changed overnight!"

The message seemed to go down in the correct form and initially reassured market participants. A seasoned Irish-European interface of financial markets wrote to Marco Buti: "Watched press conference on BBC. Went well and has been well received by commentators. Appreciated effort to explain agreement, admit regret that cannot move faster, and apology for poor communication. Impressed that OR broke vacation as UK politicians under fire for being away".

So we were able to move the focus elsewhere, for a while… But of course we knew we would—at best—only be buying time. We knew that once the summer break was over and the markets were again in full swing, we'd better be really serious and forthcoming with our revitalized comprehensive crisis response.

In the press conference, I also assumed that the ECB would continue to play a key role in managing the crisis: "Yesterday, the Governing Council announced a number of non-standard measures in order to tackle the tensions in some financial markets within the euro area". Naturally, I underlined the independence of the ECB, but I also tried to communicate a message that would give an impression that there was active coordination among the euro area operators. The Brussels correspondents were aware that I participated in the meetings of the ECB's Governing Council—albeit without a voting right—and had taken part in the meeting in Frankfurt the day before.

I also said that the Commission fully trusts that the ECB would continue to do whatever is needed to preserve financial stability in the euro area and to restore an appropriate monetary policy transmission channel. The reference to the monetary policy transmission channel was considered a particular justification for the ECB to take action in order to balance the secondary markets.

From time to time, I felt that the lack of mutual coordination was a genuine problem in the Eurozone governance. In this regard, the operation of the

Eurosystem differs, from the traditionally rather smooth relationship based on mutual interaction between the US Treasury and the Federal Reserve, which provides a more solid foundation to utilize the entire toolkit of economic policy. However, it has to be qualified that this is how it worked in normal times, which is not necessarily a primary feature in the recent period since 2016. Anyway, the Eurozone's rather complicated coordination is one of the reasons why economists educated in the United States often find it so difficult to understand the policy-making of the euro area. That's one reason why I welcomed President Herman van Rompuy's July 2010 initiative to substantially improve policy coordination among the EU institutions.

Contrary to what some commentators tend to claim, I do not think the EU Treaty constitutes a barrier to this type of coordination. In accordance with the first paragraph of Article 127, the primary objective of the ECB is to maintain price stability. However, the next clause of the same paragraph emphasizes that the ECB should support the achievement of the general objectives of the Union as stated in the 3rd Article of the EU Treaty, as long as this is not in conflict with the pursuit of price stability. And the 3rd Article reads: "the sustainable development of Europe based on balanced economic growth and price stability, a highly competitive social market economy, aiming at full employment and social progress, and a high level of protection and improvement of the quality of the environment". Thus, the ECB indeed has the possibility to act on these important "secondary" objectives of balanced growth, full employment, social progress and the quality of the environment, as long as price stability is maintained.

In July 2012, Lorenzo Bini Smaghi, by then already a former member of the ECB executive board, coined the stark choice: "Price stability is not in danger right now. The euro might be".[10] He was right at face value, though I have to add that the ECB has not reached its price stability target of "below but close to 2 per cent" since 2011, and we should not accept an asymmetric interpretation of this key policy goal.

Lessons About the Moral Hazard and Limits of Conditionality

Despite all the strenuous efforts, the Italian summertime blues and Berlusconi's gauntlet run continued. It was alleviated by the joint statement of the Eurozone Summit and EU institutions (including the ECB) to do "whatever is needed to ensure the financial stability of the euro area as a whole", which gave political cover for the ECB to reactivate its sovereign bond-purchase program, the so-called SMP. Soon the ECB began buying Italian and Spanish government bonds on the secondary market.

But the ECB and *Banca d'Italia*, led, respectively, by Jean-Claude Trichet and Mario Draghi, did not want to commit to bond purchases unconditionally. They wanted stability-enhancing structural and fiscal measures in return from the Italian government. Thus, following the ECB Governing Council meeting on 4 August, Trichet and Draghi contacted Prime Minister Silvio Berlusconi on behalf of the Eurosystem by sending a letter on 5 August in order to solicit a commitment on Italy's measures to balance its budget and speed up reforms. The letter called for Italy achieving a fiscal deficit of 1% in 2012 and a balanced budget in 2013 and required a decree law to implement these decisions by September. This was in line with the Commission's analysis. As Jean Pisani-Ferry writes, "The letter contained an extraordinary precise series of policy initiatives that the Italian government was requested to take in fields like labour markets, product markets, pensions and public finances—hardly the bread and butter of central banks".[11]

Berlusconi initially accepted the conditions—as conditions they were—for the SMP bond purchases. On 5 August 2011, Berlusconi announced plans to balance the budget in 2013, not only in 2014. This was supposed to be achieved, e.g., by far-going labour market reforms. To fill in fiscal gaps, on 13 August, the Berlusconi government issued decree law 138 which established a new 20% tax rate on interest paid for certain Italian taxable securities and dividends for ordinary shares. During the very same week, the ECB started purchasing Italian and Spanish bonds from secondary markets, buying more than €20 billion in only five days.

However, when the decree law was sent to the parliament for ratification, it lacked some of the measures that had been set as conditions by the ECB to act in the secondary markets. President Jean-Claude Trichet felt betrayed and the popular and governmental sentiment especially in Germany and Northern Europe turned very negative on Italy and on solving the Eurozone crisis by bold measures á la Big Bazooka. It thus caused big collateral damage to the Eurozone rescue efforts.

Finance minister Giulio Tremonti did not shy away, especially in our bilateral conversations and phone calls, from heavily criticizing this mode of operation of the ECB and the Eurosystem. Partly understandably, as Italy's fiscal package was substantial: spending cuts worth €54 billion were agreed by its parliament on 14 September 2011. On the other hand, the episode was a consequence of the lack of trust in the Italian government at the time, which unfortunately proved empirically grounded, since

Berlusconi's government did not uphold all the commitments it had made to the Eurosystem before the bond-buying had started.

In August, even France had a close encounter with the burning flames, when its interest rates skyrocketed. A credit downgrade and loss of AAA status was looming. France's structural fiscal deficit and weakened competitiveness had scared investors. President Nicolas Sarkozy brought the government budget session forward to August and declared he would propose a German-style budgetary-balance rule to the constitution, in order to protect France's AAA rating.

Moreover, the slowdown in growth caused ripples in France and even Germany. Merkel and Sarkozy met in Strasbourg in mid-August to discuss a common strategy to conquer the euro crisis. The markets were expecting a statement on Eurobonds, but it never came. Instead, the German and French leaders called for continued fortification of the economic union, even tighter budgetary discipline and a financial transaction tax. This broad and generally phrased package was obviously not enough to reassure the markets. As Richard McGuire, the chief strategist of Rabobank, commented: "This meeting is all stick – fiscal rule enforcement – and no carrot – a pooling of fiscal resources via a common bond".

A Recession That Could Have Been Avoided

In retrospect, the Italian summertime blues was a critical episode in the firefighting of the Eurozone crisis, as it showed the limits of policy conditionality, especially in the case of larger member states. It also revealed the problem of moral hazard in central banking activity—in particular, at least in the case where there is no clear rule-based framework for mutually binding commitments. For me, it underlined the importance of a clearly written and simple rule book for the Eurozone, certainly for the ECB operations, but also for the ESM activity. This rule book should spell out the terms of and thus facilitate an effective but conditional response to preserve financial stability. With the ECB decision on the Outright Monetary Transactions in August–September 2012 and the creation and first-round reforms of the European Stability Mechanism, such a rule book has moved on, but there is still plenty of work to do especially as regards the role of the ESM as fiscal backstop in the banking union.

Hence, the episode also highlighted the importance of a financial firewall with sufficient firepower, as was shown by the earlier experience in the United States, where this method calmed the markets quickly, as the firepower was both overwhelming and quickly available. Thus, the case was ever stronger for speeding up the reinforcement of the EFSF and turning it to a permanent, capitalized international financial institution. This was now our main goal and effort.

Thus, the search for the "lost ark" of comprehensive crisis response continued and would go on. In the meantime, the recession returned to Europe due to the damaged financial stability and the loss of confidence. It could have been avoided. This was the Impossible Triangle in action, with still too many red lines.

Notes

1. Carlo Bastasin, *Saving Europe*, 2012.
2. https://www.newyorker.com/magazine/2011/09/05/europes-big-mistake.
3. George Papaconstantinou, *Game Over*. Papadopoulos Publishing, 2016, p. 198.
4. EU's Rehn, Must Avoid Triggering Greek "Credit Event". Reuters, 8 June 2011.
5. Carlo Bastasin, *Saving Europe*, 2012, p. 288.
6. Papaconstantinou 2016.
7. Papaconstantinou 2016, p. 213.
8. See, e.g., Martin Sandbu, *Europe's Orphan*, 2017.
9. ECB, Introductory Statement, press conference, 4 August 2011.
10. Lorenzo Bini-Smaghi. *Financial Times*. A-list, 23 July 2012.
11. Jean Pisani-Ferry, *Euro Crisis and Its Aftermath*, 2011, pp. 105–106. The letter was not made public, but it was apparently leaked to and soon published by *Corriere della Sera*, the Italian newspaper.

8

The Hour of Obama—And Don Camillo

Brescello is a sacred place for many Italians. And it was such also for my father Tanu. It is the village of Don Camillo and Peppone from the novels and films of Giovanni Guareschi. One who does not bother to know about the place, does not really know the history of Europe—my father, who had only irregular access to schooling while growing up in the 1930s and never visited the place, was nevertheless very well acquainted with the Brescello village through his intensive reading passion.

I went to Brescello. The origins of the mission stemmed from the plenary session at the Italian parliament in November 2011 where I had been invited. I had a good grasp of the workings of the *Camera dei Deputati* and the *Senato della Repubblica*, since I had done frequent missions to Rome already since I started as the Enlargement Commissioner in autumn 2004. The Italian political culture was—or at least up until recently has been, and I trust still fundamentally is—strongly in favour of European integration. The country also has a lively heritage of pondering issues related to the future of Europe, as well as a practical touch on the Western Balkans. Former President Giorgio Napolitano, as senator in 2005, pressed me hard about the direction of the EU's enlargement policy, even though we in fact shared the same view of the importance of enlargement policy for the EU's external relations and stabilization of Southeast Europe. Now my role had changed, but yet we had an intense dialogue with the members of the parliament, during which they by no means let me off easy, questioning the EU's perceived lack of solidarity.

© The Author(s) 2020
O. Rehn, *Walking the Highwire*, https://doi.org/10.1007/978-3-030-34592-1_8

On my trip to Rome in November, I was working on a speech draft on my outbound flight after a long week at work. In addition to dry financial issues, I was looking for something to mentally reach out to the Italian parliamentarians and more generally other Italians, as the occasion would be filmed. From the depths of my mind, I found a snapshot image of Giovanni Guareschi's Don Camillo, whose adventures I had read as a little boy. My father Tanu's bookshelf included all of the Don Camillo books among its many treasures. My favourite, hands down, was *Comrade Don Camillo*, whose ventures in a communist-dominated delegation led by Mayor Peppone into the Soviet Union in the 1960s at the time of establishment of the Lada factories in Samara were an outstanding antidote to any potential contagion of "Finlandization". So wretched, albeit comical, were the stories painted by Guareschi about the real socialism in the Soviet Union. The Samara factories are known by the name Togliatti, which refers to the leader of the Italian communist party who sold, together with the capitalists of Fiat, Italian automotive technology to the Soviet Union, which consequently helped making the squarely boxy Fiat 124 model, via the inexpensive Lada, the best-selling car in the mid-1970s in many parts of Europe.

I began my speech in the *Camera* by telling the deputies about these reading experiences and the cultural connection built by Guareschi between Northern and Southern Europe. I then said I was certain that both Don Camillo and Peppone would have voted for Monti's government—a few days earlier the parliament had given Mario Monti a firm vote of confidence backed by a vast majority. This majority was leaning on the support from the moderate right and the centre-left. My point was obviously that Don Camillo represented the former heritage, the former *Democrazía Cristiana* or Christian Democrats, now spread between centre-right and centre-left, and Peppone the latter, the *Partido Democratico*, many of whom originate from the former *Partito Comunista Italiano*, the Euro Communists.

The message was well received. The session in the parliament was amicable in spirit, but the questions posed by the deputies were tough.

A few days after my visit to Rome, I received a friendly letter from the Brescello village, whose mayor thanked me for the reference to Don Camillo and Peppone, and invited me for a visit in his village. I replied I would accept the invitation as soon as I got the chance.

From the Stormy Summer to a Turbulent Autumn 2011

After the stormy August of 2011 came at least an equally turbulent autumn, and it kept getting worse and worse until November. The *FT*'s then Brussels bureau chief Peter Spiegel catches the paramount importance of those momentous events:

> When the history of the euro crisis is written, the Eurozone crisis is likely to go down alongside the founding Treaty of Rome, the expansion to Eastern Europe after the fall of the Berlin Wall, and the creation of the euro itself as one of the defining moments of the European project... And the period from late 2011 through 2012 will be remembered as the months that forever changed it.[1]

First, the IMF issued a warning about larger than assumed gaps in the capitalization of European banks, which gave the markets a new reason to be scared in September. Second, disconcerting news emerged on the Spanish government finances and the banking sector, which were amplified by the elections looming in October. Third, Italy was under special scrutiny by the market forces and faced rising yields particularly until Monti's government stepped into office.

I was not at my best shape in the late summer and early autumn of 2011, as my mother Vuokko's stomach cancer proceeded faster than we could have imagined. On 9–10 September, Friday–Saturday, I participated in the G7 ministers' and central bankers' meeting in Marseilles, where new efforts were made to outline an effective common strategy to overcome the crisis. Late at night, I got a call from my wife at the Mikkeli central hospital that my mother's condition had seriously worsened. I managed to book a morning flight to Helsinki, set the alarm at 4.00 a.m. in Marseille, took the connecting flights through Paris and Helsinki, and finally arrived in Mikkeli at 5 p.m. in the evening. My mother was still in her senses, and we talked for a long long time. I stayed in Mikkeli with her.

"*Aujourd'hui, maman est morte*". These laconic opening words, "Mother died today", from *The Stranger* by Albert Camus, forced themselves on my mind when my mother Vuokko passed away in the small hours of Tuesday. I had subconsciously feared this moment ever since reading the abrasive *L'Étranger*.

The market forces and the euro crisis had no respect for human emotions, which is not a part of their job description. The turbulence in the financial and government bond markets in particular kept going from bad to worse as the autumn moved on.

Furthermore, the ECB had stopped secondary-market purchases of distressed government bonds, which weakened the power of our counter-fires and reflected a broader disagreement on the management of the crisis and on the division of responsibilities between the central bank and the member states.

Carlo Bastasin criticizes the solution heavily and regrets the tensions between the ECB and certain member states. As described in the previous chapter, he considers the termination of bond purchases a "fatal mistake" for the euro area. It was certainly a big gamble, and in retrospect one may clearly see that it was not worth the gamble. On the other hand, the ECB's actions should be seen against the background that the governments of member states had not accumulated the stability reserves and provided them with more flexible tools, and finally in autumn 2011 Berlusconi's Italy itself shirked from its commitments, which was seen by the ECB as a fundamental betrayal of trust.

I experienced the ECB actions both as an insider and outsider. Insider, since I could participate in the meetings of Governing Council and give there my take on the perspectives of general economic policy, economic reforms and fiscal policy in the Eurozone as Commissioner in 2010–14. Outsider, since I was a non-voting member who had to respect the central bank's independence and was thus not supposed to take a stand on monetary policy, which was rightly reserved for the governors of national centrals banks and the members of the executive board.

In my case, the then monthly meetings of the ECB Governing Council in Frankfurt were actually a "mental holiday", precisely because for institutional reasons I could not intervene on the core issue of monetary policy, but could have the opportunity to benefit from the excellent economic analysis of the ECB staff and from the high-quality discussions on monetary policy by the members of the Governing Council. I don't usually take professional pressures personally, but especially in the years 2010–13 my life consisted of "continuous making of points"; that is, either in Brussels or in the capitals of the EU, my task was to make the argument and persuade my partners on economic policy orientation to pursue structural reforms, balance public finances or support the rescue programmes. Thus, the "mental holiday" indeed sometimes came to good use. Of course, I did my job and intervened, but at the same time I was not centre-stage.

Anyway, I could thus witness the ECB's dilemma in conditionality from a very close distance. Italy's disregard for its commitments after the ECB had purchased its government bonds illustrates the ECB's basic dilemma: How can the ECB determine the conditionality on economic policy for its support, without violating its operating principles? According to these principles, fiscal policy belongs to the member states and the Eurogroup, while the Commission is in charge for monitoring the member states, and the ECB governs monetary policy.

This dilemma was resolved elegantly by the ECB President Mario Draghi in August 2012 by passing a resolution to the effect that sovereign bond purchases by the ECB are a justifiable means to improve the transmission of monetary policy into the economy when it is undermined by doubts in the markets about the sustainability of the euro. A prerequisite for supporting purchases is a commitment by the country concerned to a reform programme and preparedness of the Eurogroup for at least a standing facility with joint ESM resources. The Eurogroup and the Commission determine the fiscal policy conditions that must be met before the ECB may, subject to its independent discretion, make supporting purchases in the secondary markets.

Obama's Hour to Lead the Eurogroup

In the Cannes G20 Summit, US President Barack Obama held several meetings in the course of the three days in a multilateral format with the Europeans. Obama, who among other things has a professional-voluntary background as a community worker in Chicago's civil society associations, now probably assumed a similar role he had played in Chicago back in the day and acted as a principal moderator, quickly posing the right questions and drawing succinct conclusions on the way forward. After the gathering, I wondered how come the US President was essentially chairing the Eurogroup meeting! And what's more, he did it rather well.

So in late October 2011, we arrived to the rainy and cold Cannes. There was not much feeling of glory that one might normally expect from the site of the famous film festival. Critical discussions centred on Greece and Italy, both of which saw their situation rapidly deteriorating. Spain remained still in the shadow, since the focus was elsewhere and there was a lack of time. Neil Irwin coins the mood well: "Italy, and to a lesser degree Spain, was seeing the exact sequence of events that had led Greece and then Ireland and then Portugal to require a rescue – except that now it wasn't at all clear whether a rescue would be even possible".[2]

Prime Minister George Papandreou was committed to overhauling the Greek economy. But he felt the pressure of street demonstrations and the political power games played in Athens as an imposing challenge to the legitimacy of his policies, which made him in October 2011 to announce a referendum on Greece's euro membership. He was playing with fire—and with the future of the Eurozone.

From the European perspective, the problem was not the referendum itself, but its impeccably impossible timing. Organizing a referendum would most likely have taken several months, probably even until January–February 2012. The resulting protracted uncertainty for several months would have been totally unbearable from the perspective of the stability of the euro area economy. Papandreou's announcement exacerbated the turbulence and lifted interest rates in the entire euro area, and it began to shadow the prospects for recovery, which were already fragile.

Other Eurozone member states reacted forcefully, even politically violently, spearheaded by Merkel and Sarkozy: the generally shared view was that Greece's rogue actions rocked the boat of the whole euro area. This was considered unwarranted—especially since Greece itself was constantly seeking help from the other Eurozone countries, whose economy it now shook by its unilateral twists.

In the G20 summit in Cannes in late October, a few days after the announcement of the referendum, Papandreou was lambasted by the other Eurozone leaders who were present. Following the forceful rejection, and since Papandreou had ended up in an impasse in the complicated and sometimes surreal world of Greek politics, he decided to resign. The Greek President Karolos Papoulias acted as an active midwife for a new coalition government, which was composed partly of technocrats and was expected to lead the country out of the crisis and facilitate a smooth transition. On 11 November, the ECB's former Vice President Lucas Papademos, an internationally respected economist and central banker, was sworn in as the new prime minister. It was an interim three-party coalition cabinet. While Papademos brought consistency and competence to Greek economic crisis management, the political transition turned out to be anything but smooth.

Papademos's cabinet included representatives from the two largest parties, the socialist Pasok and the centre-right New Democracy. The socialists' strongman and powerbroker Evangelos Venizelos, the main rival of Papandreou, replaced the latter as Pasok's leader. Antonis Samaras, the leader of New Democracy, who had relentlessly hammered the EU-IMF economic programme, decided to stay outside the government. Venizelos and Samaras knew each other well and seemed to have a close personal connection with each other. Power politics remained centre stage in Greece, although the country was in an emergency. National unity was vocally absent. This was the fundamental curse of Greece.

Over the following months, the government of Lucas Papademos was nevertheless able to take difficult decisions on economic reforms and fiscal consolidation. At the same time, backed by the support of the Eurogroup and the Commission, a more sustainable though not yet sufficient solution was sought for Greece's debt burden, in order for the country to return to a growth path.

Cometh Monti's Hour

In the course of autumn 2011, Berlusconi's standing as prime minister faltered. President Giorgio Napolitano, a veteran of taming political crises and pursuing European integration, sought a resolution that would reinstate Italy's political credibility. In the politically heated G20 summit in Cannes, Berlusconi received a broadside from his colleagues since Italy had proven incapable of correcting the course of its economic policy and shirked from the commitments it had made. The Eurozone leaders convened in Cannes in the same composition as in the previous week at the Frankfurt Opera, but this time wearing specific "*Groupe de Francfort*" nametags, which was a French attempt to institutionalize the group to mimic a Eurozone government.

Following the loss of credibility in the markets and loss of confidence among peers and in the home ground, Berlusconi ended up in a political impasse and decided to resign as prime minister in November 2011. President Napolitano appointed the former Single Market and Competition Commissioner, Professor Mario Monti to put together a new government. Subsequently, Monti convened a cabinet of experts and was nominated as prime minister in mid-November.

After his tenure as Commissioner in 2004, Monti had returned to Italy and acted as the Principal of the renowned Bocconi University in Milan, Italy's industrial and entrepreneurship capital, and as the Chairman of the Board for the Bruegel think tank in Brussels. Northern Italy is not only the home of a major proportion of successful Italian, but also European, small and medium-sized enterprises. For anyone doubting the Italians' entrepreneurial spirit and economic potential, I heartily suggest a visit to Milan, Turin or Bologna. To make a point, Monti used to call himself "Italy's most German economist".

As its first task, Monti's government decided on a bold and determined, but also inevitable programme to reform the structures of the Italian economy. A balanced budget was set as the goal for 2013. A decision to reform the pension system was made immediately. A labour-market reform was to be implemented by the end of March 2012, which partially happened. Closed professions were supposed to be opened for competition.

I decided to visit Rome immediately after Monti's inauguration in order to show the EU's support for the reform-oriented government and inquire about its future policies. In addition to the objective circumstances—a new reformist government driving invaluable decisions for overhauling the Italian economy—weighing in the scale was my respect for Mario Monti and a well justified and timed recommendation by my friend Petri Tuomi-Nikula, the Finnish ambassador to Italy. During my two-day trip on 24–25 November 2011, we had a long working session with Prime Minister Monti, and next day I gave a speech, answered questions in the Italian parliament, and closed the day with a long press conference.

Monti's government made a bold and solid start on the reforms. Immediately after taking office in December 2011, it decided on a pension reform raising the retirement age for both women and men to around 67 years. Before Christmas, it also approved a new savings package to restore property tax and raise value-added tax from 21 to 23%. In spring 2012, Monti's government, despite objection from the labour unions, pushed through a major labour market reform designed to improve the incentives in unemployment coverage, to transform periodic employment relationships into regular employment and to enable redundancies based on production-related grounds in the private sector. Initially, confidence in Italy's economic policy began to return, even though it was not yet seen in the bond yields or interest rates Italy had to pay for its public debt.

The downside of the determined action was the not completely unexpected loss of popularity of the previously very popular Mario Monti, which took its toll soon in the reduced capacity to act of his government. But the Monti government did important reforms for which it should be recognized.

Spain Emerges to the Crisis Scene from the Shadow of Italy

Spain had gotten off in relative terms easier than Italy from the turbulence of summer and early autumn 2011. This was partly because José Zapatero's socialist government was now finally taking some bold decisions, beginning in September 2010, to balance public finances and start to reform the pension system. Finance Minister Elena Salgado was called "the Iron Fist" in her home country, thanks to the perceived toughness of these measures. Support for Zapatero's socialist party had started to suffer from the fiscal policy U-turn by the Prime Minister, although the turn was clearly inevitable for the country's future fortunes. Meanwhile, economic growth was crumbling and information about large credit losses by the "*cajas*", the Spanish savings banks, and the large deficits of the provinces began to undermine trust in Spain's ability to cope with its problems.

So by the time the G20 Cannes Summit took place in November 2011, Spain's economic and financial situation had turned into dire straits. After Greece and Italy, Spain was the third crisis country waiting for the Cannes limelight. There was strong pressure on both Italy and Spain from Germany, France and the IMF to ask for a rescue programme or at least a precautionary credit line from the IMF.

This is how Paul Taylor illustrates what happened, with his lively pen:

On a rainy day in November 2011 in the hulking concrete Palace of Festivals in Cannes, where film stars strut on the red-carpeted staircase in warmer months, Angela Merkel ambushed Jose Luis Rodriguez Zapatero. With financial markets in turmoil and speculation rife that the European single currency area could break up, the German chancellor tried to bounce the then Spanish prime minister without notice into taking an International Monetary Fund bailout, according to his account of the meeting.[3]

The rendez-vous took place just few days before the 2011 Spanish parliamentary elections. Zapatero writes about it in his memoirs *El Dilema* (The Dilemma). This is how he describes the rendez-vous:

She greeted me pleasantly and almost without any introduction put forward a proposal about which we had not had any indication. Merkel asked me if I was willing to ask for a preventive credit line of 50 billion euros from the IMF, while another 85 billion would go to Italy. My response was also direct and clear: 'No'.[4]

In the November 2011 elections, the centre-right Partido Popular lead by Mariano Rajoy won an absolute majority in the parliament. Rajoy's government took office before Christmas and made its first decisions even before New Year 2012 on massive spending cuts and tax hikes, which bode well for restoring credibility. However, it did not immediately eliminate the international distrust towards Spain or the uncertainty about the shape of the country's economy and its banks.

In spring 2012, the situation in Spain gradually but rapidly deteriorated further, as loan defaults rose in the wake of a massive real estate bubble and worsening unemployment. Especially the *cajas* were reporting increasingly worse results and bigger losses, even though Spain's large and globally active banks like Santander and BBVA still made solid results. At the same time, new and worrying information emerged about the country's budget deficit, when especially the budgets and tax revenues of the autonomous regions failed to reach the projections by a long way. Instead of the projected 4%, the deficit threatened to reach 7%. The difference between the target and the reality was over 30 billion euros, and closing such a gap with expense cuts and tax rises would be politically a tough job, to put it mildly.

In March 2012, the Eurogroup had a heated discussion on the subject after Prime Minister Rajoy had unilaterally declared a 5.8% deficit target, which was significantly larger than what the Commission had recommended. Symbolically it was a rather clumsy communication act, as PM Rajoy had upstairs in the Justus Lipsius building in the European Council just been signing the EU's fiscal compact, binding it to a balanced budget, while after taking the lift downstairs to the press conference he was stating effectively the precise opposite!

In accordance with the Commission's proposal, however, the next Eurogroup meeting settled for a 5.3% deficit target. Sometimes decimal points matter, too—especially if they represent billions of euros and are heavily charged politically. New regulations that reinforced economic governance gave the crucial push, since overthrowing the Commission's proposal would have required a so-called reverse qualified majority, that is, 70% of the votes in the Council. This would have been a hard sell indeed in the Council at the time—and it would have been taken very badly indeed in the markets. Budgetary discipline prevailed this time.

Nevertheless, towards the end of 2011 the nervous turbulence in the financial markets continued. Paul Taylor, now a columnist with Politico and then European Affairs Editor of Reuters, leading coverage of the Eurozone crisis, told me privately in early December 2011 that Reuters had established a kind of "B-team", involving journalists in London and Berlin, to analyse the possible consequences of a Euro break-up. Based then in Paris, he had himself also been on reconnaissance missions to both Berlin and Brussels. A sign of times, and definitely not a good one.

Pilgrimage in Don Camillo and Peppone's Village

Following the mayor's invitation, my mission to Brescello, the town and land of Don Camillo and Peppone in Emilia-Romagna, took place the following April in 2012. We had a stopover in Brescello between missions to Florence and Milan, and spent a nice long afternoon walking down the memory lane.

The present-day Mayor Peppone, Giuseppe Vezzani of Brescello and Giorgio Quarantelli of Roccabianca, the neighbouring village, as well as Father Camillo, Don Giovanni Davolli, showed us around the village in the spirit of the book and the movie. The crucifix with Jesus, which I recognized from the movies, in front of which Don Camillo would often kneel, was still intact.

However, I declined to pose either next to the American Sherman tank standing in front of the museum or the Soviet-style sickle and hammer ornamenting Peppone's office, although the hosts and the photographers of Italian newspapers were suggesting that. The Sherman had come to Italy in 1943 with the American troops that liberated the country. It had now—still in good shape—found possibly its final resting place in Brescello.

At the end of the visit, I met the author Giovanni Guareschi's children Alberto and Carlota, who live in Roncole Verdi, a neighbouring village, next door to the composer Giuseppe Verdi's place of birth and statue. They were captivating people, who had cherished the literary and cultural heritage of their father Giovanni.

The next step was a few hours' drive and a late meeting in Milan with Spain's Finance Minister Luis de Guindos who had flown in from Madrid to give me a heads-up of what's cooking in the country. This encounter forced me back to the reality of the debt and banking crisis. Spain and its banks were returning to centre stage. Together with the Spanish authorities, we started to prepare a rescue operation.

Be that as it may, the day in Brescello, eternalised by the Finnish film director Pekka Lehto and his cameraman Mika Purola for the documentary film "In the Eye of the Storm", was a pleasant and healthy reminder that Europe does not amount only to an endless debt or confidence crisis, refugee crisis or terrorism threat, but also to a deep-rooted and enriching common cultural heritage. I'd prefer more of that.

Notes

1. Peter Spiegel, *How the Euro Was Saved*. Financial Times e-book, 2014.
2. Neil Irwin, *The Alchemists: Inside the Secret World of Central Bankers*. Headline Business Plus, 2013, p. 316.
3. Paul Taylor, *Merkel Tried to Bounce Spain into IMF Bailout—Ex-PM*. Reuters, 25 November 2013.
4. Jose Luis Rodriguez Zapatero, *El Dilema (The Dilemma)*, 2013; cited in Taylor 2013.

9

Flexing the Six-Pack

Reform is never easy. Yet, it is necessary to cope with the rapidly changing world—both in life in general and in the economy in particular.

I recall delivering the Ludwig Erhard Lecture at the Lisbon Council in Brussels in October 2010. The Council, which is dedicated to liberal economic reform in Europe, has named its main annual lecture after Ludwig Erhard, the father of the economic miracle of the post-war Germany. In my lecture, I referred to the late sociologist Ralf Dahrendorf who wrote in his great little book *Reflections on the Revolution in Europe* in 1990 that a country in democratic and economic transition needs both a constitutional leader to build up and ensure political legitimacy and another leader of "normal politics" to drive necessary economic reforms. Post-war Germany was lucky to have these leaders in Konrad Adenauer and Ludwig Erhard, the first one as the constitutional leader and the second one as the economic one.

Even though the economic challenges standing before Mr. Erhard over 70 years ago and before us after the financial crisis in 2010 may not have been comparable, I pointed out to some parallels. Quite like the post-war Germany, we needed to rebuild our European economy battered by a deep crisis. Much thanks to Ludwig Erhard and his reforms, Germany made it happen against most if not all odds. The foundation of Erhard's policy was the currency reform in June 1948, which was essentially a monetary shock therapy that suddenly freed most prices and all rationing. We know the result as *Wirtschaftswunder*—the "economic miracle".

I asked if we could perceive and conceive another "economic miracle"— this time in Europe? Luckily, there is nothing supra-natural in Erhard's

© The Author(s) 2020
O. Rehn, *Walking the Highwire*, https://doi.org/10.1007/978-3-030-34592-1_9

"miracle". The *Wirtschaftswunder* was a down-to-earth programme of economic reform, built on the principles of monetary stability and free market to encourage entrepreneurship, boost economic efficiency and facilitate job creation.

One of the lessons of Erhard is that governance and growth are intertwined. This was the rationale of reforming EU economic governance. The first phase of the economic governance reform, including six pieces of EU legislation and thus nicknamed the "six-pack", was first presented by the European Commission for consultation in May 2010 and subsequently proposed in the form of legislative measures in September 2010, and was finally adopted by the Council and the Parliament by December 2011. The legislative package had been stuck in a standstill before the summer holiday season of 2011 due to the Council dragging its feet and likewise due to the parliament's maximalist demands. In the end, however, the agreement reached after an intense haggling of a few months was ultimately in essence similar to the Commission's original proposal or even better (Image 9.1).

In addition to the six-pack and economic governance, in the years 2010–13 the Barroso II Commission pursued institutional and policy reforms with plenty of dynamism. For instance, it introduced the Annual Growth Survey, which starts the year in January with a comprehensive view of economic outlook and policy priorities, not only on economic policy but also as regards sustainable development and the social dimension. Cooperation among the Commissioners was excellent, with many progressive proposals on the policy agenda. For instance, with Michel Barnier we advanced in parallel the reform packages of financial regulation and economic governance. With Laszlo Andor, we pursued social dialogue with the trade unions and employers' federations and presented a Green Paper on how to work out sustainable, safe and adequate pension systems in Europe. With Vivian Reding, we presented a proposal to advance gender equality in the boardrooms, or more precisely, to set "an objective of a 40% presence of the under-represented sex among non-executive directors of companies listed on stock exchanges" (this was not adopted by the Council). Looking at things from inside the Commission, President Barroso was a competent captain of the ship, providing leadership in policy debates, listening to various viewpoints with an open mind, concluding the discussions with clear policy orientations and then supporting his Commissioners.

Image 9.1   The European Commission has been driving legislation for gender equality. My colleague Viviane Reding and I proposed in 2012 a directive that would have increased the presence of under-represented sex among non-executive directors of listed companies to at least 40%. However, our proposal was turned down by the member states. Not even my "Southern" hand gestures were enough to convince them (*Source* © European Union, 2012; European Commission—Photo: Georges Boulougouris. Licensed under CC BY 4.0 [https://creativecommons.org/licenses/by/4.0/])

Broad Support in the Parliament, Franco-German Resistance in the Council

In the light of the retrospective flagellation and self-flagellation (by some), it is indeed worth recalling the six-pack legislation reached out to a broad support and had a large or in fact vast cross-party majority backing it in the European Parliament. And rightly so, because the six-pack constituted a crucial building block for restoring confidence and returning the Eurozone public finances to a sustainable footing, thus helping to beat the crisis.

The parliament's rapporteurs, the Dutch Corien Wortmann-Kool for the European People's Party EPP, the Portuguese Diogo Feio also for the EPP and Elisa Ferreira for the Party of European Socialists and Democrats (S&D), as well as the Finnish Carl Haglund for the Alliance of Liberals and Democrats for Europe (ALDE) and the British Vicky Ford for the European Conservatives and Reformists (ECR), mostly skilfully and always forcefully steered the legislative package to its destination, with Sharon Bowles, Chairman of the Committee on Economic and Monetary Affairs (ALDE), acting as pilot. In the Socialist group, my fellow countrywoman Liisa Jaakonsaari provided valuable common-sense support from the flanks. Sven Giegold and Philippe Lamberts of the Greens pushed on for us to emphasize more strongly the importance of correcting macroeconomic imbalances, and rightly so. Sylvie Goulard, a French Democrat MEP and the ALDE coordinator in the Economic Affairs Committee, supported by Guy Verhofstadt, Chairman of the ALDE group and former prime minister of Belgium, was instrumental in negotiating the overall package deal. They sneaked into it, as a condition for the parliament's approval, a commitment by the Commission to produce a "Green Paper" on Eurobonds—or "Stability Bonds", as the Commission later decided to call them.

On the other hand, the Ecofin Council was seriously difficult on the governance reform. The reinforced method of deciding on sanctions was a red cloth for many member states, not least for France. As finance minister, Christine Lagarde had to oppose this essential building block of the reform. It was probably unpleasant for her, but if *la République* calls, "a lady's gotta do what a lady's gotta do"—*je ne regrette rien!* The Macroeconomic Imbalance Procedure, to which we put great expectations in terms of helping to rebalance the Eurozone economy and prevent the next crisis, was equally facing headwinds. I had strong tensions and several tough but fair exchanges of views in the Council with Germany and Wolfgang Schäuble on the definition of "excessive macro-economic imbalance", especially on the treatment of the German current account surplus. This dispute lasted for several months. In the end, in order to get the whole six-pack adopted, it was necessary to strike a deal with Schäuble, which was not perfect, for neither side. This happened in one of the tensest Ecofin meetings I can recall. It was to be an *asymmetric* solution, where current account *deficits* trigger a close look and analysis if they exceed 4%, while current account *surpluses* do the same only once they exceed 6%. The logic is that in the end of the day current account deficits are nevertheless more dangerous for the euro area financial stability than surpluses, as experienced in 2008–11, and should have indeed been noted during the pre-crisis period.

The six-pack reform of economic governance entered into force on 13 December 2011. We decided to immediately make use of the new tools. In November, I gave an advance warning of a potential breach of the budgetary deficit target in 2011–12 to a total of five countries: Belgium, Cyprus, Malta, Poland and Hungary.

I first discussed the advance warning in a press conference on 10 November 2011, and the following day I followed it up with a letter to the finance ministers of the five countries. The countries were faced with the threat of a financial sanction, if they failed to implement the recommended actions to balance their budgets and to push their deficit under three per cent. The sanction would first be a deposit and amount up to 0.2% of GDP, and it could subsequently be converted into a fine, in which case the country would lose it and pay.

For example, for Belgium, 0.2% of GDP corresponded to around 800 million euros. This may not be a huge sum, but in this case it was sufficient—especially considering that the savings required to avoid a sanction were of the same magnitude, amounting to approximately one billion (or 1000 million) euros. Hence, Belgium did have to choose between saving a billion euros and losing the same amount. By any sensible measure, there was only one reasonable answer: to save.

Of course, the political circumstances were fertile for using the potential sanction as an incentivising device, since the goal of fiscal sustainability was considered legitimate. The majority of Belgians were fed up with the country's politicians' inability to balance the economy or even to establish a politically legitimate government. Finally in December 2011, coinciding with the entry into force of the six-pack, and after record-long negotiations lasting 540 days, the coalition talks picked up new pace and were concluded by forming a new government. The Socialist leader Elio Di Rupo first managed to reach an agreement on the budget with six parties and subsequently established a new government for the country on the same basis. Just before Christmas, I met Di Rupo as the prospective prime minister and had intense negotiations with Finance Minister Steven Vanackere on the outlines of the budgetary savings and how they would be allocated.

At home in Brussels during the New Year's break on Sunday 8 January 2012, I could watch live on Belgian TV as Prime Minister Di Rupo announced both the stabilisation measures and the formation of the government. The speech was made elegantly—and most astutely—in two main official languages of the country: the expense cuts were delivered in Flemish, while the social aspects in French. What a masterpiece of segmented political marketing!

Later in January, at the New Year's reception of the royal family, King Albert II invited me to a private conversation. He expressed his gratitude for the work the European Commission had done for the stabilisation of Belgium's public finances and told me that the EU's new six-pack regulation had played a key role both in the creation of the budget and also in the normalization of the political situation in his country.

Judging on the basis of his reflections, the King also seemed to have a very clear plan ahead on how the budgetary process and the solutions to the basically linguistic community problems would now move ahead, in order to overcome the existing threats to the unity of Belgium, which was constantly challenged by some political forces, mostly in Flanders. As we conversed in French, which is my weaker working language, after the meeting I blamed myself for not having asked for a more detailed briefing in French from my civil servants—the King was extremely well briefed on all relevant details of the budget of his country. Respect!

Cyprus, Malta and Poland also rolled up their sleeves and made the decisions sufficient at the time to avoid penalty deposits. In contrast, Hungary was not yet ready for this and it refused to take the required further measures. Therefore, the Commission decided in January to propose to freeze its payments to Hungary from the cohesion fund, which was the most that could be done in the case of a non-euro country. The Council supported this stance after a tough debate. As a consequence, Hungary made the decisions in May on the required stabilization measures to push the deficit under three per cent in 2012. In June, the Commission and the Council in turn agreed to de-freeze the Commission's payments to the country.

These examples illustrate that the new rules fortifying the EU's economic and monetary union could work as they were supposed to. Of course, the rules were and are being tested on a constant basis. The more political the Commission gets, the more difficult it is for it to apply them in an objective manner—this may increase pressure to shift the task of fiscal policy monitoring to a European Monetary Fund, which has occasionally been in the drawing board in some influential quarters of the Eurozone.

The six-pack was a major step forward also by introducing the Macroeconomic Imbalance Procedure and enabling better, more substantive and more relevant, surveillance of economic reforms in the member states. However, as the monitoring in macroeconomic and reform policies is by definition mostly *qualitative* while in fiscal surveillance it is *quantitative*, the focus in the media and political debate tends to be on fiscal policy. I would prefer more focus on structural reforms and macroeconomics, which is fundamentally more important for economic health and performance of a nation. This is one key lesson from the crisis for the next Eurozone governance reform.

In 2013, two additional pieces of legislation were adopted to reinforce EU economic governance, known as the "two-pack". They gave the Commission the right to screen and propose changes to the national budgetary plans of the member states. Economic reforms are evaluated through the national reform programmes, which are annually presented to the Commission and discussed in the Eurogroup. We used this possibility with six member states right away in November 2013, starting with Finland that was not practising what it preached, and indeed deserved the hard time given to her representatives, this time civil servants of the finance ministry.

What was the impact of the reform of economic governance? This is the take of the political economist Waltraud Schelkle in 2017:

> Despite the limitations of the [Eurozone] reforms reviewed so far, it must be acknowledged that they brought forth collective action. They were swift, administratively demanding as regards fiscal surveillance, and substantively significant in the case of collective action clauses for government bonds. It would therefore be rather superficial to portray them as evidence for yet more failure to take action, as many observers in the media and in academia did.[1]

As part of the package of reforms, the Commission also committed itself to analyse the pros and cons of "stability bonds", which could be perceived as joint-and-several government securities, i.e. Eurobonds. They did not however fly at any moment in the Eurogroup or Ecofin Council. Moreover, various alternatives for reducing the heavy debt burden were considered in the Commission's policy papers, such as the idea of a debt redemption fund, originally presented by the German Group of economic Experts ("the Wise Men"), but neither that never got off the ground.

Vice-President in Charge of the Euro

In the winter 2011–12, we needed to reinforce the comprehensive crisis response that was put forward one year earlier. That was because its first version—to the extent decisions had been reached—had fallen short of the goals in some respects. This marked the second phase of the CCR: we began to defuse the economic and financial mines in the Eurozone one by one, and in doing so, gradually clearing the whole minefield. Greece's second debt restructuring and the 70% "haircut" were geared to reach a sustainable solution enabling the country to manage its debt burden. Italy and especially Spain made progress with their economic reforms.

One of the decisions to reinforce economic governance stemmed from the discussions a year before in July 2010 at the dinner organized by President Herman van Rompuy. Now 15 months later President Barroso invited me to his office to discuss "an administrative matter" at noon on 25 October 2011.

It turned out to be a combination of a job offer and a promotion. Barroso said he had thought of making me a Vice-President of the

European Commission, in charge of not "only" generally economic and monetary affairs, but explicitly and especially also for the euro. "We need to create Mr. Euro inside the Commission, not let it happen outside", he said in reference to the ongoing debate of having a Eurozone finance minister. "Besides, this has been put forward by MM. Rütte and Verhofstadt, so it should also garner support among your liberal and centrist friends", he added. Barroso knew he needed the support of ALDE in the parliament, both in economic policy and in general.

I responded by saying that I understand the communication as well as political and policy reasons for the move and thanked for confidence. Barroso concluded by saying that he would put his decisions forward either the following day in the College or in two weeks' time, after the Cannes G20 Summit.

I used the opportunity to both rationalize the work of the Commission and my own work. So I proposed to Barroso half-spontaneously in the same meeting:

> Could I make a proposal? We could be more convincing and credible in economic and fiscal surveillance, if we created a firewall inside the Commission between purely technical analysis, especially statistical data analysis, and more policy-based discretion. So I could give up the responsibility for Eurostat to a colleague, so as to separate Eurostat's statistical analysis from policy-making of the Commission.

Barroso reflected for a moment and quickly concurred that it sounds like a good idea. Subsequently, he charged Algirdas Semeta, the Commissioner for Taxation and Audit, with responsibility for Eurostat. Semeta was a former Finance Minister of Lithuania and had a strong background in statistics, so he was an ideal choice, a competent and fair colleague. Once the decision entered into force, we worked closely together in our respective fields, both respecting the fresh firewall.

Two days later, on 27 October 2011, Barroso and I were representing the Commission in the plenary of the European Parliament, in order to report on the important European Council of 23–26 October 2011. Barroso said the Summit conclusions will strengthen the role of the Community method and of the Commission in economic governance. "In effect, the Heads of State and Government have pledged to build on the measures of the six-pack and the European Semester by strengthening the Commission's role in assessing, monitoring and coordinating national economic policies and budgets". He announced that the Commission will present a comprehensive package on governance on 23 November, to include further deepening, to link financial assistance to fiscal surveillance and to present a Green Paper on Stability (Euro) Bonds. This package was intended to not only help containing the financial forest fires but also to accommodate the parliament's views.

He continued: "The Commission is ready to take on this responsibility... the independent and objective authority of the Commission is even more important, namely for the success of the Euro and reinforcement of the governance—a view often expressed by this parliament. Today, I announce that I intend to entrust Olli Rehn with a reinforced status and additional working instruments. He is to become Commission Vice-President for economic and monetary affairs and the Euro".

Barroso's decision had several effects. First, it gave me the tools to enforce decisions in the Commission, so that national vetoes by a Commissioner were no more accepted even into discussion, which had not even previously changed the substance of decisions, but had sometimes been a serious nuisance.

Second, it helped my activity of coordination inside the Commission, where I had more senior colleagues, particularly Joaquin Almunia and Michel Barnier, in the same Ecofin team. With them we always had a relationship based on substance, "let the best argument win", and I had no problems with these excellent colleagues. Barroso's decision made sure we would not face them in future, either.

Moreover, the decision effectively calmed down the debate on the axis between the Commission and Council about who should primarily represent the euro in the international context. Underneath, the issue may have remained unsettled till today, as both the Eurogroup president and Commission vice-president have a role to play in the euro's representation, but for the medium term we ensured that we didn't have to invest continuous political energy into totally useless turf wars with the Council. Of course, and stating the obvious, it must be added that the president of the ECB in the public mind and institutional governance carries the highest "stripes" of Mme./Mr. Euro, and rightly so.

The European Semester—No Holiday

The six-pack reform of economic governance also introduced systematic calendar for the Eurozone, called the European Semester. This means that in the first half of the year, policies are monitored, analysed and planned, both in the member states and EU institutions, while in the second half of the year the budgetary and reform plans for the following year are critically evaluated and debated.

Thanks to the reform of economic governance in 2010–13, the Eurozone now in principle has the necessary toolbox to identify early on any accumulating macroeconomic imbalances and worsening differences in competitiveness, and also has the powers to make proposals for their correction. These imbalances, such as a rapidly growing current account deficit or ballooning labour costs, had previously emerged from the shadows and, along with fiscal deficits (but actually even more than the deficits), constituted the root cause of the debt crisis.

Box 9.1 *Macroeconomic imbalances and current account surpluses/deficits*

What are macroeconomic imbalances all about? Take the key concepts first. Current account refers to the aggregated amount of capital flows between an economy and foreign countries during a specific period, for example a year. It covers, in addition to the surplus or deficit of foreign trade in goods (=balance of trade), also the balance of service trade (=balance on service), as well as investment income, other factor income and current transfers. Current account deficit means an increase in net foreign debt, while surplus means a reduction in net foreign debt.

Current account surpluses and deficits are part and parcel of the operation of an open international economy, and in principle they hold promise of economic convergence in a currency union by allocating surplus savings into (preferably) productive investment. But in reality they came to reflect some fundamental problems of the euro area. Over the past decade, the integrated capital markets channelled savings from countries with slowly growing domestic demand of investment to countries with burgeoning domestic demand and investments. In itself, this was not a problem, but the fact that the capital flows that emerged through this mechanism were very large, short-term (and as such, reversible) and channelled through banks, and used excessively into non-productive purposes, created cumulative current account deficits and thus became economically toxic.

This lending, particularly for construction and real estate, grew at a fast pace in the deficit countries, such as Ireland and Spain; in Greece, it was more about public consumption. At the same time, and inevitably, wages and prices in these countries rose rapidly. This created a spiral of bubble and casino economy, which fed the consumption spree of domestic demand. All this finally led to a too rapid rise in labour costs, which was soon followed by a profound loss of cost competitiveness.

Apart from strengthening the European house, the reform also created stronger national fiscal institutions in the member states. One of the six-pack's key reforms was the establishment of independent fiscal council or equivalent institution in each EU member state. I believe this will, in the long run, prove to be one of the most important governance reforms, since it will provide systematic and scientific independent analysis and advice for the policy-makers and public debate. I have seen this in action in Finland, where the Economic Policy Council, set up in 2014 at the initiative of Finance Minister Jutta Urpilainen, has done objective and analytic and thus very valuable work in assessing the government's economic policies. Led competitively by Professor Roope Uusitalo in 2014–18 and since 2019 by the experienced macroeconomist Jouko Vilmunen, it has interpreted its task rather broadly and assessed not only fiscal policy but also macroeconomic policy and structural reforms, and given advice on some specific policy issues, like education. It has not always been pleasant to the government—I can say this as a former government minister—but that has made its work legitimate and respected.

When preparing ground for the independent economic policy councils, in the Commission we benchmarked especially the Netherlands. The Dutch have a strong tradition here, with the CPB, the *Centraal Planbureau*, as an independent institution in operation since 1945. It produces independent macroeconomic forecasts, estimates for budgetary measures—and even analysis of election manifestos, which would probably not work in many countries of the world! The sustainability analysis of public finances, as well as expenditure rules and spending frameworks, has been pioneered by the Dutch. Both the legal basis of the CPB and the wide acceptance of its role in society are the essence of the Dutch stability culture.

These Dutch achievements owe much to Professor Jan Tinbergen, the first president of the CPB and the first Nobel Economics Laureate in 1969. I am tempted to say that Tinbergen did the same for comprehensive economic policy analysis than what Johan Cruyff did for football through the philosophy of total football. Europe can learn also from this Dutch model and is already applying its lessons.

This governance reform was carried out and is being applied under normal EU legislation. It is based on the EU's reality-tested Community method, which, in this context, places a major responsibility on the Eurogroup and the Commission for the monitoring of the Eurozone's economic policy, and gives all euro area member states authority in common decision-making in accordance with the founding treaty.

By contrast, the fiscal compact that was agreed in late 2011 is primarily an important political commitment device on the part of the member states to the stability culture. It requires, among other things, the inclusion of a "debt brake" directly in national legislation. At the same time, the fiscal compact overlaps to a large extent with the six-pack reform of economic governance, which constitutes the practical basis for the monitoring of economic policies of the member states.

Few considered these changes possible in spring 2010. However, they were inevitable in order to strengthen the original idea of the monetary union. Of course, the tools that have been created must also be used in a consistent and counter-cyclical manner to enable the member states to stay on a path of sustainable economic policy. Fundamentally, it requires national ownership, an issue to which I shall return in Chapter 19 when discussing the next reform of the Eurozone.

This type of new thinking and new tools has begun to bear fruit in terms of implementing a culture of economic and fiscal stability in the member states. What has been the impact of the reformed governance?

In my final press conference as Commission Vice-President in Brussels on 2 June 2014, after having been elected a member of the European Parliament in Finland only 10 days before, I could inform the media and the public that on fiscal policy we took a number of important positive decisions related to the Excessive Deficit Procedure (EDP). First and foremost, we recommended to the Council the closure of the EDP for six member states: Belgium, the Czech Republic, Denmark, the Netherlands, Austria and Slovakia. These countries had all brought their deficits sustainably below 3% of GDP, for which I congratulated them. I also reminded that in 2011, no less than 24 member states were still in the EDP. By 2014, there were 17. Once the Council adopted the Commission's June 2014 recommendations, the number fell to 11. As of this writing in summer 2019, the number of countries in the EDP has fallen to one only: Spain. France was abrogated in 2018 from the EDP, which left Spain alone in the procedure.

Moreover, if you look at the accumulated fiscal deficit in Europe since the crisis, it has fallen dramatically. The fiscal deficit of the Eurozone decreased from the heights of over 6% in 2009–10 to around 3% in 2014, and below 1.5% in 2016–17 and finally to around 0.5% in 2018. The aggregate debt level in the Eurozone has come down from 92% in 2014 to 86% in 2018.[2] Contrary to what many have claimed, this proves that the Stability and Growth Pact can be made work, if there is the right kind of will, and Europe's public finances are in fact being repaired. The more recent developments concerning Italy's fiscal stance are an exception to the trend.

Erhard's Bold Liberal Reforms

As has been seen from the country cases, finding sufficient political backing for the necessary reforms is far from easy. The political acceptance of the conditional financial assistance programmes, say in Ireland and Greece, differed hugely from each other. And it is indeed evident that economic reforms require strong political and social acceptance in the society to be effectively implemented and thus to have real impact and improvement in the living conditions. That calls for convincing communication and dialogue in the society. And that does indeed take quite some persuasion and perseverance from the policy-makers. Did we have it in Europe in 2010–14? Many doubted it. But I trusted in the end we could take those steps.

The boldness and foresight, which helped Ludwig Erhard to bring about the German economic miracle, would still have quite some use in Europe. Let's recall the story in which Ludwig Erhard was confronted by US General Lucius Clay, who had been warned by his advisors that Mr. Erhard's decisions on economic reforms were a terrible mistake. "Pay no attention to them", Erhard responded, "My advisors tell me the same thing". The reforms were carried out as planned. And the rest is history in Germany, which carries major effect in Europe still today and tomorrow.

Notes

1. Waltraud Schelkle, *The Political Economy of Monetary Solidarity: Understanding the Euro Experiment.* Oxford University Press, 2017, p. 209.
2. https://ec.europa.eu/eurostat/documents/2995521/9731224/2-23042019-AP -EN/bb78015c-c547-4b7d-b2f7-4fffe7bcdfad (on fiscal deficit).
   https://ec.europa.eu/eurostat/documents/2995521/9510404/2-21012019-AP -EN.pdf/97de2ad5-5b7e-4de9-ab36-7bbf8773aad0 (on public debt).
   See also IMF Fiscal Monitor, *Capitalizing on Good Times.* April 2018, p. 7.

10

Gasp of Air Before the Plunge

Sic transit gloria mundi—"thus passes the glory of the world". This seemed to hold true to the efforts and effects of the Eurozone decision-making under the umbrella of the comprehensive crisis response in 2011–12. The most verbally creative criticism came from the economist and later Finance Minister Yanis Varoufakis, who put it unequivocally in 2013: "As an illiterate, yellow, third category understrapper, Rehn gets his orders and is obliged to deny the IMF mistake. And he denies it".[1]

The reinforcement of economic governance, which had many dimensions and was at the core of the comprehensive crisis response, had primarily a preventive impact: dealing with the present, but focusing on the future. It serves to prevent another crisis in the future. As to the acute crisis, the new rules mainly contributed to the strengthening of confidence, which was important in order to overcome the deep instability. But despite all the reforms, the yields on government bonds of the distressed countries did not show any sign of decline in autumn 2011.

To counter the financial stress, the European Central Bank began to take bolder measures to ensure short-term funding for banks. Expansion of the long-term refinancing operations (LTRO), conducted in December 2011 and February 2012, amounting up to 1100 billion euros, alleviated pressure on the banks, so as to avoid them contracting their lending too rapidly, and thus eased the looming threat of a credit crunch. Together with the wave of reforms in the vulnerable countries and the more sustainable Greek resolution, the LTROs seemed to improve the prospects of the euro area in early 2012, giving us a gasp of air.

© The Author(s) 2020
O. Rehn, *Walking the Highwire*, https://doi.org/10.1007/978-3-030-34592-1_10

Following these measures, the growth outlook of the Eurozone for the year 2012 seemed more encouraging, and prospects for a gradual pick-up in employment also improved. The shining star of the World Economic Forum's annual summit in Davos, held at the end of January 2012, was the new ECB President, Mario Draghi, who had pushed through the decisions on the LTROs, and thus he rightly got the credit for preventing a worse credit crunch than was experienced.

The LTROs were the most significant systemic action taken by the ECB by then. However, the brief economic upswing from December 2011 to March 2012, for which we had worked so hard, was cut short by bad news from the crisis countries, especially Italy, Spain and—not least—Greece again. At this stage, the crisis was a combination of both systemic factors and country-specific factors, and the policy response had to likewise target both.

Prior to the relatively short upswing, the economic governance of the Eurozone was substantially reinforced by the so-called six-pack legislation, as described in the previous chapter. It had a positive impact on credibility of the Eurozone's economic policies. In the medium-term, it was essential for the return of confidence into fiscal sustainability in Europe. But in the short term, its positive impact was limited, and the immediate crisis symptoms kept on getting worse and worse.

Just before Christmas 2011, the chief economist of the credit rating agency Standard & Poor's, Jean-Michel Six, made a rather outrageous but—in retrospect—painfully accurate prediction: "There is probably yet another shock required before everybody in the Eurozone reads from the same page, for instance a major German bank experiencing some real difficulties on the markets, which is a genuine possibility in the near term. Then there would be a recognition that everybody is indeed on the same boat and that even German institutions can be affected by this contagion. I'm afraid this may still be required".

Of course, the Commission protested heavily on this reckless prediction by a market player. But at least he was more accurate than Nouriel Roubini, who had predicted that the Eurozone would break up either in five or even two years! However, the "yet another shock" did not come from Germany, but from Greece again. Although Italy and Spain had their fair share of financial woes in the summer and autumn of 2011, the worst turbulence soon sparked from Greece—once again. It concentrated on the six-month period between October 2011 and June 2012.

Progress Before Backlash in Greece

The EU-IMF programme for Greece has got a bad reputation over the years. However, the whole picture involves more shades of grey than only black-and-white images. In the first programme summer of 2010, there was serious progress in the implementation of the programme. As the then Finance Minister George Papaconstantinou says, "That summer, we all felt that things were moving: the cogs were slowly turning again and the machine was starting to work, sanity was being restored to a system run wild, responsibility was again the order of the day, and long-overdue changes were beginning to materialise".[2]

After the Cannes Summit in October 2011, there was again progress in Greece. Over the winter months 2011–12, Greece negotiated a substantial haircut through a debt swap with its international creditors, inspired by the Brady Plan which in the 1980s helped alleviate the Latin American debt crisis, starting with Mexico.[3] The counterpart of the Greek government was again the International Institute of Finance, led by Charles Dallara and chaired by Josef Ackermann, who together with especially BNP Paribas' effective Jean Lemierre negotiated on behalf of the large European and international banks. The voluntary debt exchange was conditional both on the achievement of a structural surplus in public finances and on a new and large haircut on sovereign debt held by private investors, who were expected to lose up to 70% of their capital through the so-called PSI or "private sector involvement", which was the euphemism for haircuts on investors' capital.

The framework for the solution was defined already in October 2011, but the details continued to be worked out and negotiated for several months. With the support of the Eurogroup, Greece—and essentially Prime Minister Lucas Papademos himself, with his very much hands-on approach of a first-rate economist and seasoned central banker—negotiated the above-mentioned additional and substantial haircuts on the country's sovereign debt with international investors, all in all resulting in the mentioned write-down of 70% on debt securities held by private investors. According to the then assessment jointly done by the EU and the IMF, these write-downs were expected to cut Greece's debt burden from over 160% of GDP to about 117%, if the economy started growing as expected and did not relapse.

While the general mood among the "commentariat" in the media and academic debate on the Eurozone problems started to become more and more populist, there were some balanced voices of reason as well. For instance, Professor Raghuram Rajan, the former Chief Economist of the

IMF and later on the Governor of the Reserve Bank of India, wrote in March 2012 in favour of sensible Keynesianism, referring to Greece:

> For Greece, government spending is the problem, not the solution. A responsible government would implement judicious austerity, firing the party hacks who were hired in the go-go years, cutting wages and pensions and restructuring itself to collect taxes and provide useful services, even while retaining transfers to the indigent and elderly. As public sector workers share the private sector's pain, national solidarity could improve.[4]

In fact, Professor Rajan largely described the goals of the EU-IMF programme. Unfortunately, its implementation was anything but plain sailing.

In Greece, the implementation of the programme got to a halt after the conservative leader Antonis Samaras effectively forced the country into new elections in April, which created further uncertainty about the country's direction. It had been quiet for a while on the Greek front, with no difficulties caused to the rest of the euro area—but this did not last long. Now it threatened again to drag the rest of the euro area along in a dangerous downward spiral.

At the same time, the situation of the Spanish banks and provinces deteriorated rapidly. Sometimes the rather clumsy and cumbersome communication by the country's government did not exactly help the situation. Greece's political crisis and Spain's economic crisis fed each other and threatened the entire euro area.

In Greece, Alexis Tsipras, the charismatic and energetic leader of the left-wing Syriza party, took advantage of the discontent of the people and lifted the party's backing to record heights. In turn, the socialist party Pasok lost the bulk of its support. After the first snap elections that were held in May, forming a government proved impossible, and the country ended up having to go to yet another round of snap elections, which were held in late June.

The Ultimate Rock-Bottom: Snap Elections and Bank Runs, While Grexit Looms

Summer 2012 was to be yet another rock-bottom, this time as serious as ever. In retrospect, this was probably the most dangerous rock-bottom of the whole long series of them. The silver lining was that it finally woke up the European leaders, both the political leaders in the European Council and the central bankers in the ECB Governing Council.

To illustrate the degree of seriousness of the Greek situation, I recall Tim Geithner giving me a call roughly a week before the June elections to sound out where we were. On substance, it was about Spain and Germany. He had urged Spain to go ahead with the recapitalization effort and EFSF (ESM) assistance. Moreover, he had encouraged Germany to endorse or outline key elements for a banking union—and to do so before the Greek elections and the G20 Summit in Mexico. Geithner and the Fed Chair Ben Bernanke provided useful advice when we in Europe were planning and building the banking union, and I usually consulted them on this issue among others when meeting in Washington or elsewhere in the conference circuit.

However, as I could have guessed Geithner's views on those matters and knew them already, the real issue for Geithner's phone call this time was a message which he expressed at surface calmly but in reality in the state of only very weakly concealed desperation: "I am much more worried about Greece now than last fall... I'm afraid we are beyond the point of no return".

That was indeed heavy stuff, since Geithner was in my eyes the ultimate international financial fire-fighter, who always tended to have an *analytical* solution to propose—to be followed (or not!) with a *political and policy* solution—which made him a most valuable "special policy advisor" for the Eurozone during the crisis. "Have we really crossed the cliff already?", I recall thinking after that. Now the red lines were in full steam to haunt the Eurozone. But we had to fight on.

The Commission had internally been preparing for some time already a worst-case scenario where Greece would either decide to exit the euro or be led by circumstances to do so. In order to avoid being faced with a question "Do you have a Plan B?", we named this fallback action plan as Plan Z. We were aware of the risk of leaks, but on the other hand we simply needed to simulate and rehearse our action plan in case of a worst-case scenario would materialize. Discipline was strong however and no leaks occurred. Subsequently, in the Euro Working Group, the influential meeting of the ministers' deputies or state secretaries, the "counterfactual" scenario was discussed for the first time in early September 2011, in case there was to be a fundamental failure to comply with the programme. In September, the mood was that "the glass was more half empty than half full" as to the implementation of the Greek programme. Especially, Germany, the Netherlands and Finland would not accept any further slippage from the policy targets by Greece.

Nine months later, it looked as if that danger was about to materialize. On 14 May 2012 at 8.30 a.m., we had a restricted meeting on Greece with my most senior staff from both the cabinet and DG Ecfin. Marco Buti,

Servaas Deroose, Maarten Verwey, Timo Pesonen, Taneli Lahti and I were elaborating the alternatives. I said we cannot afford a repeat of the 2011 situation where the ECB and Germany were at loggerheads—we now needed a small cell to lead preparations. Marco agreed and said a small group would be needed, as a bank run was a real danger. The first conclusion was to think through what would be the counterfactual, and how much it would cost for the Eurozone. Maarten Verwey pointed out that the ECB was key, since the banking system of Greece would be first under fire if there were a bank run. There was concern of other vulnerable countries: "we need to ring-fence Spain". Financial contagion was still a very much present danger in Europe.

Summing up the discussion, I crafted conclusions for our future work: Greece was heading towards new elections in June which could lead to a point of no return; it was likely that the financing of the sovereign would dry out in August, if there is no implementation of the programme, and in the short run a bank run could not be ruled out. The probability of a Greek exit was increasingly high, and we needed to get prepared for both scenarios—"we cannot afford any wishful thinking"!

My operational conclusions for my senior staff in the mid-May meeting were meant to orientate the Plan Z work in the next hours, days and weeks:

1. We must secure the rest of the EU and Eurozone by financial ring-fencing, where the ECB and ESM would have to play the key role, and direct recapitalization of banks should be moved forward.
2. We must prepare to minimize damage in Greece, where it would be inevitable to call a bank holiday, install capital controls... (and in the worst case, to think of how to keep Greece in the EU, if no more in the Eurozone).
3. We must estimate the costs of different scenarios, including the "counter-factual" (which in our prudent jargon meant Grexit).
4. We must set up a small secret group to plan and prepare both alternatives; it should include the key people from the Commission, ECB, EWG, Germany and France, and especially the ECB-Commission cooperation would have to be extremely smooth, while the IMF would have to be kept informed.
5. We must agree a common line of communication, essentially a "social contract" between Greece and the Eurozone to respect commitments and consider solidarity a two-way street; and to understand that an exit would be bad for both, but much worse for Greece and the Greeks than for the rest of the Eurozone.

Later on during the same day at 13–15 h, there was a meeting of EU institutionals called by EC President Herman van Rompuy. I gave a concise and
only slightly sanitized summary of the Commission preparatory meeting
and suggested we have to be prepared for both scenarios and secure stability of the rest of the Eurozone and minimize damage in Greece. I also proposed to set up a small secret crisis team of the EWG Chair Thomas Wieser,
Commission, the ECB and other stakeholders.

My recollection is that Mario Draghi underlined the need to effectively
prepare for contingency measures. I also recall that Herman van Rompuy
concurred, though I got the feeling that he didn't want to know… I admit it
was unorthodox, but the situation was unprecedented and sufficiently dangerous to merit such an approach. In the subsequent days and weeks, to my
understanding especially Thomas Wieser played a central role in persuading
Chancellor Merkel on the huge economic and political costs of the Grexit
for Europe and Germany.

Mid-June: Greek Elections and the G20 Summit in Los Cabos

Greece's elections on the weekend of 16–17 June 2012 garnered huge international interest. The Commission practised a complete radio silence during
the campaign. We only emphasized that the Greek people would themselves have to decide democratically, whether the country wished to make
reforms and stay in the euro, or not. Pure platitudes as any substantive political intervention in the super-heated Greek political debate would have been
counterproductive.

On the very same weekend when the Greek elections took place, a G20
Summit was held in Los Cabos on the Western coast of Mexico. Normally,
I would participate as part of Barroso's delegation in these summits, which
are always preceded by meetings for the finance ministers who were my
institutional counterparts. This time, however, I would be off-side from
the real game because of the two-day-long one-way flight to Los Cabos and
the ten-hour time difference between it and Brussels, a combination that
would have made it practically impossible to lead crisis management in the
Eurozone from the shores of the Pacific. Therefore, Barroso and I agreed that
I should stay in Brussels to lead potential crisis measures, especially in case
a bank run emerged in Greece. Barroso said to me on 29 May 2012: "I ask
you to stay here in Brussels on 17-18 June because of the potential fallout
from the Greek elections and their management".

Even more important was that the ECB's Mario Draghi decided to stay in Frankfurt and the Eurogroup President Jean-Claude Juncker in Luxembourg. We were all on alert to act immediately and together in case something nasty happened and caused contagion. We had prepared a contingency plan and consulted the Washington Group in case there would be a serious bank run on Monday morning. It was no empty paranoia: according to media reports afterwards, on Friday 15 June alone Greeks withdrew more than 3 billion euros from their bank accounts, which equals to 1.5% of its GDP! The drainage had been going on for years, but it had been still rather a "bank jog" than a full-blown bank run. The Commission's Plan Z, which was endorsed by the Euro Working Group and involved emergency measures like capital controls in case things turned sour in Greece, was ready to be activated, if needed (Image 10.1).[5]

ECB President Mario Draghi and Eurogroup President Jean-Claude Juncker stayed, like me, in Europe in June 2012 when the critical Greek elections took place during the Mexico Los Cabos G20 Summit. In February 2012, we were holding a press conference after the G20 ministers' and central bank governors' meeting in Mexico City, together with Mario Draghi and EU Presidency Denmark's Finance Minister Margrethe Vestager, who became one of the strong members of the Juncker Commission and is now Commission Vice-President.

The mid-June weekend of the Mexico G20 Summit was a very long weekend for us staying in Europe: waiting, waiting and still waiting. As we had fallback plans prepared and we just had to wait for the election result— and most of the colleagues were in a different time-zone in Mexico anyway—there was not much meaningful to do job-wise. It might have been nerve-wracking if you are into that. Anyway, I invited my daughter Silva to visit the surreally magnificent *Musée Magritte* in Brussels, which was the perfect choice as its spirit was as surrealistic as was the state of Europe on that weekend! Later on in the evening I zapped between the Greek elections forecast and Euro-2012 football games between Portugal-Holland and Denmark-Germany. Greece had defeated Russia on the previous day Saturday with the great goal of Giorgos Karougounis, which at least was a good omen.

The Greek re-election had become an outright duel between Samaras and Tsipras, where the stance towards the reforms required by euro membership was the crucial watershed. Following an intense election campaign, Samaras and the New Democracy won the elections by a margin of a few percentage

Image 10.1 Mario Draghi, Olli Rehn and Margrethe Vestager holding a press conference after the G20 ministers' and central bank governors' meeting in Mexico City (*Source* © European Union, 2012; European Commission—Photo: Johan Ordonez. Licensed under CC BY 4.0 [https://creativecommons.org/licenses/by/4.0/])

points. The new Samaras government was formed soon after the elections on the basis of the New Democracy, Pasok and a smaller Democratic Left party. Yiannis Stournaras, a respected Oxford-educated economist, was appointed finance minister. The challenge for the new government was to restore Greece's credibility in the implementation of the programme, which had come to a halt during the campaign, to make the required decisions for further reforms and programme conditions in the parliament, and thus to avoid an outright bankruptcy of the country.

While it had been a political thriller and the omens for the future were not particularly good, there was to be a period of better implementation of economic reforms in Greece from the summer onwards. But political turbulence went on, and Greece went to another snap election in 2015, which brought Syriza to power and led to an open confrontation with the Eurogroup with the game theories of Yanis Varoufakis. I was then already out of the Commission and wondered the episode from quite some distance. More on that in Chapter 16: "Aftershocks That Didn't Explode".

No Government, No Implementation—Facing Un-governability

Because of the long political vacuum due to the two subsequent parliamentary elections in a country that was in a deep economic crisis, implementation of the Greek programme was halted for months and months in spring 2012, as there was no functioning government in the country, and the country's administration on its own was not very operable, which is an understatement. As the implementation was stuck, the payment of support loans was also stuck—a reality the Greek politicians carry responsibility for. Usually in a severe crisis situation in small states, a necessary minimum degree of national consensus is found to overcome the crisis, be it a security or economic crisis. You could see this national unity and determination in Ireland, Latvia and Portugal, but not in Greece. The country lacked the minimum sentiment of national unity—e.g. to tackle tax evasion—which cost its people dearly in terms of social and economic consequences of the crisis.

This was the problem from the very start, from the very first programme onwards. Greece has a very strong entrepreneurial potential and thus capacity to create wealth. Many Greeks have succeeded in various spheres of life so the country has plenty of human innovative potential. But I have to admit that we underestimated the leadership vacuum and management challenge in Greece.

Francis Fukuyama observed the Greek saga as follows, "When the European Union and the IMF demanded structural reforms in return for a restructuring of Greek debt, the Greek government was willing to consider virtually any form of austerity before agreeing to end party control over patronage".[6]

While reforms in Greece were stubbornly slow, what was the alternative? Not suggesting a financial assistance programme? Not providing any funding for Greece from the Eurozone? I strongly doubt the Greeks would be better off with that.

In the 2015 referendum organized by the Syriza government, the majority of the Greeks rejected the programme. Soon afterwards, the country nevertheless returned to the programme path, apparently because the alternative was considered much worse. In the final analysis, the key was that the Greek people wanted to stay in the euro. But much time was again wasted. And the ordinary Greeks paid the price.

Notes

1. https://www.keeptalkinggreece.com/2013/02/14/varoufakis-olli-rehn-an-illiterate-yellow-3rd-category-understrapper/.
2. George Papaconstantinou, *Game Over*. Papadopoulos Publishing, 2016, p. 149.
3. William R. Rhodes, *Banker to the World*. McGraw-Hill, 2011, pp. 222–223.
4. Raghuram Rajan, Sensible Keynesians Know There Is No Easy Option. *Financial Times*, 23 May 2012.
5. Peter Spiegel, *How the Euro Was Saved*. FT e-Book, 2014.
6. Francis Fukuyama, *Political Order and Political Decay*. Profile Books, 2014, p. 107.

Part III

Turning the Tide

11

"Whatever It Takes" and the Banking Union

In June 2012, we entered the final turning point of the crisis, even though we couldn't realize it yet then. Too many rock-bottoms had taken their toll in self-confidence. Yes, the first 20 days of June had been a political and economic nightmare, with Greece again taking the Eurozone to the brink of a disaster. But as a silver lining that rock-bottom spurred decisive action in the last 10 days of the month, leading to key decisions over the summer. It was the summer of Inferno and Redemption.

Over the winter of 2011–12, we had continued to work on the comprehensive crisis response to support growth and break the liquidity trap where the Eurozone economy had fallen. We had also expected the ECB to do more—in return or at least in support for the consistent consolidation of public finances that was going on and which the ECB had called for (in a way as a quid-pro-quo for monetary stimulus). However, the policy mix was imbalanced, and a stronger monetary stimulus that was required to support the recovery was still pending. I recalled what Tommaso Padoa-Schioppa, one of the founding fathers of the euro, once said: "It would be unfortunate if the ECB's independence were to be confused with loneliness".

So, by now already as old hands of second-best efforts, we made initiatives at many fronts. For instance, we tried our best to smoothen the liquidity situation of Italian SMEs by giving Italy a special treatment in fiscal surveillance for an emergency measure to pay back 20 billion euros of state debt to enterprises per year, both 2012 and 2013. It was one of the achievements of the Monti government. We worked very intensively for this goal with my

© The Author(s) 2020
O. Rehn, *Walking the Highwire*, https://doi.org/10.1007/978-3-030-34592-1_11

colleague, Commission Vice-President Antonio Tajani, who was the father of the Late Payments Directive, a very important piece of legislation for European SMEs.

The Capital Boost That Didn't Bark—EIB Reinforced

Another of our initiatives was to pursue a capital increase of the European Investment Bank. We tested it with the member states in early 2012. Initially, there was no support. Then, some warming could be seen. Wolfgang Schäuble told me: "If you convince the FDP, why not". Always witty, this time he was probably half-serious, as he had political difficulties with his coalition partner in the German federal government and he tried to put me in responsibility as a fellow liberal to the Free Democrats. My influence was limited though.

After several rounds of talks we were still going nowhere. At the same time, the liquidity trap got only worse, especially for SMEs, and the ECB's actions seemed then not strong enough to alleviate the pain or break the financial fragmentation.

In May 2012, we had come to a sufficiently desperate situation to try our luck even at the cost of a backlash—that's how life often works and how progress is made. In Strasbourg, when preparing my speech at the EP plenary session in a grey and rainy Wednesday morning, I had a word with my advisor Taneli Lahti on our way from our hotel to the Parliament. "Should we not try to raise the EIB capital increase now? We don't have much to lose. Perhaps we can move the mood now".

Thus, we drafted a few bullet points in the car for my use to speak out in the plenary meeting. After the speech we drafted the text into a more precise form to correspond to the spoken word and then got it published. My speech went along these lines:

There are many measures we can take quickly to strengthen our economy and send a message of confidence. Promoting public and private investment is a cornerstone of our growth initiative.

We will first of all propose that Member States commit a further 10 billion euros to the European Investment Bank. This could unleash many times that amount in new investment. The EIB could expand its lending volume, which is a quick and effective way of channelling badly needed stimulus to the real economy.

I referred to President Barroso's proposal that was put before the EP on 28 September 2011 in his State of the Union address. Now there was momentum to get it off the ground, with a focus on financing innovative and competitive small and medium-sized enterprises, especially in countries and regions that needed it most. Moreover, I referred to the next EU budget as a Marshall Plan for Europe and suggested that the EIB and EU structural funds could be used more effectively.

We will also urge an immediate agreement on our growth-focused budget for 2013, with agreement by the end of the year on the Multi-annual Financial Framework for 2014-2020. This will be an important signal in Europe's readiness to invest in its future, into job-rich green growth and innovation-based re-industrialisation of Europe. In truth, the MFF is our Marshall Plan for Europe.

And we will look at further optimising the use of structural funds. We want to invest better and to use the funds as catalysts to boost sectors such as renewable energy sources, which have great potential but are finding it harder to access funding. Likewise, we want to support education and training more effectively.

But I said there is a fundamental problem: the EIB has reached the limits of what it can do with its current capital base. Therefore, without the endorsement of the EU member states, there would be no additional investment stimulus—a great pity.

My intervention was a catalyst for a serious debate for many months on reinforcing the EIB's lending capacity. Following the very strong drive of the EIB's active President Werner Hoyer, and still many negotiations in the Council and the Parliament, the EIB received a capital increase of €10 billion in 2013. As a result, the EIB's lending volume increased by 40% annually in 2013–15, leading to overall investment of around €180 billion over the three years, mainly targeted at innovation and infrastructure, renewable energy and the bio-economy, and at SMEs.

This provided a solid base for the Juncker Commission to launch the European Fund for Strategic Investments (EFSI) in 2014. Its overall volume, when counting both public and private investments, has been around 315 billion euros. It has transformed the functioning of the European Investment Bank and has significantly helped supporting the economic recovery in Europe.

It is evident that the investment plan should go together with a renewed drive to cut red tape, pursue growth beyond our borders through free trade, complete the single market in services and speed up the digital single market. We need a better business environment and stronger prospective demand for the companies to invest, and likewise, for the pension funds and other institutional and private investors to provide finance. That's the way to combine investment for growth and sustainable public finances that are needed for sustainable growth.

This raises the issue of investment. The green economy, e-commerce and SME lending should increasingly be the European Investment Bank's focus of lending. It is the public development bank of the EU, and one of the world's best kept secrets is that it is in fact the largest development bank in the world with a lending capacity that is several times the size of the World Bank.

Towards the Banking Union

"Can you get yourself to Charles de Gaulle for tomorrow evening?", asked my head of cabinet Timo Pesonen over the phone on Monday. It was a rhetorical question, as of course I should go. There had been a plan to organize a small preparatory meeting of the Frankfurt Group on how to start breaking the poisonous loop between the banks and sovereigns, and now the meeting was materializing.

So we drove from Brussels to Hotel Sheraton at the Paris Charles de Gaulle airport with two of my Commission colleagues on Tuesday 26 June 2012. Ministers Wolfgang Schäuble and Pierre Moscovici and the IMF's Christine Lagarde arrived in parallel, and also the Italian and Spanish finance ministers, Vittorio Grilli and Luis de Guindos, took part. Leaders' economic policy advisors participated as well, including Emmanuel Macron, who was then President Francois Hollande's policy advisor and G7/G20 representative, or "sherpa". The meeting was organized fully under the radar screen and with a low profile, but as we say back home, there was nevertheless "quite some spirit of a great sporting spectacle in the air".

Direct recapitalization of banks was the original focus of the meeting, even if the agenda was expanded to cover banking union. On direct recap, a deal was reached, though there were some hiccups later on, in fact at one level above ministers (read: the Chancellor), and our deal didn't fly as such. But it was also a decisive meeting for getting the banking union off the ground. And the banking union was a core part of the Comprehensive Crisis

Response, which we had advocated since 2010 when the CCR was originally put to the agenda.

The reason why the banking union is so important is well illustrated by the *FT* economics writer Martin Sandbu: "Incestuous relations between states and banks... – call it the bank-state complex – shoulders much of the blame for economic waste in the boom and the weakness of the recovery. By dissolving it, banking union promises a much healthier political economy in Europe and its nation-states".

The De Gaulle supper essentially prepared the Eurozone Summit that was scheduled to take place only a few days later in Brussels on Thursday–Friday 28–29 June 2012. In the summit, the euro area leaders decided on the strengthening and the next reform of the economic and monetary union, especially on building a banking union, which would dismantle the perilous link between banks and sovereign debt.

We were satisfied with the decisions, as long as we could witness them being implemented as well. The immediate reason was that since the capitalization of banks inevitably increased governments' debt ratios, confidence in governments' ability to service their debt also weakened, which further amplified the debt crisis. This needed to be turned around, and the banking union was the key answer to it.

The agreement meant that once a credible and operable banking supervision was set up for the euro area, the European Stability Mechanism (ESM) would have the right to directly re-capitalize banks without the debt granted by it adding to the debt burden of governments already suffering under market pressure. However, there was a rather immediate backlash against the agreement from Germany, Finland and the Netherlands, which could have derailed the Eurozone stabilization effort again, unless other important things had not taken place over the summer 2012.

The Commission's legislative proposal was quickly finalized and tabled in September 2012. It laid the legal foundation for a banking union, whose key components were to be, in addition to comprehensive banking regulation and supervision that were already being reformed, a proper crisis management or resolution mechanism for banking crises with clear bail-in rules, which would save the taxpayers' euros, and a more unified deposit guarantee system whose details were to be decided later on. The bulk of the relevant legislation was included in the so-called BRRD or the Bank Recovery and Resolution Directive.

The Eurozone countries also agreed to utilize effectively the already existing tools to stabilize the markets in the distressed member states. This meant a possibility for the ESM to purchase government securities either at the time of their issue on the primary markets, or alternatively, on the secondary markets, even though both cases would always require a separate decision. Despite the latter caveat which weakened its impact, this was also an important message for the financial markets that stability in the euro area would be upheld by any means necessary.

It was agreed that the necessary condition for the use of these tools would be a credible commitment to reforms by the countries that would be receiving assistance. This meant that market operations could only be used to help such member states that are willing to commit to sound budgetary policies and making structural reforms to boost growth and employment. This requirement was not mere talk, but it led to tangible decisions as well: In July 2012, Spain decided on a two-year 65 billion euro mid-term stabilization package, which equalled over six percent of its GDP. Likewise in July 2012, Italy decided on 26 billion euros of expenditure cuts to follow up the stabilization packages implemented over the previous years.

The Eurozone Summit lasted until the early hours, this time not in vain. It was already early morning at 4.35 on Friday 29 June 2012 when the Council President Herman van Rompuy closed the summit after intense haggling, resulting in important decisions, and also victories for some. The summit was concluded by Germany's Chancellor Angela Merkel, who congratulated Prime Minister Mario Monti for Italy's victory in the semi-final of the Euro 2012 football tournament.

The Summit decisions alone did not yet stabilize the Eurozone. Bond yields continued to be high, and talk about Grexit went on. The Exit talk also spread wider, including Finland. Some less than careful ministerial statements over the summer 2012 gave the impression that a *Fixit* could be seriously in the cards, which was never really the case. For instance, Roubini's Global Economics wrote in its Crisis Watch on 9 July 2012: "There are increasing doubts about the future of Finland's Eurozone membership... the purely economic considerations suggest exiting would be wiser. Only recently considerable criticism of Eurozone membership has been voiced in the Finnish media. When the public perception changes, politicians' views will change too".[1] The report forgot to mention that membership in the euro had a solid two-thirds support in Finland even during the crisis. No matter, over the crisis years I quickly learned to take Roubini's flashy headline-inducing remarks with a grain of salt. I wish the rest of the world had done the same.

But this kind of speculation fuelled plenty of fuss, uncertainty and detrimental speculation on "Fixit", which came to my face from the market forces in the largest financial centre of the world, New York City, on my mission there in August 2012. After my dinner talk and a lively subsequent discussion at Bank of America in its 5th Avenue and 42nd Street financial centre, two youthful representatives of market forces blocked me into the corner of the dining room and asked supposedly discreetly: "What is your take, will Finland exit the Eurozone already early this fall, or will it only happen later, like next year?"—What can you say to that? Well, of course I slowly explained how things really are: patience, prudence, perseverance….

The Spanish Rescue

In spring–summer 2012, Spain was facing a dead-end of going it alone and instead had to seek financial assistance from other Eurozone countries to recapitalize its banks. It is not that its economic fundamentals—at least the real-economy fundamentals—had changed so much overnight that the pressure was "justified". Rather, it was the stress in the banking and financial system, especially the "*cajas*", or the savings banks, whose governance was rather old-fashioned to put it mildly. Both Benoit Coeure and Barry Eichengreen retrospectively underline this fact:

> The spreads of Spanish and Italian ten-year government bonds relative to Germany had increased by 250 basis points and 200 basis points respectively in July 2012 compared to the one year before. In neither one of the two countries, fundamentals had changed so spectacularly to justify such drastic re-pricing of sovereign risk… The Spanish government had just embarked on a series of reforms redressing long-standing problems in the labour market and the banking sector.[2]

By early June 2012, the situation in the Spanish banking sector turned from critical to almost desperate. On 5 June 2012, I discussed with President Barroso on what to do to avoid a dead-end. We knew that Chancellor Merkel was not ready for direct recapitalization of banks, so we had to find another way forward. Prime Minister Rajoy, in turn, was expecting a quantum leap towards the banking union, but was strongly against a fully fledged adjustment programme with full conditionality. The political costs of a serious reform programme frightened the proud Spaniards.

It was time for a compromise solution, which could be based on the combination of a programme targeted especially for the repair of the banking sector, on one hand, and limited conditionality in fiscal policy and structural reforms, on the other. Barroso discussed this option with Merkel. She requested Barroso to fly to Madrid to talk to Rajoy and convince him.

As the G20 Summit in Los Cabos in Mexico was approaching in two weeks' time, there would be immense pressure on Rajoy to opt for a programme. Spain had benefitted from the cover provided by the more immediate crisis faced by Italy and Greece in the Cannes G20 Summit in November. Now there was the nasty scenario that "Rajoy will be the Berlusconi of Los Cabos".

So Barroso talked with Madrid and convinced Rajoy on the merits of a banking sector programme. In the meantime, the preparations of a possible limited banking-sector programme intensified under the radar screen in the Commission and with the Spanish authorities. Finally, following months and months of negotiations and backroom talks, the scene was set for the request of the Spanish government for a conditional financial assistance programme for recapitalizing its banks.

The final stretch of the negotiations on the programme went on, and by 27 July things were ready for a Eurogroup teleconference to decide that the other Eurozone countries would be prepared to recapitalize banks in Spain, on the condition that she would streamline its banking sector thoroughly and run down unviable banks so as to minimize the cost on European taxpayers. The EFSF/ESM programme included granting a maximum of 100 billion euros of loans for bank recapitalization to Spain. The programme design included a first-aid reserve of 30 billion euros.

I did the teleconference and presented the Commission's proposal from the Pori Jazz Festival on the Finnish West coast, which had become a standard practice during the crisis years. I thank the Pori city mayor Aino-Maija Luukkonen and the deputy mayors for letting me use their offices for the teleconference—a Europe of Regions in action! In fact, Pori is a very appropriate seat for important European decisions, as the real jazz connoisseur, Commission President Jacques Delors, honoured Pori Jazz in 1994 with his presence and participation.

What should we take away from the Spanish rescue programme? First of all, and for once, the Eurogroup and the Commission worked closely in tandem and decided to **overshoot** rather than undershoot, which was crucial for the credibility of the Spanish rescue operation and for the financial stability of the Eurozone. This was decisive to show that we were finally ahead of, or at least no more behind, the curve.

The markets took our commitment seriously and positively, realizing that we were effectively ready to recapitalize the Spanish banking sector, as the maximum figure 100 billion euros was clearly above the assumed financing needs.

In addition, the excellent preparation by the Spanish authorities, especially by the central bank, *Banco de España*, was crucial for the success of the Spanish programme. This was substantially aided by the high-quality work of the Commission mission team, led by the very competent pair of hands, Deputy Director General Servaas Deroose, and also by the IMF country team that provided technical assistance.

Draghi's Speech Brings a Truce to the Markets

As the heavy turbulence in the markets continued in July–August 2012, the member states—and market forces—began to look to the ECB for help. During his visit to London in the context of the Olympic Games in July 2012, Mario Draghi gave a more or less spontaneous speech in which he pledged the ECB's willingness to do "whatever it takes" to restore stability in the euro area and for the euro to survive. "Believe me, it will be enough", he stated, and the markets took him by his words.

But as Barry Eichengreen has pointed out, it is often forgotten that Draghi had an important preface in his sentence: "*Within our mandate*, the ECB is ready to do whatever it takes to preserve the euro" (emphasis added).[3] Not surprisingly, the ECB's new activism received heavy criticism especially in Germany. However, as time passed by and the results were undoubtedly positive, the ECB leadership could better withstand the criticism, even though it has never completely calmed down.

Meanwhile in Helsinki, two important state visits took place: both Bruce Springsteen and Mario Monti were in town in late July—early August. On 31 July at the Helsinki Olympic Stadium, the Boss played his longest gig ever, lasting 5 hours 37 minutes! One can only wonder the renewable energy and enjoy his great songs, which I've done since 1975, and now we did with my wife Merja and daughter Silva and 49,997 other fans. There was no "darkness on the edge of the town" whatsoever.

Next morning was for me a return to the reality of European contemporary darkness, as I met Prime Minister Mario Monti at the airport of Helsinki just after he had landed. We went straight to business and analysed options to bring down the prohibitively high interest rates which were now hitting hard Italy and Spain in particular. The decisions of the June Eurozone Summit had not at least yet had the desired effect in the bond markets. Mario had various options in mind, which included leveraging the ESM for this purpose by possibly using credit enhancements.

The Commission was in principle in favour, but had no vote in the ESM Board of Governors.

Conspiracies to kill the break-up risk of the euro continued in the following days. In the afternoon of 1 August, a few hours after the meeting with Mario Monti in Helsinki, I talked with Mario Draghi who was now in Frankfurt and no more in Rome to find out how he would follow up his London speech in the Governing Council. He explained his plan but was quite concerned about the probable and even strong resistance to his line. So he insisted on me speaking frankly and openly about the critical or almost desperate situation in the sovereign bond markets and the need for rapid stabilization. He was preaching to a convert, and I did so with conviction. So off to the Frankfurt financial battlefields from the sweet summer of Helsinki.

Next day, on Thursday 2 August 2012, the ECB's Governing Council convened in Frankfurt. At Draghi's proposal, the Governing Council announced that it would, as needed, be ready to undertake market operations named as Outright Monetary Transactions (OMT) in the secondary sovereign-bond markets, aimed "at safeguarding an appropriate monetary policy transmission and the singleness of the monetary policy". Contrary to some retrospective claims, the decision was taken in full independence by the ECB Governing Council, and involved a high degree of risk of back-firing. In my eyes, that makes it an even more courageous and crucial act; decisive it has always been.

The Governing Council underlined policy conditionality by stating that it could purchase sovereign debt of distressed Eurozone countries only as long as these countries pledged their adherence to clear goals in terms of fiscal policy and structural reforms. The ECB had to stress this point of rigorous conditionality by its experience in early autumn 2011 when Prime Minister Berlusconi began to actively shirk away from the commitments he had made towards changing course. As Draghi put it in his press conference on 2 August 2012:

> Risk premia that are related to fears of the reversibility of the euro are unacceptable, and they need to be addressed in a fundamental manner. The euro is irreversible. The adherence of governments to their commitments and the fulfilment by the EFSF/ESM of their role are necessary conditions. The Governing Council… may undertake outright open market operations of a size adequate to reach its objective.[4]

Following the August meeting, the Eurosystem's technical committees engaged in very intensive work and soon produced a proposal for the technical framework of the OMT operations, which was decided a month later, on 6 September 2012. In the same meeting of the Governing Council, the ECB's Securities Markets Programme that had been in use since May 2010 was terminated.

Any possible OMT operation would be considered by the European Central Bank, if and when a Eurozone government requested financial assistance. Even more rigorously, the ECB made activation conditional on the country first agreeing on a conditionality programme with the ESM. Through OMT, the ECB could, if so decided, buy government-issued bonds that mature in one to three years, provided the bond-issuing countries agree to certain economic policy measures of stabilization and reform.

That's where conditionality came into play. Conditionality would be implemented by the member states through the ESM, if or when the OMT mechanism were to be activated, which has not been the case so far. Hence, the decision-making powers and political responsibility lies ultimately collectively with the member states in the ESM. The Commission's task would be to determine the conditions of the programme for the Eurogroup and to monitor their fulfilment.

This arrangement was an essential guarantee for the ECB on the fulfilment of the conditionality that was set for the debt purchases. In my opinion, it was a fully justified solution that gave the ECB the required legal and political backbone.

As Eichengreen has noted, "The most striking aspect of OMT was that it didn't actually have to be activated to produce the desired result".[5] I would add that the logic of the OMT was the logic of the SMP turned upside down: while the SMP in 2010 was designed in the atmosphere of "old normal" by way of "speak softly and carry a modest stick", the OMT in 2012 was designed in the spirit of "new normal" by way of "speak loudly and carry a big bazooka with unconstrained firepower". This strategic turnaround was part of the ECB's learning process during the crisis, as it was a learning process for all of us.

Some columnists and pundits compared the ECB's action to Draghi playing a game of chess and waiting for the member states' next move. Although I dislike gambling and gambling metaphors having seen its social costs in too many cases, in my view stud poker, which I sometimes played in my youth on trips to away matches, is a better metaphor. Draghi already had a good hand open on the table after a few deals and—I suspect—an ace in the hole, so I guess it was a no-lose situation. That does not usually make the other players happy, who have to decide when to make a move. But unlike chess or stud poker, this is not a zero-sum game, and therefore everyone can win, together and separately.

The initial reactions among the market participants to Draghi's statement were critical or at least doubtful. At first, I felt like saying to myself, "this can't happen again!" I was scared we'd face yet another rock-bottom due to the possible lack of understanding of the ECB's supposedly clear message. However, the market situation began to improve in the course of the following day, Friday 3 August.

On the same Friday morning, I spoke at Mikkeli's marketplace in Finland to the participants of the National Homestead Day, and to the ordinary townsfolk from all walks of life who were attracted to the marketplace by the sunny weather of early August. My main point was that the market forces do not seem to have properly understood the true significance of the ECB's decision. It was the critical big bazooka now finally, I maintained, especially to the TV cameras present.

Moreover, I emphasized to my fellow folks of Mikkeli that there was no reason whatsoever to belittle the influence of a small country, and Finland in particular, within the EU. To hammer to point in: at the time at the table of the ECB's Governing Council, the seats were divided 2-2 between Mikkeli and Germany (I noted, though, that as a Commission representative I was not allowed to vote, only to speak). To be even more precise, I said the powers were divided 2-2 between Pitkäjärvi and Germany, since both Erkki Liikanen's family and mine originally hail from the same suburb of Pitkäjärvi, right next to downtown Mikkeli. I admit I was not referring to the influence of the Bundesbank on the ECB or to its 10,000 employees, which is several times more than the ECB and the Bank of Finland combined. Details, just details... But recall that when a Savonian speaks, listen at your own discretion!

Stabilization in 2012—And Return to Recovery and Growth?

In the second half of 2012, stabilization of the Eurozone started to be felt—or rather, it started to sneak in. This was to a large extent thanks to Mario Draghi's landmark London speech and the subsequent ECB decisions in August and September. The creation of the permanent ESM and the restored credibility of member states' fiscal policies and structural reforms provided important flanking support and constituted one precondition for the success of the ECB's more activist role in containing the crisis.

After the climate-wise and even more so financially and politically heated summer break of 2012, the EU's then 27 finance ministers and 27 central bank governors (Croatia had not yet joined) gathered in September in Nicosia, Cyprus, for their twice-yearly jamboree called "informal Ecofin meeting". The dark shadow of a looming financial and banking crisis in Cyprus herself was hanging over the ministerial. Most of the participants were aware of the critical financial situation of the country. The Commission had warned President Dimitris Christofias and the Cypriot government in the end of the previous year 2011 that the country was heading for a financial dead-end. Indeed, Cyprus should have, for her own sake, entered an economic adjustment programme way earlier than it finally did. Some Russian doping there was! More of this in Chapter 16.

However, the informal Ecofin did not focus on Cyprus, but rather on the overall state and near-term prospects of the European economy. Discussions focused on the pursuit of a banking union and structural reforms. Both in the meeting itself and in the subsequent press conference I tried to give a realistic but reassuring message. I recognized the downside of a delayed recovery, but underlined the upside that the rebalancing process was genuinely under way. The latter I did partly out of necessity, as that was the only imaginably honest way to present at least some good news. And good news was needed to credibly reinforce consumer and investor confidence, which in turn was necessary in order to achieve a proper recovery.

My summary was thus: "We started today's discussion with a sobering economic outlook, where economic recovery will be delayed into next year. But the rebalancing and reform in the euro area is well underway, although it will need to continue for some years to come".

In the course of the following weeks in September–October 2012, the fresh hard and soft data analysed by our economists and run through our econometric models started to show that the long-awaited stabilization was now taking place and the recovery was finally on its way to emerge and be felt. This contrasted with the previous estimates that the economy had dipped back into contraction in the second quarter of 2012, with further weaknesses expected in the third and fourth quarters. The recession did not return, and compared with the very fragile situation before the summer, in the autumn of 2012 financial tensions gradually abated. We finally started to feel some sturdy ground under our feet.

As a matter of fact, the recovery of the Eurozone emerged by stealth, after having evaded it for so long. Until mid-2012, all efforts for stabilization and restarting growth had been soon eroded. That's why it was hard to believe that we would finally be able to return to the path of recovery and growth—we had to see it before we could believe it. The exits of former crisis countries from their programmes amplified the positive effect. Reinforced economic governance provided continued solidity for economic policies and ensured fiscal sustainability.

Soon after taking office, particularly once I had come to realize the formidable challenges in communication, with which I should be able reach out equally to political leaders, ordinary citizens and market participants, I decided to opt not for cautious optimism but guarded realism, and chose the rebalancing of the Eurozone as my main narrative. Why so? Because it fitted the facts. Its virtue was substantive validity and undisputable honesty. Why realism? Simply because the rebalancing narrative showed that the large cumulative macroeconomic imbalances, related to excessive capital flows and currents account surpluses and deficits, were the root cause of the Eurozone's banking and debt crisis—and as they had accumulated over years, it would also take years to overcome them.

But equally important, the rebalancing process could be speeded up with smart and coordinated policies. That's why early on in the crisis the Commission focused on the prevention and correction of macroeconomic imbalances, which became a core part of the six-pack reform under the name of Macroeconomic Imbalance Procedure. Under it, the focus is on both surplus and deficit countries, which takes us to the origins of the euro and, more generally, of European monetary integration, where Germany and France have played a key role and where both represent a certain economic-monetary philosophy that underpins even the current tensions within the construct of the Eurozone.

I shall focus on the rebalancing question in Chapter 14 where both current account surplus and deficit countries will be analysed. I will take Germany and France as particular cases in point, simply because they were our particular policy focus over the crisis years, and because there is much to learn from their experiences.

This prompted me to take a step further in expressing confidence in the return of growth when presenting the Commission's autumn forecast on 7 November 2012, and to say that we were now finally seeing some light in the end of the tunnel: "A return to moderate growth is projected in the first half of 2013. Major policy decisions have laid the foundations for strengthening confidence".

But I continued with a warning and called for vigilance in reforms: "Market stress has been reduced, but there is no room for complacency. Europe must continue to combine sound fiscal policies with structural reforms to create the conditions for sustainable growth to bring unemployment down from the current unacceptably high levels".

Later on the same day, I gave a talk at the European Policy Centre, one of the reformist think-tanks in Brussels. The idea was to strengthen the message that Europe had returned to a positive albeit still fragile growth trajectory:

> Earlier today I presented our latest economic forecast titled Sailing through rough waters. While we expect growth to gradually return next year and firming in 2014, the European economy is undergoing a rebalancing process that will last for some time. Therefore we have to pull all levers to strengthen the long-term drivers of sustained growth.

Full Steam Ahead: Blueprint for a Deep and Genuine EMU in November 2012

While focusing on the real economy and its rebalancing, we had not forgotten institutional reforms, on the contrary. Following the success of the six-pack, we wanted to move full steam ahead in reinforcing the Eurozone.

After many months of preparations, on 28 November 2012 the Commission adopted a major policy document, *Blueprint for a Deep and Genuine Economic and Monetary Union*, which deserves to be referred to, as it provided a vision for a strong and stable architecture in the financial, fiscal, economic and political domains of the Eurozone. It was the key post-six-pack contribution by the Commission to reinforce economic governance in the Eurozone, combining solidity with solidarity. It also provided the intellectual foundation for the subsequent policy initiatives, such as the four and five Presidents' reports in 2012–15.

The goal of the Blueprint was to pave the way for a deep and genuine economic and monetary union in order to overcome the crisis of confidence that was hurting Europe's economies. We needed to give tangible proof of our willingness to stick together and move forward decisively to strengthen the architecture in the financial, fiscal, economic and political domains that underpinned the stability of the euro. In the box below the Blueprint is illustrated in a nutshell.

Box 11.1 *The Commission's blueprint for a deep and genuine EMU, November 2012*

A blueprint for a deep and genuine EMU: launching a European debate

				Secondary law	Treaty change
All along the process	Short term	Within the next 18 months	1. Full implementation of European Semester and six-pack and quick agreement on and implementation of two-pack	X	
			2. Banking union: Financial regulation and supervision: quick agreement on proposals for a Single Rulebook and Single Supervisory Mechanism	X	
			3. Banking union: Single Resolution Mechanism	X	
			4. Quick decision on the next Multi-annual Financial Framework	X	
			5. Ex-ante coordination of major reforms and the creation of a Convergence and Competitiveness Instrument (CCI)	X	
			6. Promoting investment in the euro area in line with the stability and growth pact	X	
			7. External representation of the euro area	X	
	Medium term	18 months to 5 years	1. Further reinforcement of budgetary and economic integration	X	X
			2. Proper fiscal capacity for the euro area building on the CCI	X	X
			3. Redemption fund		X
			4. Eurobills		X
	Longer Term	Beyond 6 years	1. Full banking union		X
			2. Full fiscal and economic union		X
			Political union: Commensurate progress on democratic legitimacy and accountability	X	X

Source European Commission

The Blueprint set out the path to a deep and genuine EMU, which involves incremental measures taken over the short, medium and longer term. We underlined that part of the agenda could be delivered on the basis of the current Treaties, though part of it required Treaty change. Its core elements were:

> • *In the short term (within 6–18 months), immediate priority was to be given to implementing the governance reforms already agreed (six pack) or about to be agreed (two pack). Member States were also urged to strive for an agreement on a Single Supervisory Mechanism for banks by the end of year 2012. We pointed out that an effective banking union would not only require the setting up of a Single Supervisory Mechanism, but after its adoption also a Single Resolution Mechanism to deal with banks in difficulties.*
>
> *Moreover, once an agreement on the Multiannual Financial Framework was reached, the economic governance framework was supposed to be strengthened further by creating a "convergence and competitiveness instrument" within the EU budget, separate from the Multiannual Financial Framework, to support the timely implementation of structural reforms that were important for the Member States and for the smooth functioning of the EMU. This support was suggested to be based on commitments set out in "contractual arrangements" concluded between Member States and the Commission.*
>
> • *In the medium term (18 months to 5 years), further strengthening of the collective conduct of budgetary and economic policy—including tax and employment policy—was expected to go hand-in-hand with an enhanced fiscal capacity. A dedicated fiscal capacity for the Eurozone was suggested to rely on the EU budget's own resources and provide sufficient support for important structural reforms in large economies under stress. This was to be developed on the basis of the convergence and competitiveness instrument, but would have benefitted from new and specific Treaty bases. A redemption fund subject to strict conditionality and Eurobills were proposed for consideration, to help with debt reduction and stabilise financial markets. The monitoring and managing function for the fiscal capacity and other instruments was to be provided by an EMU Treasury within the Commission.*
>
> • *In the longer term (beyond 5 years), based on the adequate pooling of sovereignty, responsibility and solidarity at the European level, it was considered possible to establish an autonomous Eurozone budget providing for a fiscal capacity for the EMU to support Member States affected by economic shocks. A deeply integrated economic and fiscal governance framework could allow for the common issuance of public debt, which would enhance the functioning of the markets and the conduct of monetary policy.*

Some of the steps in the European Commission's blueprint could have been adopted within the limits of the current Treaties. Others would have required modifications of the current Treaties and new competences for the Union.

The Blueprint was also the Commission's contribution to the report of the "four presidents" on the next steps for economic and monetary union. A final version of the report was prepared by the President of the European Council Herman van Rompuy in coordination with President Barroso, the President of the European Central Bank Mario Draghi and the President of the Eurogroup Jean-Claude Juncker, and was discussed by the European Council on 13–14 December 2012.

The report did not however lead to any new breakthroughs. Progress on reforming the Eurozone has happened mostly in the field of the banking union. Other reforms have been left into the back-burner by the member states, which is regrettable and keeps the Eurozone vulnerable. I shall return to the Eurozone reform in Chapter 19.

Notes

1. Roubini Global Economics, *Crisis Watch*. Finland and the Eurozone: Should I Stay or Should I Go? 9 July 2012.
2. Benoit Coeure 2012, cited in Barry Eichengreen, *The European Central Bank: From Problem to Solution*. BBVA, 2015, p. 13.
3. Eichengreen 2015, p. 13.
4. Mario Draghi, Press Statement, 2 August 2012.
5. Eichengreen 2015, p. 15.

12

Recovery Arrives by Stealth

The sign of times: "I am not as worried today as last year", said Chancellor Angela Merkel in Die Welt's new year conference in Berlin on 8 January 2013.

Indeed, the year 2013 started better than 2012, although the Chancellor may in her bad memories of 2012 have had rather the terrible springtime 2012 in mind… the year 2012 actually started well, but soon turned to a competition who would make the biggest contribution to Europe's collective suicide, a competition that lasted until June. Only from the Midsummer onwards started reason to prevail again, with decisive action by both the European Council and the ECB, as described in the previous chapter.

I echoed Chancellor Merkel's positive narrative in Davos in January 2013 when interviewed by Reuters' Paul Taylor. "I recall last year in 2012, Davos was full of uncertainty about the Eurozone. This year we are seeing the sentiment moving from stabilization to recovery, and that means I should get a chance to do some cross-country skiing". I couldn't help providing a Nordic metaphor, even though I am not a very keen skier—in fact, as a skier I could be described as "more eager than competent"! Be that as it may, "Brexit had replaced Grexit as Davos man's nightmare", as Paul Taylor coined that year's Jamboree of global business leaders. Paul's quip turned out to be a most insightful prediction, much to our joint regret!

I had a slightly calmer Christmas break in 2012 than normally, so I had time to take a closer look at economic analysis and fresh statistics and think through the prospects and remedies ahead. As I tend to do thinking by

© The Author(s) 2020
O. Rehn, *Walking the Highwire*, https://doi.org/10.1007/978-3-030-34592-1_12

writing, I used part of the break to draft my speech for the European Policy Centre on 10 January 2013.

Came February 2013, and it was time for the Commission's winter forecast. I continued with the message of rebalancing and gradual recovery, as the European economy was slowly coming out of contraction, a turn owed to decreased risk premia on the vulnerable sovereigns and banks in the financial markets. This signalled returned confidence in the integrity of the euro and in the determination of the member states to bring public debt back on a sustainable path.

Against my habits, I also referred to a piece of economists' favourite jargon, the "negative feedback loop" between fragile public finances, vulnerable banks and a weak macro-economy: "The negative feedback loop that fuelled the sovereign-debt crisis in the first half of 2012 has weakened, but the improved financial market situation still contrasts with the absence of credit growth and the weakness of the near-term economic outlook. The re-balancing of the European economy continues to weigh on growth in the short-term".

Staying the Course of *Austerity*— No, of *Reform*!

Considering that the prospects of recovery were still fragile, to say the least, I stressed that staying the course of reform and avoiding any loss of momentum that could undermine the turnaround in confidence was a mandatory element of stability and growth in the coming year. As I had done before, I spoke consistently about staying the course of *reform*, not *austerity*. Using reform instead of austerity was a deliberate choice from my and the Commission's side, because there is a fundamental difference in substance between the two. Economic reforms aim at boosting potential growth, while consolidation—which was especially during the crisis pejoratively referred to as "austerity"—relates to public finances.

By early May 2013, the discourse of cautious and realistic optimism about the state of the European economy had been properly established and noted in the markets, especially after the Cyprus rescue package in late March, as will be explained in Chapter 16 that deals with aftershocks of the crisis that didn't explode.

Still, when I presented the Commission's spring forecast on 3 May 2013, there was little room for complacency. The economy was set to pick up speed only very slowly in 2013 with relatively small gains in 2014 relying on increasing investment and consumption. Moreover, we expected domestic demand to remain constrained by a number of growth impediments, commonly associated with balance-sheet recessions after deep financial crises. This implied that the projected recovery of domestic demand over the next two years would remain modest.

I wanted to shift focus even more clearly than before to stronger growth and job creation. Fiscal policy was already targeting medium-term structural balance. The credit crunch was a major challenge now:

> In view of the protracted recession and high unemployment in many parts of Europe, we must really do whatever it takes to overcome the unemployment crisis. Each EU institution will need to work within its own mandate. The EU's policy mix is focused on sustainable growth and job creation. Monetary policy is accommodative and will remain so. In fiscal policy, consistent consolidation is continued, even though with a slower pace in the current economic context, while ensuring the medium-term sustainability of public finances. Next, we must resolve the financing trap of households and enterprises, especially in southern Europe, to let credit flow and facilitate economic growth by using possible ways and means at the disposal of the EU institutions, including the European Investment Bank.

I couldn't say in public that the ECB should do more, which is partly why I and the Commission focused so much on the EIB capital increase. It was a worthy goal in substance to counter the financing trap, and a worthy signal that we would welcome the ECB taking an even more active policy stance.

The process of debt deleveraging by banks, corporates and households had been going on for several year already, but it was not yet completed, and they would still have to maintain it for some years. This would continue to maintain or in some cases worsen the liquidity trap. Governments also needed to continue consolidating their public finances, although at a lower structural pace thanks to the large efforts in the past two years. Anyway, while both were unavoidable, they were obstacles to growth that were difficult to overcome in the short run. This meant we couldn't expect miracles from the ongoing process of rebalancing, a fact that required a heavy dose of realism in communication.

G7 Calls for Better Policy Coordination and the EU Banking Union

As a sign of improving times, the G7 meeting in the UK on 10–11 May 2013 was clearly calmer than for many years, and the Eurozone was no more at the epicentre. Instead of only focusing on the immediate crisis management, the meeting was more forward-looking in terms of concentrating on policy coordination and institutional reform. The meeting was also the first G7 one where Janet Yellen attended, then as vice-chair of the Federal Reserve. I had a chance to sit the dinner next to her—a wonderful personality, with a great sense of humour. We talked about the Fed's monetary policy strategy but also small-talked about Finland where she had spent some weeks in the late 1970s to lead a Ph.D. course given by James Tobin.

The meeting was organized by the UK G7 Presidency in the English countryside, at the impressive Hartwell House close to Aylesbury in Buckinghamshire. George Osborne, the Chancellor of the Exchequer, and Sir Mervyn King, the Governor of Bank of England, hosted it with the best British traditions of no-nonsense substance and unconstrained wit; this is the British style we will miss after Brexit.

It was also agreed that the meeting would not adopt a communiqué, which likewise facilitated an analytical and candid—or as it is called, "frank and open"—discussion. As Osborne said before the meeting, he wanted "to take the G7 back to its roots as a forum for advanced economies to come together for informal discussions", and that was done successfully over the two days.

In the meeting, there was a broad consensus on a policy mix that would combine a non-standard, expansionary monetary policy with a consistent fiscal policy focused on medium-term plans. Of course, there were also the usual and for some "necessary" skirmishes on global macroeconomic imbalances and the German current account surplus between the new US Treasury Secretary Jack Lew and the German Minister of Finance Wolfgang Schäuble—there was indeed quite some continuity in the proceedings, as this didn't change at all when Tim Geithner left the Treasury! I supported actively this policy mix on behalf of the European Commission, as this was in fact what we had been calling for since the first drafts of a "comprehensive crisis response" in 2010. Sometimes it was easier to discuss these matters of coordination at the G7 or IMF table than at a European one. This is how Osborne put it in his press statement:

> We discussed the recent actions taken by our central banks, of both a conventional and unconventional nature, and the role monetary policy can play to support the recovery while maintaining price stability. We reaffirmed our commitment we made in February that our fiscal and monetary policies have been, and will remain, orientated towards meeting our respective domestic objectives using domestic instruments, and that we will not target exchange rates.[1]

We discussed the importance of having in place credible country-specific, medium-term fiscal consolidation plans for ensuring sustainable public finances and sustainable growth, and the need to focus on structural deficits so as to ensure the near-term flexibility, such as by allowing automatic stabilisers to work. This meeting confirmed there are more areas of agreement between us on fiscal policy than is commonly assumed.

In my intervention, I informed the G7 colleagues on the previous year's shift of focus in EU fiscal policy coordination from nominal targets to structural fiscal balance, and the decisions in December 2012 accordingly to grant several member states, including France, Spain and the Netherlands, extra time to meet their deficit targets. I underlined the importance of structural reforms by member states, which would be supported in our economic governance and gave a preview of our 29 May 2013 package: "Focusing on reforms and imbalances, my intention is to do a Full Monty and become equally unpopular in all 27 capitals". In retrospect, I pretty much succeeded in that goal over the years 2010–14!

The next morning on Saturday 11 May I was tasked to present the EU's plans on the banking union and used the opportunity to brief my colleagues on the progress made in order to get substantive and possibly useful feedback. I had used all IMF and G7 meetings to have bilateral discussions with Ben Bernanke, who was always very helpful and insightful as to how the Eurozone banking union meaningfully could learn from the US experience. This time the introductory interventions by Mario Draghi and Janet Yellen were particularly enlightening and instructive, especially as regards the ways and means how to combine the resolution approach and bail-in principles with financial stability concerns.

In my introductory remarks, I focused on bank resolution procedures:

> The EU's approach to managing failing banks is underlying the Commission's proposal for an EU Directive on Bank Recovery and Resolution, to be agreed between the EU member states and the EP before the summer. A key issue is how to organize the private financing of bank resolution. The proposal envisages that stakeholders in the failing bank should contribute via a bail-in procedure. Meanwhile, the broader banking sector should contribute via pre-financed resolution funds.

I also explained our approach to sequencing of any possible bail-in operation in the fresh state-aid guidelines: (1) Equity, (2) Junior debt, (3) Senior debt and (4) Uninsured deposits. I indicated our likely endorsement for depositor preference, "which is particularly important following the recent decisions taken on Cyprus".

Mario Draghi maintained that why we don't take directly the US FDIC law as the starting point, as we'd need uniform rules of the game. In my view, this was a most substantive point, in fact sheer empirically grounded common sense, but it was probably considered a provocation by some. Osborne concluded the debate:

> We discussed the importance of measures being taken, or under considera-tion, in some of our economies, to ensure that credit can flow appropriately to support the economy. We agreed on the importance of ensuring that bank's balance sheets are adequately capitalized to enable them to play their role in supporting the economy, and we discussed steps being taken to establish a banking union in Europe.[2]

Unless Margrethe Vestager was available, George Osborne would have made an excellent Competition Commissioner of the European Union—it is my gut feel-ing that it would have been his dream job. Alas, the decision by his ally David Cameron to organize a Brexit referendum drastically changed the European dis-course in Britain and her relation to Europe, and as a side effect killed all chances of his nomination. For the other implications of Cameron's decision that are now increasingly seeing the light of day, I'll let you be the judge.

"The Best Joke of G7"

There were also some more-memorable-than-normal moments at the rela-tively short social parts of the meeting. The Friday dinner took place at the next-door Chequers, or the Prime Minister's mansion, with "PM Cameron's permission". We were given a round tour by George Osborne and could wonder various sorts of art and history collections of the British Empire. This included a precious collection of Napoleon's letters and muskets in vit-rines. As some members of the French contingent at the Chequers started to demand the British to return the letters and muskets of Napoleon back to *La République*, George quickly quipped: "No way, we won the war!"—So much for European unity, and so quickly back to 1815!

My contribution to the lighter side of policy-making life stemmed from the banking union. As I explained its project plan to the colleagues, I told them that we had support from the highest level of the international community, including the United Nations, referring to my recent meeting with the UN Secretary-General Ban Ki-moon in New York. The Korean pronunciation of his name goes more or less like this: **pan.gi.mun**. I told he smiled most sympathetically when I had explained to him how the banking union was progressing. Actually, I wondered why he was smiling, but then he suddenly said that he "really supports *the Ban-Kim…mmnngg…mm-Union!*"

There was a slow reaction and puzzlement before a fully fledged laughter was out in the meeting room. George declared: "Olli gets the prize for the best joke of G7!"

But the lighter side of life was not dominating my contacts. In the margins of the meeting, I had a discussion with Mario Draghi on fiscal backstops for bank recapitalization and their treatment in the Excessive Deficit Procedure (EDP). He was for understandable reasons advocating a special treatment (= exception) for the backstops, which was seen important for the recap operations. With the IMF's Christine Lagarde, we discussed Cyprus, Slovenia and the financing of bank recapitalization. With the fresh Italian Finance Minister Fabrizio Saccomanni, a highly respected former central banker, I called for concrete decisions in May so that Italy could finally exit the EU's EDP. With George Osborne, we discussed the UK's treatment in the EDP, which was always less rigorous than for the euro members, even though the UK was actually running large fiscal deficits.

That's how I typically spent my time in policy coordination in the G7 and G20 meetings, as well as those of the IMF and World Economic Forum. In those occasions, one could meet with people and get messages across, and sometimes get things moving in a very cost-effective way. Together these fora constitute a continuous concertation in global economic governance, which is definitely needed in our modern interconnected world. If you don't believe that, read Liaquat Ahamed's modern classic *Lords of Finance*, a history of the policy-makers and their mistakes in the 1920s and 1930s, and the dramatic collapse of international policy coordination that contributed to the economic catastrophe of the Great Depression and the subsequent Second World War.[3] Tim Geithner writes in his memoirs that at the height of the financial crisis he started reading Ahamed's book, but he had put it down after a few chapters, since he found it too scary!

EXIT Yes—But No Grexit!

While the talk of the town—or at least all the financial centres in the world, from New York to Shanghai, from London to Frankfurt—in 2012 was about the "Grexit" or a possible exit of Greece from the euro, in 2013 we started to talk about very different kind of exits. That is, most programme countries were gradually ready to exit from their conditional financial assistance programmes, which was a very concrete sign of the ongoing economic recovery in Europe. Ireland was the first to leave its programme in December 2013, to be followed by Portugal in May 2014.

Both countries made a so-called clean exit, i.e. they did not request a precautionary programme, which would have allowed them to return to markets with the backing—for instance, a precautionary credit line—from the European Stability Mechanism, if they countered any problems. They wanted to reaffirm the success of the adjustment programmes and especially to avoid any further constraints on their national economic and fiscal policies from the side of the Troika.

The preparations for the Irish exit from the programme started early on. Once the stabilization of the Eurozone in late 2012 was on a more solid ground, we intensified consultations with the Irish authorities on the matter. We had continuous and direct contact with Finance Minister Michael Noonan, who steered the process in Dublin with all the skill and stamina he had gathered in Irish politics over a few decades.

In the Eurogroup meeting of 11 February 2013, I reported on the Irish situation:

> I welcome the major steps taken by the Irish authorities and their continued steadfast programme implementation, as witnessed by the successful completion of the 9th review mission last week. This should help to further improve Ireland's prospects for a durable return to market funding and facilitate a successful exit from the programme by year end.

Quite early on, it became clear that the Irish would indeed prefer a clean exit. This was not the Commission's initial preference, as we would have preferred to play it safe and have a follow-up financial arrangement, supported, e.g. by the new instrument of the ESM, a precautionary credit line—maybe be supplemented by a parallel IMF arrangement. As the ESM ex-post evaluation report in 2017 correctly states, "The European Commission and the ECB asserted that follow-up arrangements were justified as the countries in all the early programmes remained vulnerable to shocks post-exit… Liquidity insurance and a continued focus on reform commitments drove considerations for a follow-up arrangement".[4] This should be fixed in the next governance reform, well before the next crisis, because there will be one—one day, some year, some decade.

However, knowing the mood in Dublin, I thought it would be inappropriate to advise Ireland publicly. Thus, we agreed a working method with Noonan so that we keep each other fully informed and consult at critical stages, and subsequently the Irish decide and make the proposal how to proceed. This is what happened.

As Ireland was the first country to exit its programme, it set a model and precedent to follow. It moved successfully to market financing. Portugal decided to follow suit, following again early consultations with the government. Finance Minister Maria Luis Albuquerque had prepared a carefully crafted plan and was very determined to execute it. My understanding was that most member states, including Germany, were not unhappy with the clean exits, because those would both enable the policy-makers to show the success of the two ESM programmes and at the same time help especially the creditor governments to avoid going to their own parliaments to ask for support for a precautionary credit line from the European Stability Mechanism, a course that was considered politically painful.

The story has a reasonably happy ending in the sense that both countries returned to the markets already before their official exits. Ireland made a successful 10-year debt issue in March 2013 at 4.15% interest and Portugal in May the same year at 5.67%. Since then, their sovereign bond yields sunk below 1.5 and 2.4% respectively by March 2015, which should be considered a major success story. The countries' economic performance also substantially improved.

Governor Carlos da Silva Costa has summarized correctly the elements of success in the case of Portugal. First, programme ownership was essential; Portugal was committed to the implementation of the programme, which was accepted by the population and conducted in a constructive dialogue with the social partners. Second, the speed and intensity of the response from the tradeables sector, in particular exports, was key to the rapid rebalancing · of external accounts. And third, the maintenance of confidence in the banking sector, especially the behaviour of deposits, was crucial in preventing the economy from collapsing with a credit crunch and avoiding capital controls.[5]

The Irish Homework, the Spanish Recovery and Return to Growth

One lesson of the Eurozone crisis is the Irish flagship recovery, which demonstrates the importance of flexibility and functionality of the real economy. The fact that Ireland lost some control over economic decision-making by becoming an EU-IMF programme country was a source of major unease for the Irish electorate. Nevertheless, Ireland has enjoyed political stability, which was a key prerequisite for the recovery. There is a prominent narrative about the Irish recovery of the crisis saying that the Irish "did their homework", meaning that after three years of sacrifice the Irish fought their way out of the crisis by implementing the reforms and fiscal consolidation. Today the Irish economy is flourishing again, preferably more sustainably than during the Celtic Tiger era. Since 2013, Ireland has grown significantly faster than the euro area as whole. Today there are some macroprudential concerns about the booming commercial real estate markets in Dublin. The departure of the United Kingdom from the European Union, especially the eventuality of the so-called hard Brexit, would hit the Irish economy quite hard, possibly knocking down several percentage points of her GDP.

During the crisis, multinational companies never abandoned Ireland. While some of the extraordinarily fast growth figures might reflect rather virtual corporate transfers of intellectual property, the country has been able to attract a considerable amount of direct foreign investments. Ireland has also been able to boost its competitiveness and diversify its economy away from banking and construction. Furthermore, longer-term growth prospects have not been dampened down by the reduction in productivity growth that has muted recovery particularly in the UK.

Ireland has benefitted from its economic growth in dealing with a high debt burden. Growth helps to reduce the debt-to-GDP ratio. As standards of living increase, the state is able to achieve budgetary surpluses to pay off the debt. In addition, growth increases the tax revenues, easing public finances still further.

The financial crisis has cast a long shadow, especially for the most vulnerable countries. But the good news for Ireland is that while unemployment peaked at 15.4% in 2013, it had fallen by almost two-thirds to 5.7% by spring 2019.[6] By and large Ireland provides a sound model of how to turn an economy around from crisis to recovery and growth. One must always learn the lessons not only of the *crises* but also of the *recoveries*. The Irish recovery is part of the broader story of the European recovery from the debt crisis. Today Ireland and other countries recovering from the crisis face the challenge to ensure that everyone gets a share when the economy improves.

As explained in the previous chapter, Spain received assistance of €41.3 billion to recapitalize its banking sector, out of the credit line of 100 billion euros reserved for her. The restructuring and resolution plans were approved by the Commission under state-aid rules and carried out over the course of

2012–14. The Spanish authorities were also strongly committed to fiscal consolidation and structural measures, in line with the Excessive Deficit and the Macroeconomic Imbalance Procedures.

Spain exited the financial assistance programme in January 2014. The recovery in Spain has been impressive. Once the GDP started to grow, the rate of growth has been strong. External deficits in countries hit by the crises have been turned into surpluses. Deleveraging of the Spanish corporate sector has been painful, but the credit quality has improved, which is witnessed in the decline of the share of non-performing loans.

Two-Pack Gives New Tools of Economic Governance

With autumn 2013 came the introduction of additional fiscal and reform surveillance tools that were based on the so-called two-pack legislative package, which had been endorsed by the Council on 13 May. In addition to demanding euro area member states to include a debt brake in their national legislation, the legislative package mandated the Commission to examine their draft budgetary plans (called Stability Programmes) and to give an opinion on them before they went to a vote in respective national parliaments. In parallel, the Eurozone member states present National Reform Programmes, which outline their structural reform plans and are vetted in connection with the budgetary plans. If the draft budgetary plans are in clear contradiction with commonly agreed fiscal rules, the Commission has the right to request the member state to review its plans. Due to earlier shortcomings in encouraging structural reforms through economic governance, increasing emphasis is now put on them and fiscal paths are made smoother, conditional to convincing economic reforms, which makes sense from the economic theory angle to support growth.

By 15 October 2013, the deadline set in the two-pack, euro area member states sent their draft budgets and reform programmes in for the Commission's early scrutiny for the first time in history. The analysis was presented exactly one month later and included Commission opinions on 13 draft budgetary plans, excluding Cyprus, Greece, Ireland and Portugal, which were still subject to a macroeconomic adjustment programme and thus exempted from this exercise. Presenting the so-called autumn fiscal package marked the culmination of several intense weeks of preparation for the first-ever examination of this kind.

The peer and Commission pressure on budgetary plans had a positive impact: the plans were mostly credible and realistic as opposed to the overly optimistic budgets we had seen over the previous years. Out of the 13 countries assessed, all countries were broadly compliant with the Stability and Growth Pact, although Italy (with a risk of insufficient progress in reducing public debt), Spain (where fiscal deficit was projected to increase in 2015) and Finland (crossing the 60% threshold of the debt-to-GDP ratio) were at risk of breaching the rules. The fact that none of the budgetary plans assessed was finally considered non-compliant showed that the member states had taken their commitments to sound public finances seriously. That boded well for future stability.

On the other hand, it was regrettable that governments were not paying enough attention to the impact of their fiscal consolidation plans on growth, notably when it came to public capital expenditure. Public capital expenditure, i.e. public investment, continued to decrease even as the first signs of economic recovery had already appeared. We treated this as a matter of urgency and, along with efforts to boost overall investments in Europe by using the European Investment Bank more effectively, it was one of the top priorities of our economic policy agenda for the rest of the mandate of the Commission.

Looking at the economy in general, growth had turned positive in the second quarter of 2013 and continued so in the third quarter. This was also the case for the crisis-ridden Spain and Portugal, who had carried out their adjustment efforts according to plan and were on their way towards exiting the assistance programmes. At the height of the crisis in 2011, there were only three member states NOT in the EDP; so 24 member states were under the EDP's special surveillance. In 2013, the number of countries in the procedure was still high at 12 out of 27; yet, by then the number of countries not in the EDP had increased from 3 to 15, and thus Europe was clearly moving in a better direction. Debt-to-GDP level for the EU as a whole was still alarmingly high at about 90%, which added to the importance of our autumn fiscal package. Equally alarming were the rising debt levels in countries like Finland that had previously seemed to cope relatively well in that respect.

The Spectre of Deflation Emerges from 2013 Onwards

While recovery was going on and gradually gaining ground, there were new clouds in the horizon: the spectre of deflation, or at least "low-flation", which referred to a sticky and prolonged period of abnormally low inflation.

Our concerns about the high debt-to-GDP were not eased by the ever-lower inflation—on the contrary. Consumer price inflation in the euro area had been falling rapidly since summer 2012, from 2.6% in August 2012 to just 1.3% in the first half of 2013 (this is the "official" inflation rate, HICP = the Harmonised Inflation of Consumer Prices; not the core inflation rate which is neutralized from the effects of the volatile energy and food prices). By November 2013, inflation had already fallen below 1.0% and seemed to continue approaching the sub-zero lows experienced post-crash in the summer of 2009.

We were thus very concerned about a prolonged period of low inflation, or even deflation, which would be most detrimental to Europe's debt sustainability—not to speak of growth and jobs. But we were also aware that our short-term tools for fixing the problem on the Commission's side were limited. The slower pace of fiscal consolidation made possible by the improved economic situation gave us some space to manoeuvre, but not nearly enough considering the scope of the problem. Our job was to keep economic reforms going despite noticeable reform fatigue and to create the preconditions and space for the ECB to make a move.

"The outlook is for a lengthy period of low inflation. However, a risk of outright deflation for the euro area would probably only be relevant if a large shock to GDP occurred or inflation expectations became unanchored", I told the ministers during January 2013s Ecofin meeting in Brussels. The drop in euro area headline inflation reflected both an easing of underlying price pressures in the wake of a prolonged slack in the economy and a lower impact of short-term factors, such as taxes, energy and food. Some member states experienced very low or even temporarily negative inflation, which was in fact an essential element of the necessary adjustment process of their competitive position. The structural reforms that had been carried out had increased the responsiveness of wages and prices to the persistent large output gaps, which helped bring down inflation.

In the short term, the effects of low inflation weren't only negative, of course. Some two-thirds of the fall in consumer price inflation since 2012 was due to favourable developments in internationally determined energy and food prices, which increased the purchasing power of consumers and investors. This trend was further bolstered by collapse in oil prices over the latter part of the year.

However, the possibility of "low-flation" turning to outright deflation was becoming an increasingly serious risk in the spring of 2013. In 2013–14, I frequently warned publicly of the dangers brought be eventual deflation, or its softer version, a long-lasting "low-flation", which would both be damaging. There was a further major worry of political nature. Geopolitics had made a nasty and most unwelcome comeback and also affected the economic climate, as in February–March 2014 Russia illegally annexed Crimea and subsequently supported war in Eastern Ukraine.

My sense of deflation danger was reinforced by the above-mentioned discussions with G7 central bankers and finance ministers in the British countryside in early May 2013. So I decided to make a rare public intervention on monetary policy—moving deliberately to the borderlines of the unwritten code of conduct between the Commission and the ECB—for two reasons: first, to raise the public awareness of the deflationary danger and call for policies to combat it; second, to provide flanking support for the ECB in case it decided to take further action. This is how Reuters reported on my speech at the Atlantic Council of Finland in Helsinki on 17 May 2013:

> Economic affairs commissioner Olli Rehn is encouraging new rate cuts, as exceptionally low inflation provides the European Central Bank room for manoeuvre. From the perspective of the low inflation rate, it is possible to continue easing monetary policy conditions. Inflation in the euro area was 1.2% in April, which is the lowest figure for three years.[7]

Following my intervention on monetary policy, which was noticed in various quarters in Europe and beyond, I expected a "frank and open" phone call from Mario Draghi. But it never came. I took that as a very good sign— in fact the best sign for a long time! Why so? Because at that very moment I could assume that the ECB—or at least its president—most probably agreed with the need for further accommodation of monetary policy and would perhaps eventually pursue quantitative easing.

Why was this an important discussion? What are the implications and why would a deflationary downward spiral have been so damaging? From the consumer's instinctive point of view, it seems not a problem, as low inflation should support real wages. But that is a deceptive argument because a prolonged period of very low inflation in the euro area, not to speak of outright deflation, would have made the ongoing rebalancing of the European economy much more difficult.

Why? It is only natural that during the crisis and its aftermath inflation should have been kept low in vulnerable reforming countries like Ireland, Spain, Portugal and Greece—and even Italy—because they were engaged in regaining their cost and price competitiveness. The problem was that a prolonged phase of low inflation in the entire euro area would make it much harder for the recovering crisis countries to achieve these objectives.

That's because the real exchange rate of the euro would have stayed high, and subsequently the efforts of the vulnerable countries to restore their cost competitiveness would have had less real impact, and moreover they would have been suffocated by the excessively slow growth in export demand.

In a nutshell, a prolonged period of low inflation would undoubtedly have made the rebalancing process in the crisis-hit countries much harder. The low-flation we nevertheless experienced was hard enough: e.g. in January 2015, consumer price inflation in the euro area was below zero, at -0.6%. Moreover, the markets were then pricing negative inflation in the time horizon of 2–3 years with the probability of over 50%. To counter deflation, monetary accommodation has been reinforced many times since. The threat of deflationary spiral was subsequently avoided. Outright deflation would have made it even worse, thus damaging for Europe as a whole. As it turned out, it has been far better for the ECB to act forcefully than to wait for deflation to happen because, if necessary, it is so much easier to prevent deflationary dynamics with quick and determined action than to tackle the problem belatedly. We don't want to be in the midst of a deflationary spiral before we take action. This is one of the key lessons of the Japanese experience.

Notes

1. George Osborne, *Chancellor's Closing Remarks at the G7 Meeting*. Aylsbury, 10 May 2013. See: http://www.g8.utoronto.ca/finance/fm130511.htm.
2. Cf. Osborne 2013.
3. Liaquat Ahamed, *Lords of Finance*. William Heinemann, 2009.
4. ESM Evaluation Report 2017, p. 59.
5. Carlos da Silva Costa, *The Challenge of Inclusive Growth*. Keynote speech at the Delphi Forum in Greece, 1 March 2019.
6. https://www.reuters.com/article/ireland-economy-unemployment/irish-unemployment-rate-revised-up-to-57-percent-from-53-percent-idUSS8N1X-N00X.
7. Rehn: EKP:lla vielä varaa helpottaa rahapolitiikkaa. *Taloussanomat*, 17 May 2017; referring to the Reuters story. See also: *Rehn. Matala inflaatio antaa EKP:lle uusia mahdollisuuksia*. Yle, 17 May 2017.

13

Basta!: Austerians vs. Spendanigans

"*Basta!*"—"You don't need to put on your earphones", shouted Elisa Ferreira, a socialist member of the European Parliament from Portugal, at me, referring to a headset providing simultaneous translation. "You just need to memorize a single word: *Basta!* This is enough!"[1]

I kept my cool and didn't enter into this quite unilateral exchange of views. It was May 2013 in ECON, the Economic Affairs Committee of the European Parliament, and the mood was even more heated than usual. Elisa Ferreira was a respected member of the committee and a competent previous rapporteur of the Macroeconomic Imbalance Procedure, at the time when the Socialists and Democrats were still actively supporting the six-pack reform of EU economic governance. In recent years, we were colleagues in our respective central banks, she in Portugal and me in Finland—and still friends on a European journey, I assume. Today, it's her turn to be a European Commissioner—best of success in reforming Europe!

At that time, when the European economy was already on the path of recovery that arrived by stealth, populists and other critics of various political colours in the European Parliament and elsewhere were lambasting the Commission and me, saying we were pushing Europe to ruin. No doubt the post-crisis economic situation was dire and unemployment high in many member states, which caused most regrettable social and human costs. But the heavy criticism was also partly the result of the IMF's multiplier debate, as the IMF's (perceived) views started to live a mythical life of their own and became politically instrumentalized.

From the other side, the Commission's focus on the structural balance of public finances in the medium term was considered excessively generous

O. Rehn, *Walking the Highwire*, https://doi.org/10.1007/978-3-030-34592-1_13

towards the countries with high fiscal deficits. And our calls for more determination to combat the danger of deflation were regarded almost as heresy, mostly in Germany. Wolfgang Schäuble did not shy away from calling my views as "nonsense". Straight talk, much appreciated—and I trust we, too, are still friends on our European journey.

Public debate on fiscal policy during the crisis may well be portrayed as a fierce political battle between the Austerians and the Spendanigans. The former refer to those who believe that fiscal sustainability—or "austerity", which is an ideologically confused and loaded word I refuse to use—is the way to return to a healthy economy and solid growth. The latter refer to those who believe that the concerns about high debt and deficits are secondary in times of recession, which leads them to believe that substantial discretionary deficit spending should be used instead to stimulate the economy, not to rely only on automatic stabilizers and some fine-tuning.

I refuse to take an oath to either of these views, as in my view there is no single issue movement that could have solved the crisis with some magic wand. Besides, to focus only on fiscal policy misses the point because, in reality, the financial repair and the pursuit of improved credit conditions, as well as the implementation of structural reforms, were at least as important to lubricate the economic engine and boost growth.

Let's look at the facts. What was the evolution of public finances during the euro crisis? Fiscal deficits in the Eurozone expanded rapidly during the global financial crisis in 2008, both due to the severe recession itself and because of the fiscal stimulus that was executed to combat the recession. As can be seen from Fig. 13.1, the Eurozone aggregate deficit reached over 6% of GDP in both 2009 and 2010, which created legitimate concerns about the sustainability of public finances. In some countries, the deficits were substantially larger, like 15.4% in Greece, which led to "buyers' strikes" and lockouts from the markets, as noted before. Decisions were taken since late 2009 to pursue country-wise differentiated fiscal consolidation. As a result, the Eurozone fiscal deficits were on average reduced below 3% by 2014 and below 1% by 2017. The latest statistically recorded aggregate deficit was around 0.5% in 2018.

As the crisis evolved in different phases, so did fiscal policies. Reading the media coverage in spring 2013, which was the period when the Eurozone moved from stabilization to recovery, one gets the impression that there was a fundamental shift underway in the Commission's economic policy. That was, however, not the case. Sometimes, austerity is in the eye of the beholder. This perception gap was down to a pervasive and persistent view that the Commission's economic policy consisted of a rigid insistence

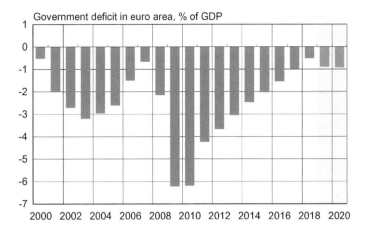

Fig. 13.1 Government deficit in the euro area, 2000–20 (*Sources* European Commission and Macrobond. *Shadowed area indicates forecasts)

on fiscal consolidation, and little more. But in reality the Commission consistently insisted that structural reforms to enhance sustainable growth and job creation were at least as important as a sound fiscal policy. As Waltraud Schelkle observed in retrospect, "The Commission looked for ways to give governments leeway to avoid pro-cyclical retrenchment, particularly by emphasizing structural reform".[2] And Europe was by 2013 making headway as regards both rebalancing and economic reforms. Many European countries enacted major structural reforms, especially of labour and product markets, during the crisis years.

The public debate of the time tended to centre round the size of the so-called fiscal multiplier, taking into account the exceptional circumstances of the financial and debt crises. The concept "fiscal multiplier" refers to the ratio of short-term change in national income to the change in government spending that causes it. Multiplier is usually positive, for instance in the scale of 0.5–1.5, which implies that one euro more spent in public finance would as a direct effect increase GDP by 0.5–1.5 euros in the short term, while one euro less spent in public finance would reduce GDP by 0.5.–1.5 euros. The growth effect of fiscal stimulus normally fades away in the course of some years; meanwhile, public debt increases, unless the growth impulse fully compensates for that. This is the trade-off policy-makers normally face.

The "exceptional circumstances" of the financial and debt crises can refer to two things: first, to the zero lower bound in monetary policy, which is assumed to reinforce the multiplier effect of government spending. Second, alternatively, it can refer to the lockout of a country from normal market financing, which makes the multiplier a less relevant concept, and can strictly theoretically speaking even turn the multiplier into a negative territory. In the latter case, the so-called confidence effects would dominate over the direct effects in fiscal policy and thus make deficit spending counterproductive. This was the case of at least Greece, Ireland and Portugal in 2010–11; Italy and Spain were at the cliff.

Much of the fiscal multiplier debate focused on the issue whether the confidence effect or the direct effect dominates, and to what extent. It is an important analytical exchange both for the theory of macroeconomics and for the often very much hands-on concrete making of economic and fiscal policy.

From the European perspective, the fiscal multiplier debate was an ongoing reflection in the Commission. I was confronted big time with it at the IMF 2012 Annual Meeting, which took place in Tokyo in mid-October 2012. It was followed by fierce debates in the European Parliament in the early months of 2013 and the revised research reports of the IMF and our dialogue with it.

The outcome of the analytical-turned-very-political boxing match was rather a draw than a knockout. In my view, it is obvious that the fiscal multipliers matter for short-term growth. What remains open is their size, and in the exceptional cases of a threat of a lockout from markets, also their direction. The conclusions depend very much on the assumptions and the modelling parameters that are used in the analysis, which have to be empirically verified in the course of the analysis.

Round One: Multipliers in Tokyo

In October 2012, the IMF chief economist Olivier Blanchard and his colleague Daniel Leigh published, without any advance warning to their (supposed) "comrades-in-programmes" in Brussels, a paper highly critical of the Eurozone's fiscal stance and general handling of the crisis. I became aware of the paper just after I had barely landed in Tokyo and was put a microphone in my mouth.

It was not pure science, as in this rather one-sided narrative the Commission was reserved the role of the bad cop. I was not ready to accept that without an argument—not least as we had designed the programmes for Greece, Ireland and Portugal in cooperation and in agreement with the IMF. This led to a six-month-long intensive debate, in which the IMF paper was politically instrumentalized by political groups in the EP and elsewhere.

It was hard to hold a balanced, analytical standpoint in that very heated political climate, but we tried nonetheless.

In Tokyo, I had to use all my already limited policy-making capital to defend the Eurozone's fiscal policy stance. In the IMF annual meeting, my line was this:

> Should fiscal consolidation be altogether forsaken to make room for fiscal stimulus instead? Even leaving aside for a moment the limits set by the EU rule-based fiscal framework, one has to ask oneself, what room for manoeuvre the EU countries would have in this respect. The response of the economy to a change in the government tax and spending plans – the so-called multiplier – should not be measured against an implicit business-as-usual scenario, but one in which the unsustainable policies revealed by the crisis are allowed to continue. It is not too difficult to imagine the reaction of capital outflows and risk premia that would quickly negate the putative benefits of fiscal relaxation.

On 13 October, the debate burst out in the IMF meetings with full force and compelled also the other Europeans to react. Wolfgang Schäuble did not hesitate to go into a counter-attack and defend Europe's policies (he never does!). He said that Europe will never get to the timeline wanted by the financial markets, which makes Europe-bashing very harmful. He reassured others that in the medium term Europe will deliver, which is shown by the fact that deficits have been halved from 6 to 3%. In his view, it was better not to create expectations that you cannot fulfil, e.g. having a banking union fully in place as of 1 January 2013. Italy's Finance Minister Vittorio Grilli endorsed Schäuble's line and pleaded others to get it—in other words, he said to this IMF colleagues that Italy simply has no fiscal space!

So we left the "multiplier battle of Tokyo" battered but not beaten. When I returned to Brussels on 15 October, I gave a brisk, spirited and perhaps slightly frustrated lecture to my cabinet and DG Ecfin senior management to be ready to continue the debate and analytically prepare for its next phase. I said we needed to have an open and critical mind for changes, also self-critical, but we should not accept false accusations and loose attacks. I was not entirely satisfied with the level of the Commission's and my department's analytical preparedness, and let it be known.

In the meeting of the College of Commissioners a few days later, I reported on the G7 and IMF Tokyo meetings as follows:

> There was also some discussion on the fiscal multipliers, but this did not lead the IMF to suggest that the fiscal consolidation paths in the EU should be changed.

On the contrary, the IMF Managing Director Christine Lagarde stressed in the concluding session that fiscal consolidation should continue as planned.

My colleagues felt that the IMF was playing its cards with two very different hands—like a classical two-handed economist. Obviously, they were not totally wrong.

With the benefit of hindsight, one may say that in October 2012 the worst turbulence in the financial markets was already about to start fading away, not least thanks to the ECB's OMT decision in September. But one could not know it for sure at the time, and that's the critical metric. Once we started to see its calming effects in the markets, we were tentatively reassured, but decided to play it safe—the simple but very valid reason was that we had so many times before been disappointed by unforeseen setbacks after supposedly decisive actions that should have logically contained the crisis. And with the well-known universal lags in fiscal policy and the problems related to its fine-tuning in a 17-member currency union, one week or one month is not a long time to make sure that the stabilization truly holds.

Moreover, with the spring 2012 shift from immediate firefighting and nominal targets to the structural balance over the medium term, the fiscal stance for 2013 was already less rigorous that met the eye of the public and policy-makers. So we assumed that we could soon be heading towards a recovery and return to growth, and we didn't want to endanger that by taking the risk of prematurely relaxing fiscal policy and potentially seeing the deadly financial turbulence return, yet again.

Round Two: Accidents Happen Even in the Best Papers

Round Two took place in the end of 2012 and early 2013. It was related to the practical implementation of the earlier decided "smart relaxation" of fiscal targets in several member states. As there was considerable scepticism among the market participants and some creditor states towards this approach, and as many countries concerned were not yet on safe waters, we decided to proceed with prudently calibrated steps and with a careful communication strategy.

While the goal was achieved, methodically it didn't work out quite like that. After the events, one could only comfort oneself with the logic that is well known in ski-jumping: even though we did not gain many points for elegance, ultimately, it is the length of the jump that is finally more decisive.

To pave the way for our calibrated approach, which would include extensions of the correction deadlines of fiscal deficits for some member states, in return for stronger measures for economic reforms, I decided to write an article and submit it to the *Financial Times*. My intention was to clarify the Commission's policy approach, but it didn't work out quite like that. I still defend the **text** I wrote—and checked—even though not the **title** which was chosen by the editor, and which I didn't see beforehand. This is how it happened.

I drafted the piece in early December 2012 with the help of my cabinet and spokesman Simon O'Connor, a very able and cool-headed communicator who has been carrying the same duties for Commissioner Pierre Moscovici. Once the draft was submitted on 7 December to the *Financial Times* and accepted for publication, the normal editing process ensued. Monday 10 December was spent in continuous negotiation between Simon and the FT editor. The edited text was finally OK, stating that the rebalancing is moving on and confidence is returning as structural reforms help rebalance the economy. After first carefully working on the piece over several days in-house and then fine-tuning it with the *Financial Times'* team, our message was neatly packed under our title of choice, *Staying the course of reform*. Going home in the evening, after giving my final green light for the piece, I was looking forward to reading the text from the FT online version.

However, it turned out quite different. "I don't like Mondays!", I recalled the lyrics of Bob Geldof and the Boomtown Rats when I saw the actual headline. It became an even less soothing Monday than normally. Instead of *"Staying the course of reform"*, which by all objective journalistic yardsticks coined the content of the article, the op-ed with my name under it now stated *"Staying the austerity course"*! Changing one single word reversed the whole meaning. The headline had not been part of the negotiation with the FT, and it didn't occur to us that such an unfair and frankly monstrous mix-up could happen this close to the finishing line.

Of course the image of the Commission's stance on dealing with the crisis was severely damaged by the FT's painful journalistic blunder—although I still refuse to believe it was outright intentional. Be that as it may, this came on top of the Commission's and also my own already tarnished reputation as the bad cop of the Eurozone. But there was no time to lay low depressed, only to carry on.

Naturally, we complained to the editors, but the damage was already done. I wrote an email to the editor-in-chief Lionel Barber and Brussels bureau chief Peter Spiegel saying: "Many thanks for running my article on the economic reform in the Eurozone in today's paper. Yet, just for the record, I must say that the headline chosen for my piece did not really reflect its content. I never used the word 'austerity' and refuse to get into the overly simplified 'austerity vs. growth' debate. Besides, it's the reforms that matter, and that's what the article was about".

Fortunately, at least the IMF's Christine Lagarde read the whole article and not only the headline. Immediately after it was out, she sent me an sms stating "Bravo!!!". The background is that we had been "conspiring" with her to put focus on economic reforms and productive investment and prepare adjusting the Eurozone fiscal stance, and she stood by me despite the mess in the press. That kind of consistency and fairness was encouraging in the otherwise precarious situation.

So what did I try to say and want to achieve with the article? First of all, I wrote that while the short-term economic outlook remained weak, there are signs that confidence is returning through the rebalancing process: "Far-reaching reforms are helping to rebalance the Eurozone economy. Progress is tangible: current account imbalances among Eurozone members have fallen markedly, as competitiveness lost by some members in the decade before the crisis is regained".

Second, I also called for a more symmetric external rebalancing within the Eurozone, which should effectively include both the creditor and debtor countries: "The European Commission has said surplus countries should implement reforms to strengthen domestic demand. Germany could do this by opening up its services market and by encouraging wages to rise in line with productivity, two of the recommendations made to Berlin by the EU Council last July".

Third, I tried to correct the damage done by Romano Prodi's infamous statement that the Stability and Growth Pact was "stupid":

> In spite of misperceptions to the contrary, the EU's reformed Stability and Growth Pact takes full account of evolving economic conditions. Each country's consolidation effort is specified in structural terms, removing the effects of the business cycle and one-off measures, and takes into account the country's fiscal space and macroeconomic conditions. If growth deteriorates, a country may receive extra time to correct its excessive deficit, provided that the agreed consolidation effort is being made. Such decisions have been taken this year for Spain, Portugal and Greece.

Doesn't quite sound like straightforward, brutal "austerity", does it?

I also informed the FT readers that the Commission is preparing a further revision of interpretation: "We also intend to explore further ways, within

the rules of the Stability and Growth Pact, to accommodate public investment in our assessment of national fiscal plans".

I coined my message in the final paragraph as follows:

> In order to overcome the crisis and restore confidence, we must continue to
> remove structural obstacles to sustainable growth and employment; pursue
> prudent fiscal consolidation; and turn bold thoughts into convincing actions
> when redesigning and rebuilding our economic and monetary union. In short,
> we need to stay the course of reform and pursue decisive reforms in our mem-
> ber states and deeper integration in the Eurozone.

I could have added to the list "I trust the ECB will intensify expansionary
monetary policy and unconventional measures". But as it is not customary
for the Commission to comment on the monetary policy stance of the ECB,
I left this to the imagination of the reasonably intelligent reader.

No surprise, the unfortunate and misleading headline stimulated angry
comments, and I responded to some of them. I won't cite them here at
length, but just take one illustrative example of my replies in the "letters to
the editor" section:

> In his letter of 13 December 2012, Andrew Watt claims that "the swing to
> continent-wide austerity in early 2011" was the reason for the downturn in the
> European economy following the recovery of late 2009 and 2010. Regrettably,
> Mr Watt mixes up cause and consequence.

> For a start, not all parts of Europe were feeling that recovery. Greece's economy
> shrank by 3.1% in 2009 and a further 4.9% in 2010, the year it turned to the
> Eurozone and IMF for assistance. It was the free fall of the Greek economy by
> April 2010 that forced the country to do so, not the other way around.

> More recently, investor and consumer confidence across the Eurozone was
> shattered by the re-emergence of financial-market stress: in autumn 2011
> due to fears of political and economic stagnation in Italy, then again in
> spring 2012 due to concerns over Spanish banks' solvency and the political
> turmoil in Greece, as a result of two successive and very turbulent election
> campaigns.

> That's why it is so important that the Eurozone continues restoring confi-
> dence. And that's why prudent fiscal consolidation must be accompanied by
> structural reforms and targeted investments to underpin sustainable growth
> and employment.

Paraphrasing G.B. Shaw, quoting oneself adds spice to conversation—and spine as well. I have quoted my own article at length, for good reasons. Not only to set the record straight, but because both the timing and the message of the article are important in understanding Europe's strategy of crisis management. It was about being patient, prudent and consistent: the rebalancing was moving forward in 2012, and in early 2013, the Eurozone economy turned to the path of recovery and growth, where it has continued, at least to the day of this writing in mid-2019. Of course, the ECB's expansionary policy has been critical in this regard.

A concrete case where the new line would have to be applied was France. Our conclusion from DG Ecfin's economic analysis and econometric studies was that it would make sense to have a longer adjustment period for France to reach the reference value of 3% in fiscal deficit, i.e. an extension of the correction deadline of the excessive deficit from 2014 to 2015, on the condition that France would engage in serious economic reforms in return. I will return to this in the next chapter.

Round Three: Debating in the European Parliament

Around the turn of the year 2012/13, fiscal policy was very much on the European policy agenda, as the debate had been stimulated by the IMF papers and EU media writing on the matter. Naturally, the European Parliament insisted on discussing it. So I was invited to the EP Economic Affairs Committee and plenary sessions in January 2013. My line on fiscal multipliers was as follows:

> We agree with the IMF that fiscal multipliers are likely to be larger than usual when households are credit-constrained and monetary policy is already accommodative. [...] Especially for countries at risk of losing market access, a lack of credible consolidation would have resulted in such a rise in risk premium that it would have easily cancelled or even exceeded the benefits of a more lenient fiscal stance. In their most recent paper, Blanchard and D. Leigh themselves very clearly caution against interpreting their findings as a call for reversing the course of fiscal policy followed since the crisis.

I was referring to the revised paper of Blanchard and Leigh, which they drafted following the criticism of the methodology in the first version. The second version omitted some outliers and moderated the conclusions, which meant a major revision to the policy conclusions.

The debate went on in the Ecofin Council, where on 12 February I presented the Commission view to the EU finance ministers under the item: "Economic situation and multiplier debate":

> Multipliers are larger when households are highly indebted and when interest rates are low. On this, there has already been consensus among economists. Beyond that, the recent studies do not provide a robust and conclusive answer, particularly because their time horizon is rather short and they cannot exclude that other factors contributed to the decline in growth that was not expected in the forecasts of most analysts in the early years of the crisis.

I also said that forecast errors may arise because either the impact or the size of fiscal change was estimated with error, or even both. Moreover, the period under analysis included both the growth effect of fiscal consolidation and that of fiscal stimulus—the IMF and the Commission agreed on the finding that the biggest growth forecast errors occurred in 2010, when most countries were implementing temporary fiscal stimulus measures after the huge fall in activity in 2009. I found it difficult to generalize from the stimulus measures to consolidation measures, as far as their impact was concerned—they were quite different beasts.

There was another related and frequent false accusation—not by Blanchard but by various other commentators—that was often aired during the crisis: that the Eurozone policy-makers would have believed in the doctrine of "expansionary austerity". Paul Krugman defines it as "the argument that cutting public spending would crowd in large amounts of private spending by increasing confidence", referring to a study by Alesina and Ardagna in 2010.[3]

I don't know of any Eurozone policy-maker who would have subscribed to this puritan view, but I do indeed know that I have never believed in such an effect. The programmes of fiscal consolidation in the vulnerable countries were designed due to the reality or serious danger of lockout from private financing and the rapidly widening sovereign bond yields and the regrettably rising borrowing costs, which would have come with rapidly rising social and human costs—not because we believed in some heavenly growth-enhancing impact of consolidation. For some Anglo-American economists who have no skin in the game in Europe's survival it was easy to make these outrageous claims.

Even Alesina himself has later specified that expansionary austerity is not a rule but rather an exception: it does not imply that every time a government reduces public spending the economy expands, only that it works in certain cases. With his co-authors Carlo Favero and Francersco Giavazzi he has shown, in a systematic and thorough empirical study, that the nature of consolidation matters: on the basis of Europe's experience in 2010–14, expenditure-based consolidation was clearly more growth-friendly than tax-based consolidation. They have also not found convincing evidence that multipliers were significantly larger during the crisis years.[4]

It is worth recalling what Markus Brunnermeier, Harold James and Jean-Pierre Landau point out as the realistic alternatives then available for policy-makers:

> The term *austerity* is a misnomer, as all the various EU packages to peripheral countries were in fact *still relaxing austerity*. Without all these packages, the adjustments required to bail out countries, particularly in Greece, would have been more savage than anything observed in practice. Of course, it may be argued that the fiscal adjustment should have been even more gradual, but domestic political considerations in creditor countries proved to be a hard constraint.[5]

In August 2013, three researchers of the IMF, Ran Bi, Haonan Qu and James Roaf, presented a research paper called *Assessing the Impact and Phasing of Multi-year Fiscal Adjustment: A General Framework*, which they summarized as follows[6]:

> The paper suggests that for a highly-indebted economy undertaking large multi-year fiscal consolidation, high multipliers do not always argue against frontloaded adjustment.

Intellectually, this "slightly" more balanced conclusion is sound and solid, and one can well live with it. Once the recalibrated research report was made public by the IMF, my senior advisor Taneli Lahti commented wryly by email: "I wonder why this paper hasn't received as much coverage as its predecessor".

Staying the Course of Reform and Sustained Growth

In conclusion, the EU's economic policy during the crisis aimed at promoting sustainable economic growth and job creation, and containing the increase in debt. To achieve these twin goals, which go hand in hand and complement each other, we encouraged the balancing of public finances through a consistent fiscal policy by reducing structural deficits over the medium term.

In line with this policy, the pace of fiscal consolidation evolved and was slowing down in Europe by 2013. That year, the structural fiscal effort was expected to be around 0.75% of GDP in the euro area—half of the previous year's number of around 1.5%. The decisions leading to this reduction were made in 2012, in line with the Commission's recommendations in spring 2012. By comparison, the United States was reducing its deficit by around 1.75 percentage points in 2013, proportionally twice as much as in Europe.

This slowing down of the pace of fiscal consolidation was made possible by three factors: first, by the increased credibility of fiscal policy which the euro area member states achieved since 2011; second, by the paramount decisions the ECB had taken to stabilize the markets with the long-term refinancing operations and the Outright Monetary Transactions; and third, by the reform of EU economic governance, which provided a solid framework for a differentiated fiscal adjustment and the advancement of structural reforms.

Thanks to these factors, the Eurozone since 2012 had the necessary room to make fiscal policy with a medium-term perspective. This was not yet possible in 2010–11, when many euro countries were in danger of insolvency, locked out from the private financial markets or in a free fall to the whirlpool of prohibitively high interest rates. Many member states had to restore their policy credibility by difficult decisions to bring their public finances onto a sustainable path. In fact, I can well concur with the 2014 conclusion of Olivier Blanchard, Giovanni Dell'Ariccia and Paolo Mauro: "The argument that fiscal stimulus can more than pay for itself, and thus decrease debt levels, seems to be as weak as the earlier argument that fiscal consolidation could increase output in the short run".[7]

In essence, in those years the European Commission provided country-specific recommendations and conducted its surveillance in fiscal policy in line with the recommendations of the IMF. This is how the IMF's own Independent Evaluation Office judged the Fund's advice in retrospect in its 2019 report: "The Fund supported the turn to fiscal consolidation from 2010, while from 2013 onwards also calling for use of space within the Stability and Growth Pact to avoid any excessive drag on growth in response to increasing concerns about lack of growth momentum".[8] And the report continued by analysing the shift from upfront to medium-term strategy: "As economic recovery remained sluggish, the Fund nuanced its message, noting that putting in place a credible medium-term strategy for fiscal consolidation could alleviate the need for upfront adjustment and urging countries to use their fiscal space and to make the needed adjustments 'as growth-friendly as possible'... Nonetheless, the overall fiscal message remained predominantly hawkish".[9]

Thus, the thinking on fiscal policy evolved in parallel in the Commission and the IMF. Against this evolution, it made sense that the Juncker Commission presented its Flexibility Communication in 2015 on dealing with debt and deficit criteria, in order to move beyond the caricatures and close the perception gap in fiscal policy. It provides somewhat smarter fiscal rules that give weight to structural reforms and productive investment. However, completely watering down the reformed Stability and Growth Pact would come with a high price. Ignoring its rules would crush the credibility of the Eurozone economic policy and erode its fiscal sustainability, which continues to be essential for economic stability and thus for sustained growth.

Certainly, there is room for simplification of fiscal rules. The most meaningful way to achieve it would in my view be to put the focus on the real growth trend and relate the debt path and expenditure to it. On that basis, a basic expenditure rule could state that expenditures should not expand faster than long-term income. Population ageing and the pension expenditure are key parameters of such kind of a simple expenditure rule. This will be discussed further in Chapter 19.

In any case, the fiscal rules are not there for nothing. If persistent high fiscal deficit and increasing public debt were a recipe for rapid economic growth, then France and Italy would have been European champions in the field in the crisis years, Japan would have been the world's first economic power and Finland would have been the Nordic champion of growth. But this was obviously not the case in 2010–14. What these countries have in common has been a persistent lack of willingness for structural reforms in the past—fortunately we have in recent years in many instances seen a correction of the course for the better.

Beyond the black-and-white caricatures of Austerians and Spendanigans, the truth is that real fiscal policy in Europe was and continues to be painted in varying shades of grey. Macroeconomic research provides valuable guidance for policy choices. At the same time, the difficult choices confronted with every decision in the times of crisis mean that pre-conceived narratives leaning only on one school of thought provide a poor guide to our complex reality. As we still face major challenges, it is in the interest of Europeans to stay the course of *not austerity*, but—yes—*of reform*, for the sake of sustainable growth and job creation.

Schäuble Bashes the "Candidate": "Nonsense!"

If the Spendanigans did not shy away from "friendly fire" against the Commission, neither did the Austerians keep their guns under control. The danger of deflation in 2013–15 revealed profound differences among the economic schools of thought in Europe. I kept on warning about deflation at both the Eurogroup and Ecofin meetings and occasionally also in public appearances. I continued this at the World Economic Forum at Davos in January 2014. What I said was not particularly revolutionary. In my Reuters interview at Davos, I maintained that inflation, which stood at 0.8% then, needed to be closer to the ECB's target of below but close to 2% to permit the necessary economic adjustment within the Eurozone:

> A lengthy period of low inflation can make it more difficult if this low infla-
> tion is caused by core Europe inflation being very low. In order to succeed
> in the rebalancing process of the whole eurozone, average inflation should be
> close to the 2 percent goal that the ECB has set.[10]

This didn't go down too well in the German Federal Government, nor in the country's finance ministry. "*Unsinn!*"—"Nonsense", stated Finance Minister Wolfgang Schäuble firmly. He said he didn't share my view because it would have meant that Europe only functions on the basis of instability and infla-tion, and "that is nonsense".[11]

As a seasoned tactician, Schäuble shifted the debate immediately to the political level: "With Olli Rehn I am no longer sure whether he is still talk-ing as a Commissioner or already as an election campaigner. If he is speak-ing as commissioner, I would clearly have to distance myself. If he is talking nonsense as an election campaigner, I have to say; 'It's better to vote for my party'".[12]

I had indicated my plans to run for a seat in the European Parliament in May 2014 and was considered a possible lead candidate—or *Spitzenkandidat*—of my liberal political family, the Alliance for Liberals and Democrats in Europe. I regarded the rising wave of populism as dangerous, and took it as my responsibility to do my part to contain this populist wave and instead proactively defend Europe and its integration, and the liberal international order. But my intervention had nothing to do with my elec-toral objectives, as I had for years been seriously concerned about the slowness of rebalancing, which was further hampered by the long-lasting state of low inflation. So the fact that my friend Wolfgang provided some "friendly fire" did not particularly help to advance a substantive conversation on the matter.

It was not always a walk in the park to pursue my way of thinking on economic policy, which consisted of a three-pronged policy mix of active monetary policy and sustainable fiscal policy, as well as determined structural policy of boosting investment and innovation and pursuing economic reforms to enhance productivity and employment. Despite political headwinds from the left and the right, I kept insisting on this three-way policy mix. We made progress, but often we only hit our heads to the wall. I didn't personally mind that, but for Europe those headwinds caused much economic and social damage, as there would have been a better and smoother way of rebalancing by way of enhanced policy action.

After being elected a Member of the European Parliament in June 2014, I continued to pursue the policy debate on the basis of the three-pronged approach, both in the Parliament and in the wider public debate. In my article entitled "The spectre of deflation" in *Europe's World* in autumn 2014, I again warned of the dangers of deflation and urged measures to resolve the liquidity trap that was affecting negatively both households and enterprises, especially in Southern Europe (Image 13.1).[13]

As a freshly elected parliamentarian and thus a free man to speak out my own views, not "only" the Commission's, I called in my article for a new pact on the pursuit of reform and provision of credit between the Eurozone countries and the European institutions, including the European Central Bank. The new reform and credit pact should have included three elements, I wrote. First, the countries that had for years delayed the necessary economic reforms, such as France, Italy, and also my native Finland, should get into high gear. Second, once France and Italy became serious about economic reform, the ECB should without any unnecessary delay go all the way to combat the deflationary spiral. And third, the surplus economies of the Eurozone, particularly Germany, should further boost domestic demand and investment, both public and private, to support economic activity throughout the Eurozone, as had for many years been advocated by the European Commission. All in all, I was recommending a first-best solution for the Eurozone, based on innovative and pragmatic coordination among all the key players in Europe. It is regrettable that this kind of economics-inspired policy optimization did not fly in Europe. But fortunately many of its elements gradually moved forward, including the pursuit of some economic reforms in member states, a massive investment programme of the European Investment Bank under the cover of the Juncker Plan and the progressive activism by the European Central Bank.

Looking back at the years 2013–15 as regards deflation-inflation dynamics, the ECB's more determined action to go for negative policy rates in June

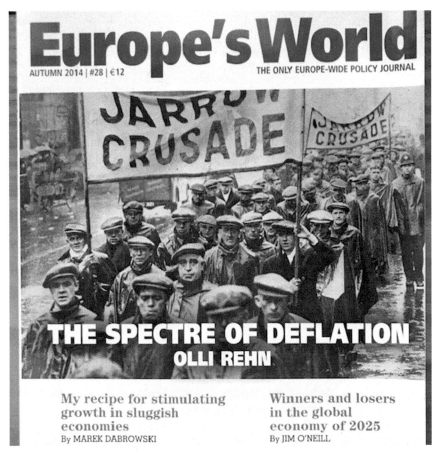

Image 13.1 Warning about the spectre of deflation hanging over Europe in 2013–15 (Source *Europe's World* # 28, 2014)

2014 and for quantitative easing with the asset purchase programmes in 2015 was a *sine qua non* for containing the danger of deflation. In the light of the recent years' economic recovery and job creation, the ECB's pragmatism has thus been vindicated.

As of this writing in mid-2019, the danger of deflation is no more there, largely thanks to the quantitative easing and low policy rates by the ECB. However, core inflation is still low and below the ECB's inflation aim. Normalization of monetary policy is waiting for its turn in the wings. It is of paramount importance to create more monetary policy space before the next recession. And once we return to the process of monetary policy normalization, it is essential to take into account the lessons of the euro crisis, especially the 2011 premature rate hikes, the 2013 turbulence following the taper tantrum and the ECB's slow reaction to deflationary dangers in 2013–14. I shall return to this matter in Chapter 19.

Notes

1. http://www.nytimes.com/2013/05/18/world/europe/europe-econo-mist-rehn-rejects-austerity-label.html.
2. Waltraud Schelkle, *The Political Economy of Monetary Solidarity: Understanding the Euro Experiment.* Oxford University Press, 2017, p. 208.
3. Paul Krugman, Good Enough for Government Work? Macroeconomics Since the Crisis. *Oxford Review of Economic Policy*, 34(1–2, 5 January 2018): 156–168.
4. Alberto Alesina, Carlo Favero, and Francesco Giavazzi, *Austerity: When It Works and When It Doesn't.* Princeton University Press, 2019, pp. 5–6, 141–147, 158–159.
5. Markus Brunnermeier, Harold James, and Jean-Pierre Landau, *The Euro and the Battle of Ideas.* Princeton University Press, 2016, p. 148.
6. IMF Working Paper No. 182, 29 August 2013.
7. Olivier Blanchard, Giovanni Dell'Ariccia, and Paulo Mauro, Introduction: Rethinking Macro II Getting Granular. In George Akerlof, Olivier Blanchard, David Romer, and Joseph Stiglitz (eds.), *What Have We Learned?: Macroeconomic Policy after the Crisis.* MIT Press, 2014, p. 16.
8. Independent Evaluation Office of the International Monetary Fund, *IMF Advice on Unconventional Monetary Policies.* Evaluation Report 2019, pp. 14–15.
9. IEO/IMF 2019, p. 16.
10. *Germany's Schäuble Raps EU's Rehn for 'nonsense' Comments on Rebalancing.* Reuters, 25 January 2014. See: https://www.reuters.com/article/us-davos-schaeuble/germanys-schaeuble-raps-eus-rehn-for-nonsense-comments-on-rebalancing-idUSBREA0O0DZ20140125.
11. Reuters, 25 January 2014.
12. Reuters, 25 January 2014.
13. Olli Rehn, The Spectre of Deflation. *Europe's World*, #28(Autumn 2014): pp. 10–19.

14

The Great Rebalancing: France and Germany

You cannot talk about modern Europe without talking about the post-war reconciliation between France and Germany; that is, *la réconciliation franco-allemande* in French, *die Aussöhnung* in German. The straight translation of the word is obviously "the restoration of friendly relations" between France and Germany, but in both languages—and in both political cultures—the word has a much deeper, more profound meaning. The German word *Aussöhnung* could as well be translated as "overcoming", referring more specifically to overcoming the bitterness of centuries-long animosity and warfare. This reconciliation was the core of the basic bargain between Foreign Minister Robert Schuman and Chancellor Konrad Adenauer in 1950, and between President Charles de Gaulle and Konrad Adenauer in 1963. It was also the philosophical underpinning of the famous hand-in-hand walk together by President Francois Mitterrand and Chancellor Helmut Kohl at the Verdun battleground—or cemetery—in 1984.

Hence, the euro has always been a political project, probably at least as much as an economic project. That's also the reason why the Eurozone reform cannot be reduced only to a technical matter on risk reduction and risk sharing, but it must be seen in the wider historical context of Franco-German reconciliation and European unification. That's also the historical context where the Community method was born and raised: the role of the European Commission evolved to a proactive broker in between the French and the German governments, in order to institutionalize the German–French basic agreement and pursue European economic and political integration leaning on their support. Later on, in the 1960s and again in the

© The Author(s) 2020
O. Rehn, *Walking the Highwire*, https://doi.org/10.1007/978-3-030-34592-1_14

1980s, the Commission's right of initiative got stronger independent wind under its wings, before in the recent decades again becoming politically more curtailed.

This historical narrative and, even more so, these historic roots were not shared or interpreted in the same way by everyone in Western Europe, especially not by the British political elite. That's one of the root causes why Brexit happened.

But the narrative evolved in other ways, as well. While the European Coal and Steel Community in 1950–51 and the European Economic Community in 1957–58 were essentially about anchoring peace in our continent, the Eastern enlargement of 2002–4 was largely about freedom for the ex-socialist peoples. Although for many of us, Europe has always been about *both* peace *and* freedom. Not least for the Finns living in the nexus of Scandinavia and the Eastern European time zone.

As I wrote in Chapter 1, while it was historic in the first place, the Franco-German reconciliation and thus the European integration project for sure also had a very strong economic dimension. This started to increasingly touch the eternally key macroeconomic question of current account surpluses and deficits.

The Macroeconomic Imbalance Procedure Enters the Scene

The European Commission raised the issue of macroeconomic imbalances, i.e. excessive current account deficits and surpluses, regularly as a priority matter, both in the governance reform and in policy recommendations. The six-pack reform of governance included the Commission's initiative on a Macroeconomic Imbalance Procedure (MIP), which after an intensive and heated debate became adopted by the Council and the Parliament in the end of 2011. The impact of these institutional changes and policy efforts has been limited, but more than just zero. This chapter also deals with those efforts, especially in relation to the two largest Eurozone economies, Germany and France. The former one is the paradigmatic case of a surplus economy and the latter one of a rather typical case of a deficit economy (at least after the terms of office of President de Gaulle).

As an analytical issue—which is always a sound starting point for economic policy-making—internal imbalances of the Eurozone are anything but straightforward, even if they are often portrayed as such. It has often been argued that the necessary economic rebalancing could be engineered in a symmetrical way between the surplus and deficit countries. That would supposedly be the first-best economically optimal solution to the problem of imbalances, not only a second-best politically possible one. However, the reality is more complex, and it is linked to the economic openness and trade channels of the Eurozone.

Much of the attention of economists and pundits has concentrated on the German current account surplus, which on average was around 6% in the immediate post-crisis years and around or above 7% in the more recent years, as shown in Fig. 14.1.

This has prompted many economists and commentators to demand more fiscal and wage stimulus from Germany, for the sake of economic rebalancing of the whole Eurozone. "If Germany only used its fiscal space and bumped more money into domestic demand, then the whole Eurozone would come smoothly out of the doldrums", the argument goes. But why is the issue more complex and nuanced?

Essentially because the Eurozone is neither a small open economy nor a large closed one, *but a large open economy that trades a lot with the rest of the world*. This was clearly outlined in an extensive in-depth study "Current account surpluses in the EU" (*European Economy* 9/2012) by the European Commission in 2012, which aimed at bringing rational analysis to the very heated debate.[1] Regrettably, economists and pundits tended to overlook the study—or not read it at all. Taking into account

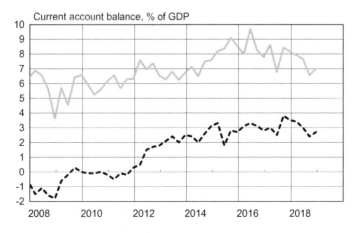

Fig. 14.1 Current account balance in Germany and in the Eurozone, 2008–18 (*Sources* Eurostat, OECD and Macrobond)

that many Commission officials have tended to be quite *dirigiste* by nature (i.e. instinctively inclined to solve policy problems by rational rules and regulations rather than leaning on market-based solutions), this study was indeed very objective and by contrast quite critical of the *dirigiste* view of the Eurozone, which paradoxically especially many Anglo-American economists seem to be holding on the matter of current account balances. But there is no visible hand that can like a magic wand deal with the macroeconomic imbalances and even them out. Current account imbalances are the outcomes of economic processes, which policies can influence, but not determine.

In the Eurozone, as a large open economy, enterprises are bound to face the challenges that come with global competition and should be able to adjust and seek out the opportunities from it. In the world economy, the real, structural competitiveness of EU member states is fundamentally based on the real factors of production and productivity, especially on Europe's innovative capacity, effectiveness of production and supply chains, and well-trained labour force.

Overcoming the long shadow of the financial and debt crises thus depends to a large degree on the capacity to turn around structural economic imbalances, in all countries in Europe. This is why structural reforms are so important for the rebalancing and growth: to improve the functioning of the goods, services, labour and capital markets. And this calls for action in and by the member states.

Rebalancing: A Slow Process of Restoring Competitiveness

While much of the debate on macroeconomic imbalances has recently centred on Germany, it is nevertheless appropriate to point out that the most urgent and painfully real problem in 2010 onwards was the lost competitiveness of *deficit* countries. It may have not been entirely right to put blame only on them, but it is likewise far too simple to put the blame solely on Germany and its current account surpluses, which has been the basic instinct of many Anglo-American economists.

The loss of cost competitiveness is shown in Fig. 14.2, which reveals the divergence in unit labour costs in the Eurozone since 2000. This was Jean-Claude Trichet's "favourite" crisis era graph, shown to the ministers in almost every Eurogroup meeting. In the countries of the so-called periphery,

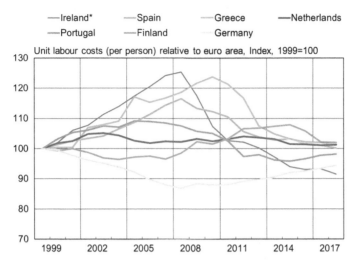

Fig. 14.2 Unit labour costs (per person) relative to the euro area aggregate, 1999–2018 (1999 = 100) (*Source* ECB, Macrobond, CSO and Bank of Finland calculations. *Based on domestic sector unit labour costs [ULC]. Data for 2017–18 approximated based on aggregate ULC)

particularly Ireland, Spain, Portugal and Greece, the unit labour costs rose sharply compared to the Eurozone average, which eroded their cost competitiveness and contributed to the widening current account deficits. The simplified root causes were the increased capital flows to the periphery countries following the introduction of the Euro and the misplaced pricing of risk to the periphery lending, enjoying the same interest rates as Germany and the other so-called core countries.

While it is rather easy to accumulate imbalances by letting the current account deficit widen and entrench, it is much more difficult to restore the balance by starting to accumulate current account *surpluses*. With a flexible (or fixed but adjustable) exchange rate, the correction can be supported and speeded up with currency devaluation. Within the monetary union, this road obviously leads to a dead end, which means that the adjustment must take place through an internal devaluation, at least if there is no federal fiscal structure in place that could provide automatic stabilizers in the form of cross-border social transfers (which the Eurozone does not possess). This implies that the process of rebalancing within the Eurozone has been relatively slow. This gradual rebalancing in the Eurozone since 2010 (in the Irish case earlier, since 2008) was illustrated in Chapter 1 in Fig. 1.2.

France as a Source of Initiative—And Imbalance

The election of the centrist reformer Emmanuel Macron as the President of France in May 2017 created great expectations of economic and political progress in France and in Europe. Macron's France is striving for a leading role in Europe, which reminds me of the remark by the historian Paul Kennedy three decades ago: "It is the French above all who have argued for a distinctively 'European' position on international economic and defence issues – and who therefore most clearly articulate the European concerns. For this reason, it is Paris which has usually taken the lead in initiating new policies".[2] At the same time, it is useful to look at the recent development and challenges of the French economy and economic policy.

Prior to the election of Francois Hollande as President in 2012, France suffered from economic stagnation, the lack of reforms and a large current account deficit (2.0–2.5% in 2010–12). Despite some efforts to the contrary, during Hollande's Presidency bold growth-boosting structural reforms remained largely absent, at least until *Loi Macron*, which made a difference in the labour market. Moreover, fiscal consolidation originally leaned too much on tax increases. The French political tradition of strikes and street demonstrations was considered to limit the room of manoeuvre of any government regardless of its political orientation. The fate of ex-Prime Minister Alain Juppé, who pursued serious economic reforms but fell to the massive demonstrations in 1997, was the key living memory among the French politicians, until the time of Macron. In the end of 2018, the yellow vests (*les gilets jaunes*) pushed Macron to a tactical retreat, hopefully only temporarily.

Thinking of France, I recall a very senior German policy-maker saying in 2013: "Germany can contribute best to French reforms by keeping our mouths shut. Globalization is difficult for France and the French people. That's also why we want to keep the United Kingdom in the EU". It is hard not to agree with this sober, realistic assessment, even if the last sentence may now sound like wishful thinking.

My relation with France stems from my appreciation of the French history and culture, as well as her contribution to European integration from Jean Monnet and Robert Schuman to Jacques Delors. I've also had the honour to work with great Commission colleagues, especially Pascal Lamy and Michel Barnier. I studied French at adult age to survive as *Chef de Cabinet* in the late 1990s in the then still rather *francophone* European Commission. Later on, I developed a close and straight working relationship with the French foreign and finance ministers during my two-plus terms in the

Commission. Besides, I've seen Michel Platini, Zinedine Zidane and Kylian Mbappé in live action on the field, including in the memorable World Cup finals at Stade de France in 1998 and the Luzhniki Stadium of Moscow in 2018. (And I've witnessed Michel Platini booed at Stade de France in July 2016, but that's another story—a sad end in UEFA for a truly exceptional football career.)

Christine Lagarde is a no-nonsense economic policy-maker of the highest global calibre and communication skills, one who stands no fools nor platitudes, has natural leadership capacity and can rally troops for the common cause, be it France, Europe or the world. She steered the IMF impeccably and will do likewise at the helm of the European Central Bank, which as a side effect has helped to break some glass ceilings.

With Pierre Moscovici, we got to know each other already when I served as Enlargement Commissioner in 2004–10, as he was one of the key players in the European Parliament and its rapporteur on Romania. Once he took office as finance minister in 2012, our dialogue on economic policy of Europe and France got intense. It coincided with the gradual recovery of the European economy, which facilitated a rethink of some elements of our common economic policies (Image 14.1).

Pierre was a very thoughtful discussion partner on these matters, and I was not surprised that he chose to pursue early on in the Hollande five-year term to be appointed my successor as the Commissioner for Economic and Monetary Affairs in the next Commission for 2014–19. He was instrumental in drafting the Juncker Commission's "Flexibility Communication", which gives more growth-based room for discretion on the application of fiscal rules, and their conditioning to investment and structural reforms.

Pierre describes me in his book *Combats* (2013) as "a liberal... but a Finnish liberal, who would be without doubt classified in France as centre-left". While my entrepreneur friends back home might get pimples due to that positively intentioned provocation, indeed as a civic and social liberal myself I take it as a cool badge of comradely solidarity. And I can reciprocate by saying that Pierre would in Finland be easily classified as centre-centre, as there is fortunately no inherent reform resistance in him!

However, despite these solid starting points, the facts are facts, and they matter: in economic and fiscal policy, the French were not always practising what they preached. That concerned the period of both Sarkozy and Hollande. The fiscal deficits were constantly at the borderline of the previously already softened requirements of fiscal adjustment. Structural reforms were not moving, at least not with the speed needed, or recommended by the Council and the Commission.

Image 14.1 Finance minister Pierre Moscovici handed the fresh French budget bill for 2014 to me in Berlaymont in the autumn of 2014. Long talks that started in Moscow in February 2013 led to a positive outcome. Pierre continued in the space of European economic policy as Commissioner in the Juncker Commission (*Source* © European Union, 2013; European Commission—Photo: Thierry Charlier. Licensed under CC BY 4.0 [https://creativecommons.org/licenses/by/4.0/])

So, in the course of 2012, we started to have a rethink on how to deal with France. That was essentially a matter of applying the EU fiscal rules as they should, which meant that the focus was now solidly on the consistent consolidation of structural fiscal balance over the medium term. The general principle now was that if the member state concerned could convince the Commission of its will and ability to pursue growth-boosting structural and fiscal reforms, then we could grant a longer period of fiscal adjustment, as long as it was credible. France was developing its economic policy stance accordingly. Against this backdrop, we decided to work with France along these lines as a "pilot case", focusing on economic reforms in the labour and product markets, which the country in our view badly needed. France had serious imbalances due to large losses in competitiveness and export performance, owing to both cost and non-cost factors.

Hence, towards the autumn and winter of 2012–13, a policy was developed that would consist of a fairly simple deal, or trade-off, of two policies. Assuming France would get serious on economic reforms, the Commission in return would give the country a two-year extension for the correction deadline of its fiscal deficit to the 3% level—instead of only one year—which meant a smoother path of fiscal adjustment. However, we had to proceed carefully, as otherwise we could have lost the support of the fiscal hawks in the Council, including the ECB and Germany and its allies.

Consequently, before Christmas 2012 I decided to test ground by spinning for background of the possibility that we might do the 2-year extension from 2013 to 2015. So I talked with Philippe Ricard, the experienced and competent correspondent of *Le Monde*, who immediately realized a good story, which besides fitted his own Keynesian mindset that is characteristic of the French centre-left. My article in the *FT* just a few days before on 13 December 2012 was directly related to this operation with France—as a supposedly astute way of making more leeway in fiscal policy in return for economic reforms—to which I will come back in Chapter 16.

As a quality paper, *Le Monde* ran a correct headline on 21 December 2012: *Déficits: Olli Rehn envisage un "ajustement plus doux" pour la France,* i.e. "OR envisages a softer adjustment for France". Philippe Ricard wrote: "In the Eurozone where growth is slipping, if not disappearing, Olli Rehn, the Commissioner for Economic and Monetary Affairs, clarifies that the return of fiscal deficits to 3% of GDP is a reference and keeps the door ajar to more flexibility in the implementation of fiscal policy".

Libération, the newspaper close to the Socialist Party and President Hollande, took the pass and wrote on Christmas Eve 24 December 2012: "Austerity: Brussels suggests flexibility, Paris declares for rigour". Jean Quatremer, a broadly respected correspondent in Brussels and a staunch European federalist, wrote: "Paris, even more austere than Brussels? When Commissioner for Economic and Monetary Affairs, Olli Rehn, suggested last Friday that France could be granted more time to put her public finances in balance, Prime Minister Jean-Marc Ayrault reaffirmed on Saturday his strong will to respect the goal of reducing the public deficit to 3% of GDP by the end of 2013".

A Moscow Deal with Moscovici

As described in the previous chapters, in the beginning of 2013 we started to feel that a recovery was gradually gaining ground, at first only a modest and fragile recovery. In January–February 2013, our dialogue with Pierre Moscovici got more intense. The crucial meeting to agree a way ahead in partnership was arranged in mid-February, of all the places in Moscow, where we both took part in the G20 conference of finance ministers and central bankers, Pierre representing France and me the EU. I prepared the meeting thoroughly with my officials, and we came up with a two-page note on concrete economic reforms, based on the Council recommendations to France in December, which I presented to Moscovici as a condition for granting the 2-year extension. The note concentrated on the labour market reform to improve the flexibility and cost competitiveness of the French economy, on the product market reform to increase competition in many sectors, the review of public expenditure and reforms in the network industries, such as railways and communications.

Pierre took a basically positive view of the envisaged comprehensive and two-pronged solution. He had been speaking to the same direction for some time. In his book, he describes the "immense diplomatic efforts" starting from the summer 2012 and intensifying in the first half of 2013 "to change the parameters of the European debate without turning the table around" (*"changer les paramètres du débat européen sans renverser la table"*). So there was an evident meeting of minds on the economic policy stance, which helped to find a common conclusion. We concluded to work on that basis and decided to come back in due course with further building blocks, once the French officials had had a chance to prepare concrete elements of reforms that could convince us and the Eurozone member states.

Soon afterwards President Hollande set the stage along the same lines, by admitting that the fiscal target probably could not be reached. As David Marsh wrote on 18 February 2013, "With a Gallic mix of pragmatism, President Francois Hollande has set the stage. He has admitted what most people knew anyway: there is little chance that France will meet its growth and budget deficit targets this year".

Marsh is a seasoned observer of the Eurozone, having written an important volume of the euro's construction and previously of the Bundesbank. He correctly linked the economic reforms and the deadline extension, although even he missed the December indications for the prospect of a two-year extension:

France needn't fear direct European repercussions. Paris faces merely a polite rap across the knuckles. Olli Rehn, the EU's monetary commissioner, carefully signalled last week that countries such as France and Spain may be given an extra year – until *2014* – to meet their deficit targets, if they can prove that they are making efforts in structural reforms.[3]

But on substance he certainly hit the right point.

So the preparations went on. We met again with Moscovici in Dublin on 12 April 2013 in the margins of a conference. I said it was not very helpful that we needed to revise the deficit forecast upwards from 3.7% for the ongoing year 2013, since according to the fresh data from INSEE, the French statistical office, the deficit target for 2012 was not met. On the other hand, I recognized positively that France was just about, as a borderline case, expected to meet the average annual structural effort in fiscal consolidation over 2010–13, by achieving close to but below 1% (the Council had recommended structural effort 2010–13 to be "above 1% of GDP"). So I urged France to fully implement the budget for 2013 and reach the targeted structural effort for 2013, which was at 1.4% of GDP.

At the end of the meeting with Moscovici, we discussed the possibility of moving the correction deadline to *2015*, on the condition that France would intensify structural reforms along the lines of the Moscow deal. This was tentatively agreed and we got reassurances by Moscovici on the delivery of concrete reforms. We concluded that a structural fiscal effort of minimum 1.25% would be needed, which is equivalent to around €25 billion in consolidation measures. This was supposed to be achieved 2/3 by expenditure cuts and 1/3 by revenue increases.

In the end of May 2013, after preparing the ground with the governments, I stated in an interview with the German Press Agency DPA that "the pace of austerity can slow down in Europe". I didn't use the word "austerity", but on substance the message was correct. France was clearly going to be a case in point. In the course of preparations, I consulted with Wolfgang Schäuble who was supportive.

In May 2013, President Hollande visited Berlaymont. Barroso asked me to play the bad cop at the luncheon with him—I didn't mind doing so and spoke in a frank and open manner on the stagnation of the French economy and the unfortunate stalling state of economic reforms. President Hollande did not deny this.

In the end of May, the Commission finally recommended a two-year extension to the correction deadline for France, together with Spain, Slovenia and Poland, and a one-year extension to Belgium, the Netherlands and Portugal. I gave a speech on this to explain it more thoroughly in the European Semester Conference on 29 May 2013. On France I said, "the recommended adjustment effort over 2014 and 2015 is slightly lower than being made this year… in return, it is very important that France uses this additional time to tackle its underlying competitiveness problem". Thus, the deal was sealed and made public.

What should be the verdict of this experiment, which was a pilot case of linking the pursuit of structural reforms to a more medium-term path of fiscal adjustment? In retrospect, depending on the eye of the beholder, the glass can be seen as half-full or half-empty. Some structural reforms, such as in pensions and labour costs, have moved forward. The progress of *Loi Macron*, which aimed at a broad-based liberalization of product and services markets, including shopping hours, and the rest of the reformist policy agenda of President Macron seemed to illustrate that reform is indeed possible in France. Whether this is a pipe dream after the violent street demonstrations is one of the crucial questions for the future of Europe. In any case, I wish the best of success for reformers of the new generation, where the hope of the economic and societal revival of France—and probably Europe—now rests.

As said, our approach with France in 2012–13 was a very deliberate experiment in conditionality, aiming at boosting economic reforms, rather than focusing only on fiscal targets. At least the experiment showed the limitations of policy conditionality. What would be a better way? In the ideal world, one should be able to construct conditionality so that the implementation of reforms is proven first, and that the extension of reaching the fiscal targets is made dependent on the delivery. But in the real world, these two dimensions move in parallel, and an absolute distinction between the "done" reforms and "future" consolidation cannot so easily be done.

The German Question Returns Through the Persistent Surplus

In his little but substantive book *The Paradox of German Power* (2016), the political scientist Hans Kundnani describes Germany's role in Europe today as a "semi-hegemon", but with important qualifications:

> Germany is not a European hegemon – nor can it be one. Rather, it has reverted to something like the position of "semi-hegemony" it had in Europe between 1871 and 1945 – but in "geo-economic" rather than geopolitical form. At the same time, there has emerged a new form of German nationalism, which is based on exports and the idea of "peace", and a renewed sense of German mission.[4]

So, Germany is mostly a geo-economic power, whose modern national self-identity rests on the notions of peace and exports—we could add democracy to the list. Moreover, Germany is fundamentally anchored to the European community and works much through EU institutions. What we witness today is what the Nobel-winning author Thomas Mann described as the "European Germany" rather than a "German Europe". Even the financial and debt crises and Germany's emergence as "semi-hegemon" have not profoundly changed that achievement.[5]

Yes, there are dissenting voices to that pro-European consensus, too. Notably, the right-wing populistic party *Alternative für Deutschland* (AfD), which combines anti-Europeanism and anti-immigration, has garnered support since the euro crisis hit Europe by criticizing the financing commitments Germany has made and the unconventional policies the European Central Bank has undertaken to contain the crisis. But there are other kinds of voices, as well: many citizens and politicians in Germany are calling for more committed and determined European policies by Germany. For instance, Joschka Fischer, a founding father of the Greens and a former foreign minister, has said that the crisis should make Europe move forward and the status quo is no alternative any more. He has been a vocal critic of the muddling through approach and coined it thus: "Germany does not know how to deal with the leadership and responsibility which have fallen to her shoulders, but which she has not wished to carry".[6] The latter standpoint of Joschka Fischer seems to have carried the day in the 2019 European elections where the Greens surged from 10 to 20%, thus becoming the second political force in the country.

Much of the discussion of Germany's role centres round the question of large current account surplus and also the fiscal debt brakes. What was behind the large surplus? A key factor was the deepening of European integration in the past 10–20 years, which helped strengthen Germany's industrial competitiveness, in many ways. First, the creation of the euro prevented the German exchange rate from appreciating to reflect the large surplus. Second, integrating Central and Eastern European companies and workers to its production chains allowed Germany to diversify and benefit from a large pool of well-educated and relatively low-cost labour. And third, financial market integration and interest rate convergence drove international capital flows, which mirrored these current account developments.

Equally important, adjustment channels are influenced significantly by global economic interdependence. Germany has specialized in products that are in demand in the rest of the world. The country is highly competitive on both quality and price. High savings and low investment in many sectors have contributed to the large and persistent current account surplus.

Moreover, around a third of the German current account surplus is explained by returns on assets accumulated abroad in the years before the crisis, when excess savings in Germany and other core countries were redistributed throughout the Eurozone and further afield. Instead of boosting productivity-enhancing investment which would have enhanced sustainable growth, they largely ended up fuelling the credit booms and subsequent asset and housing bubbles in recipient countries. That mispricing of risk was detrimental to both sides: the catastrophic busts that hit the peripheral economies led to losses for the German banks themselves, adding to those incurred from their investments in toxic US assets. Meanwhile, investment in Germany had fallen from 21.5% of GDP in 2000 to around 17.4% in 2013,[7] a lower share than in other Eurozone countries.

In the crisis years, Germany's current account surplus almost halved vis-à-vis the euro area. On the other hand, over the same period, Germany's surplus with the rest of the world almost tripled. The structural shifts over the past 30 years imply that peripheral Eurozone countries, particularly in Southern Europe (unlike Central and Eastern Europe), are less integrated into Germany's trade structures than is commonly thought. The Commission study from December 2012 found that more dynamic domestic demand in Germany would only have a very limited *direct* impact on the current account of countries such as Spain, Portugal or Greece.

In July 2013, like in many other years, the EU's Council recommended Germany to open up the bottlenecks to the growth of domestic demand. In particular, Germany was advised to create the conditions for sustained wage growth, for instance by reducing high taxes and social security contributions, especially for low-wage earners. The idea behind the recommendations was to enhance Germany's economic dynamism, for which the country should further stimulate competition in services—construction in particular, but also in certain crafts, as well as professional services—in order to boost domestic sources of growth.

These suggestions may not sound like revolutionary reforms, but their implementation would nevertheless have contributed significantly to the rebalancing of the entire euro area economy, in order to do it faster and with smaller damages than only in slow motion, which would in the final analysis also have been in line of Germany's own interests.

There are other pressing challenges too. *Energiewende*, the energy transition, will require an improved regulatory framework to unlock private investment in energy networks. Boosting investment in infrastructure will help sustain domestic demand also in the longer term via its positive impact on productivity.

All this investment would be a great service to Europe—and to Germany herself. It would enhance Germany's economic performance in the long run, as well as to reduce the inequalities that had accumulated over the previous years. Needless to say, the positive impact was seen to reach also other Eurozone countries through mutually beneficial rebalancing. In particular, a rise in German domestic demand would have reduced the upward pressure on the real exchange rate of the euro and thus easing access to global markets for exporters in the periphery.

On the other hand, there has been some positive rebalancing impact from the wage increases and the ECB's non-standard measures. In addition to the significant pace of German wage increases nearing 3% yearly, the exchange rate issue was alleviated in the last months of 2014 and early 2015 thanks to the depreciative effect of the ECB's large-scale quantitative easing programme. This continued in the years 2015–17 and contributed to the reinforced growth in Europe.

A Bundesbank study published in January 2017 shows that ECB bond purchases caused a devaluation of 6.5% in the euro against the dollar between October 2014 and the end of 2016, with most of that devaluation happening before the bond-buying programme was even announced in late January 2015. While recognizing this effect, the Bundesbank went on to downplay its importance: "The bond purchases of the Eurosystem had no significant additional effect on the exchange rate other than signaling effects and related expectations". In fact, by the end of 2016, the euro had fallen by 20% against the dollar since late 2014, partly due to a tightening in the Federal Reserve's own monetary policy.[8]

Of course, after a couple of years in a crisis mode we knew well that Germany isn't the only country whose policies had spillover effects, good or bad, on the rest of the Eurozone. By 2013–14, we were thankfully much less occupied by immediate firefighting. However, the general outlook of slow growth remained worrisome, as did the then looming threat of a deflationary spiral.

Is a Win-Win German–French Economic Strategy Plausible?

In my view, striking a balance between the two economic policy camps—to encourage Germany to take steps to lift domestic demand and investment, and France to embrace reforms in its labour market, business environment and pension system to support competitiveness—would trickle down to the rest of the Eurozone and provide stronger growth and jobs, which would in turn help lower social tensions in crisis-hit countries.

In retrospect, statistics show that the surplus turned to growth again in the last couple of years. However, this we could not yet know at the time of making the recommendation in 2012. Early on, then Finance Minister Wolfgang Schäuble countered this in the Commission's home ground in Brussels, in the Brussels Economic Forum, on 18 May 2011. I had invited him to be the keynote speaker there to hold the first-ever Tommaso Padoa-Schioppa lecture, to the dislike and consternation of some of my more federalist colleagues in DG Ecfin, who thought that almost inappropriate; however, in my view, it was indeed more than appropriate that we would listen to Schäuble who is a committed European, a key leader of the Eurozone fire brigade and the finance minister of the largest creditor!

I introduced Wolfgang Schäuble by referring to his long-lasting European conviction, illustrated by his co-authorship of the Lamers-Schäuble 1994 paper on the core Europe and multi-speed integration. I couldn't help also referring to the classic distinction by philosopher Isaiah Berlin of statesmen to the foxes and hedgehogs, where "the fox knows many things and the hedgehog knows one big thing"—I said Schäuble combines the hedgehog's long-lasting commitment to the European construction with the fox's parliamentary and political astuteness. I am not sure if he liked my appreciative wit, although he should have—it was genuine.

Schäuble made an expected but nevertheless sharp pre-emptive counter-attack against the European Commission's initiative regarding the setting up of MIP. We expected that the MIP would give the Eurogroup and the Commission credible policy tools to focus on how to channel the current account surpluses to a better and more productive use for growth and jobs in the Eurozone. Let Schäuble speak for himself:

> Yes, we have to avoid overly large imbalances between member states. But no, this cannot take the form of successful countries voluntarily limiting their competitiveness... The only workable course is for those countries in the Eurozone that are somewhat weaker, to become stronger. We can help them, but we cannot do their job. Besides, one does not resolve one's own problems of competitiveness by asking others to become less competitive and one cannot permanently close the gap between expenditure and income by asking others for more money.

It is easy to conclude from Schäuble's words that the Commission's recommendations on the rebalancing of the German current account surplus were not an easy sell politically in Germany, where I often received criticism during the crisis when I continued to raise the issue of imbalances in the public debate. This is because the Germans unfortunately tend to perceive this so that the EU wants to weaken their competitiveness, which is amplified by the media debate. Of course, that is not the goal, which is the strengthening of domestic demand and productive investment by eliminating bottlenecks and structural obstacles.

During my years in the Commission, I responded to my German critics in terms they do understand: if FC Bayern München plays against FC Barcelona, the correction of imbalance does not mean that Bayern should play worse in order to even out the game for Barcelona (not to say Barcelona would necessarily need it, at least with Leo Messi!). Instead, the purpose here is not a zero-sum club battle but to create a European win-win team, which means that the best possible team is built from the best players in each team's defence, midfield and offence. Despite my best communication efforts in the language of the game where the Germans are masters, I think I ended up in a temporary political offside, at least in Germany.

"Wachstum durch Wandel"

Nevertheless, I continued to make the point regarding the excessive surpluses, year after year, which calls for quite some stamina to overcome the accumulating frustration. I preached the sermon in the packed press room of the Commission, responding to German journalists' questions full of criticism; I preached in Germany itself, as well as in other member states. A case in point was the conference speech at the lion's den, i.e. at Deutsche Bank in the context of the IMF annual meeting in Tokyo on 12 October 2012:

> It is essential that also countries with current account surpluses should pursue structural reforms to remove unnecessary constraints on domestic demand and investment opportunities. Thus, the Commission has recommended to Germany to allow wage-growth in line with productivity, to use its fiscal scope for growth-enhancing investment and to enhance labour market participation, especially of women.

The response in the audience was somewhat dualistic: among the international banking community very positive, while among the German component cordial but not enthusiastic. Yet, I noted positively that the wage agreements in some important sectors (especially IG Metall) in Germany foresaw nominal wage increases of close to 3% for 2012, which at 2% inflation implied at least some real wage increases.

Further to make the case for a balanced approach on Germany, I wrote a blog[9] (3 July 2013) in which I analysed the root causes and economic implications of Germany's current account surplus. Later on in the fall 2013, I continued the substantive discussion with the German financial and political leadership, or at least readership, through a similar article in the Frankfurter Allgemeine Zeitung entitled *Was Handelsüberschüsse mit dem Euro zu tun haben*[10] (11 November 2013).

At the suggestion of my senior adviser Peer Ritter, for my blog I chose a headline *Wachstum durch Wandel*—or "Growth through Change", which I find a most descriptive expression to illustrate the German success. Besides, it rhymes perfectly with the two other expressions of the recent history of Germany: *Wandel durch Annäherung* ("change through rapprochement"), which was the key logic of Willy Brandt's *Ostpolitik*, and *Wandel durch Handel* ("change through trade"), which became the post-Cold War catchphrase; or as Gerhard Schröder put it, "economic exchange" would lead to "societal change".[11]

In my article, I reminded the readers that fourteen years previously, *The Economist* had written of Germany: "As economic growth stalls yet again, the country is being branded the sick man (or even the Japan) of Europe". This, it was argued, was "inevitably casting a cloud over Europe's single currency…for Germany accounts for a full third of the euro countries' output". The Economist went on to list the reasons for Germany's malaise, including "a byzantine and inefficient tax system, a bloated welfare system and excessive labour costs".

It is easily forgotten today where Germany came from at the turn of the millennium. At the start of the euro in 1999, Germany was undergoing a dual adjustment process: first, to unification, with unemployment rates in Eastern Germany still around 20%, and second, to the opening of markets of its Central and Eastern European neighbours. Facing low potential growth, the German corporate sector deleveraged and tried to raise profitability with direct investment in other European countries. This intensified the integration of Central and Eastern European economies into the German production chain. At the same time, the labour market was reformed, many unemployed got jobs, and wage moderation occurred. Social partners also took responsibility and included opening clauses in wage agreements.

This process coincided with the introduction of the euro. Consequently, the Eurozone periphery was experiencing falling sovereign risk premia at a time when financial markets were integrating into the EU. The increase in the capital flowing from the core of the Eurozone to its periphery came as debt, not foreign direct investment, and it went disproportionately into non-tradable sectors, contributing to overheating. Since the boom came to an end in 2007, peripheral countries' current account deficits have narrowed substantially.

The German government was obviously not too happy of the Commission's activity, but at least it did not complain publicly. At the same time, it expected—at least in between the lines—that as the largest contributor to the crisis containment and stability mechanisms, it would not be sanctioned. I found it better to work in partnership to rationally convince Germany to engage in a more proactive rebalancing process, rather than doing something completely against her nature.

This kind of dialogue was needed in the summer of 2011, when the Ecofin Council was stuck among the EU member states and with the European Parliament on the critical thresholds for triggering an in-depth study of macroeconomic imbalances. This became an issue of vital national interest to the German Federal Government, as it did not want to be too easily reminded of its large surplus.

As the dispute was blocking the adoption of the six-pack reform of economic governance, we had no other option than to seek for a decent compromise. In the Ecofin Council in July 2011, I made a proposal on behalf of the Commission to set the threshold at 4% for deficit countries and 6% for surplus countries. After some sharp words, Wolfgang Schäuble agreed. This deal was obviously prepared beforehand, but we were not sure of Germany's final position.

For sure, the second-best asymmetric deal was less than perfect, even if there is sustainable justification to put the bar lower for deficit countries whose problems can more suddenly hit the country and create negative spillovers in the rest of the Eurozone. But at least the avenue was now open for the six-pack and thus for a reinforced economic governance, to tackle macroeconomic imbalances.

The Responsibility of Germany and France for the Eurozone

As the two largest Eurozone economies, Germany and France together hold the keys to a return of stronger, sustained growth and higher level of employment in Europe. Obviously, the macroeconomic imbalances and policy differences between Germany and France did not surface suddenly from any vacuum, nor stem only from the economic fundamentals like the distinct production structures. Instead, they are the product of deeply entrenched and quite distinct paradigms of macroeconomic goals and policy, stemming from the traditional interventionism and *dirigisme* in France and from the stability culture and ordo-liberalism in Germany.[12]

In a nutshell, a smoother process of rebalancing, as such desirable, would call for reforms in the labour market, business environment and pension system to boost competitiveness in France, and for structural measures to strengthen domestic demand and especially to boost domestic investment in Germany. This is what the European Commission recommended once the six-pack had reinforced economic governance and gave us new tools under the MIP, and its country reports and in-depth reviews. The impact was limited.

But if Germany and France together were to concretely implement what the European Council has, at the Commission's initiative, recommended to them, they would do their greatest service to the rebalancing of the entire European economy by providing stronger growth, creating more jobs and reducing social tensions—and would also help rebalance the world economy. All these would certainly help to reduce populist pressures in democratic politics. While the Eurozone's institutional reform often dominate headlines, the countries' reform and policy efforts in the real economy are even more important.

Tietmeyer's Legacy on the Economic and Political Union

In early July 2013, I flew to Frankfurt once again, this time for a reason that I particularly appreciated, namely to give a keynote speech at a symposium in honour of Professor Hans Tietmeyer, who had just turned 82 years and was retiring as Chairman of the New Social Market Economy Foundation, a prestigious economic think tank in Germany. Tietmeyer passed away in 2017 at the respectable age of 86 years, peace be upon him. As an influential State Secretary of the German Ministry of Economic Affairs in the 1980s and later on as Vice-President and President of the Bundesbank in the 1990s, Tietmeyer had warned that monetary union requires a strong capacity for structural adjustment. The experience of the German monetary union after the reunification was still fresh in memory.

In Frankfurt after the conference, I had a chance over lunch to listen to and discuss with Professor Tietmeyer. I could tell him that we had first met over 20 years ago, although I didn't expect him to remember that, as I was part of a delegation of the Finnish Parliament. We were preparing for Finland's EU accession negotiations, and the analysis Professor Tietmeyer gave to our Economic Affairs Committee on the EMU was both intellectually rigorous and policy-wise realistic, even sobering.

In my speech, I underlined the necessity to reform economic governance for the sake of reinforcing the stability culture and thus sustainable growth in the Eurozone. Reacting to it, Professor Tietmeyer pondered whether it was a mistake to discard economic governance when EMU was created. But in his view there was no other alternative if Europe wanted to create the EMU at all, because the then Finance Minister Theo Waigel was "a prisoner of this own constituency in Bavaria, and he could not pursue a political union". I interpreted this as support for those institutional reforms we initiated to reinforce economic governance and, by and large, implemented in the course of the crisis years of 2010–13.

A propos, I recall a very similar discussion, but from the French angle, in the French *Assemblée Nationale* with Eduard Balladur, ex-Prime Minister who was chairing the Foreign Affairs Committee in the mid-2000s. The same goes for Jean Arthuis and Sylvie Goulard, very close and competent colleagues from the European Parliament in economic policy-making, and Arthuis also a former budget minister in 1995–97.

All in all, while valuing high the contribution of Germany and France, one of the critical lessons learnt from the crisis is that Europe is by far too a valuable creature to be left to these two alone. Following the structural weaknesses that were left to the Eurozone construction in the Maastricht Treaty, there were many unfortunate events, such as the breach of the Stability and Growth Pact in 2003–4 and the Deauville doomsday in 2010, as well as many other moves of crisis management by the duo. Furthermore, Germany and France carry a fair share of responsibility for the fact that Eurozone reform has not really moved forward in recent years—no major reforms have been decided since the banking union, or since 2013.

In these days, one actually wishes that at least the German–French duo was able to take the institutional initiative and provide leadership for the Eurozone, of course with the other EU member states and institutions closely involved and empowered. The policy initiative of the 14 German and French economists in early 2018 was an encouraging and intellectually strongly grounded, synthetic move to the right direction. The governments of Germany and France have not matched the level of boldness and the capacity of consensus of their economists. We have the right to expect that the leaders of the Germany and France could follow the lead of their compatriot economists and agree on the next stage of a necessary reform of the Eurozone, which I will discuss in Chapter 19. And this positive perspective also calls for an active Commission that takes initiative to this effect, and it also underlines the Community method as the critical way of taking decisions. In my view, that is one of the essential medicines against contemporary populism and to combat a dangerous disintegration of Europe.

Notes

1. http://ec.europa.eu/economy_finance/publications/european_economy/2012/pdf/ee-2012-9_en.pdf.
2. Paul Kennedy, *The Rise and Fall of the Great Powers*. Fontana Press, 1988, p. 630.
3. David Marsh, OMFIF Commentary on 18 February 2013.
4. Hans Kundnani, *The Paradox of German Power*. Oxford University Press, 2017.
5. Kundnani 2017.
6. Joschka Fischer, *Epäonnistunut Eurooppa*. Into, 2014, pp. 90–91.
7. http://www.economywatch.com/economic-statistics/economic-indicators/Investment_Percentage_of_GDP/.
8. http://www.reuters.com/article/us-ecb-policy-bundesbank-idUSKBN1571AO?il=0.
9. http://ec.europa.eu/archives/commission_2010-2014/blogs/rehn/germany-wachstum-durch-wandel.html.
10. http://www.faz.net/aktuell/wirtschaft/gastbeitrag-was-handelsueberschuesse-mit-dem-euro-zu-tun-haben-12657154.html.
11. Kundnani 2017, p. 82.
12. On German macroeconomic tradition, see, e.g., Bratsiotis and Cobham (eds.), *German Macro: How It's Different and Why It Matters*. European Policy Centre, 2016.

15

Baltic States Set Sail Against the Wind

I have to admit that drawing fresh Estonian euros out from the ATM in downtown Tallinn with the country's Prime Minister Andrus Ansip in the freezing cold just after midnight in the New Year's Eve of 31 December 2010 was one of the coolest—or chilliest—experiences in my term as Commissioner for Economic and Monetary Affairs. That moment symbolized two decades of democratic and economic transformation of Estonia and crystallized its European orientation.

While the Eurozone was burning, the Baltic states were moving on and kept on bringing their economies back to the path of recovery following the damaging impact of the financial crisis. All three of them, Estonia, Latvia and Lithuania, became members of the Eurozone in 2011–15: Estonia in 2011, Latvia in 2014 and Lithuania in 2015. Because no Grexit or other exits from the Eurozone took place during the crisis, contrary to what many Cassandras were predicting, the Eurozone's membership actually grew from 16 to 19 members.

Taking a longer-term historical perspective, the recent three decades in the Baltics are an inspiring era of freedom and progress.

I first travelled to that then forgotten corner of Europe by crossing the Bay of Finland from Helsinki to Tallinn in May 1982, in fact to celebrate my regained personal freedom just a few days after ending my military service as a fresh second lieutenant in reserves—which made me compare the fate of the Baltics under the Soviet Union to that of Finland, a free and independent Western democracy. This was less than a decade after the historic Helsinki Accords were signed in the summer of 1975 and around the time when the stagnation of the Brezhnev era culminated. The Baltics have

© The Author(s) 2020
O. Rehn, *Walking the Highwire*, https://doi.org/10.1007/978-3-030-34592-1_15

come a long way since then, and their EU membership has been a key building block for their successful democratic and economic transformation. The Baltic states are by and large also an economic success story, although the recent scandals related to money laundering have tarnished their reputation. Their clean-up through rigorous anti-money laundering activity is an essential challenge for the Baltics, as well as for their Nordic neighbours.

Estonia's Road to Freedom—And Europe

Since the mid-1980s and the start of the Gorbachev's *glasnost* and *perestroika*, I became a regular political tourist to Estonia. We organized a first-ever Finnish-Soviet youth event called "Peace to the Border" in Tallinn in May 1986 and brought a number of Finnish rock bands including the legendary *Sielun Veljet* (the "Soul Brothers") across the Bay of Finland, with great success. Then I could for the first time witness that the Estonian hosts were actually not following the lead of the Moscow crowd, despite there being the top leadership of Komsomol present. The half decade 1986–91 became the period of gradual political liberalization and proactive nation-building for Estonia, so that most of the then Soviet Republic's societal structures became manned by independence-minded individuals, from the newspapers to trade unions, up to the party machine (in singular, as there was only one party allowed, *Eestimaa Kommunistlik Partei*, EKP; the local branch of the CPSU). The Song Festivals mostly of choir singing became in essence annual demonstrations of the common will to keep up the Estonian heritage.

At the time, we Finns thought and some even bragged that we "knew" the Soviet Union. However, the Estonians knew it better, as they lived inside that Union and directly knew its weak spots and structural decline. In 1988, Siim Kallas, then the deputy editor of Estonia's main newspaper *Rahva Hääl*, put it bluntly when he told a seminar audience in Turku, Finland: "The Soviet Union will disintegrate". That caused plenty of confusion and disbelief among the seminar participants and in the public debate that followed. It has been said that very few in the Finnish audience really understood that he truly meant what he said[1]! And it was not a linguistic problem, as Kallas speaks perfect Finnish. Siim Kallas was one of the fathers of the "IME", the independent economic programme for Estonia, and since independence the central bank chief, finance minister and prime minister of the country. In 2004–14, he served as vice-president of the European Commission who was a great colleague and became a close friend.

Soon after the collapse of the Soviet Union in 1991 and the declaration of independence by the three Baltic republics, they started to approach their European perspective—and the Europeans were welcoming, by and large. The critical early step towards the EU was membership in the Council of Europe. As a young MP in 1991–95, I was chairing the Finnish delegation in its Parliamentary Assembly, where we worked intensively to bring forward the membership of the Baltics states in the organization. Estonia was accepted as member in spring 1993, which was a sunny, bright and great day in Strasbourg and one of my best European memories.

In the mid-1990s, free trade agreements with the EU entered into force in all three Baltic states, triggering an unprecedented economic restructuring and convergence. More comprehensive Europe Agreements soon followed, granting additional access for Baltic products to the EU's single market and providing the Baltic states substantial economic aid. Beyond economic liberalization, the Europe Agreements also facilitated cooperation in many areas from science and education to tourism and transport, from environment to financial services, from public procurement to customs and judicial cooperation, so on.

By the end of the 1990s, fully fledged EU accession negotiations were well on the way. In May 2004, a total of ten countries, including Estonia, Latvia and Lithuania, joined the EU as part of the Eastern enlargement, its largest single expansion. The Baltics ensured Western security guarantees by joining the NATO as well.

The Baltic Enlargement of the Eurozone in 2011–15

Overall, at least after the Latvian EU-IMF economic adjustment programme in 2009–12, the Baltic trio has a credible record of sound economic and budgetary policies, and their deficits and public sector debt are among the lowest in the EU. This is the case not only as regards the determined policy action that all three took in the wake of the financial crisis, but also as regards their remarkable legal, democratic and economic transition since regaining independence in that dramatic summer of 1991. The experience of the Baltics is an encouraging demonstration for other Eurozone countries that prudent macroeconomic policies and bold economic reforms can create a virtuous circle that brings growth and prosperity.

In the Baltic states, the first two decades of the 2000s will be remembered as a time of deep integration to Europe. By May 2014, or the 10th anniversary of the Eastern enlargement, Estonia and Latvia had become part of the EMU, with Lithuania swiftly following suit and adopting the single currency from 1 January 2015, thus completing the "Baltic full house" in the euro area.

Estonia was the first Baltic state to fulfil the so-called Maastricht criteria, including low debt and low deficit and stable inflation, which are the prerequisites for entering the final stage of the monetary union. The country's dedication and hard work were recognized by all in the European Union on 13 July 2010, when the Ecofin Council decided that Estonia was ready to adopt the euro in January 2011. The country had made a vigorous effort in the middle of the deepest global economic crisis of recent history and had emerged from it with a robust fiscal stance and by far the lowest public debt level in the EU. This owed much to Estonia's flexible economy and its ability to adjust under a fixed exchange rate for already two decades (Image 15.1).

In the discussions of the Eurogroup in 2010, there were some sceptical voices and even opposition as to the sustainability of Estonia's economic

Image 15.1 Commission Vice-President Siim Kallas, former prime minister of Estonia, is withdrawing fresh and dry newly-printed Estonian euros from the ATM in the freezing downtown Tallinn on New Year's Eve 2011 (*Source* © European Union, 2011; European Commission—Photo: Raigo Pajula. Licensed under CC BY 4.0 [https://creativecommons.org/licenses/by/4.0/])

performance and membership. I defended Estonia with a simple but forceful argument, referring to one of the key criteria of euro membership: "Can you as current euro member states with 75% public debt on average really tell 'no' to a candidate country with 7.5% public debt? That's where Estonia stands today". With this swipe, the debate on Estonia's capacity to meeting the criteria was cut short.

Unsurprisingly, the positive news coming from Estonia was largely overshadowed by the worsening market confidence and the deteriorating economic situation in Greece, Portugal and Ireland at the time. Still, the Estonian accomplishment was and is a demonstration of the vitality of the monetary union and of the validity of its underlying principles. It underpinned the role of the euro as a medium-term policy anchor and confirmed that sustained policy efforts and a long-standing record of stability-oriented policies generate concrete results.

At the same time, it was clear that the euro adoption entailed major economic challenges for Estonia—as for any country. The major challenge for Estonia is to avoid the re-emergence of a boom-and-bust cycle similar to what occurred before the crisis in the early 2000s. The prolonged growth above economic potential in the first half of the decade was partly caused by a unique combination of factors, not likely to occur again in the foreseeable future. These factors related to early transformation included the economic transition and restructuring of the past two decades and the rapid financial deepening and accession to the EU, which opened new markets and helped modernize the regulatory environment. But they also led to the emergence of over-optimistic expectations among economic agents and an unsustainable, credit-driven domestic demand boom, coupled with excessive wage and price increases and a high current account deficit.

What can Estonia do to ensure a more balanced growth in the future? In my view, there are two main factors for a more sustainable growth.

First, it will be important to keep unemployment on a declining path and to ensure that skills evolve in line with the needs of the Estonian economy. Active labour market policies and educational systems that respond to the labour market needs are vital in raising productivity.

Second, Estonia has adopted a successful culture of fiscal prudence and sustainable public finances. I am convinced that a preservation of this culture will be truly beneficial for its citizens and for the Euro area as a whole.

Estonia is already well known as a frontline digital country thanks to its *eEstonia* approach. I also believe Estonia has useful experience to share in this respect with other member states, especially as *eEurope* is still in the making.

Latvia Comes Back from the Brink and Joins the Euro

On 5 June 2013, the Commission published its assessment of Latvia's readiness to adopt the euro. I was able to announce that in our view, Latvia met the conditions to join the single currency:

> Latvia's experience shows that a country can successfully overcome macroeconomic imbalances, however severe, and emerge stronger. Following the deep recession of 2008–9, Latvia took decisive policy action, supported by the EU-IMF-led financial assistance programme, which improved the flexibility and adjustment capacity of the economy within the overall EU framework for sustainable and balanced growth. And this paid off: Latvia is forecast to be the fastest-growing economy in the EU this year.

I added a general point on the euro: "Latvia's desire to adopt the euro is a sign of confidence in our common currency and further evidence that those who predicted the disintegration of the euro area were wrong".

The official seal of approval for Latvia's EMU membership was given by EU finance ministers in the Ecofin Council in the following month, on 9 July 2013.

How did Latvia come about from the deep crisis to fast growth again?

Since the nadir of the crisis in 2009, Latvia managed a very difficult economic adjustment process. I have no illusions about how hard the global financial crisis hit the Latvian people in 2008–9 in terms of the quickly falling GDP and rapidly rising unemployment. Wages were reduced by over 10% and the economy contracted by over 15% in 2009. Unemployment and labour force emigration initially soared.

The situation was deemed so dire in the end of 2008 that the IMF economists recommended currency devaluation and leaving the euro peg. This is understandable, as this has always been part of the IMF toolbox, and in the case of a country that is *not* a member or a candidate for a currency union, it usually provides with a more rapid and less painful adjustment—though with significant side effects too, e.g. for domestic SMEs with currency loans, especially in the era of free movement of capital. The Commission, boldly steered by then Economic and Monetary Affairs Commissioner Joaquin Almunia, and the ECB however firmly resisted this advice and instead recommended an internal adjustment, which would be hard in the short run but make the economy more resilient in the longer run. Latvia chose the latter alternative. In the case of Latvia, this worked.

This is the assessment of Jean Pisani-Ferry, one of the most prominent European economists and a founding member of the Bruegel think-tank: "Internal devaluation is not impossible to carry out. Latvia, a small Baltic country, managed to pull it off rather successfully following the financial crisis of 2008-2009… IMF economists recommended abandoning the euro peg and devaluing the currency. Latvia, backed by the ECB and the European Commission, rejected the advice… and decided instead to embark on an energetic process of internal adjustment".[2]

In 2016, Vivek Arora, an IMF official who participated in the post-financial crisis fire brigade, wrote in the ex post assessment that the IMF adapted its programme design as the crisis unfolded. He also concludes, in my view correctly, that "if the exchange rate is not available as a tool to help the economy adjust to shocks, we may need to prepare for longer programmes with more financing".[3]

In fact, maintaining the euro peg was crucial for the necessary financial stabilization that underpinned the later success of the Latvian EU-IMF adjustment programme. Confidence in the financial system, the lack of which triggered the crisis in 2008, was quickly restored. Latvian authorities remained firmly committed to the long-standing monetary and exchange rate arrangement. They also took major measures for financial system stabilization, particularly by restructuring ailing banks, while prudential supervision and regulation were strengthened.[4] But as we learned in early 2018, there were major problems in the banking sector and supervision. The US authorities found that the Latvian ABLV bank had been involved in money laundering, and the ECB's Supervisory Board declared it failing or likely to fail, which led to its winding up, as it was not in the public interest to save it. This calls for strengthening of financial supervision in Latvia, as well as reinforcement of European competences to combat money laundering more effectively.

In any case, in 2009–12 the determined implementation of the EU-IMF-led assistance programme helped Latvia to reform and to return to economic growth, probably more quickly than either the Commission or IMF initially thought. Indeed, Latvia became the fastest-growing EU economy in 2012. The Baltic tiger set an example for other European countries struggling with getting their economies running again, even though one cannot neglect the flipside of substantial emigration and brain drain, nor many remaining challenges, including high social inequality.

Not that it was an easy ride. I recall many difficult discussions with Valdis Dombrovskis, the clearly focused and bold Prime Minister of Latvia in 2009–13, on the pace of fiscal consolidation. I trust there are no hard feelings left, and the Commission's firm approach was taken as an encouragement to "do the Full Monty" and help the economy turn around quicker. Valdis Dombrovskis was re-elected in 2012 with 60% support, and in 2010–14, he served as my successor as Commission Vice-President for Economic and Monetary Affairs, with great distinction.

The Latvian reform programme has been used by contrasting schools of economic thought to prove their point. Dombrovskis responded to Paul Krugman who insisted that the programme was too harsh and could not succeed: "Krugman famously said back in December 2008 that Latvia is the new Argentina, it will inevitably go bankrupt, and now he has difficulty apparently admitting he was wrong".[5]

The Bank of Latvia together with the IMF held a conference in June 2012 on the most pertinent topic of "what lessons should the European policymakers draw from the adjustment experience of Latvia and the Baltics?" The panel included key policymakers of the crisis era, e.g. Christine Lagarde and Mario Draghi. On my behalf, I congratulated Latvia for the solid completion of the EU-IMF programme and the successful return to the markets. In my view, it proved the point that economic adjustment is possible without currency devaluation. I underlined this was the beginning of a long journey towards a sustainable economic and financial model, which can be turned into long-lasting success. I summarized the lessons of the crisis in Latvia for the rest of the Eurozone by underlining four issues: first, maintain cost and real competitiveness ("flexibility is an asset, *flexicurity* even better"); second, pursue a rigorous financial sector repair; third, keep up fiscal prudence and build a buffer to resist business cycles; and finally, watch out and prevent macroeconomic imbalances, also by the means of macro-prudential instruments that were then under development.

Lithuania's Turn to Join the Euro in 2015

After Latvia's successful euro adoption, the focus among the Baltic states shifted to Lithuania. On 4 June, the Commission published its 2014 Convergence Report in which it concluded that Lithuania fulfilled the Maastricht criteria and was ready to enter the final phase of the monetary union.

As I was heading to the Commission press room, I had only days earlier begun the last month of my 14-year career as a Commission official. So it was time to take a longer perspective and look back. It felt appropriate to hold a press conference presenting some very concrete results of the progress that had taken place over the past decades. I referred to the profound adjustment that had taken place in the Central and Eastern European economies, as we were celebrating their joining the EU almost exactly 10 years ago. In 1994, their income per head amounted to less than half of the EU's. In 2004, this ratio had increased to 58%. But in 2014, the income per head of the 2014 wave of accession was reaching 72% of the EU.

As far as Lithuania was concerned, its readiness to adopt the euro reflected its long-standing support for prudent fiscal policies and economic reforms. That reform momentum, driven in part by Lithuania's EU accession ten years previously, had led to a significant increase in prosperity: the country's per capita GDP has risen from just 24% of the EU28 average in 2004 to 52% in 2018.[6]

Against the background of the continuing crisis in Ukraine, it can now be more clearly seen that the development of Central and Eastern Europe could have played out very differently—and the hard work behind their democratic transitions should not be taken for granted. And certain developments, e.g. in Hungary and Poland, regrettably show that democratic transition is not irreversible. In any case, the success of the Baltic states in their political and economic transformation proves that European integration, properly used, has been a powerful driving force for stabilization, democracy and prosperity. This force should be maintained.

Just One—Or None?

I recall a discussion some time in 1997–98 with Andris Piebalgs, a very good Latvian colleague, who then served as the permanent representative of his country in the EU. That was a time when Estonia had a chance of becoming a candidate country, which was not yet considered a realistic status for Latvia and Lithuania at that point in time. My friend Andris insisted that we should support all three Baltic states, not only one, to become a candidate country. I recall responding that "now the choice is not one or three, but one or *none*". In fact, Estonia's status in the first group of six countries who started the negotiations on EU accession served to open the gates of Europe for all Baltic states and paved the way for their EU and euro membership.

Today, Europe and the world are in quite a different shape compared to the end of the Cold War and the Baltics' turning point in 1991 or compared to the EU's Eastern enlargement of 2004. Geopolitics has become predominant, and the Russian power politics are causing legitimate security concerns in the Baltic states. We in Europe are living with populism and fragmented political systems that create challenges of ungovernability. The Baltics have got their taste of that, as well. But in any case, all three Baltic states are today inside the economic and political core of Europe, including the NATO security umbrella. And that should be an encouraging and reassuring fact for the Baltics and good news for Europe as well.

Notes

1. Jarmo Virmavirta, Suomessa ei 1980-luvun lopulla tajuttu, kuinka lähellä Viron uusi itsenäisyys oli. *Turun Sanomat*, 20 July 2009.
2. Jean Pisani-Ferry, *The Euro Crisis and Its Aftermath*. Oxford University Press, 2013, pp. 117–118.
3. Vivek Arora, *Five Lessons from a Review of Recent Crisis Programs*. iMF Direct—The IMF Blog, 11 July 2016.
4. See, e.g., Gabriele Giudice, *The Adjustment in Latvia*, a slide set presented in the ELIAMEP conference, Poros, 8 July 2011. Giudice was the Commission's mission chief in Latvia in the critical years, and later on in Greece.
5. Markus Brunnermeier, Harold James, and Jean-Pierre Landau, *The Euro and the Battle of Ideas*. Princeton University Press, 2016, p. 147.
6. http://appsso.eurostat.ec.europa.eu/nui/submitViewTableAction.do.

16

Aftershocks That Didn't Explode—And the Brexit Bomb

While the most explosive years of the Eurozone crisis were over by spring 2013, many aftershocks still popped up in 2013–15 that endangered progress made until then. However, none of them—which can be seen more clearly now in retrospect, though not at the time when they were happening—did not explode to our face nor shake the still fragile recovery. But they could have done so, and that's why they should not be ignored in the writing of the history of the crisis.

This chapter discusses the events in Cyprus, Slovenia and Greece. The first of the aftershocks was the Cyprus banking crisis in the winter of 2012–13, although it had brewed for many years. It shook the country and its people, but did not derail the ongoing recovery in the Eurozone. In any case there is much to learn from it on how to deal and how *not* to deal with banking crises. The other financial-political aftershocks were Slovenia in 2012–13 and Greece (again) in 2015.

Cyprus: Crisis in the Oversized Banking Sector

Don't tell me there is no financial contagion. The discussions of a Greek debt write-off in Greece in late spring 2011 had immediate consequences for Cyprus. Fitch carried out a triple-notch downgrade and Standard & Poor's a one-notch downgrade on Cypriot sovereign debt at the end of May due to Cypriot banks' heavy exposure to Greek sovereign bonds. This led to a rally of increasing two-year spreads with the German bund, which reached their

© The Author(s) 2020
O. Rehn, *Walking the Highwire*, https://doi.org/10.1007/978-3-030-34592-1_16

new record-high of 2548 basis points in September 2011, blocking Cyprus from the international capital markets.

When considering the root causes of the Cyprus banking crisis, it is clear that her problems built up over many years. At their origin was the oversized banking sector (almost 1000% of GDP, roughly the same relative magnitude as in Iceland or Ireland) that thrived on attracting foreign deposits—not least from Russia—with very favourable conditions. The banking problems were aggravated by poor practices of risk management and banking supervision. Lacking adequate oversight, the largest Cypriot banks built up excessive risk exposures.

Cyprus was also fighting excessively high deficits. Cyprus' government balance went down from −5.3% in 2010 to −6.3% in 2011. Concerns of Cyprus' fiscal position materialized in July when Moody's downgraded the country's sovereign bonds by two notches. Demetris Christofias, the President of Cyprus, carried out a government reshuffle on 5 August and appointed Kikis Kazamias as the new finance minister. Christofias hailed from the nominally communist AKEL party, which did not make him a natural expert of international capitalism—unless you count his Marxist-Leninist roots for that. In his party office in 2005, I recall meeting V.I. Lenin in the form of a bust, and facing the red flag and a hammer and sickle. It would have felt rather surreal unless I had the experience of facing his Soviet comrades in the context of international youth cooperation in the 1980s. In practical politics though, AKEL was broadly similar to a normal centre-left party in Europe.

During the hot summer months, we had our hands full in finding a solution to financing a new programme for Greece. The Eurogroup meeting scheduled for 11 July 2011 threatened to be fractious, but given the pressing time constraints it was essential to make progress in creating a consensual and operational model for private sector involvement and an agreement between Greece and its creditors.

A part of our work was addressing possible contagion effects. On top of charting ring-fencing measures for other vulnerable countries, we had to have a plan in case the developments in Greece resulted in a disorderly outcome. We were well aware that the negative spillovers to Cyprus would have necessitated immediate arrangements for external financial assistance—the island's banking problems and consequent fiscal and macroeconomic imbalances were included in the reports and country-specific recommendations under the first European Semester in June 2011. With this in mind, the idea of Cyprus requesting a precautionary programme had been on the table in our internal meetings already well before the agreement on Greece's second rescue package that included private sector involvement.

Greece's rescue package on 21 July 2011 had major ramifications to Cyprus. To counter the increasing fears of Cypriot banks failing, the Central Bank of Cyprus strengthened capital requirements in July and domestic banks made an effort to increase their capital bases throughout the year. Nevertheless, our risk analysis showed that any haircut on Cypriot banks' Greek government bond holdings would cause the banks a gap of several billions of euros in funding needs. Concerns were also raised of risks linked to foreign deposit deleveraging, which we considered a possible second-round effect if confidence in the banking sector were to wane.

I expressed very serious concerns about the economic and banking situation in Cyprus to Finance Minister Kazamias in early November 2011. I told him that the Commission had carried out advanced preparations ahead of a possible Cypriot request for a precautionary programme, which would be unavoidable unless the persistent problems were immediately addressed. This was intended as the last wake-up call to Cyprus and its leadership. But accepting the fact that Cyprus was in need of a programme was a bitter pill to swallow for Cypriot politicians, and much time was wasted. The same story as with other programme countries, all over again.

The most burning issue was the overly inflated financial sector and the special relationship of Cypriot banks with Russia. Between the 2007–10 period alone, Russians had channelled—through banks—some €30 billion worth of funds to Russian-owned companies in Cyprus, a lion's share of Russian total foreign transactions. Due to the scale of this partnership, and the importance of the financial sector for the then Cypriot economy, Cypriot officials were anything but enthusiastic about having the Troika present their proposals for financial sector reform.

By fall 2011, the situation was looking dire. Cyprus needed money to refinance its debt, but the country had become de facto blocked from the international capital markets. Cyprus was running out of funds by early 2012.

From Russia with (Not Much) Love

But Cyprus had yet to play its (perceived) trump card, which came from Russia—probably with not much love. In October 2011, Cyprus requested and got a €2.5 billion loan from Russia, with an interest rate of 4.5% for 4.5 years—this was an attractive deal as Cyprus' 10-year benchmark bond traded on a yield of over 10%. The deal was meant to cover Cyprus' medium-term financing needs and avoid liquidity strains on local commercial banks.

Meanwhile, a Eurozone programme would have provided a much cheaper loan with ca. 2–3% interest rate. But that would have required an adjustment programme, which didn't suit the government.

The Russian loan made Cyprus even more dependent on Russian money and influence. In the face of a possible assistance programme, the deal made Cyprus' negotiation position more complicated: To what extent would they heed Russian interests if it came down to a bail-in?

Fast-forward to 2013. The Russian roulette came back if not with vengeance but certainly with significance in the resolution of the crisis in 2013, as correctly described by Professor Panicos Demetriades, who served as the Governor of the Central Bank of Cyprus during the heat of the crisis in 2012–14:

> The message [from Moscow to Nicosia] was that the Russians would be ready to contribute to help save Cyprus but the contribution should be limited to no more than 10% of their deposits… No one mentioned they were taxing the poor to protect not just Russian oligarchs but also the business model from which the Cyprus elite made their money. Nor that higher interest rates may have reflected increased risk.[1]

The year 2012 began with the financial world's eyes on Greece, again. The negotiations for a second economic adjustment programme went on until the final agreement was reached on 21 February 2012. The 53.5% haircut to private investors' Greek governmental securities had detrimental effects to the Cypriot banking sector, which had invested a lot into Greek bonds. The Bank of Cyprus, the biggest bank on the island, lost €1.8 billion and Laiki, the second biggest bank, lost €2.3–2.5 billion—around 60% of the banks' total equity.

Thus, the year 2011 came to a close without a request for assistance from Cyprus. After difficult negotiations, the government passed a budget law for 2012 in mid-December that included a significant number of consolidation measures with the aim of reducing government deficit from 6.3% of GDP in 2011 to 2.5% in 2012. These measures were a big step in the right direction, especially in terms of the criteria set to Cyprus in the excessive deficit procedure.

The significant weakening in the capital adequacy of Cyprus' two largest banks resulted in Moody's slashing the island state's credit rating to junk status in mid-March. Moody's was the second credit rating agency to do so after Standard & Poor's similar decision in January. Fitch, as the last of the three major credit rating agencies, followed suit on 25 June, which meant that Cyprus' bonds were disqualified from being accepted as collateral by the ECB, effectively cutting the country's access to financial markets.

After the Russian doping was running out by winter 2012–13, Cyprus started to turn to the Eurozone to cover its financing needs. On the same day when the last downgrade in credit ratings took place, i.e. in the mid-summer of 2012 or five days before it took over the EU's rotating presidency, Cyprus asked for a bailout from the EFSF/ESM to obtain financing to recapitalize its banks amid increasing risks.

It was estimated that a rescue package worth around 17 billion euros would be needed. Only the funding to recapitalize the banks would require around 10 billion euros. But the Eurozone member states were not ready to print money just like that. Binding external constraints were decided, which limited the room for manoeuvre: the member states made it absolutely clear that programme financing should not exceed 10 billion euros (out of the 17 billion euros).

Following a mandate from the Eurogroup, the Commission then began working on an adjustment programme for Cyprus with the ECB and the IMF. The progress was slow due to disagreements about the extent of necessary structural reforms and fiscal measures between the Troika and the Christofias administration. An agreement on the reforms was finally reached in November 2012 and many of them were voted through parliament before Christmas.

Agreeing on the reform agenda was only the first step on a bumpy road. The economic situation in Cyprus kept on getting worse in early 2013. There had been significant outflows of deposits from Cypriot banks since the beginning of the year.

On 20 February 2013, I called Wolfgang Schäuble and said to him:

> The situation in Cyprus has deteriorated significantly during the last week. There have been remarkable outflows of deposits last week and this Tuesday the outflows have accelerated. In case there is no deliberate action from the Eurogroup to reverse this trend, we may soon reach a situation in which the Cyprus authorities will be forced to declare a banking holiday and freeze the deposits, followed by capital controls. This can happen any moment. The Troika has intensified technical preparations to be ready, if this scenario materialises. In fact, we may have crossed the Rubicon already.

I recall Schäuble largely agreeing with the analysis and saying that they have also been monitoring Cypriot deposit outflows. The concerns were widespread in the markets. Among the financial sector analysts, there was a large consensus that the two largest banks Laiki and Bank of Cyprus were bankrupt and should be wound down. And among the finance ministers, there was the sentiment that the Central Bank of Cyprus had taken a lot of risks through the Emergency Liquidity Assistance (ELA), accepted by the ECB, and it was needed to deal with those risks now. Many finance ministers were also of the view that the ECB blocking the bail-in for Ireland (and the private sector involvement for Greece) was a mistake.

Among the creditor member states, the views were converging: (1) the two biggest banks should be wound down (in line with the IMF position), (2) the corporate tax rate should be increased to the level of Ireland (12.5%), (3) the IMF must be on board with financial assistance, and (4) if Russia is ready to take over a bank, then Russian involvement is acceptable; otherwise it doesn't play a big role (N.B. these events took place more than one year before the annexation of Crimea). The Commission did not share all these views, but we had to know them for planning a reasonable solution—there was no perfect way forward any more.

In January 2013, the Eurogroup had elected a new Chair, Jeroen Dijsselbloem, who had just two months before been appointed as the Dutch Minister of Finance. He had a tough baptism of fire, as he had to jump to a fast-moving train of the Cyprus rescue. But he quickly learned the trade and became a broadly respected Eurogroup Chair, whose worldview is that of an economic reformist and fiscally responsible policymaker with a social-democratic background. Soon we learned to work well together. When I faced public criticism due to the Commission's consistent implementation of economic governance and fiscal rules, or outright opposition from some member states under scrutiny, Jeroen was always fair and supportive.

In the Eurogroup of 11 March 2013, I said it was important to strive for the conclusion to a programme with Cyprus shortly after the presidential elections scheduled for mid-February. There had been a toxic leak of an early version of a Troika working document, which mentioned a full bail-in option. The leak had only increased the urgency, not least since Cypriot banks lost a whopping €750 million over the first week after the leak. We knew we were walking on a very tight rope, because there was heavy political pressure from Germany and the IMF to have a substantial, although still partial, bail-in, in some form, in order to reach an agreement on a programme. On the other hand, we had no other choice but to publicly dismiss the full bail-in option to avoid inciting panic in the markets.

A very complicated discussion on how to cover the financing needs of Cyprus took place over the winter months. The Troika had a hard time getting past the red lines that a group of member states, including Germany, had vis-à-vis the package worth around €17 billion of which €10 billion were needed to recapitalize the banks and the rest to cover the fiscal needs of the state. Two strong external constraints reduced room for manoeuvre: the fact that the IMF insisted on a debt-to-GDP ratio of not more than 100% by 2020, and the fact that key Eurozone member states including Germany made clear that programme financing should not exceed €10 billion.

This implied that at least €6 billion financing gap needed to be covered by bail-in of some sort. Our preferred line in the Commission was to protect the insured deposits under €100,000 and introduce a higher levy on uninsured deposits, usually held by wealthier persons and companies. However, soon it became clear that the high levy of around 15% on uninsured deposits (i.e. those above €10,000) was not acceptable to the Cypriot decision-makers.

By March, the economic situation had deteriorated so badly that the scenario of the more gradual economic adjustment was not on the cards anymore. Especially, the state of the banks worsened rapidly. Soon it became clear that the second biggest bank, Laiki, had to be resolved immediately. The risk of a complete collapse of the entire banking system—and thus a sweeping loss of deposits and savings and a disorderly default of the sovereign—was about to materialize. That would have been a disaster for Cyprus and the Cypriot people.

During the Eurogroup discussion on the night of 15–16 March 2013, various options were explored with the leadership of Eurogroup Chair Jeroen Dijsselbloem and exceptionally also by the European Council President Herman van Rompuy, who was actively brokering a package with President Nicos Anastasiades of Cyprus.

After a fairly chaotic night, ultimately the Cypriots committed to cover the financing gap of €5.8 billion by introducing a levy of 6.75 and 9.9% on deposits. It was the strangest policy discussion and decision I have been involved (I've *had to* be involved, more precisely): a decision was **taken**, indeed in a passive voice. The ad hoc meeting that prepared the decision was not properly organized, and no one knew who would be responsible for making the proposal. I had no mandate from the Commission. No one wanted to claim the birth-right nor commitment to it afterwards.

Ultimately, it all eroded in the subsequent days when the Cypriots during the Eurogroup conference call on 18 March refused to amend the structure of the levy to exempt insured depositors entirely, in spite of the encouragement of the rest of the Eurogroup and the Troika. It became clear that the high levy (15.6%, instead of 9.9%) which this would have implied on uninsured deposits (= the deposits above 100,000 euros) would not be acceptable to Cypriot leadership.

Following the rejection of the levy by the Cypriot House of Representatives on 19 March, Laiki came under massive pressure and the priority became for the Cypriot parliament to adopt bank resolution and capital restriction laws, and then to get an agreement on a programme to avoid an outright default of the state. In the ten days up to the agreement in the Eurogroup on the 25th of March, when the key elements of the programme were agreed, the banks remained closed. When they re-opened, the Cypriot authorities imposed capital controls to avoid the flight of deposits—a justifiable move given the tough circumstances the island was facing.

So by the time of the Eurogroup met again, there were in our view no longer any optimal solutions left on the table, only hard choices—and an imperative to reach a viable agreement with no further delay.

The agreement that was reached on Sunday night largely reflected the original IMF proposal. Even if the agreement was not our preferred option, the priority then was to implement it as well as possible: to minimize the negative impact on the economy and financial stability, and help Cyprus to move forward.

The programme was designed to support Cyprus over the period of 2013–16 in overcoming the burden of the past and correcting the excessive economic imbalances from which it was suffering. It aimed at ensuring a smaller but resilient and transparent banking sector. Reforming the legal framework for anti-money laundering and ensuring its effective implementation was a key element in this respect, and a necessary condition for ESM funding.

In fiscal policy, the programme facilitated the elimination of Cyprus' excessive deficit over four years. It also outlined a broad agenda of structural reforms to create conditions for the renewal of the Cypriot economy, building on its strengths, such as its well-educated and skilled labour force and tradition of entrepreneurship.

What, in retrospect, is the verdict of crisis management in Cyprus in the light of the recovery? According to the European Commission analysis in the autumn of 2017, "Economic growth has exceeded expectations in recent quarters... forecast to reach 3.5% in 2017 and... remain robust over 2018–19. Unemployment is set to continue falling... on the fiscal side, headline surpluses are expected to occur in 2017–19, underpinned by a favourable macroeconomic environment".

Sounds good, and it is certainly better than most of us expected in 2013. However, there is a downside still, which is the slower recovery of the banking sector. Nobody expected that the Cypriot banking sector would return to the extremely unhealthy and unsustainable pre-crisis conditions, but there are still major challenges left to complete the financial repair. The amount of bad loans is high, the profitability of banks is weak, and the capital buffers are, at most, mediocre. But within the sound macroeconomic context, this should certainly be manageable.

What Are the Essential Lessons Learnt from the Cyprus Crisis?

First of all, Cyprus became, unintentionally but on her part not that innocently, the first testing ground for an effective bail-in, which was made a rule for the Eurozone banking union. While a shock initially, the bail-in has helped to protect the taxpayer as intended and resulted in a milder contraction than a traditional bailout.

Don't delay the adjustment, is the other lesson. Prevention is always better than correction or mitigation. The European Stability Mechanism should be developed accordingly. In my view, a viable alternative would be a short-term ESM facility of precautionary nature, probably with a lower degree of conditionality.

With regard to Cyprus' future, let me admit I take it also very personally: I recall having worked hard for five years as Commissioner for enlargement to facilitate the reunification of the country. I regret that there has been no decisive progress recently. Namely it is still worth recalling that the reunification of the island would give a major boost to the economic and social development of Cyprus.

Slovenia's Economic Turnaround in 2012–13

Slovenia, a small and beautiful country in the northern pocket of the Adriatic Sea and at the gate to the Western Balkans, and a former part of both the Habsburg Empire and Yugoslavia, emerged into the radar screen of the financial fire brigades in the course of 2012. I knew the country well, as I had mediated in 2008–9 on the border dispute as regards the Piran Bay between Slovenia and Croatia.

Following an analysis of the Commission in spring 2012, I thought a public warning was needed, to give backing to the country's government for rapid decisions to re-balance the economy. In a speech on 15 June, I said that there are serious imbalances in Slovenia as to corporate debt, banking stability and external competitiveness. Some policy action was taken in late 2012. Notably, the Slovenian parliament adopted a pension reform on 4 December 2012, while a seemingly populist referendum request, which would probably have derailed the solution, was avoided.

However, the threat of un-governability haunted Slovenia in the form of a very low hurdle and correspondingly easy access to call a referendum. For instance, in December 2012 the country's public sector trade unions filed a referendum request regarding the budget the parliament had already approved for the 2013/14 fiscal year. Even the adopted budget was on the soft side and was expected to lead Slovenia to miss its correction deadline with the deficit of 3.9% of GDP, while public debt was forecast to breach 60% of GDP in 2014.

Even more serious problem was the large amount of bad loans and the major needs of recapitalization in the Slovenian banking sector. For this, a "bad bank", i.e. an asset management company, was considered a solution. Moreover, the then ongoing labour market and constitutional reforms were subject to political risk.

By late 2012, the Slovenian government had proposed an asset management company for banking rescue and to deal with the large amount of bad loans in the banking books. However, at that time implementation questions still remained. The banks needed fresh capital, but we were aware that the raising of financing would be difficult as long as there was uncertainty around rescue measures.

I made these points to Prime Minister Janez Jansa at the Berlaymont on 14 December 2012. I told him privately but bluntly that the Commission staff thought that Slovenia could not manage its economic and banking challenges without a financial rescue programme, including of course the normal conditionality, and many member states shared this view. I repeated this to the new Prime Minister Alenka Bratushek in February 2013 soon after she was appointed. It was not an empty pledge, as our staff and most member states shared that view, which was not necessarily mine. Only with a very determined programme of corrective actions could Slovenia overcome its economic problems without a rescue programme.

In the following months, the economic and financial situation of Slovenia still got worse and worse. In the Dublin Eurogroup meeting on 12–13 April 2013, I signalled that the macroeconomic and financial imbalances in Slovenia are excessive and aggravating and needed to be addressed urgently:

> With negative economic trends and substantial risks stemming from high corporate debt and deleveraging, the inter-linkages with the sovereign are aggravating the case of Slovenian banks. These risks are compounded by the limited

adjustment capacity in the labour and capital markets and due to an economic structure dominated by state ownership. Recent rise in the bank and bond spreads and the downgrade of the Slovenian banks pose an additional problem for the government, who faces debt redemption in June. Recapitalization of banks adds to the challenge of the public sector funding. These are the main arguments for a programme.

It was straight talk in as plain and broken Finnish "rally English" as possible. I made this as the last wake-up call before Slovenia indeed would have no other alternative than to go for a programme. However, I could also provide the last olive branch by saying that "in the Commission's view there is a chance to avoid a programme, if you urgently provide a credible policy response in the forthcoming National Reform Programme, starting with concrete actions already in the coming weeks".

I referred to concrete measures in the consolidation of public finances, the banking sector strategy, and structural reforms and state-ownership. In the banking sector, we called for a transparent and reliable asset quality review and stress tests of domestic banks. In addition to these immediate measures, in 2014–15 we requested an expenditure review of public finances, a clean-up of the banks' balance sheets with the help of the bad bank, and full privatization of state-owned banks.

In the course of 2013, after much procrastination in Slovenia and desperation in our quarters, a little miracle happened. It was indeed a very close call, and e.g. the Central Bank Governor Bostjan Jazbec said still in November 2013 that he cannot rule out a request for a rescue programme, as the recession was deeper than expected.[2] So from early 2013 onwards, Slovenia began taking decisive action to address its serious economic weaknesses. To the surprise of many, it made progress and could thus avoid a rescue programme. In May 2013, I could state that the Commission recommends a two-year extension to the correction deadline of public finances. Moreover, the government took measures to improve cost competitiveness and started a serious clean-up of the banking sector.

By and large, the banking repair was a success story. Against this backdrop it is striking that Governor Bostjan Jazbec was brought under investigation for alleged irregularities by the central bank during the banking sector overhaul in 2013. The ECB took legal action against Slovenia due to the infringement of independence and confiscation of documents in the central bank. As of this writing the case is still open.

What was the outcome of these bold policy actions? As said, Slovenia avoided a rescue programme and returned to the path of recovery and growth sooner than anybody expected. This further underlines the importance of financial stability for sustained growth. This is how Reuters reported on Slovenia in June 2017: "Slovenia returned to growth a year after the bank overhaul and the government expects the economy to expand by 3.6% this year from 2.5% in 2016, mainly due to a rise in investment, exports and domestic spending".

Slovenia's rapid economic recovery is a classical case in point of a small country taking decisive and united action when facing almost a mission impossible. The country and its people got their act together at the eleventh hour. From the other Europeans, that deserves due respect and appreciation.

Game, Set and Match—The Rise and Fall of Game Theory in Greece

In 2015, with yet another snap elections, the situation in Greece turned again to yet another drama. The difference to the period of 2010–12 was indeed that now in 2015 it was purely political and self-inflicted, while in the earlier phase it was partly due to external conditions of the global financial crisis and partly due to long-lasting structural problems in the Greek economy and body politic (Image 16.1).

As I was calling for national unity in Greece, I also tried to stay in contact with the opposition. In December 2013, I met with Alexis Tsipras, the leader of Syriza, who soon became the Prime Minister of Greece. Tsipras had his speaking points on an iPad, which didn't feel overly revolutionary or Marxist, and we had a constructive, almost friendly bilateral meeting in my small office in Strasbourg.

But it was not to be only plain sailing, which nobody of course expected. The victorious Syriza movement in 2014–15 wanted to challenge the functioning principles of the euro. It aimed at, especially when Tsipras entrusted Yanis Varoufakis with the Ministry of Finance, "revolutionizing" the economic and legal framework of the Eurozone. Varoufakis was supposedly playing a prisoner's dilemma and threatening the Eurozone with a unilateral Grexit, but ended up in a six-month shadow-boxing dogfight with the Europeans who refused to enter the ring and watched calmly from the outside. The outcome was a no-brainer.

Referring to the events in Greece in 2014–15, Commissioner Pierre Moscovici has argued that the second programme (2012–15) could have been completed if the New Democracy-PASOK coalition government had agreed to the social security reform and to the value-added tax increase for

Image 16.1 Alexis Tsipras, then opposition leader on Syriza, pictured in Strasbourg in December 2013 with "an illiterate, yellow, third category understrapper" [to paraphrase Professor Yanis Varoufakis] (*Source* © European Union, 2013; European Commission—Photo: Mathieu Cugnot. Licensed under CC BY 4.0 [https://creativecommons.org/licenses/by/4.0/])

the islands in 2014, which could have saved Greece from much political turmoil. Yannis Strournaras, the finance minister in the reformist coalition government of 2012–14 and the current Governor of the Bank of Greece, concurs halfway with Moscovici by saying that "assuming rational and realistic behaviour from both sides, a third programme could have been avoided". He has calculated that the cost of the events of 2014–15 were in the magnitude of 86 billion euros for Greek taxpayers, based on the debt sustainability analysis conducted by the IMF: whereas Greek public debt in 2022 would have been 105–110% of GDP according to the 2014 analysis, the ratio was projected a 160–170% of GDP in 2015. The extra cost was caused by politics and equals to the difference of approx. 55–60% of GDP. So the Varoufakis game-theory laboratory experiment cost Greece and the euro area some 86 billion euros.[3]

I have not much to add to what has already been written about the episode, since I was not at the epicentre of the events any more, as I was serving in my parliamentary duties after being elected to the European Parliament in May 2014. In fact, George Papaconstantinou, one of Varoufakis' predecessors, coins it well:

Despite their bravado, the Greek government and its game-theory experts were badly outplayed. They played straight into the hands of those who were willing to see Greece exit. The rest of the Eurozone waited patiently for the game to play itself out.[4]

While the second Greek crisis of 2014–15 was an unnecessary and irresponsible political drama, which put Greece at the risk of having to leave the Eurozone and derailed the ongoing economic recovery of the country, it had one positive consequence. It cleaned up the air from exit debates in the Eurozone. Brexit is another story, and its roots deeper in history, as I will discuss below.

Still the "Troika"—Or Rather a European Monetary Fund?

In Chapter 1, I referred to the Impossible Triangle as the *modus operandi* of the Eurozone rescue programmes. I was painfully aware of the problems in policy design and coordination. Let "the other side of the table" testify on the workings of the "impossible triangle". George Papaconstantinou, the finance minister of Greece at the time, has written in his perceptive testimonial *Game Over* (2016):

> The Troika also had problems. The three institutions had never worked together before on such a programme... The Eurozone was putting up most of the money, so one would expect the Commission to be pre-eminent. Nevertheless, the financing arrangement meant that it had to ensure that the decision to be taken would be palatable even to the most difficult of the Eurozone countries... Bringing the IMF into the arrangement explicitly questioned the competence of the Commission and its ability to reassure the markets. This gave the Fund a weight in the negotiations larger than its one-third share in the financing... Despite the allocation of roles, there were tensions; on a number of occasions, negotiations had to be suspended until the three institutions could agree among each other.

I can confess that Papaconstantinou's analysis, by and large, corresponds to my experience. Yannis Stournaras had similar views:

> It is natural to have tensions in such a difficult negotiation. But it always stayed within the bounds of politeness and civil debate. Poul Thomsen, as head of the IMF mission in Greece, the institution with the toughest stance, had his views, and I, as Minister of Finance, had mine... in the end, we always

worked out [the differences]. Valuable time was lost, of course, but I hope we have all learned our lesson and are now wiser about how to better shield the euro area by improving its architecture.[5]

The essential lesson we should in my view learn from this is that the Eurozone still needs to upgrade its own capacity to act. We must make the ESM decision-making more effective and rapid, and provide it with new tools of precautionary nature.

The need to improve the functioning of the EU-IMF Troika was accelerated by the criticism of the European Parliament, especially against the participation of the IMF in the Troika. Hence, in order to straighten the lines and improve the execution, I suggested for Mario Draghi and Christine Lagarde to meet and discuss these at the level of the principals of the three institutions. The key conclusion was that all three institutions committed themselves to the tripartite cooperation and forward-looking, timely execution of the programmes. An exit strategy of the programme countries to market financing was broadly agreed. To tackle communication problems, it was agreed to have a "hotline" to settle possible disagreements rapidly at the level of principals. All this helped to improve the atmosphere and get the three institutions work better together, both at the headquarters and especially on the ground.

On the IMF participation, I said we initially had our doubts, but we have learnt to live with it and appreciate the Fund's professionalism, and will defend it in the EP. Lagarde willingly admitted that the IMF takes part with a smaller share of funding but larger influence—it's not their problem. (Well, true enough.) She pointed out that from the IMF standpoint it was really peculiar that a central bank is part of the Troika, not subject of a programme. (Quite a smart counter-attack!) The ECB had two special points of concern: first, the IMF is needed in the Troika, since the member states do not trust the Commission, which is regarded as political; second, no sudden breaks from bushes with the other institutions, like the IMF fiscal report on Greece.

My sentiment after these meetings, and taking into account the debates in our joint hearing in the EP, was that in the short term the IMF would still have to take part in any possible Eurozone financial rescue programme. But in the medium-to-long-term, both the ECB and the IMF were not natural overseers of a Eurozone programme; the ECB since it would almost inevitably be drawn to broader policy decisions that would risk compromising its central bank independence, and the IMF since it is not considered appropriate by the rest of the world that it should have to put money on the table to rescue richer Eurozone economies. This has obvious implications for the Eurozone reform. I will return to this matter in Chapter 19.

Brexit: Collateral Damage or a Flanking Explosion?

While these intra-Eurozone aftershocks did not end in a financial or economic explosion, another kind of massive political explosion took place on the North-Western fringes of the Continent, soon after the worst was over in Europe: Brexit.

It has been claimed that Brexit would have been collateral damage of the euro crisis, as the British people supposedly reacted to uphill struggles of the Eurozone and didn't want to be associated with the EU any more. I find that by far too simplistic. Rather, it was a flanking explosion that coincided timewise with the euro crisis.

During the euro crisis, the British approach to the Eurozone development was in fact transformed to a more constructive direction, compared to the country's traditionally restrictive, even opposing view on the single currency. In 2011, at the height—or trough—of the crisis George Osborne, then Chancellor of the Exchequer, stated that the "remorseless logic" of monetary union takes the single currency members in the direction of greater fiscal union. "I think we have to accept that greater Eurozone integration is necessary to make the single currency work and that is very much in our national interest. We should be prepared to let that happen". Osborne admitted that this flew in the face of traditional British policy.[6] I wish Osborne had been right in his prediction, as we haven't seen a quantum leap in Eurozone reform!

While the euro crisis, and the global financial crisis before that, played a role in changing the mindset of public opinion in Britain (and elsewhere), it hardly was a decisive factor. Instead, the long and winding road to Brexit was paved by the politically acrimonious British (primarily English) debate over the past three or four decades, further fuelled by the country's mostly Eurosceptic yellow press. The EU is certainly not faultless, but also not the kind of monster that it has been portrayed as by much of the British media or the country's Eurosceptic commentators and politicians. During my one-and-half decades in the European Commission, I found that in no other EU member state was it so difficult—virtually impossible—to lead an analytical and substantive debate on Europe than in the UK. To my regret, British pragmatism and English empiricism were conspicuous with their absence.

Yet Britain in Europe is a subject about which I speak with particular interest, as I have a very special relationship with Britain. I have great affinity and affection for the country. My mother was an English teacher. I have a degree from a British university. Two of my cousins have British passports. I've watched the English and Premier League all my life. I am a lifelong supporter of Manchester United. And I have been an equally strong supporter of Britain being fully and actively engaged in the European Union, a Union of which it should be an essential part.[7]

As of this writing, the answer to the question "To Brexit or not to Brexit, and how?" is still anything but clear. Anyway we know that there will be substantial economic and political damage, mostly for the UK but also for the EU.

The closest partners of the UK, like the Finns and other Nordics, do much regret the UK's decisions to leave the Union. After the Brexit vote in 2016, a Finnish friend of mine wrote to me with sadness: "Did I waste 30 years of my life? Perhaps". He has devoted a big part of his life to European integration and counted on Britain's role in it and, even more fundamentally, on Britain's role in the wider Western security and economic community. Many of us share the same feeling and disappointment.

But feelings cannot prevail over reason, as the EU must defend its own interests and fix today's and tomorrow's Europe. During the process of Brexit negotiations, patiently led on the EU side by Michel Barnier, it has been important that the EU has not let the whole of Europe slide into prolonged political and economic turbulence due to the Brexit mess, which is Britain's mess and should not be made Europe's. It is the legitimate right and indeed profound responsibility of EU leaders to contain the contagion from the UK and keep the turbulence in Europe as small and short as possible. The EU is not a charitable organization, but a community of nations that has to look after its member states' and citizens' interests.

In some ways, the UK's relationship with Europe is still conditioned by her imperial past and island status. In most of Europe, in smaller and even large member states, but less so in Britain, it is widely recognized that as a political community the European Union has stronger clout in world politics than individual member states. In our time of trade tensions or even trade wars, the EU's common trade policy and single market provide strong backbone to maintain favourable trading conditions for every member state. Combatting climate change would be much more difficult without the joint and bold approach of the EU. Even the EU's biggest member states are not great powers by global standards but need the backbone of the EU.

Sentiment among the Eton and Oxbridge-educated English political establishment is quite different, which tends to be characterized by the dictum of Lord Palmerston soon two centuries ago: "Nations have no permanent friends or allies; they only have permanent interests". That approach may have worked in the distant past in a divided Europe, but it is in a fundamental contradiction to what the EU today is all about—the essence of the EU is having "permanent friends and allies"!

For over four decades by now, Britain has been stronger thanks to its membership of the European Union: more dynamic economically, more equitable socially, and more influential in world affairs. But it has clung to the memory of its imperial height, the remnants of which have not left the collective consciousness in many corners of the world—and not in Britain itself, in many ways.

To illustrate Europe's importance for Britain, in my view Dr. Simon Sweeney from the University of York hit the nail on the head when he wrote as follows:

> What did the EEC/EU ever do for us? Not much, apart from: providing 57% of our trade; structural funding to areas hit by industrial decline; clean beaches and rivers; cleaner air; lead-free petrol; restrictions on landfill dumping; a recycling culture; cheaper mobile charges; cheaper air travel; single market competition bringing quality improvements and better industrial performance; break-up of monopolies; Europe-wide patent and copyright protection; no paperwork or customs for exports throughout the single market; freedom to travel, live and work across Europe; funded opportunities for young people to undertake study or work placements abroad; labour protection and enhanced social welfare; smoke-free workplaces; EU-funded research and industrial collaboration; European arrest warrant....

I must stop here for the sake of space, as he listed dozens of other things that the EU has brought for Britain. But he summed it up well:

> All of this is nothing compared with its greatest achievements: the EU has for 60 years been the foundation of peace between European neighbours after centuries of bloodshed. It furthermore assisted the extraordinary political, social and economic transformation of 13 former dictatorships, now EU members, since 1980… We must play a full part in enabling the Union to be a force for good in a multipolar global future.

That's the point. And the European Union is stronger today because of Britain's tremendous contribution to it. Our economy is more open and dynamic as a result of Britain's liberal instincts, which have been an important counterweight to the regulatory reflex which still sometimes surfaces.

The single market we have built up over the last three decades owes a lot to those liberal instincts. But let's be clear about one thing: the single market needs rules, regulations and strong and effective institutions in order to function properly. Without those, there is no single market. Prime Minister Margaret Thatcher understood this when she signed the Single European Act and had it ratified.

Therefore, it would be in everyone's interests for Britain to be an active player in European decision-making. This is a game in which, if I were a British citizen, I would want my country to be playing as a midfield playmaker rather than watching from the sidelines. No one ever scored goals sitting on the bench.

Be that as it may, the most regrettable human consequence of Brexit is that the votes cast by older generations will take away from younger British citizens a lot of future opportunities to travel, study and work in Europe. While realizing that the inherent logic of Brexit-polarised UK body politic is taking the country towards a hard Brexit, the perspective of younger generations is one important reason why there are many in Europe like me who would wish that the UK could in the course of the process decide to stay very close to the European family.

To my mind, the most reasonable and just about realistic alternative for now would be to negotiate a customs union-type agreement between the UK and the EU. That would serve as a very close bridge between the two unions, until the UK decides to return to the European community of nations—during the next generation.

Notes

1. Panicos Demetriades, *A Diary of the Euro Crisis in Cyprus: Lessons for Bank Recovery and Resolution.* Palgrave Macmillan, 2017.
2. Reuters, *Slovenian Central Bank Chief Warns of Looming Bailout*, 15 November 2013.
3. Interview with Yannis Stournaras, *Kathimerini*. English edition, 23 August 2018.
4. George Papaconstantinou, *Game Over*. Papadoulos Publishing, 2016.
5. Interview with Stournaras, *Kathimerini*, 2018.
6. https://www.ft.com/content/e357fe94-b2ec-11e0-86b8-00144feabdc0.
7. See also my speech at Policy Network, London, 28 February 2013. https://europa.eu/rapid/press-release_SPEECH-13-174_en.htm.

Part IV

Learning the Lessons

17

The Jury Is Out: Fiscal Multiplier vs. Financial Accelerator

In past years, there have been intensive political and academic debates on the lessons of the crisis and on the policy mixes to contain and overcome it. Southern European interpretations have tended to call for more solidarity and the pooling of the debt burden, while Northern European analysis has underlined the need to build a stability union and stick to fiscal prudence and structural reform. Of course—and fortunately—there are many contributions that overcome this South–North divide.

Leading retrospective analyses of the Eurozone's performance during the crisis focus on both institutions and policies. Among the main institutional explanations are the structural shortcomings and unfinished construction of the economic and monetary union, such as the weakness and/or false twist of the Stability and Growth Pact or, from another angle, the lack of a lender of last resort due to the supposedly limited mandate of the European Central Bank. Another recognized effect is the original sin of Maastricht in terms of not providing any Eurozone-wide banking supervision, macro-prudential instruments or a financial stability mechanism.

Excessive fiscal rigour ("austerity"), the slow pace of structural reform and the cumulative macroeconomic imbalances and indebtedness are among the main policy-related explanations, even if they may have been rooted in the construction of the EMU. Macroeconomic imbalances are considered the usual suspect—rightly in my view, since this time it was not so different. As Richard Baldwin et al. describe it, the root causes of the Eurozone crisis were "the imbalances [that] were extremely unoriginal – too much public and private debt borrowed from abroad".

© The Author(s) 2020
O. Rehn, *Walking the Highwire*, https://doi.org/10.1007/978-3-030-34592-1_17

In this chapter, I will assess how these policy-related explanations perform in the light of empirical evidence of economic growth and fiscal balance. The analysis is based on OECD data on economic growth and fiscal position of both the Eurozone and the United States in 2009–15. Note that the data for the Eurozone are in aggregate and represent the general government balance in the respective jurisdictions. The statistical comparison is supplemented by real-world historical observations of the time that are considered relevant for policy outcomes.

In analyses of the management of the Eurozone debt crisis, the main explanatory parameters are usually the following: (1) fiscal policy; (2) monetary policy; (3) structural reform; (4) debt sustainability; and (5) financial instability. Let me provide some examples of these lines of reasoning.

First, fiscal policy. As discussed in the previous chapter, many analysts and commentators have been highly critical of the fiscal policy pursued in the euro area in 2011–12. For instance, the former ECB Vice-President Vitor Constâncio said in his reflective farewell speech in May 2018: "What really was responsible for the recession of 2012/2013 was the coordinated fiscal consolidation in which all member states engaged". He is correct in regard to the asymmetric economic adjustment in the Eurozone, as the deficit countries were not able to boost growth through fiscal stimulus or higher wage increases, while the surplus countries did not want to, as pointed out in Chapter 1. Despite the Macroeconomic Imbalance Procedure, created by 2011, there were no policy instruments, such as ones through which the Commission could require a more symmetric rebalancing process or a better-calibrated aggregate fiscal policy stance. However, we must also note that the ECB Governing Council itself was calling for even more rigorous fiscal consolidation than either the Ecofin Council or the European Commission. Namely, the ECB Governing Council consistently and continuously fired its call for more rigorous fiscal consolidation, like in this statement in September 2011:

Turning to fiscal policies… *to ensure credibility, it is now crucial that the announced measures be frontloaded and implemented in full*. Governments need to stand ready to implement further consolidation measures, notably on the expenditure side, if risks regarding the attainment of the current fiscal targets materialize… *All euro area governments need to demonstrate their inflexible determination to fully honour their own individual sovereign signature*, which is a decisive element in ensuring financial stability in the euro area as a whole. (emphasis added)

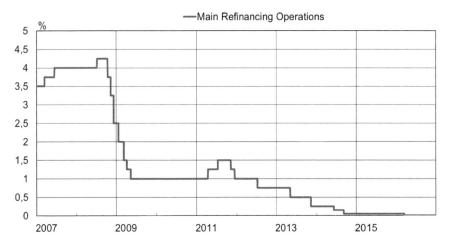

Fig. 17.1 The Main Refinancing Operations Rate (MRO) in 2007–16 (*Sources* ECB and Macrobond)

The forceful wording of "inflexible determination" stands out as the ECB's guiding principle of more rigorous fiscal consolidation, or as some would put it, of austerity. Right or wrong, it is hard to see how this position of the Governing Council could be considered *less* rigorous in calling for fiscal entrenchment!

The second line of argument is the criticism against the ECB rate hikes in spring and summer 2011. As illustrated in Fig. 17.1, the key policy rate (= Main Refinancing Operations Rate, MRO) was raised in April 2011 (0.25%) and in July (0.25%), so 0.5% in total. But these rate hikes were reversed in full in the same year when interest rates were lowered in November (−0.25%) and December (−0.25%).

This criticism is in line with the likes of Carlo Bastasin and James Surowiecki, mentioned in Chapter 8: "a fatal mistake", "like kicking the economy when it was down". This has been argued by many other commentators over the years, both at the time and in hindsight. Constâncio, who served as Vice-President of the ECB in 2010–18, also admits in retrospect that the rate hikes were a mistake, although he points out that growth was solid then (though I don't recall that) and inflation rising.[1] When looking at the period carefully, one can see that core inflation only picked up in spring 2011, and at that time, GDP growth had already stalled. Even though headline inflation peaked at 3% in 2011, the weakening economic outlook started to reduce the underlying inflation pressures. I find the critique of the 2011 rate hikes quite inevitable and reasonable. But that is certainly not the whole explanation, considering the size of the hikes, the increases in the borrowing costs and the magnitude of the recession.

A third argument could be the lack of structural reforms in the member states. It is indeed true that reforms were a core part of the solution to overcome the Eurozone's slow growth. But I would not subscribe to the view that the lack of structural reforms as such was ***the primary root cause*** for the financial and debt crises. Rather, the slow rhythm of reforms has hindered productivity and job creation. Having said that, there is no empirical evidence that this precisely would have triggered the crisis or the double-dip.

Fourth, debt sustainability. The *FT* economics writer Martin Sandbu, in his intelligent book *Europe's Orphan*, lays the blame on those Eurozone policy-makers who resisted debt restructuring in spring-summer 2010. In an ideal world—in a world without damaging spillovers and financial contagion, and rid of institutional constraints—this argument has definitive merit. However, when regarding debt restructuring as the silver bullet to resolve the euro crisis, Sandbu neglects the political economy constraints which stemmed from the "impossible triangle" or the divisions among the member states and EU institutions on the matter in 2010–11. He also vastly underestimates the contagion effect, which was in full swing in Europe until fall 2012.

Hence, I am tempted to say that Sandbu has a strong point in theory, but hits off mark in practice—which erodes the foundations of his analysis in the real world. Having said that, Sandbu is right in his conclusions by underlining the paramount importance of building a solid banking union and applying a bail-in and resolution regime, which would also make it more realistic and credible to expect some form of debt restructuring as a standard practice in crisis management in the future.[2]

Fifth and finally, as indicated above and further developed below, the collapse of financial stability was in many ways a crucial factor in triggering and aggravating the crisis. Its seeds were sown by the macroeconomic imbalances of the 2000s. The crisis strangled interbank lending in 2008–9 and again in 2011–12, and led to prohibitive borrowing costs for the vulnerable euro member states. It was also, in retrospect, an obvious intellectual neglect by the economics profession, as Olivier Blanchard noted wryly in 2013: "It has become a cliché to say that macroeconomic thinking understated the role of financial factors in economic fluctuations".[3]

Moreover, some of the necessary remedies aimed to prevent future financial crises similar to the one of 2007–9, such as higher capital requirements and other more stringent prudential regulations, may also have amplified the credit crunch that was experienced in the Eurozone after the financial crisis and through the debt crisis. As Charles Goodhart has noted, "In particular, the requirement to raise equity ratios quickly and dramatically... with no strong direction, in the EU at least, on *how* this was to have been achieved was partly responsible for the deleveraging and slow growth of both bank lending and deposits since 2009".[4] This is in fact the same kind of criticism that Mario Draghi expressed against the false sequencing of crisis management measures, referred to in Chapter 6.

Which of these explanations carries the most weight in the light of empirical evidence? We can compare the explanations during three distinctive periods of the crisis: 2008–10, 2011–12 and 2013–15. Furthermore, by comparing the respective stages and policy outcomes in the Eurozone and in the United States economies, we can meaningfully try to assess the relative weight of these various explanations. Below, the evolution of GDP growth on the one hand, and of the cyclically adjusted government primary balance on the other, is compared between the Eurozone and the United States. The concept of "cyclically adjusted fiscal balance" refers to the fiscal balance (= the surplus or deficit of public finances) where the effect of the business cycle is neutralized, and thus reveals the policy-induced fiscal stance based on decisions by the government. There are well-known lags in fiscal policy impact on economic growth that stretch from months to years.

1. Financial-crisis recession (2008–10)

As we can see from Fig. 17.2, in terms of the cyclically adjusted fiscal balance that was explained above, both the United States and Eurozone reacted to the first phase of the financial crisis in 2008–9 with a substantial fiscal stimulus programme.

In the United States, the stimulus was more than twice as strong as in the Eurozone, as the change in the fiscal balance was −2.3% of GDP in the United States vs. −0.8% in the Eurozone in 2008, and −3.4% in the United States and −1.3% in the Eurozone in 2009. In line with expected short-term fiscal multipliers, growth dipped more in the Eurozone than in the United States—the difference in 2009 was 2 percentage points as the US growth rate was −2.5% and the Eurozone rate was −4.5%.

Even though there were other factors at play, we can conclude that the growth outcomes in 2008–9 are consistent with the smaller fiscal stimulus applied in the Eurozone. In other words, the fiscal multipliers seemed to have behaved "normally" in the early period of the financial crisis, apparently reacting logically to the fiscal stimulus provided by the governments on

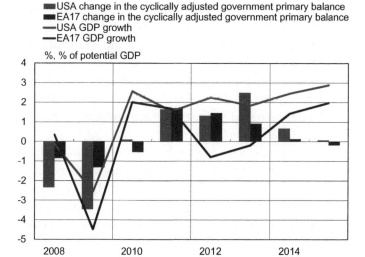

USA change in the cyclically adjusted government primary balance
EA17 change in the cyclically adjusted government primary balance
USA GDP growth
EA17 GDP growth

%, % of potential GDP

Fig. 17.2 GDP growth and fiscal policy in the United States and Eurozone, 2008–15 (*Sources* OECD, Macrobond and Bank of Finland calculations)

both sides of the Atlantic, nearly in the same manner as would be instructed in an Economics 101 class.

2. Debt-crisis recession (2011–12)

Does the same story hold in the trough of the Eurozone debt crisis? Apparently not, if we are to believe the empirical evidence. Some things did seem to change, and the most powerful factors were probably other than fiscal policy.

Let us look at the trough of the crisis in 2011–12. The recovery was still rather even in the United States and Eurozone when moving from 2009 to 2010, despite the Eurozone's smaller fiscal stimulus in 2009. In both cases, we can assume the normal time lag in policy effect. But the surprising fact, at least in the light of the general thrust of the ex post debate, is that the aggregate fiscal policy stance in the critical year 2010 was less contractionary in the Eurozone than in the United States. The change of the cyclically adjusted fiscal balance in the United States was positive, i.e. +0.2% of GDP, while it was marginally expansionary in the Eurozone, i.e. −0.5%.

In 2011–12, the change in the aggregate fiscal balance was clearly positive and thus contractionary, and even of the same magnitude, in both jurisdictions (in 2011 +1.7% in both and in 2012 1.4% and 1.5% in the United

States and the Eurozone, respectively). While the growth rate was virtually parallel between the United States and the Eurozone in 2011 (1.6% vs 1.7%), in 2012 it suddenly dropped to the negative territory (−0.8%) in the Eurozone while remaining firmly positive (+2.2%) in the United States. Consequently, the Eurozone recovery was delayed by two years from 2011 onwards, as it only gradually returned to growth in the course of 2013.

3. Turnaround and recovery (2013–15)

At the time of writing, the Eurozone economy has been on the path of recovery and growth, at first weak and fragile, for six years since spring 2013. This revival followed the setting up of the European stability mechanisms (ESM) in 2010–12, the member states' commitment to consolidate public finances which helped contain the panic in financial markets, as well as the landmark decision of the ECB to commit to Outright Monetary Transactions (OMTs) in August–September 2012 and, in 2015, to the implementation of quantitative easing. The ECB's OMT decision was taken as a reaction to the recession in 2011–12 and against the backdrop of the renewed turbulence in the summer of 2012, which represented the worst trough, or the deepest rock-bottom, of the Eurozone debt crisis.

From 2013 onwards, the Eurozone has continued with its gradual recovery, which in its first stage was weaker than in the United States. Despite this, its fiscal stance was less contractionary than in the United States in 2013–15. For instance, in 2013 the change in the Eurozone fiscal stance was +0.9%, while in the United States it was +2.5% (the larger positive figure indicating stronger consolidation and thus a more contractionary fiscal stance).

From 2014 onwards, the correlation between fiscal policy and the growth rate has started to behave more logically again and we are now witnessing a gradual return to "normality".

Bernanke's Financial Accelerator Theory as an Explanation

It seems that during the rock-bottom of the crisis in 2011–12 the normally consistent correlation between aggregate fiscal stance and growth rate falls down in the euro area, in light of the OECD data. Why is that—what could be the logical explanation for the second wave of the recession in the euro area?

If one subscribes to a fiscal explanation of the Eurozone weakness in 2012 and 2013, then variation of fiscal policy multipliers could help explain the outcome. As we know, fiscal policy was tightened most in the peripheral countries who had no fiscal space, and much less in the core countries. It is plausible that when the channel of financial intermediation is not functioning properly, as was the case in the peripheral countries, fiscal tightening may have a larger effect on demand than when financial markets function normally. Yet, one can bring under question whether this difference alone could be large enough to explain the much weaker growth in the Eurozone as a whole than in the United States in this period. After all, the countries that were forced by markets to tighten their fiscal policies were in most cases relatively small ones.

Thus, one probably should search for at least a supplementary explanation elsewhere. An obvious alternative to a fiscal explanation is either a monetary or financial one—or a combination of the two. What, then, can they reveal of the impact on growth?

The period when the Eurozone growth performance really started to weaken relative to the United States—the second half of 2011—coincides with a widening gap between the long-term interest rates between the Eurozone and the United States. Part of that is accounted for by the increase in the ECB policy rates. But an eventually more important factor was the intensification of the euro area banking and debt crisis, which was felt in the financial markets and reflected in the significant increases of the spreads between the bond yields of the vulnerable and the core countries, as illustrated in Fig. 1.2.

High sovereign bond yields had a damaging impact on growth in the countries concerned. Refinancing costs of the banks increased and asset values decreased, which weakened the availability of collateral, led to a more rapid deleveraging and caused a financial squeeze in the private sector. In addition, a vicious circle set forth in the public finances: higher yields increased public sectors' financing burden, accentuating insolvency fears as well as the anxiety that the sovereigns could not guarantee the functioning of the banking sector if it were to face solvency problems.

This sounds very much like **the financial accelerator**, a concept introduced and developed by Ben Bernanke as a leading scholar of the Great Depression, long before becoming chairman of the US Federal Reserve. The gist is that "recessions tend to gum up the flow of credit, which in turn makes the recession worse". This implies that during recessions, banks lend more cautiously as they are burdened by losses, and at the same time borrowers become less creditworthy since their finances deteriorate.

Consequently, credit becomes constrained, which hits household purchases and business investments, thus amplifying the recession. All this puts economic activity in a reverse gear.[5]

In a similar vein, Charles Goodhart underlines the central role played by financial intermediaries for monetary policy transmission. As he points out, financial intermediaries, especially banks, are responsible for intermediation between the central bank and economic agents, and many agents primarily access the financial sector via such intermediation. This is not normally captured by today's economic or econometric models: "If the transmission mechanism, via banks and other non-bank financial intermediaries, is seriously impaired, then so will be the efficacy of a given interest rate policy change – a point that most formal models miss".[6]

Several scholars of the Eurozone debt crisis have come by and large to similar conclusions. In her study on the real rate of interest and a long history of boom-bust cycles, Hélène Rey emphasizes the role of global financial cycles. Of these, she gives particular weight to the boom phase of boom-bust cycles and underlines the importance of understanding more fully the crisis periods in which financial constraints may be binding and amplifying the shocks hitting the economy, leading to deleveraging and depressed aggregate demand.[7] Likewise, Gavyn Davies has stressed the critical role of financial conditions indicators (FCIs) when assessing the likely impact of monetary policy: "The [latest] IMF study shows clearly that changes in FCIs can be helpful in predicting GDP growth up to 12 months ahead, especially when a significant tightening in the FCI predicts an increase in recession risk".[8]

These empirical findings, as well as the IMF analysis, indicate that the financial stress felt in Eurozone member states could have affected its real economy with a time lag that is seen in GDP figures cumulatively in roughly 12 months' time. Interestingly, an independent evaluation report of EFSF/ESM financial assistance has concluded that where the conditional financial assistance programmes of the ESM in the stressed countries were implemented effectively and upfront (i.e. Ireland and Spain), the banking sector was stabilized and returned back to profitability on average in seven quarters ($= 21$ months).[9] The stabilization of the banking sector was necessary in order to recover lending to enterprises and households, and thus create conditions for sustained growth.

This interpretation is supported by facts as we look at the events that preceded or coincided with the alleviation of the financial stress. ECB President Mario Draghi's speech in London in July 2012, promising "to do whatever it takes to save the euro – and believe me it will be enough" had a rapid impact on the yields of the vulnerable euro countries. Soon after, in August–September 2012, the ECB's Governing Council took decisions on the provision of OMT as deemed necessary, and the euro crisis gradually subsided—even without resorting to the actual use of these OMT interventions.

After Draghi's speech, the ECB had to back his words with concrete decisions and communication, and carry out the role of a lender of last resort—or, more accurately, "the balance sheet of last resort", as it has been referred to by Papadia and Välimäki.[10] Since then, the ECB has stood behind fundamentally solvent individual member states in the critical sense that it can buy sufficient amounts of sovereign debt if the yields suggest redenomination risks—but only on that condition, and provided that the fiscal sustainability of the given sovereign was facilitated by an ESM's economic adjustment programme. The word "redenomination" refers here to the potential threat of a break-up of the euro.

The redenomination issue is related to the nature of the Eurozone as a monetary union. As Adair Turner has observed, a dramatic consequence of the redenomination risk previously perceived during the crisis was that, on average, the Eurozone countries had to pay higher interest rates than, for example, Japan, although the average public debt in Japan was 138%, while in the Eurozone it was "only" 74%. Consequently, the Eurozone had to keep fiscal deficits at mere 2% of GDP compared to 6–7% in Japan, the United States and the United Kingdom.[11] This can be regarded as a *redenomination constraint* that prevailed then in the Eurozone.

Likewise, Paul De Grauwe refers to the market panic and the absence of lender of last resort as the root cause of the double-dip recession: "This second recession in the Eurozone is the result of the structural problem in the currency union… The absence of central banks to support national governments led to panic in many markets and forced the governments to implement overly strict austerity measures".[12]

The redenomination constraint was clearly a profound downside factor during the crisis, as it curbed the possibilities of a more expansionary or Keynesian fiscal stance, or even maintaining a consistent and slower pace of fiscal consolidation in the first years of the debt crisis. On the other hand, while nothing to cheer about and certainly avoiding any complacency, its upside consequence is that the Eurozone economies are today on average much less indebted than, for example, the United States, China or Japan, as shown in the IMF 2018 Fiscal Monitor.[13]

Regrettably, only few economists provided solid and pertinent intellectual ammunition for changing the monetary policy course at the time. As an exception, in 2011–13 Paul De Grauwe wrote a few articles that influenced the thinking in many quarters by articulating the arguments in favour of the necessary lender of last resort in a currency union.[14] Discussing the unnatural increases in sovereign interest rates of certain euro countries during the initial stage of the debt crisis, he boiled the problem down to the constraints of the ECB, which due to its perceived mandate was not considered able to actively respond to market panics as the lender of last resort, not only to banks but more broadly to the economy, including the sovereigns. He regards this as the fundamental systemic shortcoming in the Eurozone's institutional architecture. Lesson: Institutions matter, again!

As an antidote to this original sin of the EMU, De Grauwe argued that the ECB needed to act as the lender of last resort, even if it was never made explicit in the Maastricht Treaty. Perhaps even the opposite, according to some. In his view, a central bank must do what a central bank must do: to carry out the function of lender of last resort in a monetary union, for the sake of financial stability that is essential for sustainable growth and job creation. While recognizing the merits of De Grauwe's work on the lender of last resort, I wouldn't agree with his further view that the ECB should become the unconditional supporter of weak governments,[15] which would lead to unbridgeable moral hazard and amount to monetary financing forbidden in the EU Treaty.

Links to Fiscal Policy and Financial Repair

While certainly essential, the ECB's actions alone did not change the course of the Eurozone. The measures taken to calm down the financial market turbulence by first creating the ESM and later on the decision to set up a banking union were also necessary building blocks for the turnaround. It is also worth recalling that the crucial decision made by the ECB in August 2012 on OMT, regarding purchases (or "outright transactions") in secondary sovereign markets of bonds issued by Eurozone member states, was based on a thoughtfully crafted policy conditionality. Any OMT programme was declared to be conditional on an economic adjustment programme of the recipient country, to be provided and designed by the ESM.

Also, the OMT decision was made possible by the pursuit of returning to reasonable fiscal prudence in the Eurozone. The six-pack reform of economic governance had already enabled this approach. In addition to that, both Germany and the ECB called for an even more rigorous anchor of fiscal prudence. This gave birth to the fiscal compact in spring–winter 2012, starting from November to December 2011.

As the Financial Times reported on 1 December 2011, a serious last-minute rescue plan for the Eurozone started to take off after Mario Draghi said that a fiscal compact could pave the way for a more aggressive European Central Bank response to the Europe's ongoing debt crisis. As Draghi told the European Parliament, an agreement binding governments to strong rules on public finances would be "the most important element to start restoring credibility" with financial markets. "Other elements might follow, but the sequencing matters", he added. As a newly installed ECB President, Draghi also argued that a fiscal compact could act as a long-term anchor for confidence, which would also boost investor trust in the short term. Draghi's comments on the sequencing and fiscal compact were interpreted so that the ECB could reinforce its bond-buying programme SMP after the forthcoming European summit on 9 December 2011.[16] For this reason, Jean-Claude Trichet as President of the ECB had already previously searched for guarantees of the member states' ability to ensure the sustainability of their fiscal policies.

I can say with conviction that the European Commission was never a big fan of the overly rigorous fiscal compact. The Commission preferred the six-pack reform to reinforce the economic governance of the Eurozone, which was in line with the Community method, and in line with making the Stability and Growth Pact smarter and fiscally reasonable. But for the sake of facilitating the ECB's room for manoeuvre and activism, the Commission had to play rhythm guitar for the fiscal compact. At face value, it was yet another second-best. On the other hand, no harm was done on substance, and essentially, it was Draghi's astute move to expand his room of manoeuvre for the common good.[17]

In sum, the financial accelerator theory, or should we in this case say "**the financial *decelerator***", better explains the Eurozone's recession and weak growth performance than other explanations. The Eurozone vacillated and acted slowly, offering too little financial firepower when the crisis hit. Hence, the financial system was out of oxygen for too long to support credit (see Fig. 17.3).

On the other hand, once the crisis had hit in September 2008, the United States almost immediately switched to crisis mode to implement very expansionary monetary policy and fix the badly damaged banking and finance system. The repair of the United States' banking system was conducted in 2008–10, whereas in the Eurozone the financial repair only seriously took place in 2012–14.

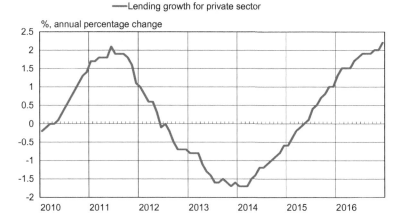

Fig. 17.3   Credit growth in the euro area (*Source* ECB. *Note* Loan stocks adjusted balance sheet transfers and securitisation)

Conclusion

There are several lessons to be learned from the strenuous experiences of the financial deceleration of the Eurozone for economic governance and financial firefighting.

An essential conclusion drawn by the then policy-makers (including myself) was that convincing financial repair was necessary so that the Eurozone could return to a sustainable path of recovery and growth. This pushed the Eurozone to build a banking union, which has advanced well, but is still a work in progress.

At a more theoretical level, the euro crisis reflects the key argument of the maverick-turned mainstream economist Hyman Minsky: while stability is destabilizing, the effect can be contained by an apt use of regulation and policy—but even that can never be permanent, and policy will have to continually adjust to new circumstances. So, as much as the reform of Eurozone economic governance in 2010–12 was necessary to correct the flaws in its original design, it was incomplete from the start, which is why the reconstruction of EMU cannot wait forever.

Another lesson is that when there is an emergence of a major threat of recession or deflation, or both at once, monetary policy must be used forcefully to bring back higher employment and normal inflation. This is how Ben Bernanke puts it:

[There are] some enduring lessons of the Depression for central bankers and other policymakers. First, in periods of recession, deflation, or both, monetary policy should be forcefully deployed to restore full employment and normal levels of inflation. Second, policymakers must act decisively to preserve financial stability and normal flows of credit.[18]

At times, the ECB was rather slow, or restrained, in taking action. Nonetheless, it acted decisively in the autumn of 2008 and, especially, again in the summer and fall of 2012, then fighting the danger of deflation from 2014–15 onwards.

Economic policy-makers must act decisively and with dynamic force to secure stability in the financial system and to maintain normal credit flows. The ESM was conceived in 2012, which together with the OMT commitment of the ECB belatedly created the much-needed "Big Bazooka", based on the bold but bitter experiences from its weaker predecessor EFSF that was given birth by a caesarean section in May 2010. But alone they were obviously not enough to contain the crisis.

The central banks cannot do all the heavy lifting: the capacity for real-economy adjustment is crucial in a monetary union. Hence, national economic policy matters. Policy coordination in the Eurozone should support this endeavour.

More will be said in Chapter 19 on the lessons learnt in safeguarding financial stability and supporting stronger, sustained growth and job creation in the Eurozone. Before that, in the next chapter, we return our gaze to some "misadventures of dismal science", to see what issues the economics profession has faced in these tough and turbulent times, and how it has succeeded in dealing with them.

Notes

1. See Vitor Constancio's comprehensive and in-depth analysis of the ECB's monetary policy history in his speech in Malta in 2018: https://www.ecb.europa.eu/press/key/date/2018/html/ecb.sp180504.en.html.
2. Martin Sandbu, *Europe's Orphan: The Future of the Euro and the Politics of Debt*. Princeton University Press, second edition, 2017. See especially Chapters 3 and 7.
3. Olivier Blanchard, 2013. See: https://voxeu.org/article/rethinking-macroeconomic-policy.
4. Charles Goodhart, Financial Crises. In David Chambers and Elroy Dimson (eds.), *Financial Market History: Reflections of the Past for Investors Today*. CHA Institute and the University of Cambridge, 2016, p. 193.

5. Ben S. Bernanke, *The Courage to Act: A Memoir of a Crisis and Its Aftermath*. W. W. Norton, 2015, pp. 35–36. See also Ben S. Bernanke, *Essays on the Great Depression*. Princeton University Press, 2000, pp. 5–38; 70–160.

6. Charles Goodhart, *The Optimal Size for Central Bank Balance Sheets*. Central Banking, 25 October 2017.

7. Hélène Rey, *The BIS Andrew Crockett Memorial Lecture: The Global Financial System, the Real Rate of Interest and a Long History of Boom-Bust Cycles*, 2017, p. 7.

8. Gavyn Davies, The Message from Financial Conditions Indicators. *FT*, 30 July 2017.

9. EFSF/ESM Financial Assistance. Evaluation Report, 2017.

10. Francesco Papadia with Tuomas Välimäki, *Central Banking in Turbulent Times*. Oxford University Press, 2018, p. 141.

11. Adair Turner, *Between Debt and the Devil: Money, Credit and Fixing Global Finance*. Princeton University Press 2016, p. 158.

12. Paul De Grauwe, *The Limits of the Market: The Pendulum Between Government and Market*. Oxford University Press, 2017, p. 146.

13. The IMF Fiscal Monitor, April 2018.

14. Paul De Grauwe, Managing a Fragile Eurozone. VoxEU, 10 May 2011. See also Paul De Grauwe and Yuemei Ji, *Panic-Driven Austerity in the Eurozone and Its Implications*. VoxEU, 21 February 2013: http://www.voxeu.org/article/panic-driven-austerity-eurozone-and-its-implications. A useful summary of the articles can be found in a revised form in De Grauwe, *The Limits of the Market: The Pendulum Between Government and Market*. Oxford University Press, 2017, pp. 117–130.

15. As quoted in Papadia with Välimäki, *Central Banking in Turbulent Times*. Oxford University Press, 2018, p. 283.

16. Ralph Atkins and Hugh Carnegy, Draghi Hints at Eurozone Rescue Plan. *The Financial Times*, 1 December 2011. See: https://www.ft.com/content/87b3db16-1bfc-11e1-9631-00144feabdc0.

17. On argumentation, see President Mario Draghi's Ludwig Erhard Lecture, *The Euro, Monetary Policy and the Design of a Fiscal Compact*. Berlin, 15 December 2011: https://www.ecb.europa.eu/press/key/date/2011/html/sp111215.en.html.

18. Bernanke 2015, pp. 35–36.

18

Misadventures of Dismal Science

Underlying the euro crisis—and I am intentionally referring to *a **euro** crisis* instead of just *a euro **area debt** crisis*—there have been some misadventures in the economic science, by which I mean such interpretations and arguments that have proven to be outright false or badly on a shaky ground.

The system errors of the euro stemmed from certain paradigms of economics that have proven seemingly mistaken, leading to policy mistakes. Hence, the title of this chapter is not to denigrate the "dismal science" (as Thomas Carlyle called economics in 1849), but to challenge some of the beliefs of this beautiful and indispensable discipline on the basis of the lessons learnt during the crisis.

However, any responsibility in this respect is obviously shared. The system errors also stemmed from the flaws in the institutional design of the EU and the normal political pressures from the member states that together are inclined to lead to second-best compromises. As it happens, these do not always lead to the first-best policy outcomes. The critical political economists Magnus Ryder and Alan Cafruny go as far as saying, "Traditional theory not only failed to anticipate the crisis but has also had very little to say about Europe's inability to resolve it".[1]

At the early stage of the crisis, a common misrepresentation of the euro crisis was to treat it only as a morality play, where the past sins are punished by default or disciplined by sanctions. However, the euro crisis was not just a Greek drama: its roots lie in the systemic problems of the monetary union, which were not recognized or acknowledged in the first two decades of the euro in 1990–2010. On the basis of the practical experience of the crisis

© The Author(s) 2020
O. Rehn, *Walking the Highwire*, https://doi.org/10.1007/978-3-030-34592-1_18

years and the related debate on economics, two tenets in particular seem erroneous.

First, in the construction phase of the EMU—and contrary to what many observers have in more recent years claimed[2]—very much focus was placed on the theory of optimum currency area and the asymmetric shocks resulting from the different structures of production in the countries emphasized by the theory. Meanwhile, surprisingly and regrettably little attention was devoted to financial flows and the macroeconomic imbalances facilitated by those financial flows. There were many economists who argued that the balance of payments does not matter in a currency union. Not only that: apart from the current account deficits, the possibility of a crisis in the financial system did not deserve the attention it should have deserved. And astonishingly little attention was paid to the ability of financial markets to amplify economic shocks, even though a certain Ben Bernanke had proven already in 1983 that this was a central cause for the deepening of the Great Depression.[3]

By neglecting the paramount importance of macroeconomic imbalances, such as excessively large current account deficits and rapidly rising labour costs that were brewing in the deceivingly benign context of the integrated financial market and uniform interest rate level, the Eurozone was sleepwalking to a classical financial crisis of its own. Their impact on the financial stability of the euro area economies proved much more damaging than was continuously assumed in the 2000s.

Second, at the time of euro's creation, there was a strong belief in the ability of the Stability and Growth Pact together with the market forces to maintain effective budgetary discipline and prevent excessive private indebtedness. The threat of rising interest rates was assumed to force a Eurozone country to stabilize its public finances, avoid imbalances and improve its cost competitiveness. However, in retrospect we can see that both the policy rules and the market forces badly failed in this task. This was in fact accurately recognized in the Delors Report in 1989:

> Experience suggests that… access to a large capital market may for some time even facilitate the financing of economic imbalances. Rather than leading to a gradual adaptation of borrowing costs, market views about the creditworthiness of official borrowers tend to change abruptly and result in the closure of access to financing. The constraints imposed by market forces might either be too slow and weak or too sudden and disruptive. Hence countries would have to accept that sharing a common market and a single currency area imposed policy constraints.[4]

Quite some wise words in the light of the euro's crisis in 2010–12! It was a pity that these warnings were not followed at the Maastricht negotiations in 1990–92 or when the SGP was set up in 1996–97. Only once the Macroeconomic Imbalance Procedure was constructed in 2010–11 were these warnings taken into account—more on the MIP and its limitations below.

As far as the market forces are concerned, this may have been partly caused by their (more or less) rational expectations that the EU would still bail out member states facing insurmountable financial stress, even though the EU Treaty explicitly banned it. That may have created distorted incentives and contributed to the mispricing of risk in sovereign bonds. Moreover, the assumption of the rational power of the market forces was based on the theory of optimal operation of self-regulating, efficient financial markets that prevailed at the time. The obvious lesson is that the institutions and incentives have to be designed so that they help orient the market forces to meaningful directions—you may call it "market discipline".

Furthermore, the EU's Stability and Growth Pact that was supposed to maintain fiscal sustainability in the member states along with market discipline was watered down right at the first opportunity, when Germany and France breached its conditions in 2003–4, supported by the then Italian EU Presidency. This created long-lasting credibility problems to the economic governance of the euro.

Theory of Optimum Currency Area and Asymmetric Shocks

The first misadventure, the overemphasis of the theory of optimum currency area, took place about 20 years ago and lasted long. While this theory as such has obvious merits, its general application in the Eurozone in the twenty-first century can be questioned due to the changing circumstances. Essentially, the theory of optimum currency area emphasizes the significance of asymmetric shocks, normally country-specific, which would cause a serious adaptation problem for an individual member state, when the interest rate level is bound by the decisions of the entire currency area and the foreign exchange tool—i.e. currency devaluation—is eliminated from use. Within the currency union, labour mobility and income transfers have been regarded as key elements to adjust to asymmetric shocks.

Generally, an economy living on a single commodity and its refining industry, and therefore exposed to cyclical fluctuations of this particular commodity, is assumed to be particularly vulnerable to asymmetric shocks. This is logical and is often called the "Texas phenomenon", since the difficulties of the oil-rich state of Texas in adjusting to the often large fluctuations in crude oil prices in the US dollar union (i.e. in the absence of a state-level Texan currency of its own) has been considered a classic example of an economy susceptible to asymmetric shocks.

During the 1990s, the theory of optimum currency area received a new boost, as some researchers like Jeffrey Frankel and Andrew Rose started to advocate a view that a monetary union can lead to ***endogenous convergence*** among its member states.[5] Assumption was that increasing trade among members of the monetary union would also lead to higher correlation of their business cycles. Hence, the euro area could develop into an optimum currency area even if it was not one before its inception.[6] Paul Krugman (1993) offered an opposite view: common currency would cause countries to specialize more, which would then make their aggregate business cycles less similar than before.[7]

Ultimately, the questions related to endogenous convergence are empirical. Did business cycle correlation increase within the monetary union? Was the change in this correlation different inside the monetary union than between, say, other EU member states? Campos, Fidrmuc and Korhonen offer evidence that business cycle correlation in Europe has generally increased after the introduction of the euro, and this increase in business cycle correlation is larger for the countries that adopted the euro in 1999.[8] This would support the view that endogenous convergence is taking place, but it is also true that the effect can vary from country to country, and it is not clear whether this is endogenous or caused primarily by other factors.

The theory of optimum currency area was at the core of economic debate also when the pros and cons of the EMU were weighed up in Finland.[9] This was understandable as Finland at the time was even more dependent on the cyclical forestry industry than it is now, and the Nokia phenomenon in the technology sector was still picking up speed. I made my own contribution too, by writing the following passage, based on my doctoral dissertation in 1996, two years before the Finnish Parliament decided to endorse Finland's accession to the EMU:

> In contrast, when I consider it from Finland's perspective, my answer is uncertain and conditional. The EMU – if used right – may prove a means of ensuring stable economic development and a stable currency for Finland.

But if used incorrectly, for a remote and cyclical open economy, the EMU may prove a straightjacket which will prevent the economy from managing flexibly the consequences of international economic fluctuations or failed economic policy.[10]

I have no reason to pretend that I have been "right" all along, but one can clearly see that the persistent economic recession of 2011–15 resembled that prognostication. Finland is a rare case of a true asymmetric shock due to several and simultaneous structural setbacks in the past decade—I am referring to the downfall of Nokia's mobile business, the long decline in demand of the paper industry products and the economic slowdown in Russia, which were amplified by the loss of cost competitiveness since 2005–7 due to expensive wage agreements.

At the time of this writing, after half a decade of virtually zero growth, the Finnish economy has been on a recovery path since 2015, thanks to the stronger export demand in the Eurozone economy and the correction of her own cost competitiveness. It took a long time for the Finnish body politic and social partners to recognize the problem and also to act on it. The test has been passed, by and large, but with quite some procrastination. The competitiveness pact that was negotiated by February 2016 and ratified by the social partners by June of the same year was a litmus test whether Finland can live within the framework of the single currency. The pact entered into force in 2016 and has so far delivered, as the unit labour costs per hour declined by 6½% relative to main competitor countries in 2014–17, and the economy has recently been growing again close to the potential output, with the growth rate of 2–3% per annum for 2016–18.[11]

Most other countries in trouble in the Eurozone were rather hit by *a symmetric and system-wide shock* by the financial crisis in 2007–9 and the debt and banking crisis in 2010–12. However, the financial system again played the critical role: while the shock was symmetric, the degree of vulnerability in the euro area member states varied a lot, depending on their economic and financial resilience. Once the shock revealed these vulnerabilities, the financial markets reacted rapidly, and in the integrated markets, their compound effect was indeed very strong.

This called for a systemic response (as described in Chapter 6), but inevitably also bold national responses by individual member states to put their own house in order. That is, even if the main cause of the crisis may have been a systemic one and thus required a systemic response, many corrective and mitigating policy measures, such as correcting structural budget deficits and pursuing painful structural reforms, nevertheless had to be undertaken in and by the member states. In that sense, it was difficult to distinguish between the symmetric and asymmetric (idiosyncratic) dimensions of the crisis. Life is not always fair—one critical lesson of the crisis is the paramount importance for each member state to realize her own responsibility for her economic and social development. Collective action in the Eurozone may support the member states in this task, but there is no guarantee of this in the current institutional architecture, and hence, it would be short-sighted and indeed irresponsible to neglect building up one's own economic resilience.

Macroeconomic Imbalances Were Brushed Aside

In comparison with asymmetric shocks stemming from the production structure, a much more serious and difficult problem has proven to be the macroeconomic and financial imbalances that emerged in particular during the first decade of the twenty-first century. **Most economists focused their attention on the production structure, while the real problem was actually left hiding in the financial system**.

Likewise, there was a great deal of analysis about the twists and turns in monetary policy, but insufficient attention to finance and banking. This was also linked to regulation. For instance, the uniform regulatory treatment of different euro area sovereign bonds before the crisis probably contributed to banks' apparently excessive demand for government securities.[12] Harold James has drawn attention to these shortcomings of neglecting finance and banking before 2010:

> The first ten years of the Euro's existence were overshadowed by two long-running sagas, both of which attracted a great deal of public attention and seemed to define the struggle over the currency: struggles over the character of monetary policy and who made it, and struggles over competitiveness. The debates deflected attention from the main issues, the unsustainability of Europe's (and the world's) approach to banking and the effects of the financial-ization explosion on public credit.[13]

Most strands of economics and political economy neglected the central role played by the capital flows and financial system in the modern world economy. This is striking as the root cause for the financial crisis can be found in the excessive *financialization* of the world economy. By "finan-cialization" is meant the vastly expanded role of financial motives, financial markets, financial actors and financial institutions in the operation of the economy—a process whereby "financial services take over the dominant economic, cultural and political role in a national economy".[14]

Of course, the fact that the EMU and euro were conceived largely as a political project, explained in Chapter 1, played an important role here. Many economists understandably endorsed the EMU for wider reasons of European integration. An example is provided by Paul Krugman, who in 1990 wrote as follows:

> I find it quite reasonable to guess that Europe is too large, diverse and poorly integrated to benefit economically from a single currency. I also think that a single currency for Europe is an excellent idea. Economic efficiency is not everything. A unified currency is almost surely a necessary adjunct of European political unification, and that is a more important goal than the loss of some flexibility in the adjustment.[15]

Fast-forward 22 years, and Krugman is profoundly critical of not only the Eurozone economic and policy performance, but also of its capacity to survive as a policy project and its inherent, endogenous tendency to institutional self-destruction:

> What's interesting is that the euro itself created the asymmetric shocks that are now destroying it [via the capital flows it engendered]. Not only have they created something incapable of dealing with shocks but the creation engendered the shocks that are destroying it.[16]

As said before, I'd consider the shock the euro faced in 2010–12 rather as a systemic shock than a series of asymmetric shocks. Be that as it may, the neglect of financial flows was a fundamental flaw of both policy-makers and economists. As the ECB's former Vice-President Vitor Constâncio has rightly coined the EMU as designed at Maastricht, "No one had thought about the possibility of capital flows 'sudden stops' with the European monetary union".[17] Likewise, Schelkle criticizes the contemporary crisis literature of comparative and international political economy for this critical omission: "The financial system as an explanatory variable is conspicuous by its absence in these explanations. The growth regime literature does not look for national or regime-type differences in financial systems [along the lines of Zysman and Hancke], which would have been a natural starting point".[18]

The very same omission goes for the standard macroeconomic models.[19] These models tend to assume that credit markets work without frictions, which was hardly a realistic assumption during the financial crisis, when the deleveraging of the banks' balance sheets and the subsequent squeeze of lending or even a credit crunch damaged the credit channel and monetary policy transmission. This omission seriously weakens the guiding capacity of the benchmark macroeconomic models for the actual decisions in economic and monetary policy.

My critique should not be regarded as a general criticism of macroeconomic models, which are essential instruments in making economic and monetary policy, even if they should indeed be regarded as analytical instruments, not as policy-defining straitjackets. The macroeconomic models are rather good in extrapolating from the past trends and recent data, and the now-casting models based on data analytics are an interesting supplement in forecasting the current rhythmic of the economy.[20] But their shortcoming is the insufficient capacity to identify discontinuities in the complicated real world that is not linear and stationary, but rather complex and full of uncertainties. This is probably what Queen Elisabeth II meant when she asked "why nobody saw it coming?" in the wake of the financial crisis in 2008–9.

For the purpose of identifying and simulating discontinuities or the breaking points in otherwise smoothly perceived economic development, we should try to continuously draw wisdom from the lessons of economic history. And from political history as well, for that matter, since many of the economic disruptions are in fact caused by political changes and uncertainties. For instance, when considering booms and busts, it rarely is the case that "this time is different"—more often than not when you see a bubble, it is a bubble—whether of a bitcoin, a dot.com or a tulip bulb!

David Vines and Samuel Wills propose a solution to add financial parameters, like credit growth, to the benchmark macroeconomic models. As they say, this would help "capture leverage". Whatever the exact method, this should indeed be done to upgrade the relevance of the benchmark models—which is being or has been done as risk and stability analysis in macroprudential policy, e.g., by the European Systemic Risk Board. This would help integrate the "financial accelerator" to the macro models, in line with the concept and still valid analysis of Ben Bernanke et al. (see Chapter 17).

Relevant examples can be found in the crisis countries. Although in the case of Greece the crisis was largely but not only about the public sector, both Ireland and Spain suffered primarily from serious macroeconomic imbalances, which stemmed from excessive private lending growth and a boom-and-bust crash especially in the construction sector. These were fed by strong capital inflows and the rapid decline in interest rates and shrinking of interest rate spreads against Germany after the turn of the millennium.

By 2010, the party was truly over as to bonds and rates. The disappearance of interest rate spreads proved unfounded. In retrospect, we witnessed a profound mispricing of risk by market forces.

Paradoxically in today's light, these capital flows were seen, at least initially, as a sign of (positive) economic integration within the EU. There was a presumption that financial integration promotes financial development and thereby contributes to a higher long-run level of productivity.[21] Some member states were seemingly catching up the difference in living standards and domestic output by faster growth. The euro offered them a better access to the capital markets and lower debt-servicing costs to finance their growth.

If the investments enabled by this "unnaturally" inexpensive lending had been directed at producing goods and services of high productivity, no problem would likely have emerged. Quite the opposite, this would have spurred higher productivity and faster growth of the less-developed Eurozone countries and supported the catch-up of development differences, which has been the very aim of economic integration in the name of convergence. Higher productivity would have allowed wage growth without a detrimental effect on competitiveness. This is what seemed to happen in the EU's emerging economies of "new Europe", as the countries of Eastern and Central Europe were rapidly catching up and converging with the more mature economies of "old Europe".

However, the bulk of capital flows in the Eurozone was misallocated to less productive activities, such as the rapid expansion of construction output, which gave rise to real estate bubbles in Ireland and Spain. Also, some Eastern European countries experienced unsustainable booms (such as Latvia), but they turned out much more flexible in their adjustment than the so-called peripheral Eurozone.

The Eurozone was late in realizing these unsustainable trends. They were addressed in the joint EU discussions on economic policy only after ten years of the launching of the euro, when it was noted, still very carefully, that some elements of the differences in inflation, growth and external positions can be traced to the dynamics of structural convergence in living standards ("real convergence"), but definitely not all of it.[22] In other words, divergences in economic development did not stem only from the real economy, but at least as much from financial flows.

The economic and societal price of the unrecognized macroeconomic imbalances has been huge. In retrospect, more attention in the euro area should have been paid to the unsustainable capital flows associated with single monetary policy ("one size fits all"). While policy rates were uniformly set for all euro countries, the market rates were affected by the capital flows that pushed them down, which contributed to the overheating of the housing market and created real estate bubbles, with damaging consequences to growth and jobs. That's why since 2010, and in particular since the construction of the banking union started in 2012, an immense amount of policy-making capital has been invested in developing effective macroeconomic policies that could help prevent that kind of bubbles and excessive booms that usually end very badly. This has implied that central banking today is increasingly based on two pillars, monetary policy and macro-prudential policy. Macro-prudential policy has gained importance in the world of unconventional monetary policy, where negative interest rates and quantitative easing have been essential for credit growth and economic recovery, but where negative side effect, e.g., bubbles in the housing markets should be avoided. This is work in progress all over the world; in the Eurozone, the national Financial Supervisory Authorities, the ECB's Supervisory Mechanism and the European Systemic Risk Board are mandated in this task.

Another factor underlying the imbalances was the deviation of price competitiveness among the Eurozone countries. During the first decade of the twenty-first century, Germany was able to restore its price competitiveness especially thanks to its labour market reforms and the German manufacturing industry building up production chains in Central and Eastern Europe, utilizing cost advantages. Meanwhile, in the deficit countries, the consumption frenzy and the real estate bubble did inflate wages and erode price competitiveness, as productivity growth did not match cost increases.

Figure 1.4 in Chapter 1 illustrated the current account surpluses and deficits in the euro area countries in 1999–2020, showing that once the imbalances peaked in 2007–8, a rebalancing has been in progress since then. It has meant mostly that the deficit countries adjust their economies through wage moderation and/or reducing labour costs, and through fiscal consolidation. In Ireland, this started in 2008 and led to the restoration of price competitiveness by 2012. Spain, Portugal and also Greece followed suit with the help of conditional financial programmes.

How about the surplus countries? What have they done to restore the equilibrium of the euro area economy—or to create a better first-best equilibrium? This was the subject of Chapter 14 that dealt with the question of coordinated rebalancing between the surplus and deficit countries, especially with Germany. Suffice to say here only that the rebalancing—or economic adjustment, more bluntly—has taken place mostly in and by the deficit countries. The surplus countries have their institutional and other constraints—like the German constitutional debt brake—that prevent them from entering into stronger reflationary activity.

Since 2010, substantial adjustment especially in deficit countries has taken place. The accumulated internal and external imbalances constituted a massive challenge. Most deficit countries had to bring their current accounts to surplus in order for their external debt to start decreasing. This required, apart from declining domestic demand, an improvement in cost competitiveness. This was also the goal of the EU and IMF's programmes. Unlike what is often claimed and perceived in the public debate, these programmes did put a great deal of emphasis on economic reforms, not just the adjustment of public finances, in order to boost medium-to-long-term growth.

Proactive Correction of Imbalances

Under the six-pack legislation adopted in 2011, the Commission is tasked with monitoring the balance of the member states' economies and to issue a warning, if a balanced development threatens to falter, for example, due to reckless mortgage lending or wage rises outpacing the developments in productivity. Based on the reports, the Commission issues policy recommendations, which are discussed and usually approved by the Council, which represents the member states. The objective is to identify the emergence of imbalances in time, so that proactive measures can be taken in the member state concerned in a timely fashion before they accumulate to an uncontrollable extent and hence pose a threat to the stability of the euro.[23]

In June 2012, the Ecofin Council concluded the first round, where all 27 member states were first assessed, and 12 states were subsequently taken under a thorough scrutiny. Based on the assessments, the Ecofin Council issued warnings to Spain and Cyprus on very severe imbalances and to Italy, France, Slovenia and Hungary on severe imbalances. The recommendations were tailored for each country, focusing especially on the functioning of the labour markets and service production, as well as on the reinforcing of the resilience in the banking system. The recommendations raised the essential economic reforms onto the national policy agenda in the countries concerned. And in countries like Spain and Cyprus, they soon became building blocks of the conditional financial assistance programmes.

The underlying rationale of the recommendations under the Macroeconomic Imbalance Procedure stemmed from both economic analysis and historical experience. By historical, I refer to the countries that did undergo substantial economic reforms in the earlier decades and have overcome the downturns normally with smaller damage to growth and employment. These countries include Denmark, Ireland and the

Netherlands in the 1980s, Finland and Sweden in the 1990s, and Germany during the first decade of the twenty-first century.

In Chapter 14, I referred to Germany's current account surplus and recent wage developments. In its analysis, the Commission did not limit itself to the deficit countries, but made recommendations for surplus countries on how they could support the balancing of the euro area economy. To Germany in 2012 and in the subsequent years, the Commission after very careful analytic deliberation presented three material and specific recommendations: firstly, wages in Germany should rise in line with productivity to support domestic demand. Secondly, Germany was encouraged to take advantage of the low funding costs of its public economy and invest in education and research supporting growth. Thirdly, the Commission urged Germany to increase women's labour participation rate by removing taxation obstacles and increasing the availability of full-time day-care and basic education. The Ecofin Council supported all these recommendations.

These recommendations may not sound like revolutionary reforms, but their implementation would have nevertheless contributed significantly to the rebalancing of the entire euro area economy. Thus, the rebalancing would have proceeded more quickly and with smaller damages than only in slow motion, which would in the final analysis also have been in the line of Germany's own interests.

What can we conclude, finally, on the overall impact of the Commission recommendations under the Macroeconomic Imbalance Procedure? It is evident that their impact is more limited in reaching the intended policy goals than the recommendations under the Stability and Growth Pact, which focuses on public finances. There are two reasons for this. First, the current account deficits depend much more indirectly and usually slowly on the decisions of the national policy-makers than the fiscal balance. Second, the legitimacy of sanctions is weaker than in the SGP, and thus, they remain as recommendations. This shows the limits of economic governance and policy coordination.

Theory of Efficient Financial Markets: Science or Religion?

Another misstep of economics is related to the functioning of financial markets, in particular the theory of efficient financial markets. The finger has been pointed at both bankers and policy-makers. Economics and economists have also had their share of the criticism. Mainstream economics failed to see to what excessive risk-taking and lending expansion on risky and shaky grounds would lead. According to Paul Krugman in 2009, referring particularly to the efficient market hypothesis, much of the previous 30 years of macroeconomics before the financial crisis was "spectacularly useless at best, and positively harmful at worst".[24]

Or as the macroeconomist Willem Buiter wrote in the aftermath of the global financial crisis: "Standard macroeconomic theory did not help foresee the crisis, nor has it helped understand it or craft solutions... Indeed, the typical graduate macroeconomics and monetary economics training received at Anglo-American universities during the past 30 years or so, may have set back by decades serious investigations of aggregate economic behaviour and economic policy-relevant understanding. It was a privately and socially costly waste of time and other resources".[25]

Likewise, Paul De Grauwe, a distinguished monetary economist, was rather merciless to mainstream macroeconomics after the 2008 shock: "Mainstream macroeconomics has become a system of beliefs, some will say a religion, about rational and fully informed agents operating in efficient markets. The accumulation of facts that refute the mainstream macroeconomic models has become so strong that only the most fundamentalist believers will want to cling on to these theories".[26]

At the beginning of the millennium, US monetary policy of the Federal Reserve was based on a firm conviction of technology-based eternal growth. The justification for this conviction was, in addition to the rapid rise of information technology production, also the strong growth of productivity through all production and services as a result of the ubiquitous utilization of IT. But the growth of productivity was only partly true. And in any case, the monetary policy conclusions drawn from the assumed "eternal growth" and "bursting the glass ceiling of growth" were soon proven wrong.

The policy that the Fed then pursued was aimed to tell the markets that it would not tolerate a downfall in the markets—instead, if necessary, it was prepared to provide put protection for asset prices and prevent a decline in the markets by adding monetary liquidity. This was known as the "Greenspan Put", which indeed implied a fair degree of moral hazard. It was related to the belief that in the context of rapid and persistent economic growth, not only a high level of asset prices but also full employment could be achieved thanks to the strong productivity resulting from the IT breakthrough, without accelerating inflation placing any constraints on economic policy. Had that belief—essentially "this time is different"—turned out to be true in the end, it would undoubtedly have been something revolutionary!

However, every party comes to an end. Alan Greenspan, who led the Federal Reserve for 20 years, admitted in a Congressional hearing in 2008 that his theory had indeed a fundamental construction defect: the markets were not self-regulating after all! This is pretty much equivalent to the Pope telling that God does not exist.

In the light of these confessions, in the line of fire is especially the theory of efficient markets, which is based on the very straightforward assumption that the prices of goods, also financial products, are always and everywhere just at the correct level, from the welfare-maximizing standpoint. But what if this assumption does not hold true? This is what, e.g., the 2017 Nobel Laureate and one of the founding fathers of behavioural economics, Richard Thaler, thinks: "My conclusion: the price is often wrong, and sometimes very wrong". Referring to the US home price and housing bubble, he points out that in the United States, where home prices were rising at a national level, some regions experienced especially rapid price increases and historically high price-to-rental ratios. If both lenders and homeowners had been perfectly rational "Econs" instead of behaviourally bounded "Humans", they should have behaved rationally and noticed those warning signals and expected a fall in housing prices. But none of this reversion happened; instead, people continued to behave "as if what goes up must go up even more". The result is now known.[27]

In case we concur with the analysis of behavioural economics, we should have serious reservations about the core belief of the efficient market hypothesis that "price is always right". Consequently, this would simply undermine the key assumption of the 1980s financial market liberalism that financial markets always function efficiently and are able to self-regulate themselves. When one recalls the turmoil on Wall Street in 2007–9 and its long shadow cast on the world economy, it seems even quite reckless and irresponsible to expect the markets always function efficiently and balance themselves rapidly.

This misadventure relates not only to the study of finance but also very much to macroeconomics. Richard Thaler states that if he were to pick up the field of economics that would most benefit from adopting behaviourally realistic approaches, it would be the field where behavioural approaches have had the least impact so far: macroeconomics. As he coins it: "John Maynard Keynes practiced behavioural macro, but that tradition has long since withered".[28] Thaler is right—many misadventures might have been avoided if behavioural approaches had had more impact in macroeconomics. A better understanding of Humans (as opposed to Econs only) is essential in the making of monetary and fiscal policy.

The "Minsky Moment" Arrived Out of the Blue

Besides Keynes, the critics of excessive financialization rediscovered Hyman Minsky, and rightly so. Before the crisis, Minsky (1919–96) was a nearly forgotten economist whose main thesis was that stability itself contains the seeds of instability. He postulated that a lengthy period of economic growth creates such high expectations of future growth that it induces rapid lending expansion. Minsky argued that financial markets create their own internal dynamics which cause waves of credit expansion and thus an inflation of goods, which leads to credit contraction and a decrease of asset values, that is, deflation. Even though, according to Minsky, the goods market has a natural tendency to find balance, the financial markets have an in-built inclination to cause forceful rises and equally violent collapses.

The analysis of the financial crisis has given birth to a rapidly burgeoning production line of economic policy literature.[29] Minsky was vindicated in the debate. In autumn 2008 after the collapse of Lehman Brothers, the concept of "Minsky moment" surfaced in the discussion on economic policy. It refers to the moment where lending suddenly turns from increase to decrease and then surges into a downward spiral. This may lead to a liquidity trap postulated by Keynes in his general theory and to a recession, or even a downright depression of the real economy.

Minsky is merciless when discussing the movers and shakers of economic policy of his own time, the 1960s and 1970s, who in his view undermined the economic theory and policy revolution started by Keynes. Rejecting its fundamental assumption that financial markets could turn unstable did in Minsky's view erode the very foundation of Keynes' entire general theory. In the course of the 1970s, the neo-Keynesian synthesis of economics became the culprit in Minsky's mind, because it leaned on the theory of efficient markets and rational expectations. In Minsky's view, this emerging reinterpretation of Keynes' theory turned the radical Keynes into an apostle of new conservatism, which was used to promote the inequality of income and consumption that took place at the expense of social justice.

An illustrative anecdote comes from a smart critic of financial capitalism, George Cooper, who is not a Wall Street Occupier or a theoretician at a Marxist study group, but a finance-sector professional with a successful investment background—a London investment banker who has worked at Goldman Sachs and Deutsche Bank. Cooper describes how Minsky was forgotten in the economics discussion after the mid-1970s. Cooper says he purchased his own copy of Minsky's "sold-out classic"—which it was up until the 2008-reprint—in a Pennsylvania library where it had laid without any readers since 1977, branded "REMOVED FROM USE".

Minsky may have been described as an eccentric character—never got to know him personally so can't judge—and he was a researcher who was not generally respected or even known in the mainstream of economics. He did not teach at a top-tier university, but in the Midwest at the relatively peripheral Washington University in St. Louis. One lesson to be drawn from this is that the value of no person's work should be depreciated merely on the basis of its "peripheral" origin.

Paul Krugman describes his relationship with Minsky by stating that today many economists, Krugman himself included, acknowledge the groundbreaking significance of unstable financial markets. Krugman continues his intellectual self-flagellation: "Yet these days many economists, yours truly very much included, who were relative newcomers to Minsky's work, wish that we had read it much earlier".[30]

I join Krugman and count myself into the group of late-born Minskyites. Although, as a real economy guy, I have always had an instinctive doubt against any excessive trust in the efficient functioning of the financial markets, I had previously not found sufficiently convincing analytical justifications for it in economics literature. My doubts were especially based on my experience in the constant heat of high-pressure crisis management as policy advisor to Prime Minister Esko Aho during the Finnish banking crisis in the early 1990s. It was learning by doing and included the creation of a stability fund and an asset management company, or a "bad bank". But it was also a traumatic experience for all of us who went through it, being forced to clean up the mess created in the second half of the 1980s—even if training-wise it certainly was an educating experience with a view to my later duties, which is a very modest silver lining.

In his search for culprits to the financial crisis, Cooper puts blame onto a broader group, stretching from the decision-makers of economic policy to the international academic community of economists: "If blame must be laid anywhere it must be placed at the collective feet of the academic community for having chosen to continue promoting their flawed theories of efficient, self-regulating markets, in the face of overwhelming contradictory evidence".[31]

Cooper hangs much of the responsibility around the neck of Paul Samuelson, one of the prime Nobel Laureates in Economics. In Samuelson's seminal economics book written in the 1940s, which later became the world's most-read textbook on economics, Samuelson equates the functioning of the financial markets directly with the functioning of the goods market: "What holds true for the market for consumer goods, also holds true for the market of factors, such as labour, land and capital".

But what if that is not true? This would undermine the crucial assumption that financial markets, too, always function efficiently and regulate themselves. Charles Goodhart has coined the difference of product and financial markets: "[T]he failure of bank X is an extraordinarily bad signal for creditors of banks W, Y, and Z, which are thought, rightly or wrongly, to have similar asset structures to (or be owed money by) bank X. In most sectors of the economy, the failure of a firm B benefits, on balance, similar firms A, C, and D via a reduction in competition and overcapacity. The reverse is true in banking, where contagion trumps competition. When a bank fails, the immediate response is to explore which other bank is next in line to come under pressure".[32] Thus, Goodhart is critical of the recent bail-in approach in bank resolution, which in his view could lead to enhanced contagion.

Thinking Outside the Box: Modern Monetary Theory and the Blanchard Debate

In recent years, especially as the low interest rate environment and the effective lower bound have been constraining monetary policy, more and more attention has been put on fiscal policy and its capacity to help revitalize the economies that are suffering from subdued growth that is clearly below the potential output.

One school of thought that has made its way to mainstream conversations is Modern Monetary Theory (MMT), which offers fiscal dominance as a solution to slow growth or to secular stagnation. Proponents of MMT argue that countries that can print their own currencies do not need to default and hence not worry about their deficits; instead, they can happily borrow and finance any government spending. If the result is inflation, then just raise taxes or cut spending. By doing so, this approach would dramatically swap the roles of fiscal and monetary policy, as it is normally the central bank's job to ensure that prices are stable and the economy is in full employment (the Fed's explicit mandate). The proponents of MMT would make the fiscal authority in charge of both.

While being always ready to think outside the box, and recognizing that MMT is "an attempt to create a consistent body of thought within the wider post-Keynesian literature", MMT is still not a consistent, empirically tested economic theory. As has been rightly pointed out by the *New York Times* columnist Josh Barro, there is no magical money tree involved. "The economy is not constrained by its ability to obtain dollars, but the economy is constrained by real limits on productive capacity".[33]

Besides, and what is part of the standard economic theory, fiscal policy has always a role to play in establishing sound economic environment. But that does not mean that the central bank should finance the government debt. In the Eurozone, the division of labour between monetary and fiscal policy is well established in the EU Treaty. I do not see that in any G20 economies, the legislative situation would be different to ours. It is hard to see that any responsible policy-maker would be willing to expose the citizens and the economy of his or her country to such experiments. Would you hold bonds of a country that followed such experiment?

Another recent conversation is the "Blanchard debate" on the growth-enhancing debt-based financing of fiscal deficits in the low interest rate environment, which may be linked to "secular stagnation", or structurally prolonged low growth. Olivier Blanchard argued in his 2019 Presidential Address of the American Economic Association that welfare costs of deficits and debts are smaller than commonly thought.[34] According to him, looking at the historical times series, the interest rate is very frequently below the growth rate ($= r - g < 0$), "the norm rather than the exception in the United States in the past", which should be taken as an opportunity to finance spending while keeping debt stable or reducing it, thanks to the higher rate of growth. Were this the case, then debt-based fiscal stimulus would be a silver bullet.

However, there are quite serious counter-arguments to Blanchard. Charles Wyplosz has coined two of them in his empirically grounded research paper "Olivier in Wonderland". First, the differential of interest rate minus growth rate ($r - g$) is not the norm but is very volatile, and when the differential shifts from positive to negative, the debt accumulation process switches rapidly from stable to unstable. This is reminiscent of the so-called deficit bias hypothesis, which points out that governments pay insufficient attention to the longer-term effects of fiscal deficits. Second, if the primary deficit is sizeable (and/or the debt is large), the debt is likely to increase fast, as both debt service and the primary balance work in the same negative direction. Furthermore, as a result of these factors, and if the policy advice to increase spending assuming you can afford it without risk is heeded, this is likely to lead to pro-cyclical fiscal policies.[35] In fairness, it has to be underlined that Blanchard himself says that his purpose in the lecture is not to argue for more public debt, but to have a richer discussion of the costs of debt and of fiscal policy than is currently the case.[36]

Consequently, neither MMT nor debt-based financing of deficits provides a silver bullet. More research is needed on the options in fiscal policy before policy-makers are ready to jump into uncharted waters. In my view, one focal point of research should be the quality of expenditure from the growth-enhancing perspective. Moreover, population ageing is something that has structural ramifications to public finances especially in the rapidly ageing societies like Japan and in Europe. Besides, population ageing affects monetary policy, where it is a major factor that lowers interest rates. The reasons for the decline of the long-term real interest rates are linked to changes in the saving-investment balance in the advanced economies, both in Europe and globally. In any case, it is clear that the role of fiscal policy is stronger in the current low rate environment, which calls for a better policy mix in the Eurozone than is the case today. We will return to this in Chapter 19.

Anyway, policy mix does indeed matter for both short-term and long-term economic and social development. While an effective, coordinated use of fiscal and monetary policy can provide a sound counter-cyclical response and thus dampen detrimental economic fluctuations, it can also support the conditions for longer-term economic well-being, social inclusion and sustained employment.

Even though cyclical fluctuations refer to temporary movements, their effects may persist for a long time. In this context, the key element is the extent to which unemployment increases in a cyclical downturn. As a rule, a cyclical rise in the unemployment rate may have long-lasting effects on unemployment, especially if labour market institutions do not support the unemployed in regaining work.

During cyclical downturns, in particular, it is common to refer to the ideas of the economist John Maynard Keynes and urge fiscal stimulus, including by taking on further public debt. This may be justified from the viewpoint of stabilization policy, if the country concerned has fiscal space. However, it is regrettably often forgotten that fiscal policies should be tightened in good times, and this omission leaves us with a very *half-Keynesian approach* only. I wonder if it would be appropriate to call for *comprehensive Keynesianism*: in other words, once fiscal buffers are replenished in good times, they can be effectively utilized in times of a recession.

Keynes' Third Way and the Limits of the Market

This discussion on policy alternatives brings us to the heart of economic-political philosophy and the gates of the great analytical divide in economics. Milton Friedman, the founding father of monetarism, swears by efficient markets. Keynesian theory, on the other hand, regards financial markets as unstable.[37] Who draws the longer straw? And what could be the consequences of economic policy?

Paul De Grauwe ponders the pendulum swing between the market and the state in his small but weighty book *The Limits of the Market*.[38] He takes distance from full-blooded capitalism and makes a strong case for mixed economies, for an economics of balance. While recognizing the evident benefits of market mechanism, he lists examples of the limitations of the market economy: income inequality may undermine the legitimacy of the market economy; the herding behaviour of financial markets may lead to instability; climate change is a result of neglecting economic externalities. "Capitalism is a corrupted form of market economy", as the Finnish statesman Johannes Virolainen put it in the 1940s.

In my view, pitting the state and the market simply only against each other does not do justice to neither of them. In reality, instead of only competition between the two, there is a strong degree of *complementarity*, and besides, there is the third pillar of *community* that is important for the continued legitimacy of the political system based on free markets and democracy, as argued by Raghuram Rajan.[39] As seen from the collapse of "real socialism", the state cannot provide good life for its citizens without the market and without a working price system to allocate resources efficiently to enhance economic and social welfare. At the same time, the market cannot truly function well without the state that enables free enterprise, protects property rights, guarantees legal contracts and corrects market failures.[40]

The rule of law is indeed the basic function of the democratic state and a prerequisite for a true market economy. In Western and Northern Europe, it is supplemented by the pursuit of social justice and the aim of relative equality of income through redistribution—this is why the modern European state is regarded as *a social market economy*, also enshrined as a concept in the EU Treaty. In the social market economy, the task of democratic politics is to set the rules of the market and open up civic development for every person.

When making his case, De Grauwe compares the Great Depression of the 1930s and the Great Recession of the late 2000s. He recalls that both periods saw the state constrain the market and strengthen the role of the public sector in managing the economy. Growth and employment in the global economy, however, recovered significantly faster after the 2008 financial crisis. De Grauwe credits the contribution of economics to this remarkable achievement. Its diagnoses of the causes of the financial crisis were largely correct, and the resulting monetary and fiscal stimulus policies in 2008–9, implemented with international policy coordination, helped prevent a deflationary cycle and restore overall demand.

This is a sound reminder of the importance of economics and why, despite the criticism of recent years for the inability of economists to predict the financial crisis, we sure still need the dismal science. Indeed, one lesson learnt of the crisis is that while it is important to recognize the second-best constraints of decision-making in a given institutional context, at the same time it is of paramount importance that the economists and economics continue to seek and argue for first-best outcomes.

Nowhere is this as urgent today as in combatting climate change. Mark Carney, Governor of the Bank of England, has referred to "the tragedy of the horizon": the impact of climate change is felt far in the future, while the costs of its mitigation are immediate, and thus we lack the right incentives to fix the problem. Economists might talk about "time inconsistency". For the past couple of centuries, economic growth has also implied equivalent growth in the emissions of CO_2. And historically, economic growth has gone hand in hand with the increase in welfare. Thus, by limiting carbon emissions without any structural change we would also limit the welfare of our citizens. Instead, we need to figure out how to continue enabling our economies grow, while at the same time effectively cutting down our emissions. Some countries have already managed to weaken the link between economic growth and emissions, but for the future of our planet, the link needs to be cut across the world.

Economics and economists can provide valuable input on what is the "common good" for the society and citizens, by way of their analyses that combine economic theory, empirical evidence and statistical methods. The study of economic history and political economy provides essential elements of a well-informed overall research programme. As the consummate economist and central banker Stan Fischer said in a recent lecture, "I think I've learned as much from studying the history of central banking as I have from knowing the theory of central banking and I advise all of you who want to be central bankers to read the history books". A stronger focus on economic and financial history would probably have inspired the policy-makers to take the credit cycles more seriously and learn from the experiences of the 1929 crash and the Great Depression. Besides, as Kevin O'Rourke has pointed out, economic history enables students and policy-makers alike "to recognise that major discontinuities in economic performance and economic policy regimes have occurred many times in the past, and may therefore occur again in the future".[41]

Economics for the common good is obviously linked to democratic politics. While there is normative content in economics in the welfare theorems and economic efficiency, democratic politics is the sphere where values compete, and the elected politicians have the right and responsibility to take value-based decisions. Jean Tirole, the 2014 Nobel Laureate of Economics, has said, "Economics is a science of the means, not of the ends". For him, the role of economists is "not to make decisions, but to identify the recurring patterns structuring our economies, and to convey economic science's current state of knowledge".[42]

Yet economic policy is never made in a social vacuum. Keynes is a prime case. As Minsky pointed out, Keynes was no technocratic theoretician but a real-life intellectual, a profoundly societal animal who persistently pushed his economic and social agenda. Keynes coined his programme in three goals: economic efficiency, social justice and individual freedom. He wanted to save the Western way of life and its freedoms from both socialism and capitalism, which is why he welcomed the third way. To promote these values, Keynes built his general theory. It constitutes the foundation of macroeconomics and remains a great inspiration today, as the Western way of life is facing the nasty threats of authoritarianism and populism.

Notes

1. Magnus Ryner and Alan Cafruny, *The European Union and Global Capitalism: Origins, Development, Crisis.* Palgrave Macmillan, 2017, p. 10.
2. For instance, Overtveldt 2011 ibid. makes this claim.
3. Ben Bernanke, Nonmonetary Effects of the Financial Crisis in the Propagation of the Great Depression. *The American Economic Review,* 73(3, June 1983): 257–276.
4. Committee for the Study of Economic and Monetary Union (Jacques Delors, Chairman), *Report on Economic and Monetary Union in the European Community.* Presented in 17 April 1989, p. 20.
5. J. Frankel and A. Rose, The Endogeneity of the Optimum Currency Area Criteria. *Economic Journal,* 108(1998): 1009–1025.
6. Francesco Paolo Mognelli, *The OCA Theory and the Path to EMU.* In Marco Buti, Vitor Gaspar, Servaas Deroose, and João Nogueira, *The Euro: The First Ten Years.* Oxford, 2010. It is worth noting that Jeffrey Frankel and Andrew Rose even predicted that euro member states could ***retroactively*** fulfil the conditions of belonging to an optimum currency area, even if they failed to meet them in advance! They also anticipated that this would lead to strengthening economic convergence, or to a decrease in differences in levels of growth and living standards.
7. Paul Krugman, Lessons of Massachusetts for EMU. In F. Torres and F. Giavazzi (eds.), *Adjustment and Growth in the European Monetary Union.* Cambridge University Press, 1993.

8. N. Campos, J. Fidrmuc, and I. Korhonen, Business Cycle Synchronisation and Currency Unions: A Review of the Econometric Evidence Using Meta-Analysis. *International Review of Financial Analysis*, 61(2019): 274–283.

9. For example, the expert working group led by Professor Jukka Pekkarinen (1997) paid a lot of attention to the theory of optimal currency areas.

10. Rehn 1996, p. 69.

11. See, e.g., the OECD Economic Outlook for Finland, February 2018.

12. Helge Berger, Giovanni Dell'Ariccia, and Maurice Obstfeld, *Revisiting the Case for Fiscal Union in the Euro Area.* IMF Policy Document, Draft, 2018, p. 15.

13. James 2012, p. 393.

14. One of the first authors to coin the terms "*financialization*" is Kevin Phillips in 2006 in his book *American Theocracy: The Peril and Politics of Radical Religion, Oil, and Borrowed Money in the 21st Century.* For a concise but useful discussion on the concept, see Wikipedia under "financialization".

15. Paul Krugman, *Currencies and Crisis* (1993); the article referred to was originally published in Paul de Grauwe and Lucas Papademos (eds.), *The European Monetary System in the 1990s.* Longman, New York, 1990.

16. Paul Krugman, interview in *The Financial Times.* FT 26.5.2012, Life & Arts, p. 3.

17. Vitor Constâncio, *Completing the Odyssean Journey of the European Monetary Union.* Remarks at the ECB Colloquium on *The Future of Central Banking.* Frankfurt am Main, 16–17 May 2018.

18. Schelkle, p. 184.

19. The benchmark New Keynesian model—the "DSGE" (= Dynamic Stochastic General Equilibrium) in the economists' jargon—relegates finance and credit to the background, as David Vines and Samuel Wills note. See David Vines and Samuel Wills, The Financial System and the Natural Rate of Interest Rate: Towards a "New Benchmark Model". *Oxford Review of Economic Policy*, 34(1–2, 5 January 2018): 252–268.

20. See, e.g., the macroeconomic columns of Gavyn Davies in *FT* with Fulcrum's analysis and the Bank of Finland's recent now-casting model: https://helda.helsinki.fi/bof/handle/123456789/14979.

21. See, e.g., Philip R. Lane, *EMU and Financial Integration.* The Euro at Ten—Lessons and Challenges, Fifth ECB Central Banking Conference, 13–14 November 2008, pp. 82–115.

22. See *The EU Economy: 2006 Review, Adjustment Dynamics in the Euro Area—Experiences and Challenges.* European Commission, 2006.

23. As part of the legislative reform, the so-called Macroeconomic Imbalances Procedure was created with clear set of rules. Information on the procedure and the rules are found on the Commission's website at: http://ec.europa.eu/economy_finance/economic_governance/macroeconomic_imbalance_procedure/index_en.htm.

24. Paul Krugman as quoted in the *Economist*, 16 July 2009: http://www2.econ. iastate.edu/tesfatsi/CritiqueOfEcon.Economist2009.pdf.

25. Willem Buiter, *The Unfortunate Uselessness of Most "State of the Art" Academic Monetary Economics*. Vox, CEPR Portal, 6 March 2009.

26. https://econoblog101.wordpress.com/2009/07/31/paul-degrauwe-on-cconomics-fail/.

27. Richard Thaler, *Misbehaving: The Making of Behavioural Economics*. Allen Lane, 2015, pp. 250–253.

28. Thaler 2015, pp. 348–349.

29. Among the critical school of thought, the most convincing contributions comprise *The Origin of Financial Crises* (2008) by George Cooper on the general causes of financial crises and the reprint of Minsky's classic *John Maynard Keynes* (2008), originally published in 1975. Both of these works are largely building on Keynes' milestone volume *The General Theory of Employment, Interest and Money* (1936) and reinterpreting it. Whereas Keynes' General Theory is the Old Testament of this faction, Minsky provides the New Testament and Cooper the Catechism. If one is interested in the root causes of the financial crisis but has not studied economics, it is advisable to start with Cooper and proceed to Minsky—and after having come that far, it is worthwhile to delve into Keynes' seminal work, too.

30. Krugman 2012, p. 43.

31. George Cooper, *The Origin of Financial Crises: Central Banks, Credit Bubbles and the Efficient Market Fallacy*. Harriman House Limited, 2008.

32. Charles Goodhart, Financial Crises. In David Chambers and Elroy Dimson (eds.), *Financial Market History: Reflections on the Past for Investors Today*. CFA Institute and University of Cambridge, 2017, pp. 190–191.

33. Inês Goncalves Raposo, *On Modern Monetary Theory*. Blog, Bruegel, 22 February 2019.

34. Olivier Blanchard, *Public Debt and Low Interest Rates*. The AEA Presidential Address, January 2019: https://www.aeaweb.org/aea/2019conference/program/pdf/14020_paper_etZgfbDr.pdf.

35. Charles Wyplosz, *Olivier in Wonderland*. Vox CEPR Column, 17 June 2019.

36. Blanchard 2019.

37. At least if one follows the interpretation of Minsky rather than Samuelson!.

38. Paul De Grauwe, *The Limits of the Market: The Pendulum Between Government and Market*. Oxford University Press, 2017, 165 pages.

39. Raghuram Rajan, *The Third Pillar: How Markets and the State Leave Community Behind*. Penguin Press, 2019.

40. For a more thorough discussion on the complementarity of the state and the market, see, e.g., Jean Tirole, *Economics for the Common Good*. Princeton University Press, 2017, pp. 160–161.

41. Kevin O'Rourke, *Why Economics Needs Economic History.* Vox.eu Column: https://voxeu.org/article/why-economics-needs-economic-history.
42. Jean Tirole, *Economics for the Common Good.* Princeton University Press, 2017, pp. 8 and 164.

19

Lessons of the Crisis for Eurozone Reform

This book concurs with the argument that institutions do indeed matter for policy outcomes: for sustainable growth, for steady job creation, for better living conditions to our citizens—as well as for the maintenance of peace and liberty in our continent and beyond. And institutions evolve continuously, reflecting both the economic and political conditions of our time while simultaneously further shaping them. As Karl Polanyi, one of the greatest political economists of all time, reported: "History was geared to social change: the fate of nations was linked to their role in an institutional transformation".

This also goes for the European Union and the Eurozone. Institutional transformation of the EU, or reform of the Eurozone, is anything but only a "technical" matter. First of all, it matters to European citizens, as the capacity of the Eurozone to function effectively is essential for sustainable growth, job creation and social progress. But it is also profoundly related to Europe's standing and influence in the world. In our contemporary world, where the United States has turned inwards, Britain is badly divided internally and pushing itself away from the rest of the European community, Russia is trying to reassert its influence with old-school geopolitics, and China is getting ever stronger and more authoritarian, it seems Europe will take the forefront in championing the case for multilateralism and a liberal international order. However, to succeed, we need to put our own house in order first. The Eurozone reform is therefore critical for this broader endeavour to strengthen international institutions and global governance, which is at the heart of Europe's peace project.

© The Author(s) 2020
O. Rehn, *Walking the Highwire*, https://doi.org/10.1007/978-3-030-34592-1_19

Against this backdrop, it is warranted to analyse the lessons learnt from the Eurozone debt crisis discussed in this volume. It provides a wealth of lessons of general application that should not be ignored. Besides, economics offer us generally valid lessons regarding the consequences of macroeconomic imbalances if and when excessive indebtedness and/or real estate booms and busts do appear. It is a fallacy to believe in the insinuation that "this time is different"—the ironic title of the Reinhardt-Rogoff milestone[1]—which we heard repeatedly during the dot-com boom in the late 1990s and likewise along with the subprime boom of the 2000s.

The preceding chapters have explored these lessons through a series of sequential narratives and political-economic analyses. Their clear message is that our post-recession legacy leaves us with much work to do in order to make the euro area function better.

What then are the most essential lessons to draw from the crisis for the Eurozone reform? The FT columnist Martin Wolf has said insightfully: "The recovery is… an opportunity for reforms, at both national and Eurozone level. The question is which reforms to choose".[2] Based on the crisis experience, I would argue that the following seven lessons are key issues for reinforcing the EMU and the Eurozone:

1. Throw away Groucho Marx: once you are a member of a club, you'd better make it function—and even better if you can make it function well and effectively, to the benefit of every member of the club.

The early twentieth-century film-maker Groucho Marx was famous for musing that he would refuse to join any club that would have him as a member. Sometimes during the crisis as Commissioner, I got the feeling that some of the euro area member states were indeed thinking like Groucho Marx, behaving rather as outsiders than as members. The sense of common ownership of the European project—be it the fiscal rules, economic reforms, the stability mechanism, or the then still nascent banking union—was sometimes quite limited.

But to be fair, there was a lot of policy learning for most of us who were responsible for policy-making in the euro crisis. Over time, the ownership by euro area member states evolved for the better, and in 2012 it facilitated decisive moves in the European Council and the ECB Governing Council. It was indeed an evolutionary learning process, in which the decision-makers gradually realized that concerns of financial stability and thus the union's future were in fact even more important than concerns of moral hazard, without belittling the importance of the latter.

The starting point for any consequential reform of the euro area is therefore simple: since the euro area member states are committed to their membership in the common project, it is better for each of them that the euro area functions well and effectively. Thus, each member state has every reason to support a solid foundation of the euro that can withstand economic headwinds and support sustained growth. It is no use getting nostalgic over the bygone 1990s by repeating the lines of the 1982 Clash classic *Should I stay or should I go* for the umpteenth time.

Instead, we should look forward and ensure that the euro's architecture is solid enough to support economically and ecologically sustainable, as well as employment-friendly growth in the economies of all member states. That's why we should get Eurozone reform underway and actively set its directions in anticipation of preventing the next crisis in the euro area before it starts. It is not much use to embark on any *catenaccio* defence or stand watching on the sidelines.

Again, the issue is anything but "technical", even if the nuts and bolts of the reform must be prepared for them to truly work. Rather, it is a matter of expressing the joint ownership and political will to ensure the euro's future. The technics will follow from that fundamental statement, with full commitment—like with Draghi's speech in July 2012.

2. Financial stability was grossly neglected before the crisis. Completing the banking union is a necessary but not sufficient precondition to achieve the required stability, and this stability should be the key priority in the Eurozone reform. The banking union would be reinforced by membership of non-euro EU countries, like Denmark and Sweden, who would themselves also benefit of it.

It is the critical lesson of the financial and debt crises that stability of the financial system is crucially important for the macro-economy, i.e. for sustainable growth and employment. The worst rock-bottom of the crisis followed the worst phase of market turbulence, which raged untamed until the European Stability Mechanism (ESM) was put in place and the ECB took its role as the lender of last resort.

The crucial importance of financial stability was grossly underestimated when the EMU was first created, and it generally continued to be underestimated in the run-up to the financial crisis. Daniel Gros has correctly noted that financial stability proved to be the "neglected stepchild" of the Maastricht Treaty. As a result, we Europeans paid a bitter price in the form of a double-dip recession in 2008–12 and suffered years of high unemployment aggravated by this recession.

The distorted functioning of the banking system did profoundly shake financial stability in Europe in 2007–12 and was amplified by eroding confidence in the debt sustainability of many member states. The link between the banks and the sovereigns created the toxic financial doom loop that fuelled the flames of the crisis. To counter this, the banking union project was launched in 2012.

Since then, substantial progress has been made in the area of the banking union, as the Single Supervisory Mechanism and the Single Resolution Mechanism have been established. This has contributed to significantly improved financial stability in the euro area. Now the central task, though not sufficient alone, is to complete the banking union. What we still need to do is two things: first, to create a solid fiscal backstop for the bank resolution fund, which has been decided in principle but is still lacking the necessary specifics; and second, to build a common European Deposit Insurance Scheme. To be politically feasible, these will require convincing measures of risk reduction, and possibly some co-insurance features in their construction, at least in the first phase.

This prerequisite also urges us to solidify the missing elements of the banking union. Accepting the principle of bail-in reinforces the importance of a sturdy and credible resolution mechanism. Why is this so? Because the bail-in rules imply that a solvency crisis of any large "systemically important" bank would be dealt with by bailing in shareholders and senior investors and putting the bank into resolution, not by sending the bill to taxpayers. In order to prevent banking crises from occurring and, where necessary, resolve them effectively, a contingency financial arrangement guaranteed by the member states is needed as a liquidity backstop.

Regarding common deposit insurance, a guarantee trust of national funds has been proposed as a compromise. This would mean mutualized reinsurance of national deposit guarantee funds for the proportion exceeding the liability of each member state's own deposit guarantee scheme. This could be a useful interim solution, but when banks get more international and operate across borders in the euro area, this being the underpinning tenet of the banking union, it will not suffice.

There is also a positive spillover from completing the banking union that goes beyond the banking sector and affects sovereign finances as well. If financial stability can be assured with the help of an effective banking union that is based on the bail-in principle, it should reduce the need for public support for countries that are in economic difficulty and thus reduce the risk of an explosion of public debt due to banking problems. This implies that potential government debt crises can be resolved more smoothly without overwhelming fears of contagion to the financial system as a whole.

Thus, our goal should be a strong banking union based on the bail-in principle, which means that the private sector and investors should bear the losses for bank failures so that taxpayers would not be required to foot the bill for them. In the banking sector, we can no longer live in a world of moral hazard, wherein the profits are privatized and the losses socialized, i.e. borne by the government. And "borne by the government", of course, is a lousy euphemism for "the taxpayer footing the bill".

At the same time, we must balance the legitimate concerns of moral hazard by putting enough weight on financial stability. Today, the combination in the EMU is not optimal, hurting both, though especially damaging financial stability. As Schelkle states, "The protracted euro area crisis suggests that the monetary-fiscal union of fiscally sovereign states errs on the side of preventing moral hazard".[3] It is of paramount importance that the bail-in principle is compatible with financial stability and well-capitalized banks.

And if we proceed wisely, these can be made compatible. Legacy bank problems at the national level should not be shifted to the euro-area level— instead, member states should work them out on their own. The key is to have a credible roadmap and concrete action in reducing non-performing loans (NPLs). Spain used its ESM programme effectively and has reached the euro area average of 5% in NPLs of the total stock of loans. Italy started belatedly and has reduced the share of NPLs from 16% to below 10% since 2016. This is not insignificant. Now the challenge is to maintain the positive trend of NPL reduction.

Completing the banking union also involves a geographical, or rather a geo-economic, dimension. Banks can already operate across borders in the EU, and in the future their lending operations are likely to become less concentrated in particular countries. Such a cross-border context is already vastly the reality in the Nordic countries, where the large banks in Denmark, Finland and Sweden operate across national borders with a branch structure, i.e. with a single banking license located in one of the countries. This is only one example of the kind of structures the future may bring to all of Europe, facilitated by the growing importance of real-time, mobile instant payments and other forms of digital banking, where geographical distance is becoming increasingly insignificant.

A natural corollary of cross-border banking operations, especially in Northern Europe, is that the EU countries not currently taking part in the banking union—of which particularly Denmark and Sweden spring to mind—would benefit and be welcome to join the institutions of the banking union through appropriate cooperation agreements. This would bring Denmark and Sweden the benefits of smoother integration into a larger financial space and a fully level playing field in financial regulation and supervision, and in the implementation of rules. It would also bring them benefits in terms of participating in the policy-making of the banking union and enhance Nordic influence in general and in a healthy way in the European Union.

3. For the sake of preserving financial stability in a crisis, and to prevent future crises, the EMU needed a big bazooka and a sufficiently sturdy lender of last resort. These should be further enhanced and developed, in order to make them as effective as possible to tame market panics, while ensuring that their institutional framework is clear and legitimate.

Another lesson, fundamentally related to financial stability, is to recognize the critical importance of the lender of last resort in a sovereign's liquidity crisis or when the banks are facing a general bank run—both for solvent sovereigns and for solvent financial institutions in the case of market panic. In practice this means that any jurisdiction must possess a *big bazooka*, so that a central bank, a separate stability fund, or both, have the tools to come to the rescue in a crisis and contain even a major market panic.

I recall Tim Geithner saying in one of the critical moments of the crisis that "you can't solve a financial crisis by only solving its causes; you have to take the catastrophic risk out of the market". He is right: successful crisis management cannot afford excessive orthodoxy in digging to the root causes of the crisis. In other words, you don't start with a court case if the house is on fire, you send a fire brigade in first!

Furthermore, one of the essential lessons of the crisis is that prevention is always better than correction. That's a further reason why an effective and rapidly reacting big bazooka that can provide liquidity assistance is necessary, as it helps by its very existence in proactively and permanently pre-empting a brewing financial crisis.

Why is such a big bazooka needed? Because financial markets are not always and automatically efficient and self-corrective, but prone to "animal spirits" and herd behaviour that are often self-reinforcing and occasionally capable of fomenting panic, as Keynes and Minsky illustrated. No doubt, the issue of moral hazard is important and the systemic incentives in EMU have to be built accordingly. But if we focus solely on that, the Eurozone will be too fragile to stand the next crisis.

In the event that the euro area faces market turbulence, the big bazooka currently comprises the ESM and the European Central Bank (ECB) together. The ESM is primarily the lender of last resort for sovereigns—to be more precise, for *solvent* sovereigns—but it also has a potential role in preserving the stability of the financial system, especially when its tasks will be expanded to take the role of a liquidity backstop for the Single Resolution Fund. The ECB is primarily the lender of last resort for the banking and financial system—not for member states—when a market panic looms and needs to be (pre-emptively) contained. It has been said that the ECB did during the crisis become the "balance sheet of last resort" for the Eurozone, which has some justification.[4]

However, it has to be added that by taking the decision on the Outright Monetary Transactions (OMT), the ECB has widened its role to be a lender of last resort for the Eurozone in its entirety in the case of a clear-cut redenomination risk: that is, only if and when there is serious speculation about a break-up of the Eurozone. Policy conditionality is embedded to the OMT rules, which helps control the moral hazard. Conditionality would be organized by connecting any OMT action to a programme of the ESM. Squaring the circle is thus made so that the ECB would not have to dwell into national politics.

This ECB-ESM arrangement includes a carefully crafted but reasonably clear division of labour between the two institutions, each in line with its own mandate. It also requires a fair share of burden-sharing, in full respect of the EU Treaty. Without such an effective though complicated big bazooka, it would have been virtually impossible to maintain financial stability, and as a result the euro area could have disintegrated with dramatic ramifications not only economically and financially but also politically and socially. In economic terms, that would have led to a serious recession and mass unemployment. In political terms, it could have led no less than to a possible collapse of the EU. This would have risked bringing Europe back to the year 1914 or 1939—the end of Europe as we know it today.

Preparing for the event when the euro area will next experience market turbulence, the ESM should be further developed by reinforcing its capacity to take decisions and extending its toolbox with a more effective and workable precautionary credit instrument. A pertinent benchmark is provided by the IMF's Flexible Credit Line (FCL), which was rather successfully used during the crisis by three countries, Colombia, Mexico and Poland, as a crisis-prevention instrument against market turbulence. None of the three countries had to draw on these lines, as the FCL provided an effective backstop for them and strengthened market confidence during the time of elevated risks.[5]

In my view, the primary reform now needed is one enhancing the functionality and capacity to act of the ESM in market turbulence. But I willingly recognize there are other proposals on the table as well. One is to change the name of the ESM to a European Monetary Fund, EMF. Would it be justified? To my mind, the nameplate is far less important than the substantive improvements in the functioning of the ESM. Besides, the ESM has become a positive, solid brand, based on the high integrity and professional quality of the institution and its staff, under the competent leadership of its managing director, Klaus Regling.

Another reform proposal relates to the institutional dimension. To increase accountability, the European Commission has proposed to integrate the ESM into the EU Treaty and put it under parliamentary control of the European Parliament, in a rather similar way as the ECB is—mostly focusing on the full right of getting and demanding information. On the other hand, the Commission proposal would maintain the key executive functions in the hands of the Board of Governors. This includes the decisions to approve of conditional financial programmes and the appointment of the managing director. Hence, the Commission proposal is actually less of a great federalist leap forward than some fear and others wish.

4. Post-crisis, following the realization that financial stability can only be neglected at our own peril, macroprudential policy has essentially become the second key pillar of central banking today, alongside monetary policy. Every country must find a macroprudential policy toolkit suitable for performing purposeful and well-targeted policies, and in general these toolkits should be made more comprehensive and wide-ranging than today. However, macroprudential toolkits are insufficient in many countries due to ongoing structural changes, like the growth of the non-bank financial sector and non-traditional loan products.

Monetary policy in the euro area is conducted by looking at the area in its entirety and is based on the ECB's price stability mandate, which limits its capacity to "lean against the wind" in cyclical terms and to pre-empt financial stability risks. Meanwhile, macroprudential policy is largely at the discretion of the national authorities and is intended to target particular national, regional or local conditions, especially in the housing markets, and thus help prevent booms and busts. It is intended to target particular cyclical or structural risks which could, when realized, threaten the stable functioning of the financial system and credit provision.

In recent years, the macroprudential *analysis* has started to cover an increasing range of issues and instruments. However, this has not yet been fully mirrored in actual macroprudential *policy*. These policies have focused quite narrowly on strengthening the resilience of systemically important banks and setting caps on new housing loans to contain excesses in mortgage lending and household indebtedness. For a new, evolving policy field, this focused approach may have been justified. But in the pursuit of preventing future financial crises, there is always a risk of fighting a past war.

Financial systems change, and the changes bring new risks. That's why for instance the IMF and the European Systemic Risk Board (ESRB) have recommended widening the range of instruments in the macroprudential toolbox.[6] In this context, there are some structural changes to which macroprudential policy-makers should pay more attention.

For instance, the traditional dominance of banks as providers of credit and finance has started to weaken in Europe and some other parts of the world. The growth of the non-bank finance sector has taken different speeds and forms in different countries and regions. A notable example is of course China, where the size of the non-bank finance sector was about 10% relative to annual GDP a decade ago. Now its size is over 100%.

In Europe, an increasing share of lending is provided by investment funds, insurance companies and the providers of consumer loans. To illustrate this, the total assets of the euro area investment fund sector grew by about 170% between 2008 and 2017. An expanding investment fund sector enhances cross-border risk sharing and deepens the bond and equity markets in Europe, which as such is a positive trend. However, according to various metrics, investment funds have started to take more credit risk and invest in less liquid assets, which may cause new risks to financial stability. It is essential to guarantee a level playing field in the same type of activities in regulation and supervision to both banks and non-banks.

Another development is that the relative importance of traditional loan products has decreased, at least in some countries. Take Finland as an example: the composition of the household loan stock is rapidly changing as a result of the slow growth in traditional housing loans and a much quicker increase in housing company loans and in consumer loans. The housing company loans are, in essence, housing loans, but in certain cases with less transparent risks for the borrower. Consumer loans, in turn, are easily available and aggressively marketed to vulnerable customers with poor credit records. This is a major social problem already.

Despite the strong increase in non-bank lending and non-traditional loan products, macroprudential tools in Finland can currently only be targeted at traditional housing loans and credit institutions' capital buffers. Macroprudential toolkits are insufficient in many other countries as well. Every country of course has its own macroprudential risks and needs to find a macroprudential policy toolbox that is suitable for its own specific circumstances. The Bank of Finland has strongly advocated the introduction of new macroprudential tools for containing household debt accumulation in Finland. The new instruments should ideally cover all loans and all lenders.

For example, a cap on the loan applicant's debt-to-income ratio at loan origination—the DTI-cap—would be a welcome addition to the Finnish macroprudential toolbox.

Furthermore, we should not neglect the effects of certain global megatrends on macroprudential risks. For instance, rapidly expanding urbanization is widening the regional differences in local housing markets and creating house price bubbles in some of the fastest-growing cities. Digitalization is creating previously unknown challenges to macroprudential policies, as with the emergence of new players like FinTech and especially BigTech companies, new types of credit channels and changes in interconnectedness are affecting systemic risks in finance. And one of the even too "hot" topics in the macroprudential field is the long-term impact of global warming on financial stability. These will call urgent and focused attention by macroprudential policy-makers.

Apart from the focus of analysis and choice of instruments, there is yet another important dimension in macroprudential policy: institutions do matter. In other words, as macroprudential policy tends to be unpopular with the electorate and business groups, in some countries the institutional arrangements facilitate more rational (and usually bolder) macroprudential policy than in others. Usually, the more technocratic and less political the institutional arrangement, the bolder the policies adopted. This dilemma is worth discussing more in-depth in the international fora.

Meanwhile, I find the debate on whether macroprudential policy should be formally part of the central banks' mandate as mostly exegetic, even theological—macroprudential policy is de facto the second pillar now, and de jure this fact has in Europe been anchored in the EU's secondary legislation, both as to the role of the financial supervisory authorities in the member states, and of the ESRB. "Form follows function", as we functionalists tend to say.

5. You have to get the policy mix right for the Eurozone. That calls for better fiscal policy coordination and a monetary policy framework that better fits the "new normal". Coordination is by no means in contradiction with central bank independence. "Independence should not be confused with loneliness", as has been rightly pointed out.

The long shadow of the Great Recession is a reminder that all EU member states and all EU institutions will need to work within their mandates for the common goal of boosting sustainable growth and the high level of employment. At the same time, the level of public debt in the EU is elevated, having risen on average from 60% of GDP before the crisis to above 90% during it, while slowly being reduced, being today circa 85%.

This makes for dual objectives in economic policy: we need to support sustainable growth and job creation, while in parallel pursuing the consistent consolidation of public finances. The EU's policy mix should reflect these goals.

The example of Japan is illustrative: it has proven that there is no silver bullet—or single arrow—to bring sustained and higher economic growth. Instead you have to make all the relevant arrows fly, including monetary, fiscal and structural ones. Despite comprehensive and commendable efforts of Japan's "Abenomics", one of its essential lessons is that monetary stimulus alone cannot lift a slow-growing economy, unless productivity-enhancing economic reforms are initiated and implemented. In Europe, this would call for boosting investment, pursuing economic reforms and improving the quality of public finances from the EU member states, while the ECB continues to execute consistent and effective monetary policy.

Of course, we have to recognize the limitations of time and space and avoid excessive generalization. Policy-making is always bound into a certain time and space, not least economic policy. But there are certain general principles that are still valid. One of them is the need for a better policy mix in the Eurozone.

As to **fiscal policy**, frontloaded consolidation was necessary in the acute phase of the debt crisis in 2010–11 in the crisis countries that had lost market access or had run out of fiscal space. It helped stabilize public finances and restore the credibility of fiscal policy, in a situation where many euro area sovereigns were locked out from the private capital markets, or were about to be. But once credibility was built up by 2012, consolidation could proceed with a slower pace. Today, the Eurozone member states have very different fiscal positions: there are some that have fiscal space and can use it in a downturn, while there are others that have very limited fiscal space and thus need to continue the consistent consolidation of public finances, with the goal of ensuring the structural sustainability of public finances over the medium term. In any case, the EU's fiscal rules can be made simpler, and they should focus essentially on medium-term growth performance and debt sustainability, and be made more counter-cyclical. The most promising route for reforming the fiscal rules is to introduce an expenditure rule (see point 5 below).

Monetary policy has entered the territory of unconventional measures since the crisis hit, and especially since 2014–15 it has been expansionary and thus boosted the recovery of the Eurozone. It still remains very accommodative in mid-2019—the experience of premature interest rate hikes in 2011 is a warning signal of what otherwise might happen. But monetary policy cannot be "the only game in town". Increasingly, the responsibility should be on the shoulders of member states' governments, in regard to both fiscal policy and structural reforms.

As of writing this in mid-2019, the normalization of monetary policy is on hold and in fact reversing, due to prolonged, pervasive uncertainty in the world economy, which is largely caused by the ongoing trade tensions, or trade wars. Returning to the process of normalization one day will be conditional on the sustained adjustment of consumer price inflation. Considering the return to normalization, it is indeed better to be safe than sorry as long as the Eurozone suffers from substantial economic slack and the price stability target of "close to but below 2 percent" is not achieved in a sustained way over the medium term. Apart from the ECB's own history of rate hikes, the Fed experience is a useful reference point, including the risks that materialized in the form of "taper tantrum" in spring 2013. These speak in favour of gradual and prudent normalization, with pertinent communication.

Right now, central banks must pay attention on the short term due to the current headwinds. The ECB recently responded to the prolonged uncertainty by reinforcing its accommodative monetary policy stance. Looking ahead, the Governing Council stands ready to adjust all of its instruments, as appropriate, so that inflation converges towards our inflation aim in a sustained manner.[7]

But we must also take a longer perspective. The ECB—much like other central banks—operates in a new environment where long-run trends, such as population aging, lower long-term interest rates and climate change have become key policy issues. The central banking community needs to better understand their implications for growth, employment and inflation dynamics, so that we can deliver more effectively within our mandates. Several central banks, including the Federal Reserve, are currently reviewing their monetary policy frameworks.

Would it be pertinent and useful for the ECB to do a strategy review as well, as I suggested in my speech in Helsinki in October 2018?[8] We may find pertinent arguments for that. Firstly, monetary policy is done in an economic environment that looks very different from that of 16 years ago, when the ECB last reviewed its strategy. Secondly, monetary policy is done with tools very different to the ones of 16 years ago. And thirdly, it is a good practice to periodically bring the brightest minds in the academic community together with practical policy-makers to evaluate our monetary policy strategies. Certainly one critical question is whether the ECB should adopt an explicitly symmetric inflation target of 2%, so that inflation may vary around it in both directions in the short term, while converging to the target in the medium term. The process of strategy review can, once successful, enhance our common understanding of the goals and tools of monetary policy.

The "**normalization**" of monetary policy is in fact a somewhat misleading concept—or at least there is the risk of misunderstanding. The gradual and patient withdrawal from unconventional measures, once restarted, will not mean going back to the old pre-2008 world. This applies to monetary policy itself and even more so to its operating environment. Nominal rates will likely remain at a lower level than traditionally, reflecting the decline in the working-age population and lower productivity.

Instead of normalization, I'd prefer to talk about **the journey towards a "new normal" or a new equilibrium.** It should be a more sustainable one, with a much greater focus on financial stability. Since the beginning of the crisis, the Eurozone and its international partners have done a lot of work to strengthen stability in many areas—from financial oversight to building a banking union. These achievements should be maintained, but more work is still ahead to strengthen the Eurozone's architecture: to lay down a foundation for sustainable growth and better employment, which must be the ultimate goal of economic policy.

The call for serious **economic reforms** isn't just loose talk that is more theoretical than practised. It is based on empirical evidence, and I am not referring only to Ireland or Latvia, which have reformed their economies successfully, even though some pundits have dismissed these achievements "because they are only small states". Spain, for instance, reformed its previously very rigid and dualistic labour market in 2012, and has since seen a positive impact on new jobs supported by restored competitiveness and strong export growth. And that's not to speak of Germany, the Netherlands, Denmark or Sweden at an earlier stage.

That's why many EU member states would benefit from getting their economic reforms into high gear. This goes for France and Italy, both great countries with plenty of entrepreneurial and innovative potential waiting to be liberated to more productive uses. Meanwhile, the surplus economies of the Eurozone, particularly Germany, would in a recession benefit from boosting domestic investment, both public and private. This would also support economic activity throughout the Eurozone, as has been advocated by the European Commission and the IMF.

Germany is not the only country whose policies have spillover effects on the rest of the Eurozone. Germany, France and Italy, the three largest economies, hold the key to stronger, sustained growth and job creation in Europe. If Germany can optimize domestic demand and investment, while France and Italy embrace reforms to their labour markets, business environments and pension systems in support of their economic and industrial competitiveness, these economies will do a great service both to themselves and to the entire Eurozone.

All this calls for **better policy coordination** than has been the case. President Herman van Rompuy's initiative in 2011 of increasing coordination among the Eurozone institutions was a right step that gradually over time significantly improved things. In my view, the Eurogroup could for example use the Macroeconomic Imbalance Procedure more effectively to provide the Eurozone better coordinated economic and fiscal policies across the member states.

Clear communication is likewise essential. The ECB began using forward guidance in July 2013 when its Governing Council said that it expected interest rates to remain low for an extended period of time. Since then the formulation of the ECB's forward guidance has been adapted, and it now clarifies the Governing Council's intentions not only with regard to the expected future path of the ECB's key interest rates, but also to the horizon of its asset purchase programme. This kind of forward guidance practised by the ECB since 2013 should in fact be regarded as a worthwhile benchmark to all Eurogroup and Eurozone policy-makers, even if the immediate market effects are most visible in monetary policy which therefore needs particular sensitiveness and shrewdness. Communication should be clear, consistent and forward-looking—and first of all, credible, so that it has real effect.

In the Eurozone, a more prevalent problem during the worst years of the crisis was the continued cacophony of public statements from various players, all of whom, in principle, could hold the right to veto policy decisions which gave clout to their comments. That's one reason why it was essential to improve coordination among the EU institutions, as was done since the summer of 2010. Since then, and since the crisis has been tamed, the previous problems have been much less prevalent. But that may not last forever, which is why this could also be an argument in favour of a "Eurozone finance minister", which—while politically difficult for many member states—would combine the positions of the Eurogroup chair and the Commissioner for Economic and Monetary Affairs, in the same way as the post of "EU foreign minister", the High Representative for EU foreign policy so to say, has been constructed. But this could work only if the member states decided to give the EU finance minister real powers in the institutional architecture.

There is also another argument in favour of that if real powers were involved: the external representation of the Eurozone in global governance.

For too long, and still today, the Eurozone has punched badly below its weight in global economic governance, for instance in the G20 and IMF context, because it is speaking with numerous voices that are often disconcerted. During the crisis years, we did aim at improving the internal coordination of the Eurozone before each major international meeting of the IMF or G20. But there is still some way to go here.

6. Fiscal rules should be sufficiently simple to ensure that, in normal circumstances, we can be certain in advance that they will be adhered to when budgets are prepared. They should also be made more counter-cyclical and supportive of structural reforms and encourage national ownership of healthy public finances. An expenditure rule could focus clearly on debt sustainability and probably serve better as an operational fiscal policy guide than the current metrics of the structural fiscal balance.[9]

In future, the economic and monetary union can work smoothly only if the public finances of all member countries are credibly on a sustainable footing. A functional combination of fiscal policy rules and market discipline related to government borrowing is necessary to achieve this. Fiscal rules should be sufficiently well-designed and simple to ensure that, in normal circumstances, we can be certain in advance that they will be adhered to when budgets are prepared.

In the conduct of fiscal policy, using rules that support sustainability has become commonplace since the 1990s. According to the IMF, nearly 100 states are already applying national or supranational fiscal rules. Fiscal rules have been linked with a more steady development of budget deficits. In the EU countries, budget deficits have been reduced during the recent period when fiscal policy supported by the reformed rules has been effectively applied. When fiscal rules operate correctly, they do indeed support the conduct of responsible fiscal policy, long-term sustainability of public finances, and the objective of keeping public debt financing costs low. The goal of the EU's fiscal rules is to ensure the sustainability of public finances and, within that framework, to enable sufficient fiscal room for manoeuvre to stimulate the economy in a member state in recession.

Not enough attention was paid to the level of public debt before the financial crisis. During the recession that was caused by the crisis, debt levels rose sharply due to stimulus measures and weak macroeconomic development, and in the most vulnerable countries the risk premia also started to rise sharply. This led to a negative spiral in which a number of countries ultimately had to tighten fiscal policy, even though economic conditions were difficult. This should be avoided in the future.

The EU's fiscal rules have last been revised relatively recently, in 2011. While the body of rules has produced results, it has however become rather extensive and sometimes inconsistent. Interpretation of the rules, with the flexibility options available, has become very complex and often difficult to predict.

More simple fiscal rules would probably serve debt sustainability better, and also increase transparency and facilitate ex-post verification of the applied fiscal policy. In the best case scenario, this also enhances the predictability of fiscal policy and its credibility in the eyes of the public. In exceptional situations, the rules need to allow flexibility, but this should be based on predetermined and consistent criteria.

The expenditure rule is essentially a benchmark rule, which helps contain the net growth rate of government spending at or below a country's medium-term potential growth rate. The expenditure rule can usefully be defined as a medium-term ceiling for the real growth of general government expenditure, set in relation to the estimated future economic growth and taking into account the stock of public debt. Such a rule would probably serve more effectively as an operational fiscal policy guide than the current rule that is based on the structural fiscal balance.

The so-called automatic stabilizers, such as increased expenditure through unemployment insurance in an economic recession, are important mechanisms of economic adjustment in the Eurozone countries. The expenditure rule would not prevent the operation of automatic stabilizers.

The expenditure rule supports responsible fiscal policy, as we have seen in countries like the Netherlands, Sweden and Finland where it has been used over the past decades. Recent research by the IMF has come by and large to a similar conclusion: the compliance rate of expenditure rules is greater than that for budget balance rules, especially if it is directly under the control of the government and the rule is enshrined in law or in a coalition agreement. Empirical research also indicates that the presence of expenditure rules is associated with stronger fiscal performance, i.e. a higher primary balance and countercyclical fiscal policies.[10]

Finally, it is essential to underline—even repeat—the paramount importance of national ownership of responsible fiscal policies. Both an expenditure rule and an independent fiscal council can be valuable tools for that goal—but they are only tools, which should be used well. It is worth quoting the director of the IMF's Fiscal Department, Vitor Gaspar, and his co-authors: "One extreme and dangerous manifestation… is the expressed perception by many analysts that European fiscal governance releases countries from their national responsibilities. Nothing could be further from the truth: fiscal policy is, first and foremost, a national responsibility".[11]

Several EU member states have in fact lived in line with Gaspar's recommendation and used the EU rulebook as an instrument to reinforce national ownership of fiscal policy. Belgium, Denmark, Luxembourg and the Netherlands introduced national expenditure rules in 1992 in response to the EU's Maastricht Treaty and its debt and deficit rules. Sweden and Finland followed suit after becoming members of the EU in 1995.[12] Germany went so far as to introduce a constitutional debt brake, which has recently been discussed in Germany and criticized for its excessive rigour that may prevent the country from meeting its national needs of public investment.

An expenditure rule could well be applied across the EU by including it in the next reform of the Stability and Growth Pact. It could help redress one major problem: before the crisis, the rate of expenditure growth exceeded the growth rate of potential output in many countries, and there were no adequate buffers. Particularly when economic growth is strong, there are all the good reasons to pay attention to fiscal responsibility. Good times should be used for building fiscal buffers.

7. In building the Eurozone as a stability union, the main responsibility for the economy and economic policies should rest with the member states, while this should be combined with the insurance provided by common structures, especially as regards ensuring financial stability.

In the final analysis, the responsibility of member states for their own economic policies—sustainable growth and employment—is what matters. Institutions matter, but likewise, the real economy matters, and it is profoundly decisive. As there is no EU federation in sight, the reforms done in the member states in support of sustainable growth and employment are indeed vital. The Eurozone architecture should work sufficiently well and reliably that it could genuinely encourage and enable its member states in achieving these economic goals.

Going forward, we have the Commission's policy paper, the initiative of the French president and the non-paper of the German Ministry of Finance on the table. The Commission paper focuses on the completion of the banking union; the French one on an ambitious programme of economic union; and the German one on market discipline. None of these alone will carry the day. The next reform of the Eurozone should aim at producing a synthesis between, on the one hand, the core principles of "German" economic philosophy, which calls for incentives and rules, and those of "French" economic philosophy, which emphasizes insurance and stabilization.

Here, I use the quotation marks deliberately, as these national adjectives are only labels for two economic philosophies, not owned just by the two countries.[13]

I found a recent joint policy paper of leading French and German economists, published in January 2018, most pertinent and substantive, with its call for a constructive rethinking of the inherited national positions on the question of the future development of the EMU. The group defines its priorities as follows:

> Reform of the euro area is needed for three reasons: first, to reduce the continued vulnerability of the euro area to financial instability; second, to provide governments with incentives that both encourage prudent macroeconomic policies and deliver growth-enhancing domestic reform; third – and perhaps most importantly – to remove a continuing source of division between euro area members and of resentment of European institutions... which has contributed to the rise of anti-euro populism and which could eventually threaten the European project itself.[14]

France has traditionally pursued additional stabilization and risk-sharing mechanisms in the Eurozone. Germany meanwhile tends to underline that the problems in the Eurozone stem rather from misguided domestic policies and instead tends to call for rigorous enforcement of fiscal rules and more market discipline.

Creating a European synthesis means building a stability union that underlines each member state's own responsibility, while recognising the necessity of joint structures to preserve financial stability. To ensure that each member state is responsible for its own economic policy, the rules and incentives should be designed accordingly and be made simpler than today. Meanwhile, there needs to be a sufficient joint capacity to preserve financial stability in the face of market turbulence. Moreover, steps towards further sharing of risk should be equally matched with further steps to reduce risk. This goes for both public finances and the banking union.

One important example of this kind of synthesis would be to agree creating euro area safe assets and combine it with changes in the treatment of banks' sovereign exposures to reflect credit or concentration risk. The recent initiatives, as the one by the German–French group of economists, to create safe assets differ from the various earlier proposals in 2010–12 to create Eurobonds, including by the European Commission, particularly because the recent suggestions would not rely on member state guarantees to ensure safety. Why would such safe assets be needed? If designed well, they have the potential to provide various benefits for the Eurozone: to produce safe assets in large-enough volumes to crowd out sovereign debt on bank balance sheets, to neutralize any disruption of regulatory changes in the treatment of sovereign exposure of banks and to contain a perceived shortage of safe assets in Europe. The thinning of the German Bund market is already causing shortage of safe assets in Europe, which alone would be a valid reason to create euro area safe assets. But they would also help in strengthening the global role of the euro and to create a large, liquid bond market in Europe, which would obviously be supportive of financing and investment in the real economy and its economic-ecological transformation.

For example, in case some form of concentration charges on the banks' sovereign exposure were introduced, it would create a disincentive for a bank to continue holding excessively large and thus risky portfolios in the sovereign bonds of one certain member state, say Italy. Consequently, the demand for European safe assets could be significant, if well-designed. But of course this reform would require still much product development and further building of consensus. Finally, the demand for them would depend on the investors.[15]

In the context of fiscal policy, to smoothen business cycles in the euro area, it has been proposed to set up a macroeconomic stabilization function for the Eurozone by creating a euro area fiscal capacity, for instance based on an unemployment insurance scheme. It would aim at stabilizing investment spending, which is usually hit first in a recession. This certainly has intellectual merit from the macroeconomic point of view. At the same time, there are analytical and practical counter-arguments. Many argue that the already existing "automatic stabilizers"—or national budgetary expenditure such as unemployment benefits that automatically increase once the economy is hit by a recession—already play a significant counter-cyclical policy role, and do so more strongly in the EU than in the United States, as the welfare state is generally stronger in Europe. Others point to implementation problems related to fine-tuning of counter-cyclical policies, which is a problem in general in fiscal policy even in sovereign states, not to speak of a 19-member euro area, which does not have a central fiscal authority, but only weak coordination. Still others are worried of a more fundamental issue, which is that the well-meant social transfers intended for stabilization in the trough of the economic cycle would risk turning into permanent transfers, thus eroding the legitimacy of EU policy as has happened in many member states that have large inter-regional transfers, like Italy (Mezzogiorno), Spain (Catalonia) or Belgium (Flanders/Wallonia).

An alternative to a fiscal capacity as stabilization function is a specific competitiveness and convergence instrument, which would support member states in the pursuit of economic reforms and improved competitiveness, but not provide social transfers. This was already proposed by the European Commission in 2012. In my view, it would be a meaningful supplementary element to the financing provided by the European Investment Bank, which is a well-tested development bank and should continue to carry the bulk of responsibility for EU-level public investment. The European Council in December 2018 endorsed the idea as a compromise and asked the Eurozone finance ministers "to work on the design, modalities of implementation and timing of the budgetary instrument for convergence and competitiveness".[16]

In conclusion, we need to move on with the ever-changing evolutionary Union. My thesis is that the Eurozone will not become a federation or transfer union—but neither will it break up just like that because of not becoming one. There is a realistic third way forward by combining risk reduction and risk sharing.

This volume has shown that the past decade of walking the highwire of the financial and debt crises was a real stress test for the European Union. Even so, Europe was able to muddle through the challenges it faced. But in no way should we diminish the remaining challenges, even if Europe is again on its feet. The EU should be getting poised for renewal and thus for better meeting its basic functions.

The dichotomy of "federation or death" has been put forward too often and frequently for propaganda reasons. Some columnists and other pundits have made it their brand name over the crisis years.[17] But it is fake news. The euro area will not survive by simply becoming a federation or transfer union, but neither will it break up just because of not becoming one. Life is seldom black-and-white.

Instead, there is an evolutionary third way—we need a sense of both direction and realism. The essential guiding principle in reforming the Eurozone economic governance should be that steps towards increased solidarity through co-insurance and risk sharing are combined with increased responsibility. Solidarity can only be built on solidity, for the sake of both economic sustainability and political legitimacy.

In my view, the most promising and thus preferable option for the Eurozone reform is to build the kind of stability union that leans on a balance between, on the one hand, the member states' own responsibility for their economies and economic policies, and on the other, common European-level economic policy co-ordination, with its insurance coverage of joint structures providing risk management. Based on this kind of solid architecture, it is then up to policy-makers to work out a well-functioning policy mix that supports sustainable growth and job creation.

Notes

1. Cf. Reinhart and Rogoff, *This Time Is Different: Eight Centuries of Financial Folly*. Princeton University Press, 2009.
2. *Financial Times*, 27 September 2017. See: https://www.ft.com/content/451d26e6-a264-11e7-b797-b61809486fe2.
3. Waltraud Schelkle, *The Political Economy of Monetary Solidarity: Understanding the Euro Experiment*. Oxford University Press, 2017, p. 304.
4. Papadia, Francesco, with Tuomas Välimäki, *Central Banking in Turbulent Times*. Oxford University Press, 2018, pp. 140–141.
5. https://www.imf.org/About/Factsheets/Sheets/2016/08/01/20/40/Flexible-Credit-Line?pdf=1.
6. See e.g. the Global Financial Stability Report 2019 of the IMF (April 2019): https://www.imf.org/en/Publications/GFSR/Issues/2019/03/27/Global-Financial-Stability-Report-April-2019 and the ESRB Strategy Paper 2016: https://www.esrb.europa.eu/pub/pdf/reports/20160718_strategy_paper_beyond_banking.en.pdf.
7. An empirical analysis of the ECB's past reaction function can be found in Maritta Paloviita, Markus Haavio, Pirkka Jalasjoki, and Juha Kilponen, *What Does "Below, but Close to, Two Percent Mean?" Assessing the ECB's Reaction Function with Real-Time Data*. Bank of Finland Research Discussion Papers, 29/2017.
8. https://www.suomenpankki.fi/fi/media-ja-julkaisut/puheet-ja-haastattelut/2018/governor-olli-rehn-monetary-policy-normalisationin-the-world-of-uncertainties/.
9. This section on the expenditure rule and fiscal policy has benefitted much from the work done by the economists at the Bank of Finland—my particular thanks go to Jarkko Kivistö. It is also based on my own experiences as a practical policymaker during the crisis.
10. Till Cordes, Tidiane Kinda, Priscilla Muthoora, and Anke Weber, Expenditure Rules: Effective Tools for Sound Fiscal Policy? In Vitor Gaspar, Sanjeev Gupta, and Carlos Mulas-Granados (eds.), *Fiscal Politics*. IMF, 2017, p. 317.
11. Luc Eyraud, Vitor Gaspar, and Tigran Poghosyan, Fiscal Politics in the Euro Area. In Vitor Gaspar, Sanjeev Gupta, and Carlos Mulas-Granados (eds.), *Fiscal Politics*. IMF, 2017, p. 469.
12. Cordes et al., pp. 305–306.

13. The distinctive elements of German and French economic policy philosophies are elegantly described by Markus Brunnermeier, Harold James and Jean-Pierre Landau in their important volume *The Euro and the Battle of Ideas*. Princeton, 2016.

14. Agnès Bénassy-Quéré, Markus Brunnermeier et al., *Reconciling Risk Sharing with Market Discipline: A Constructive Approach to Euro Area Reform*. CEPR Policy Insight Nro 91. https://cepr.org/sites/default/files/policy_insights/PolicyInsight91.pdf.

15. See especially the report of the working group led by Governor Philip Lane. ESRB High-Level Task Force on Safe Assets, *Sovereign Bond-Backed Securities: A Feasibility Study*. European Systemic Risk Board, January 2018, and Jean Pisani-Ferry and Jeromin Zettelmeyer (eds.), *Risk Sharing Plus Market Discipline: A New Paradigm for Euro Area Reform? A Debate*. A VoxEU.org Book. CEPR Press, 2019.

16. See Reuters report on the December 2018 European Summit: https://www.reuters.com/article/us-eurozone-future/eu-to-drop-stabilization-as-use-for-euro-budget-keep-convergence-competitiveness-draft-idUSKBN1OB1TP.

17. I am referring, not only but for example, to FT's Wolfgang Munchau, who undoubtedly is the master of this kind of branding and of catastrophe scenarios without a federation! I need to thank him for inspiring me to continue defending the euro.

Part V

Looking Back, Looking Forward

20

Epilogue

Fast-forward to 2019. Much has happened in the economy and politics of Europe since 2014, where the narrative of this book mostly ends. The Old Continent has by now undergone a full decade of crises, in plural, and its economic, social and political landscape is indeed very different today compared to the one that existed before 2008.

The financial and debt crises have cast a long shadow due to their social and human ramifications. They were succeeded by a refugee crisis that led to deep political cleavages and further fuelled the rise of populism in Europe. Russia's turn to power politics with the annexation of Crimea and the war in Eastern Ukraine have challenged Europe's security. What's more, the UK voted in its referendum of 2016 to leave the European Union. The list does not stop there: the United States under President Donald Trump's "America First" policies have since 2017 taken a nationalist turn and mentally resigned from the liberal international order that she herself initiated and successfully pursued after the Second World War.

All these developments are challenging the values of democracy, civil liberties, the rule of law and politico-economic integration that constitute the European way of life and its model of society. Politically, a populist, nationalist agenda is tempting to many. Socially, the values of tolerance, liberalism and inclusion are under threat.

As the distinguished historian Anne Applebaum has written about post-war Europe, "For roughly forty years, the nations what we used to call Western Europe were all bound together by a similar decision: as a group, they chose democracy over dictatorship, integration over nationalism, social

© The Author(s) 2020
O. Rehn, *Walking the Highwire*, https://doi.org/10.1007/978-3-030-34592-1_20

market economies over state socialism".[1] Now, this "group decision" of European nations is being seriously challenged, from both inside and outside.

Since 2004, after 10 years in the frontline of European policy-making, it had already become crystal clear to me well before the 2014 European elections that the rise of populism and nationalism would invade the political discourse and challenge the future development of the European Union. That also posed a personal dilemma: Could I look for a more reflective, tranquil life in academia or civil service, or should I do my part to defend Europe in that more hectic, intensive political arena? What road should my calling to public service lead me onto? It was not an easy choice, as years at the frontline had taken their toll on me and my family.

As a result of profound reflection and intensive discussions with my family and friends in the course of the winter of 2013–14, I decided to run for the European Parliament in the May 2014 elections. I was also elected as the other lead candidate of the Alliance of Liberals and Democrats for Europe (ALDE), on the side of Guy Verhofstadt—to provide a functionalist defence for Europe and its economic and social integration to balance Guy's formidable federalism and more political focus.

It was however no simple feat, as I had not campaigned in the rough and tumble of democratic politics for years, and nobody can ever consider their election by any means "guaranteed" in a liberal democracy (though it is another story in a "managed democracy"!). So I did a half-year campaign across the country and in many places elsewhere in Europe and met thousands of people in the market places, town hall meetings and through social media. It required a certain mind shift from the semi-professorial method of a Commissioner to the more upfront and accessible approach of a stand-up politician and, with it, the capacity and will to dive deep into the political debates with the citizens and voters on the ground, to contain populism and move to a counter-attack for Europe. Following a long and intensive, but mostly rewarding campaign that I undertook with great people, the election night was nerve-testing, as always. In the end, I got the third highest vote in the country and thus a safe and strong mandate among the 13 MEPs elected from Finland.

In the European Parliament, my group elected me to the ALDE negotiation team for the term 2014–19. I was among those who wanted to endorse Jean-Claude Juncker's appointment as Commission President, if his Commission programme would be mindful of the liberals' key policy goals and commit to reform the EU in line with the philosophy that Europe should be big in big issues and small in small issues—which implies focusing on the essentials, particularly on safeguarding peace and security and creating conditions for sustainable growth and job creation, while intensifying the efforts to cut red tape and reducing bureaucratic burden. Likewise, a bold and consistent climate and energy strategy were a key priority for us. Juncker agreed and committed himself to a well-crafted policy programme. So we supported him.

Politically, the Juncker Commission did by and large live up to its commitments. Nevertheless, the populist wave has continued, amplified by the refugee crisis. Pinpointing a single root cause is virtually impossible, but it seems that a combination of increased economic insecurity and perceived threats to traditional ways of life has provided the main triggers for populist surges. Moreover, epoch-making changes in the media landscape, stemming from social media and powered by artificial intelligence, have revolutionized the dynamics of communication and political discourse. Whether we like it or not, we are currently living with populism all over Europe—and we need to learn how to distinguish between pure demagoguery and outright authoritarianism, on one hand, and the signals of legitimate dissatisfaction, on the other, by containing the former and being responsive to the latter.

But there must be limits to accommodation. If unchecked, populism breeds or may lead to authoritarianism and/or "illiberal democracy" (which is a contradiction in terms, as it is neither liberal nor democratic). By and large, we can identify three stages in the transformation of populism. The first stage can be described as a *recognition of protest*. That's how, for instance, the Finnish Rural Party, the predecessor of the True Finns, got started in the 1960s, as a protest movement against the world's speediest structural change from agriculture to industrialization and from the rural to the urban way of life with a parallel liberalization of social values. In the second stage, once populist parties have gained support, there are ever stronger demands for *policy change*. For instance, the Danish People's Party has insisted on more restrictive immigration policies, which has been adopted by successive governments and other political parties in Denmark. Similar developments have taken place in other EU member states. In the third stage, there is a push for *regime change*, towards an illiberal democracy and/or authoritarian regime, usually starting by curbing the key liberal institutions, such as a free press and an independent judiciary. In Hungary and Poland, democratic methods are used to this effect, to undermine democratic substance. Probably we can describe authoritarianism as the highest stage of populism—unless it slides further. Racism and fascism must have no place in our political life in Europe. No respect to disrespect.

Even in their democratic forms, the economic and social policies of populist parties seldom provide real or viable solutions, and the populists' impact on political institutions tends to be corrosive. The rise of populism has already led to an increased fragmentation of the European political systems, which has often made it much more difficult than before to form functioning coalition governments and to carry out economic and political reforms. This threatens to create a truly vicious political circle.

The 2019 European elections were an important checkpoint of Europe's political sentiment. While living with populism, which once more scored well again, e.g. in Italy and France, the pro-European forces were able to come back and maintain a functional majority in the European Parliament. Even though the European People's Party and the Socialists and Democrats lost their traditional outright majority, the liberal centre of Renew Europe and of the Greens made electoral gains, which can make the pro-European majority solid and workable. So politically countervailing forces are at work.

But in the field of economic development, Europe has since the financial crisis fallen behind the G2 powers of the United States and China. This regression is obviously detrimental to the continued improvement of living standards and social cohesion in Europe. It is also damaging to the EU's global role and its relevance to global governance, which depend on its economic dynamism and political unity.

I regarded the rise of populism, on one hand, and the renewal of economic dynamism on the other, as the key challenges for Europe and my native Finland—and as a challenge that can best be met through successful economic and employment policies in the member states. Because of that, I joined the then opposition leader and Centre Party chairman Juha Sipilä's economic team in Finland and subsequently agreed to run for a seat in the Finnish Parliament to which I was elected in April 2015. The Centre Party emerged as the clear electoral winner with 21% of the popular vote. However, the populist True Finns party scored 18%, almost as strongly as in their breakthrough election four years before. As it would have been virtually impossible to form a coalition government without them, the Centre Party leadership decided to take a chance and try agree on a common programme with the True Finns, thus integrating them into decision-making and responsibility (and sure, if possible, taming them). So, while returning to politics in order to defend Europe and contain populism, it was no small paradox that I ended up in coalition talks negotiating for the Centre Party with the populist True Finns and their leader, the populist-in-chief Timo Soini. I knew him as a socially populist conservative from youth and student politics of the 1980s before he started flirting with anti-European and anti-immigration sentiments. Now, we were formulating the new government's policies on Europe and the euro.

After quite some wrangling, the programme of the Sipilä government was finally agreed on by the end of May 2015. Its EU policy stance could be described as realistically pro-European, with wordings like "Finland is an active, pragmatic and result-oriented member state that will seek, in a constructively critical and cooperative way, to combine the national and joint European interest in Finland's EU policy". No federalist poetry, perhaps, but it provided a functional basis for pragmatic EU policy. The constraints it created for the role of an active and results-oriented member state were however never truly tested, as the EU's development remained in slow motion during the period of 2015–19. But at least no harm was done to the support for the euro, as the Finns seem to value their single currency highly. According to the 2019 Eurobarometer, as many as 80% of Finnish citizens support the euro.

In recent years, I was nevertheless surprised of Finland's almost unquestioning eagerness to commit itself to the so-called new Hanseatic League, which includes the Netherlands, Ireland, the Baltic states and the Nordic EU countries. All of them are honourable countries, and certainly it is good to have partners, but as the Hanseatic League has portrayed itself largely as a group of saying "no, no, and once more no" especially to the reforms of the Eurozone, it is difficult to see that automatically joining its positions would advance either Europe's or Finland's case. Would it not be better to be open to cooperation with other member states as well, and aim at becoming a proactive bridge-builder to find common, realistic European solutions?

During the coalition talks, I worked as kind of a jack-of-all-trades in the areas of European and also economic and industrial policy. At one point during the height of the talks, I flew to Brussels at the request of Prime Minister-designate Sipilä to meet with Commissioner Pierre Moscovici to negotiate—or clarify—with the Commission the economic policy stance of the prospective government. I explained to Moscovici that we needed to build a Keynesian bridge by smoother, less rigorous consolidation of public finances than a literal interpretation of the Stability and Growth Pact would have required, in return for structural reforms and a social pact that will correct our cost competitiveness and boost growth in the medium term. When I had almost finished my argumentation, neither of us could help letting out a simultaneous, sympathetic chuckle—as we realized at the same moment that we were having nearly the exact exchange of views that we had in Moscow in February 2013, the only difference being that now our roles were completely reversed! Anyway, Pierre Moscovici could consider supporting our approach once it would be further specified into concrete economic reforms and budgetary decisions, as this was the way how the Commission's applied the Stability and Growth Pact. "I told you I am a big fan of the Commission's Flexibility Communication", I said to Pierre when I was on my way out of his office. Case settled.

Economic policy programme of the Sipilä government was finalized in the last two days of talks. The final versions of the programme were literally "writings from the basement", as ex-PM Matti Vanhanen was banging the keys of his laptop in one basement room of *Smolna*, the Government Banquet Hall, and I was banging mine in another room, each completing one chapter of the programme. Two ex-summer reporters were at work, corresponding to our training.

Overall, the coalition talks of 2015 were tough but successful, and once the three-party centre-right government had been formed, I served in 2015–16 as the minister of economic affairs for Finland. Objectively, the Sipilä government did well in economic and industrial policy and was able to lift the Finnish economy from the doldrums of stagnation to a new era of stronger, sustained growth. It negotiated a competitiveness pact with the social partners, both trade unions and employers' federations, which helped reduce unit labour costs by 6½% over several years. It stabilized public finances with a four-year plan and decided on tax cuts as part of the pact, targeted to lower-and-middle-income wage earners. It conducted a basic income experiment, which however was constrained by shortage of funding and constitutional considerations. It liberalized the shopping hours virtually completely with a short and clear law, after three decades of piecemeal change and a heavy patchwork of accumulated and bureaucratic legislation. And it assembled a bold but consistent comprehensive climate and energy strategy, which keeps Finland in the top class for renewables and circular economy, in both Europe and the world.

All these policy measures contributed to the revival of Finland's economic growth from zero to 2–3% and to the rise of her employment rate from 68% to above 72%. Moreover, despite difficult decisions to balance public finances, the level of income inequality in Finland continues to be among the lowest in the world, according to international comparative studies.[2] Even the True Finns' ministers carried boldly their responsibility, which in no small way contributed to their internal split and the takeover of the party by the more extreme wing in 2017. However, towards the end of the government's term, there were many uphill struggles, especially as the flagship healthcare reform was blocked by the opposition and constitutional experts and as some active labour market policy measures of activating the unemployed became a red cloth and a handy political weapon to trade unions. So politically the government was knocked out in the 2019 elections and replaced in June 2019 by a centre-left-green coalition, led first by the SDP leader Antti Rinne as the new prime minister, and after his resignation in December 2019, by Sanna Marin.[3]

Against these experiences, what can liberal democracies do to deal with the present populist pressures? In my view, the first and foremost way to defend liberal democracy is simply to pursue principled, consistent and well-argued and well-managed policies that help solve practical problems of our ordinary citizens—be they related to employment, economic growth, environment, immigration or climate change. I don't believe that a majority of our citizens would be against receiving immigrants as such or against tackling climate change in a rational way—on the condition that the policy process and its implementation are indeed well managed and fair, so that the citizens can trust that it is done in the interests of the whole society.

I had first-hand experience of both chaotic and managed policy processes during the refugee crisis, in the autumn and winter 2015–16. The influx of people to Finland (which received the fourth largest number of refugees in the EU in 2015) was not under anybody's control in the first months of the crisis, which created a wave of understandable discontent among the Finns. In addition to refugees and asylum seekers, the flow of people also included organized traffic through the Eastern and Western border crossings of enterprising people mainly seeking better economic and social conditions. So we spent hours and hours sorting things out in the eavesdropping-protected basement chamber of the Council of the State in the Security Committee, chaired by the President of the Republic, Sauli Niinistö. It was as a result of the systematic work by the Ministry of the Interior, the much improved coordination within the state administration over time by the Border Guard and other agencies, as well as negotiations in line with international law in Brussels, Stockholm, Oslo and Moscow, that we were able to manage the flow of immigrants and put a decent system of reception in place by early 2016.

But our citizens' trust in liberal democracy depends also very much on how democratic politics is conducted in our countries. In our contemporary societies, we suffer from a fragmented and polarized discourse where social media, cultural bubbles and single issues dominate, which breeds closed political bastions and makes analytical and civilized democratic dialogue an uphill struggle. Thus improving our liberal democracy that is the cornerstone of political Europe calls for revitalized citizen dialogue and for modernized, reformed political parties, which should engage the citizens in new ways that are appropriate for the information society and social media culture that we live in today. Such modernized parties should be able to compose consistent long-term policy programmes based on philosophical ideals and broader policy visions with popular touch, which could pull together the civil society to constructive action, instead of pure populism or indeed outright nationalism. That could be the way to steer our societies and democracies towards a more sustainable future, in every sense of the word.

But we need to keep in mind the broader and very fundamental political perspective as well. More and more often, the Enlightenment values, which underpin the European societal model, are now being challenged both politically and socially, both from the inside and from the outside. President Vladimir Putin recently called liberalism "obsolete", which should serve as a wake-up call to all Europeans, if somebody is still sleepwalking. The choice between liberalism and authoritarianism has become crystal clear: liberalism and liberal democracy are at the heart of the European way of life.

As a central banker since 2017, I fully recognize that these issues do matter immensely also for the central banks. My personal path brought me to the Bank of Finland, as I wanted to get back from micro-economics to macroeconomics and to be more involved in European decision-making. If anything is my passion, it is European economic policy-making and its relation to macroeconomics and to the broader economy and society at large. It is clear that the central banks do not live in a vacuum, but they are reflections of the society at large—independent reflections and actors. As the great economist Joseph Schumpeter once wrote: "The condition of the monetary system of a nation is a symptom of all its conditions".[4] What Schumpeter said about a nation, goes today as well for Europe as a whole, for our economic and monetary union. What happens to our single currency is a reflection of the state of our union and its economy, of its society and its democracy. So we have to take a broader perspective on the need of structural and institutional reforms in the member states and the EU.

This brings us back to the euro. The sovereign debt crisis revealed serious design flaws in the economic and monetary union. Major reforms were done to reinforce economic governance and thus resilience of the Eurozone and its ability to secure financial stability, sustainable growth and opportunities for employment.

But our economic and monetary union is still very much unfinished business. Many policy questions and institutional issues remain. How to complete the banking union? What kind of fiscal capacity will best serve strong, sustained growth? How to make the fiscal rules more counter-cyclical? What kind of European safe assets could fly in decision-making, to have liquid financial markets and pave the way for the euro's global role? These are examples of the often complicated issues related to the future of economic and monetary union, and addressing them will be an interesting quest and, above all, a most meaningful mission.

It is evident that Eurozone reform is very much linked to the overall future of Europe and its Union. The pursuit of reinforcing the EMU is a part of a broader endeavour to strengthen Europe, not only in the financial but also in the economic and political sphere. As Europeans, we should recognize the urgency of this effort, especially now as the role of Europe as the standard-bearer for liberal democracy has become even more critical than it may have been some years ago.

One essential, final note must be made. While institutional reform is important, Europe needs to work towards sustainable growth and job creation on all fronts. Moving from immediate firefighting to rebalancing and reform has been the key tenet of European economic policy over the past years, since the passing of immediate crisis conditions of 2010–12. Now, it is time to get on with a new gear in these endeavours.

Managing immigration better and reinforcing Europe's external and internal security are key policy challenges for Europe in the coming years. But so is the need to boost an economic and industrial revival of Europe. It should be based on an ever stronger focus on—and investment into—innovation and research and thus enhanced productivity. Furthermore, Europe's economic revival needs to be combined with the greatest challenge of our generation: tackling and mitigating climate change. It calls for a consistent strategy from the EU on how to pursue economic and ecological transformation of our societies and enterprises, from fossil fuels to renewable energy, from the production of waste to circular economy.

Putting the green real economy and economic reforms truly centre stage means that we should build the kind of Europe that opens up our citizens' opportunities to innovate and create new businesses and thus new jobs. We should also continue to work for a Europe that promotes and seeks growth beyond its own borders through free-trade agreements, despite the current protectionist headwinds; for a Europe that combines entrepreneurial drive and a stability culture; for a Europe where citizens and businesses can benefit from a genuine single market, not only in goods but also in digital and traditional services; and for a Europe that guarantees civil rights and social justice in the digital age.

These are the concrete, functionalist goals for sustainable growth and job creation—and fundamentally for human development—that do really matter to our citizens in Europe, which should always be our yardstick. They should be supported by rock-solid financial stability that can be enabled by completing the banking union.

Such a progressive policy agenda can help make Europe relevant again and keep it moving on. In the future, we need less of just muddling through and more of consistent and goal-oriented progress, in areas where it truly matters to our citizens.

Notes

1. Anne Applebaum, The Lure of Western Europe. *The New York Review of Books*, 6 June 2019 issue.
2. Petri Mäki-Fränti, *Tuloerojen viimeaikainen kehitys Suomessa*. Suomen Pankki, 17 May 2019: http://kirstu/sp/Julkaisut/Et/et2015/Julkaistut/20190517-Analyysi-Tuloerojen-viimeaikainen-kehitys-Suomessa.pdf#search=kajanoja%20gini. Lauri Kajanoja, *Kasvua ilman eriarvoisuutta*. Kansantaloudellinen aikakauskirja 1/2017, pp. 22–41: https://www.talousti-eteellinenyhdistys.fi/wp-content/uploads/2017/03/kak-1-2017-Kajanoja.pdf.
3. The Rinne government, like the Marin government since December 2019, is composed of the Social-Democratic Party, the Centre Party, the Greens, the Left Alliance and the Swedish People's Party.
4. "Der Zustand des Geldwesens eines Volkes ist ein Symptom aller seiner Zustände."

Name Index

Subject Index